THE FAMILY GUIDE TO BETTER FOOD AND BETTER HEALTH

"More than a family guide to nutrition, it is Everyman's Guide to Nutrition. An outstanding treatise."

—Dr. Paul A. Lachance,
Associate Professor of Nutritional
Physiology, Rutgers University

ABOUT THE AUTHOR

Ronald M. Deutsch, author and lecturer with special interest in the fields of medicine and public health, has written six books and over 200 articles for major magazines. He is also a frequent speaker to groups of professional nutritionists, physicians, home economists and food technologists. Mr. Deutsch served on the President's White House Conference on Food, Nutrition and Health.

"Written in a conversational style, its practical tips and nutritional information for all ages and types of man will help make you a more enlightened consumer."

—**Forecast For Home Economics**

"**THE FAMILY GUIDE TO BETTER FOOD AND BETTER HEALTH** should be read, understood and followed."

—**Los Angeles Herald-Examiner**

THE FAMILY GUIDE TO BETTER FOOD AND BETTER HEALTH

Ronald M. Deutsch

Illustrations by Diana Dennington

Foreword by Dr. Philip L. White
Director, Department of Foods and Nutrition,
American Medical Association

This low-priced Bantam Book has been completely reset in a type face designed for easy reading, and was printed from new plates. It contains the complete text of the original hard-cover edition.
NOT ONE WORD HAS BEEN OMITTED.

THE FAMILY GUIDE TO BETTER FOOD AND BETTER HEALTH
A Bantam Book / published by arrangement with Meredith Corporation

PRINTING HISTORY
Meredith edition published June 1971
Family Book Service edition published June 1971
A Book-Of-The-Month Club alternate selection 1971–1973
Article excerpts appeared in Better Homes and Gardens, Family Circle and Reader's Digest
Bantam edition / December 1973
2nd printing .... January 1976 3rd printing .... August 1977
4th printing .... August 1979

For information address: Meredith Corporation 1716 Locust Street, Des Moines, Iowa 50336

ISBN 0-553-13259-8

Published simultaneously in the United States and Canada

Bantam Books are published by Bantam Books, Inc. Its trademark, consisting of the words "Bantam Books" and the portrayal of a bantam, is Registered in U.S. Patent and Trademark Office and in other countries. Marca Registrada. Bantam Books, Inc., 666 Fifth Avenue, New York, New York 10019.

PRINTED IN THE UNITED STATES OF AMERICA

CONTENTS

Foreword
Preface

Section I: YOUR FOOD AND YOUR HEALTH 1
Chapter 1: What You Don't Know Can Hurt You 3
Chapter 2: How Well Do You Eat? 12

Section II: HOW FOOD BECOMES LIFE 35
Chapter 3: The Creation of Food 37
Chapter 4: Protein and the Secrets of Life 52
Chapter 5: Choosing Proteins 71
Chapter 6: Choosing Foods for Life 97

Section III: THE NUTRITIONIST ON THE SCALES 169
Chapter 7: Were You Born To Be Fat? 171
Chapter 8: How and When We Grow Fat 188
Chapter 9: How to Prevent Fatness 201
Chapter 10: How Much Should You Weigh—and Eat? 216
Chapter 11: Curing Overfat 239

Section IV: THE NUTRITIONIST IN THE SUPERMARKET 279
Chapter 12: What Is Missing from Our Food? 281
Chapter 13: Is There Poison in Our Food? 295
Chapter 14: Reading Labels for Health and Profit 308

Section V: THE FOOD SCIENTIST IN THE KITCHEN 325
Chapter 15: Preventing Foodborne Illness 327
Chapter 16: Getting the Most Out of Our Food 342

Section VI: THE DOCTOR LOOKS AT EATING AND ILLNESS 357
Chapter 17: What Do You You Know about Digestion and Indigestion? **359**
Chapter 18: Your Food and Your Heart **379**

Section VII: FOOD, GROWTH AND AGING 395
Chapter 19: Food for the Pregnant and Nursing Woman **397**
Chapter 20: The Things Kids Eat **406**
Chapter 21: Food in the Later Years **422**

Conclusion: The Food in Your Future 428

Appendix A: Food Composition: The Nutritive Values of Foods 433

Appendix B: List of Recommended and Not Recommended Books 471

Index: 477

FOREWORD

by Dr. Philip L. White

Consumer concern about the quality of America's food supply has never been greater. That concern is expressed in a variety of ways. Some people have tried to learn more about nutrition so as to cope with the staggering array of foods; others, in bewilderment, have retreated into fads, cults and unusual regimens, such as vegetarianism. For the latter we have great concern, because all too often the vegetarians' understanding of nutrition does not permit them to nourish themselves well. But what about the former, those who wish to learn? What sort of information is available to help them learn? Actually there is a vast amount of information available—highly selective, widely scattered, mostly in the form of pamphlets, and not always reliable. Good books on nutrition are hard to find.

The problem for the beginning reader in nutrition is to distinguish between established fact and what is merely the author's opinion—often phrased as though it were a fact. Much of our present framework of nutrition is actually based upon qualified judgment. It is from this that concepts develop.

Ronald Deutsch has achieved a fine blend of basic knowledge and fundamental concepts. What helps the reader is that he lets you know when he is dealing with facts and when he is describing a concept. This book, then, is an honest guide to better food and better health. To help the reader over rough spots, the author has used pictorial conceptualization of technical material. The way the book is presented, one can skip the tough parts for the time being, go on and then return for thorough mastication later on—a neat way to do it.

Mr. Deutsch asked me to read his manuscript for accuracy. This I did with great pleasure, sandwiching it in when I could evenings and over a weekend. I would like to share my reactions with the readers of *The Family Guide to Better Food and Better Health.*

I am deeply impressed with the depth of treatment. No reader could help but be aware that the book is based upon an extensive knowledge of the subject presented in a warm and vital manner. I searched carefully for omissions, misinterpretations or overemphasis, and found precious little to criticize.

The book will do much to help those who seek a positive approach to good health. It likewise should dissuade others from going the way of the food faddist.

There has been little assessment of the physiological consequences of our way of eating. It is difficult to determine whether serious malnutrition does exist to any significant degree. We have better information on dietary practices than on the biochemical and medical changes which may result from poor eating habits.

If there is malnutrition in this country it is usually due to failure to choose meals from a variety of foods, rather than inability to purchase adequate and appropriate foods. It is as though people expect any old food to nourish them. Now to these determinants of malnutrition—poverty, ignorance and indifference—I like to add a fourth for consideration, permissiveness. This seems to express best what happens in the dietary of young people, even when under parental guidance. Young people are permitted to pick their own way through the dietary maze by permissive parents. The results all too often are tragic.

The Family Guide to Better Food and Better Health fills a void that has existed all too long. Until now there has been no totally acceptable, comprehensive book on nutrition for the layman. I think now we have one.

PREFACE

Over the last long months, when friends would ask why I had taken on a hermit's life, and I explained about this book, I got an almost invariable response: "Nutrition. That's certainly a controversial subject these days, isn't it?"

At the time, with something urgent to be researched or written always on my desk (really the dining table, because I had used up all the desk space in the house), I merely muttered politely and changed the subject. But now, with the dining table almost cleared, I would like to respond. Despite all the hullabaloo in the popular prints, despite all the conflict, nutrition is not, in the main, a controversial subject.

There are a few controversies, of course, and the reader will find them plainly labeled as such in this book, with both sides represented. But the basic scientific tenets of what food is, what man needs from it and how he gets it are generally agreed upon among true and qualified scientists. It is only the unqualified who fly in the face of this basic science. It is the enthusiasts, the faddists, the quacks, the promoters, the miracle-minded, the fear-ridden who today raise most of the dust which makes so much of nutrition *seem* controversial to the layman.

For example, it may surprise some people to find that the whole "organic food controversy" is not a controversy at all in government agencies and in university laboratories, that, in general, additives do not excite panic in the breasts of physicians and biochemists, that scholars and scientists do not take very seriously the growing anxiety that the food in the supermarket is somehow made barren of the stuff of life. These "controversies" are largely needless or minor concerns.

This is not to say that there is no need for concern of any kind about food and health. There are real concerns, as we shall see, but the vast majority have answers which are agreed upon, except for detail.

I write this, as I do all of the book, as an experienced

reporter in the field, but not as a nutritionist. In so saying, I forego a temptation; for anyone may call himself a nutritionist without fear of penalty. A nutritionist is merely one whose occupation is nutrition, by dictionary definition. So all you need do to acquire the title, technically, is to busy yourself with the subject.

In this book, however, the title "nutritionist" is bestowed more carefully. It is used as professionals use it, to mean a person with advanced training in those sciences which deal with the effects of food on health—on bodily growth, function and survival. Such a person has appropriate degrees and titles in such disciplines as biochemistry, medicine and physiology.

The sources of this book are nutritionists, in the special and meaningful sense of that word. And in the main, they are nutritionists speaking not out of personal opinion, but as spokesmen for groups, in which role they tend to be objective and conservative. They have the kinds of qualifications which, as I have learned in 20 years of reporting and interpreting scientific questions, make them reliable sources—that is, sources as free as possible of self-interest, treacherous extremes and misleading distortions, because what they say is constantly subject to the review and criticism of their colleagues.

Many who press public opinion toward viewpoints which may not be in the public interest make an avocation of discrediting the sources of which I speak. To do so, they commonly resort to vague, winking innuendo that suggests pay-offs, ruthless hidden motives and the like. The American Medical Association is a favorite scapegoat. Yet this is the professional association of the same men to whom you trust your life when you are ill. And while the Association takes on a political role with which you and I may or may not agree, this has nothing to do with its *primary* role, which is the excellence of medical practice and the uplifting of the public health. And in scientific questions of health, the AMA has proven itself as dependable an authority as exists. To whom else should the reporter turn?

The AMA's Council on Foods and Nutrition, frequently referred to in this book, is a committee of experts chosen by their peers and constantly changing. And there are similar committees to which I refer. For example, in 1940 the National Academy of Sciences-National Research Council established its Food and Nutrition Board as an advisory body. It assembles distinguished scientists from all pertinent fields to make some of the judgments of a sort necessary in any science, such as those involved in setting up the well-known Recommended Daily Allowances of modern nutrition. To suggest the scope of this Board, one of its committees—on food protection—includes eight subcommittees with some 60 members.

Other groups which offer composite views of nutritional questions include the American Dietetic Association, the American Dental Association, the American Heart Association, the American Home Economics Association, the Institute of Food Technology, the American Diabetes Association, and such groups of medical specialists as the American Academy of Pediatrics, the American College of Obstetricians and Gynecologists, the Academy of General Practice and others. Such are my primary scientific sources, and in most basic matters of nutrition, they are in agreement. So are what are probably the world's most extensive university faculties in the field, those of Harvard University's School of Public Health and the University of California. I have frequently, both over the years and for the special purpose of this book, sought the guidance of these faculties in writing about nutrition, as I have the other groups I mention. They have always been generous, and in 20 years I have yet to catch them in serious scientific error.

Another group of sources is governmental. It includes the U.S. Department of Agriculture, the U.S. Public Health Service, the National Institutes of Health and the U.S. Food and Drug Administration. Most of the statistical matter in this book derives from the work of these agencies. The World Health Organization and the Food and Agriculture Organization of the United Nations are two other gathering places for reliable information about food and health. None of these agencies is in basic disagreement with my other sources about the vast majority of questions concerning the nutritional sciences. And I would add as valuable resources a number of state university extension services and health agencies.

This long list suggests the panoply of what is sometimes known as "orthodox nutrition." It has its controversies, but it states them plainly. It considers itself neither infallible nor inflexible. Indeed, it is in constant change. The material of this book is largely the base orthodox nutrition has built for its progress toward greater knowledge and health. I cannot find better on which to place my trust, or yours.

Laguna Beach, California R.M.D.
1971

SECTION I

Your Food And Your Health

CHAPTER 1

What you don't know can hurt you

"The plain fact is," the President of the United States told us as he opened the recent White House Conference on Food, Nutrition, and Health, "that a great many Americans are not eating well enough to sustain health."

The statement was appallingly true, those of us knew who had been planning the Conference in the preceding months. And we also knew that the President was not speaking only of the poor. He was talking about the families next door to us, about their youngsters on the way to school and their relatives in comfortable retirement.

We knew that there was plenty of good, healthful food for everyone in America, and that well over 90 percent of the people had the money to buy it. Yet we had read the conclusion of Dr. Arnold Schaefer, who heads the National Nutrition Survey: "We have been alerted by recent studies that our population who are 'malnutrition risks' is beyond anticipated findings, and also that in some of our vulnerable population groups . . . malnutrition is indeed a serious medical problem."

We knew that these groups could not necessarily be delineated by money, by education or social standing. We knew that malnutrition affected millions in very subtle and deceptive ways—and that aside from the direct question of health, the nation's food was the source of enormous economic cheats, as well as unmeasurable needless worry and effort.

True, on the one hand, we faced the stark problems of the poverty-starved minority. But, as the President summed it up, "On the other hand we are dealing with problems of education, habit, taste, behavior, personal preferences."

More specifically, the Conference's panel on popular education, with which the author of this book served, agreed: "It is clear that a great many of our citizens lack the necessary knowledge—both rich and poor, educated and uneducated.... In fact, the gaps in our public knowledge about nutrition, along with actual misinformation carried by some media, are contributing seriously to the problem of hunger and malnutrition in the United States."

In fact, when the author was writing the report to the White House on food deception and misinformation, that panel gave him unanimous approval to begin: *"No other area of the national health probably is as abused by deception and misinformation as is nutrition."*

This book is written to try and bring the best and newest light of science to those real and practical food matters which trouble the typical American family—and which threaten both its good health and its purse, in ways open and carefully hidden, in matters vexingly apparent and insidiously unsuspected. The aim is to provide the knowledge which is the best personal defense against the problems brought out at the White House Conference by doctors, by nutritionists, by educators, by consumer advocates and government agencies, by responsible industry and law enforcement.

Since our troubles with food are real and immediate, the answers in this book are intended to be practical and specific. Where scientific knowledge is not yet complete, and is perhaps controversial still, the author has sought the best-qualified judgments as to sensible, practical action. And he has also tried to present, as clearly as possible, the basic scientific principles and concepts, so that the reader can make his own intelligent judgments about the real choices he faces every day.

For many of the most important problems uncovered were not the kind that can be solved by law or government order, by business reform or scientific discovery. In the long run, eating is a very personal matter. What is needed is personal understanding, personal demand, personal change.

Where food problems lie

What kinds of problems do we face in our food? They were spelled out formally in the panel meetings in Washington. But they were suggested more dramatically in the stories traded by the experts at meals and coffee breaks and late-night rap sessions. These tales formed a melting pot of fact—from significant small incidents and little-known truths to national scandals and the headaches of giant industries.

A billion dollars is being spent each year on the school lunch program, and more is being earmarked. Yet a federal study, detailed in a later chapter, showed that, at a dismaying percentage of the schools, the resulting meals were nutritionally inadequate. Moreover, when the meals were nutritionally correct, the food choices of the students resulted in a tremendous waste of important nutrients and a lunch which fell well short of what they needed.

In a short decade, the national per capita consumption of fruits and vegetables suddenly nosedived a whopping ten percent. Meanwhile, the eating of sometimes questionable snack foods was zooming.

In the 1950s, the physical softness of our schoolchildren became a national worry. Presidential concern had led to a gigantic fitness program. Yet today, the number of obese children seems to have risen not less than a *third*—until one child in five is medically fat, and as many as half the adults in our cities are now overweight.

Worry about fatness has dealt a blow to potato consumption. Yet few people know that, ounce for ounce, a potato is no more fattening than an apple. Experts are worried about the tuber's undeserved bad name—because among its other little-known food values, the potato supplies nearly 20 percent of the nation's vitamin C.

Milk consumption is also dropping because of weight-consciousness. In 1955 an average household drank 46 cups a week of milk in various fluid forms. In only ten years, that number dropped to 39 cups. It is probably two cups lower at this writing, with the greatest drop among adults. The result? We are fatter than ever, anyway. But most Americans, even children, do not get enough calcium in their diets.

Even some of the simplest nutritional matters go begging for attention. Goiter—an enlarged thyroid gland—is thought by many to be a thing of the past. But doctors at the Conference warned there are still "appreciable levels in the so-called 'goiter belts' "—states such as Michigan, Wisconsin, Washington and Oregon. A tiny bit of iodine in our salt stops goiter. "Still," one panel reported, "about half of the table salt sold in this country is not iodized."

As the bits and pieces fitted together at the Conference, it became clear that there are many serious gaps in America's nutrition—and gaps that looked easy indeed to close. Teenage girls, infants, the elderly, pregnant women and breast-feeding mothers were among the most important danger groups.

How false food ideas cheat us

Ironically, Americans probably have greater interest in food and health than ever before. But pathetically, what is perhaps the most acutely concerned group also seems to be among the most seriously endangered and flagrantly cheated.

These are the folk who, by the millions, are convinced that some miraculous elements are being robbed from their food, and that a vicious commerce is cold-bloodedly adding poisons to what they eat. And they are beginning to convince much of the rest of the populace that there is indeed some magic in their "health" foods, their "natural" eating and their self-prescribed pills and supplements—that the supermarket shelves are stocked with what amounts to nutritional hemlock.

Yet, ironically, these worriers are often seriously threatened by their own curious ideas and dietaries. At the Conference there were tragic stories of such people depending on queer eating systems to cure them of deadly diseases such as heart ailments and cancer. Some of their "doctors" actually held that it was never germs which caused disease, but food processing. The author heard many such tales. And they matched his own experiences—such as one meeting with a young woman, who was carrying a baby, and said: "You see, I don't have to expose him to all those awful immunizations. As long as I keep him on a 'mucusless' diet, he can't get polio or measles or anything."

Such appalling ideas, moreover, are increasingly accepted by the progressive and liberated young. By some quirk, "organic" food—a meaningless term—has been adopted into the important ecology and conservation movements.

Needless "health foods" and supplements sell at shocking prices, and the annual bill is running well over a billion dollars. A 20-cent can of applesauce gets to be worth 50 cents with an "organic" label. "Natural" vitamins and minerals can sell for three or four times the cost of the pharmaceutical product, from which they are indistinguishable, except that the "natural" items tend to have less dependable potency and purity.

Yet these cheats are minor compared to others in the food marketplace. At the Conference we listened to reports of weights-and-measures deceptions which are running into billion of dollars, and include grossly inaccurate measuring cups and spoons sold for household use. For example, the Bureau of Standards finds that rarely does a carton of milk hold a full quart, and that meat prices are commonly boosted by packaging techniques. And experts explain that the inability to read food labels commonly results in the housewife's making poor choices for value, an inability exploited to a whopping extent.

We found misleading advertising is a major source of wrong food ideas, and that some overenthusiastic and outmoded nutrition teaching in the schools compounds the problem. In some food areas, such as breakfast, the total impact of the advertising, though it does not actually lie, is misleading to the public.

Again, some simple knowledge can easily make the consumer aware of deception by implication. But again, most of us do not even know that a "minimum daily requirement" is *not* what nutrition scientists actually recommend; that such words as "protein" and "carbohydrate" can embody a wide range of food quality; that some food factors touted on the labels are so common that one can scarcely avoid them if one eats at all; that some nutrients are added to a product not so much to make it better food as to keep it from spoiling.

The degree of misunderstanding was illustrated nicely in a recent attack on the refinement of wheat by an otherwise competent science editor. Among other things, he protested that refining removed 78 percent of the sodium in wheat and that "without sodium to bathe in, the cells of the body will either dry up or swell to the bursting point."

That has a pretty worrisome sound. Unless, of course, you know that wheat is an unimportant source of sodium, that the ordinary diet provides more than twice as much sodium as we need, and that many doctors are concerned that we consume far too much, certainly not too little, with our liberal use of table and cooking salt.

The same author was unhappy at the calcium removed "during the processing of the flour from which white bread is made here in America." Again, nutritional knowledge would have eased his mind, and those of his readers. The typical adult calcium recommendation is 800 milligrams a day (much higher for pregnant women and for children, as much as 1,400 milligrams). A slice of *whole wheat* bread (which is made without the losses complained of) provides some 23 milligrams of calcium, about 2.5 percent of adult need and 1.5 percent for a growing boy.

White bread, even if *un*enriched, provides some 19 milligrams of calcium a slice. So a slice of whole wheat bread yields four extra milligrams of calcium. That difference, all that the writer is worried about, is about the amount of calcium in the quantity of milk which dribbles down a typical child's chin.

(These values are true as this book goes to press.

However, the reader should know that a vastly more important enrichment program is planned for bread, which would include substantial amounts of calcium and other nutrients. With such bolstered enrichment, enriched white bread would become far more nutritionally impressive than ordinary whole-grain bread in a number of ways.)

This kind of error is not only a commonplace in the public prints; it is of a very minor order. Recently, one so-called "nutrition expert" was given some pages in a national magazine which serves at least eight million American women. He was calling for gross dietary changes, slashing carbohydrate consumption to the bone. (The dangers of so doing are cited in a later chapter on weight reduction.) His reason was a claimed national plague of *hypoglycemia* (low blood sugar) with some ten million victims. Curiously, however, the American Medical Association said the nation's doctors were aware of no such problem. And medical textbooks, while referring to hypoglycemia, gave its incidence as quite small and its causes as tumors of the liver and other disease states, not dietary error.

How food knowledge can protect you

While false alarms trouble the food consumer almost to distraction at times, and while loud boasts and tricky claims pick his pocket and peril his good health, many a real problem goes unsolved.

For example, most of us do not know the facts of foodborne illness. We do not realize how many incidents of digestive upset, often debilitating, are the result of estimated millions of cases of salmonella infection. We do not know that much of these, and other similar infections, can be prevented. It is the rare American who even knows, when he confronts a leftover in the refrigerator, that the more serious forms of spoilage or infection rarely reveal themselves through odor, taste or appearance.

There is a persistent theme that runs through nearly all the problems of adequate diet, of food wholesomeness and safety, of food choice and the deceptive marketplace. It is that most of the time, simple scientific knowledge and common sense are all that we need to protect us.

To provide that knowledge is the first purpose of this book, with answers to the day-to-day concerns about food, the questions which automatically arise as choices are made. Is the food I am putting on my family's table tonight giving them maximum support for making the most of their bodies? Is it safe from disease and from poisons? Does this package really contain all the food value it is implied to offer? Did I pay too much? Why do I seem to keep getting fatter no matter what I eat? Is there something I can do to keep my children from having to fight the overweight battle all their lives? Should I let my teenage daughter diet? How far should I really go with all this cholesterol talk? What am I doing that gives me indigestion or constipation so often? Should we all be taking vitamins?

The book's second and no less important aim is to provide the reader with the knowledge of common problems which are more or less concealed from most consumers. Here are the unpublicized marketplace cheats and the important facts veiled by vague and technical labels. Here are the invisible threats of foodborne illness, the little-known dangers of certain common self-treatments for digestive ills, the facts of hidden ailments in the digestive tract, the widely accepted myths and superstitions about eating. Here, in fact, is a lamentably little-known shadow world of food and health. Here is the truth of how government protects us in ways many of us do not even suspect, and how it does not protect us in ways which most of us mistakenly expect.

The author's effort has been to compile, from the best available sources of science, commerce, technology and government, answers to the questions most asked about food and health—and to other questions which, most Americans are unaware, *need* to be asked.

Plainly, not all the answers are complete or final, nor are they likely to become so in our time. But we must still make practical choices. Food is life, and life will not wait. So here are the best judgments for this moment in time, as made by the men and women whose training and experience permit them to choose with reason and with knowledge. It is the author's fond hope that thus will the reader be enabled to do the same.

CHAPTER 2

How well do you eat?

Nutritionists agree that the typical American dietary, as supplied from supermarket shelves, incorporates all that the human body needs, and in plenitude. But most of us, hearing this, wonder.

After all, we are not necessarily typical. Do our own special tastes and distastes allow us good nutrition? Maybe we won't eat salads or fish. Maybe we can't pass up a candy counter. Maybe the thought of breakfast turns us cold. Maybe we can't make do with less than ten cups of coffee a day, or three or four snacks.

Do our individual styles or beliefs block us from good eating? Maybe we live alone and hate to bother about meals. Maybe religious or spiritual dictates—from kosher rules to vegetarianism—direct our choices.

Do personal health problems distort our dietaries? Are we in nutritional trouble because we eat so as to manage our ulcers or allergies, chronic digestive problems, gout, diabetes, heart disease, skin diseases, acne, high blood pressure or overweight?

Check your diet for health

The American Medical Association's Dr. Philip L. White, who directs the Association's Department of Foods and Nutrition, has developed a simple, practical way to find out whether our personal dietaries provide all that we should have in the way of nutrients. Somewhat adapted and detailed here, his quiz can tell you much about where you and your family stand nutritionally.

Start with yesterday, and match what you ate to the food groups listed. Remember, *serving sizes* are important. Note them well. A serving of meat, for example, is only three ounces on this test. So if you ate a nine-ounce steak, it scores as three servings. If you had a skimpy meat sandwich, it may well have been less than a three-ounce serving, so put down a fraction. But don't forget that the two slices of sandwich bread make two servings from the bread-and-cereal group—or that the small pat of butter or margarine on bread should be scored in the "fat" group.

If you want to take a little more trouble, you can get much more accurate information about the adequacy of your eating by following the method used by nutritionists when they take dietary case histories. Since one day is probably not really typical, they try to get a detailed picture of three days or more. Using this method, you can get a clearer idea of your own average food intake, and apply that average to the scoring chart which follows.

You should record the number of servings you have eaten, in each category.

Food Group	Day 1	Day 2	Day 3
A. Milk or Milk Products. (In cups) One cup of milk or yogurt or 1½ cups of cottage cheese or two-three scoops of ice cream, or a serving of hard cheese (such as Cheddar) equal to about a one-inch cube.	___	___	___
B. High-Protein Foods. (Servings) A serving is a three-ounce portion of any meat, fish or poultry, or two eggs. These can be alternated with a cup of dry peas or dry beans or lentils, with four tablespoons of peanut butter or the 60-odd nuts used to make the butter. Cheese may also be used here if it is not used in Group A.	___	___	___
C. Green and/or Yellow Vegetables. (Servings) A half cup is a typical serving. Dark-green or deep-yellow vegetables are the best sources of the several nutrients supplied by these foods.	___	___	___

Food Group	Day 1	Day 2	Day 3
D. Citrus Fruits, Tomatoes, and Other Good Sources of Vitamin C. (Servings) A serving is six ounces of citrus juice, with more of tomato juice preferred, an orange or half grapefruit, two generous cups of frozen lemonade, or a medium tomato. Two-thirds cup of strawberries can be a replacement, a sixth of a medium watermelon, or half a papaya. Or, if you have extra servings from some foods in Group C, they can be applied here, in one-cup amounts of raw cabbage, collards, kale, kohlrabi, mustard greens, spinach and turnip greens.	___	___	___
E. Potatoes and Other Fruits and Vegetables. (Servings) A serving is a medium potato, ear of corn, apple, banana or usually about one-half cup of such items as cooked, canned or frozen carrots, peaches, pineapple, apricots, beets, lima beans, cauliflower, small salad portion of lettuce, etc.	___	___	___
F. Bread, Flour and Cereals. (Servings) One serving is a slice of bread, an ounce of ready-to-eat breakfast cereal, one-half to three-fourths cup of cooked breakfast cereal, cornmeal, grits, macaroni, noodles, rice, spaghetti, a two-inch biscuit, three-inch cookie, slice of cake, or muffin. (All baked goods should be made with enriched or whole-grain flour; otherwise they may not do their job in this group.) A doughnut, four-inch pancake or half a waffle also serve.	___	___	___
G. Butter or Margarine. (A serving is a tablespoon.)	___	___	___
H. Fluids. (One-cup servings) Includes all primarily water-based drinks, such as water, milk, fruit juice, beer, coffee, tea, ades, carbonated soft drinks.	___	___	___
I. Sugar Foods. (Servings) One serving is interpreted as three teaspoons of added sugar (as to coffee, fruit), a half-ounce of hard candy, marshmallow, caramel, slightly more chocolate. One tablespoon of honey, molasses, two one-inch mints, a tablespoon of syrup (chocolate, maple, corn, etc.), jam or jelly.	___	___	___

What your diet score means

Now score yourself, or any other member of the family except the very young child, against this scale:

Food Group	School Child	Preteen & Teen	Adult	Aging Adult	Your Score
A	2–3	3–4 or more	2 or more	2 or more	——
B	1–2	3 or more	2 or more	2 or more	——
C	1–2	2	2	1 (at least)	——
D	1	1–2	1	1–2	——
E	1	1	1	0–1	——
F	3–4	4 or more	3–4	2–3	——
G	2	2–4	2–3	1–2	——
H	3–4	3–5	3–5	3–5	——
I	None Needed	None Needed	None Needed	None Needed	——

What can you learn from your score? First of all, any excess over the suggested amounts is acceptable, or even desirable, provided only that the total number of daily calories is not making you gain weight.

The absence of any of the groups (except "I") may leave you with an important nutritional deficiency, as follows:

Protein is the primary value of Group B and one of the main values of A. A deficiency here is most serious. For while the other groups provide some proteins, they are of a relatively minor quantity and quality. Many Americans do not get much dairy protein, but they more than make up with Group B proteins, which can be just as good. In fact, a Group B serving has approximately twice as much protein as a Group A serving. So if you are lacking in Group A, you can erase the protein minus for one A serving with half a B serving.

But other special values in Group A are harder to replace. For example, the calcium content. This is especially important to growing children and the aging and pregnant or breast-feeding women. They would require more than two cups of broccoli to replace one cup of milk. Four eggs or 15 slices of bread would also be replacements. The total calcium in the overall dietary might be made up (in ways which will become clear as you read this book), but it is hard to be sure. And nutritionists are worried about serious calcium shortages in the national dietary.

In cold-climate winters, milk is the best of very few sources of the needed vitamin D. Other merits of milk —besides calcium, and vitamin D in that special occasion—are more likely to be balanced off by good, varied eating.

The proteins that Group B provides are very hard to make up for, without consuming a great deal of Group A or *very* large amounts of low-protein foods. An adult, for example, might get the quantity of necessary protein from about 30 slices of bread or 30 servings of spaghetti. But even then the *quality* would probably be inadequate. (Low-protein foods tend to have a narrow range of the essential amino acids and thus are of poor protein quality.)

Missing servings of the vegetables in Group C is common. They can be replaced by other foods, but it takes knowledge and care. The national problem of insufficient iron is partially due to the common absence of deep-green vegetables. And other reasons for the importance of Group C will appear as you read, along with the ways you can compensate for missing servings with other food groups.

Groups D and E are easier to make up for, *sometimes* by exchanges with one another. But again, you ought to know what you are doing to avoid subtle and meaningful losses. If the Group C fruits and vegetables are missing, too, real deficiencies can occur. Even aside from the nutrient values, the lack of bulk can create problems with mechanical digestion and elimination.

In the usual American dietary, the grains of Group F are not usually missing. But as weight-consciousness grows, so does a mistaken avoidance of this group. We will see that this food group is not just "starch" as many people believe it to be. Its values can be replaced by a mix from the vegetable and protein groups, in terms of B vitamins, iron, calcium and the like. But it is a lot safer just to use Group F foods.

The fats of the G group are easily replaced by those in milk products, meats, eggs and the like. Yet the G group is included as a safety factor, for fats are essential to good nutrition. (In practice, Americans tend to use too much fat, as we shall see in discussions of overweight and heart disease.)

There are ways to get around the need for extra fluids, such as those listed in Group H. Many of our foods—milk, meats, fruits and vegetables—have most of their weight in water. But we shall see that man is still, in many ways, a kind of sea creature. His own weight is still mainly water, and the balancing of that water content is essential to his health. Myths and superstitions cause quite a few Americans, very mistakenly, to cut back on fluids in certain situations, such as in weight reduction. These cutbacks are not only useless but risky.

Group I is a major source of food energy in America. We have a sweet tooth. Concern about fatness has caused us to cut back on fats and on high-carbohydrate vegetables such as corn, beans and potatoes. But our per capita use of sugar stays the same, now adding up to well over 20 billion pounds a year. If you are a typical American, you are taking in close to 100 pounds of plain sugar a year. While sugars—and other sweeteners such as honey and syrups—do supply pure energy value, they carry practically nothing else with them. The same energy value in other foods confers important nutrient bonuses, often in areas in which many of us tend to be lacking. As pleasant as Group I is, we don't really need it.

From this quick review, you can get an idea of how adequately you and your family eat, according to the best understanding of modern science. If your eating is nutritionally adequate or even better, do bear in mind that excess has its own dangers. Be sure to check your weight by the newer methods described in the weight-control chapters. Don't make the mistake of relying on old height-weight charts. And you should know that, even if your weight stays the same, your percentage of fatness may be changing considerably, creating extra health risk.

It should be clear that Dr. White designed this test with a double purpose. It is to tell you what is going wrong and how to make it right. Unless you have some special health problem, or are a pregnant or nursing woman, *a matching score means that you are getting every nutrient you need to make the most of our body's hereditary potential.*

Special foods and supplements cannot maximize your potential any further. And they cannot change it. If you are able to match this recommended dietary, moreover, and you have some health complaint, it is unlikely that any food or food supplement will produce a cure.

Doctors do use foods and diets in their treatment, of course. But rarely is this the only therapy. We shall see in detail what foods can and cannot do for illness. For the moment, it is well to take note of this statement by the Council on Foods and Nutrition of the American Medical Association, a statement confirmed by all of responsible nutrition science:

"The term 'health food' and equivalent claims or statements to the effect that food gives, or assures health are vague, misinformative and misleading. An adequate or complete diet and the recognized nutritional essentials established by the science of nutrition are necessary for health, but health depends on many other factors provided by such diet, or nutritional essentials. No one food alone is essential for health. There are no health foods."

Does your diet match your neighbor's?

It might be interesting to get some idea of how your nutrition score matches up to American averages. So here are the most recent findings of the U.S. Department of Agriculture on what the average American adult does in fact take home from the market. These findings are here broken down according to the food groupings in our test, with the amounts transposed to the serving measures we have used. These scores are based on averages for adult men and women between the ages of 20 and 34. Childhood dietaries are looked at more closely in a later chapter. The fractions are approximate, to simplify your reading and comparison.

		Men	Women	Your Score
Group A:	Milk Products	1⅓	⅞	——
Group B:	Meats, Eggs, High-Protein Foods	5	3¼	——
Group C:	Green and Yellow Vegetables	1/7	1/7	——
Group D:	Citrus Fruits, Tomatoes, and Others as Above	⅓	⅓	——
Group E:	Potatoes and Other Fruits and Vegetables	1½	1	——
Group F:	Breads, Flour and Cereals	7–8	5–6	——
Group G:	Butter or Margarine	1¼	¾	——
(Note: other fats and oils consumed double the average servings shown above.)		(1¾)	(¾)	——
Group H:	Fluids	3	2½	——
(Note: research on fluids is not complete because it does not include water, milk, juices or alcoholic drinks.)				
Group I:	Sugar Foods	3	2¼	——

These scores make the pattern of America's food choices relatively clear. We are obviously a protein-eating people, and grain-cereal eaters with a sweet tooth. The fruits and vegetables which our land yields so plentifully go begging. The result is that many Americans' nutrition is rated as poor or minimal in some respect.

Why minimal nutrition can be unsafe

Exact information on how food omissions affect health in America is woefully lacking. At this writing, some of the first good studies of nutrition and health are under way. Yet even these are aimed, not at the average American, but at the poor.

Most of our existing information, for example, is based on how much food was *available* within the famly, not so much on what was actually eaten, and by whom. But recently, three researchers surveyed the dietary food studies we do have and formed a composite picture for the *Journal of Nutrition Education*.

That picture was measured against the "recommended dietary allowance" calculations established by the Food and Nutrition Board of the National Research Council. This board represents the best that the nation can muster in informed nutritional fact and opinion. It reviews all nutritional and medical knowledge, to set safe standards of dietary practice and intake and resolve scientific controversy in the field. RDA levels, in the words of the board, are "a formulation of nutrient allowances for daily consumption . . . adequate for the maintenance of good nutrition." These levels are the ones used by nearly all nutritionists in planning and assaying diets.

RDA levels are not minimums. They are designed with a safety margin "planned to provide a buffer against the needs of various stresses and to make possible other potential improvements of growth and function."

How important is that buffer? It can be crucial. Food needs vary with stress. That stress can be due to work, weather, disease, injury or emotion.

Some of these problems can be seen most clearly in children. When a child gets an acute infectious disease—such as pneumonia, tonsillitis or rheumatic fever—his levels of vitamin A drop. Even vaccination against smallpox or measles can have this effect.

Intestinal inflammations of the most common type change B vitamin use. Levels of ascorbic acid drop in such infections as flu, malaria, measles, tuberculosis and typhoid. Experts believe such phenomena are common, though not a great many diseases have yet been studied in this light.

The body's protein needs and its use of protein vary significantly when infection strikes, or as a result of injuries or surgery. Many people realize this, but are not aware of the profound effects that emotion can have on nutrition. One woman in a hospital was getting a very carefully controlled amount of protein and doing fine, when she suddenly got word that her son had been wounded in combat. All at once she went into what is known as *negative nitrogen balance,* indicating a lack of dietary protein. A week later, still on the same diet, she heard that the boy was safe and sound, and she swung into positive balance. Like effects have been measured in MIT students during final examinations. And in one striking test, subjects on a scientifically controlled feeding formula which they did not like developed negative nitrogen balance. When exactly the same protein was given to them in a food form they liked, the balance became positive.

Such facts suggest why scientists do not consider nutritional minimums to be enough. Counting on those minimums to protect us is a little like calculating just how much water one ought to use on a long hike, and then setting out across the desert with not a drop more. You're in fine shape as long as everything goes as expected. But what if the temperature rises, if there's a hill you hadn't counted on, if you miss the trail, if you sprain an ankle?

Yet on most food packages, the percentages of human need are stated, not in terms of the RDA, but in terms of the MDR. This "minimum daily requirement" level of nutrition was established by the Food and Drug Administration to try and clear up some of the confusion about marketing claims. An MDR is a level required to prevent symptoms of actual deficiency, with a *small* safety margin.

Now that we have some understanding of RDA and MDR, it should be fairly plain why those who study the nutrition of various groups match dietaries against the RDA. (The full charting of these allowances may be found in Appendix A of this book.) Let us see what the composite of American diet surveys showed.

What does America's diet lack?

More than half the subjects surveyed in some 25 different studies had food intakes which gave them less than RDA levels of calcium, iron, thiamine (a B vitamin) and vitamin C. Almost half were lacking in niacin (another B vitamin). Over 40 percent got too little riboflavin (a third vitamin B factor). And about a third were missing RDA levels of vitamin A. For the most part, these seven nutrients, of about 50 known to be needed in human nutrition, were the only ones studied.

At this writing, Department of Agriculture officials say many problem areas are not getting better, but worse. For example, in ten years our household consumption of milk, milk products, fruits and vegetables dropped about ten percent.

In 1955, only 60 percent of the families surveyed had met federal definitions of good diet. In 1965, with income and food expenditure up, only 50 percent of the families rated "good," a decline of some 17 percent.

In 1955, on the other hand, "poor" ratings were given to the diets of 15 percent of this American family sampler. Ten years later, the number rated "poor" was 21 percent, an increase of 40 percent.

Was money the key to good diet? Not necessarily. Experts have concluded that education is the real key, and that richer families' diets look better in part because these tend also to be better-educated families. Even so, about ten percent of those in the top financial group were given "poor" ratings.

It is true that there were three times as many "poor" diet ratings among those at the poverty end of the scale, with family incomes of less than $3,000 a year. But a third of those families nevertheless managed to earn "good" ratings, while spending far less at the grocery store. The poor proved that people could eat well on no more than one dollar a day per person.

Our nutrition does not seem to be making much headway as our incomes rise. We spend a decreasing percentage of our pay to eat; the national average is now down well below 20 percent, and at $15,000 a year it is only 12 percent of income.

Nutritionally, our food selection grows narrower, too. With the average number of kinds of products sold in our supermarkets up in the last 20 years from 3,000 to more than 8,000, we manage to get less real nutritional variety.

More and more, we become beef eaters; ham, pork, lamb and veal appear less and less in the shopping cart, though our poultry consumption is up. We eat fewer eggs; breakfast is becoming more and more the forgotten meal. The USDA reports that the standard American breakfast for adults tends to be toast and coffee; for children, it is cereal and milk. (This breakfast change also helps account for the decline in pork products used.)

The amount of wheat used for consumer products is down about a pound a year per person. Corn consumption is rising, but much of this is due to the use of corn syrup as a sweetener, and so we do not get the nutritive value of much of that corn.

Money seems to buy us more snacks, which supply us with a big share of our calories and quite a small share of our needed nutrients. We are now spending well over *two billion dollars* a year on potato chips, pretzels, corn chips, nuts, crackers and similar snacks. And we wash them down with about half a billion dollars' worth of *diet* soft drinks alone, not to mention the hundreds of millions of cases of regular soda pop.

Not that snacking itself is so bad. But our snack choices are quite questionable.

The big boom in fats

One of the major indications of these changes is that we are increasingly a nation of fat eaters. We fry a great deal of our food, especially treats, snacks and eating-out or take-home meals. Any American who thinks about it is probably conscious that the explosion in take-out food stands has become really big business, and that the food sold is very often cooked in fat—fried chicken, fried potatoes, fried fish, fried shrimp, fried Chinese noodles. Sold along with it is food very heavy in fat content—gravy, pie, biscuits, ice cream, cheesecake, pizza.

Many people do not realize, however, that other popular foods which are thought of as high-protein are also fat-rich. Beef, for example, is fat meat. Commonly, more of its calories are in fat than protein. And our love affairs with the hamburger and hot dog are fatty relationships. The standard serving of ground beef in the "regular market mix" provides about 285 calories. Of these calories, more than 180 are in fat. And food stands and coffee shops are often not loath to use a fatter grind. It still makes an "all beef" burger.

Our huge consumption of luncheon sausage products is crowned by the fat of the frankfurter. But on the way up the scale, an ounce of all-meat bologna has 16 calories in protein, 63 in fat; an ounce of liverwurst gives you 20 calories in protein, 72 in fat; and most pork luncheon meats are similarly composed. Dry salami, in an ounce, offers 28 calories in protein, about 100 in fat. And a hot dog which contains 24 calories in protein drips with fat to the tune of 126 calories.

As a reference point, one ounce of luncheon meat is only one slice, or perhaps just a little more. A slice doesn't make much of a sandwich, so we double, triple or quadruple it. As a further reference point, the recommended dietary allowance (RDA) for an average adult's protein offers about 240 calories. So when luncheon meats are used as an important protein source, we take in a lot of fat. To get all our protein from hot dogs alone, for example, we would have to eat about ten a day, and this would give us fat with a caloric value of 1,260 calories!

Such factors add up to a damaging distortion of many Americans' dietaries. And that distortion is costly. For as we shall soon see, when we discuss weight control, the body has remarkable automatic controls over appetite. These controls appear to restrict our eating to just about the quantity of food we need to survive and function. So when we load our meals and snacks with the concentrated caloric values of fats, we narrow the slots into which foods carrying other vitally needed nutrients must fit.

How habits and tastes change our nutrition

America is changing its food culture. And the new meal patterns seem to be those that lead away from good nutrition.

Today, reassured by certain kinds of advertising, soothed by the thought that she and her husband are getting too fat anyway, Mother plugs in the breakfast coffee pot and tells the kids to pour some dry cereal into a bowl. If she is food-conscious, she may stir some orange-flavored powder into water (mentally equating its sugar calories and vitamin C to orange juice). Then, believing that she is covering any nutritional gaps, she hands multivitamin pills all around.

Here we have one reason for the growing importance of the coffee break: it is simple hunger. Dinner last night was at six. By 10 A.M. this morning, 16 hours have passed since the last true meal. So we fill in with coffee and sugar and a sweet pastry.

Lunch at noon is very likely to be a fat-rich hamburger and French fries, a sandwich of fatty luncheon meats or the like. A slice of lettuce and/or tomato may be the concession to the fruit-and-vegetable world.

If the man of the house is in a really good job, one of his rewards may be the expense-account lunch. This lets him have the more carefully prepared sauces and baked goods, which his wife is less and less likely to make at home. He can also indulge a taste for fatty steak and roast beef. He may even, as a concession to his widening waistband, leave the potato and peas on his plate. They, he thinks, are "starchy" and therefore "fattening." That way he can have room for dessert. He may even add a little cottage cheese, since that is "slimming."

Of course, if he orders some specialty dish from the large menu, something else may happen. Unknown to him, many good restaurants now buy prepared and frozen menu-enlargers. They are popped into an electronic oven and quickly brought to serving condition. The packagers prefer to save on expensive meat and extend the meal cheaply by using much fat in sauces or breadings—which also have the merit of covering the degraded texture and flavor of the frozen meat and vegetables (which may not be nutritionally injured but usually taste as if they are).

The same thing is true of many of the convenience foods which are purchased by his wife. Butter or cheese sauces are common ways to distract from the lack of fresh-tasting quality. In the TV dinner, for example, the processor has to do *something* to make the dehydrated mashed or sliced potatoes taste a little better, or taste at all. The nutrition is largely there, but gravy, or *au gratin* sauce or hollandaise, or seasoned and fat-thickened stuffing, becomes essential to consumer acceptance. These ingredients also add nicely to bulk and net weight at low cost. Pure starches also help to thicken up the meal. The result is the food "feel" to which we are becoming accustomed.

"Convenience" food can magnify the problem

Let us look at what is actually going on inside some packages of convenience foods, especially the main dishes. To suggest how they meet our appetite demands, we will measure their components in terms of caloric value.

Frozen beef goulash, in one sampling, offers about 85 calories in protein, 67 in carbohydrate, 113 in fat. "Sliced beef with gravy" has 80 calories in protein, 20 in carbohydrate, 118 in fat.

Perhaps we want to go low-calorie. So we turn to less fatty meats of poultry or fish. We buy turkey with "dressing and gravy": 96 calories in protein, 62 in carbohydrate, 100 in fat. The haddock comes with cream sauce: 83 calories in protein, 29 in carbohydrate, 81 in fat. The shrimp is "Newburg," and it gives us 55 calories of protein, 31 of carbohydrate and 138 in fat.

In still more of a hurry, we might go to a main dish in a can, or in a combination package with a dry premix to which hot water is added. Chicken a la king provides about 84 calories in protein, 40 in carbohydrate and 252 calories of fat. Chili con carne (without the beans) offers 83 calories in protein, 46 in carbohydrate and 265 in fat.

We omit main dishes which have noodles or vegetables as part of the package. We keep to those to which one is likely to add a carbohydrate such as rice, potato or noodle (with a fat such as butter to make them more palatable), a vegetable, beverage and dessert.

Note that the convenience main dishes honestly provide what would be a third of our protein for the day (as adults). But look at the fats and carbohydrates which we must take with them. And remember that we may have already omitted any important protein source from one meal of the day (breakfast) and eaten a fatty lunch. The built-in potential for dietary distortion becomes quite clear.

The reader should not be misled in one respect, that of the hoped-for protein content of the day's food. Contrary to what many people believe, under very good conditions, protein will make up only about 15 percent—certainly no more than 20 percent—of the dietary. Aside from the useful, but nonnutritive, factors we eat—such as fiber, water and ash—the rest of our food *must* be divided between fats and carbohydrates as the vast bulk of nutrient weight.

The trouble with many convenience protein foods is that they are already heavy with fats and carbohydrates. We want and need the latter dietary elements, but we must demand some extra benefits with them. When the carbohydrate, for example, is pure vegetable starch, it is perhaps taking up meal space that might go into a serving of carrots.

Those carrots give us about 30 calories in carbohydrate. They also give us a gram of vegetable protein, which helps assure important protein variety. And with them comes a bonus of a good deal of calcium, ten percent of our vitamin C, small but meaningful percentages of needed B vitamins, some iron and a day's supply of vitamin A. They also confer some crude fiber which our intestines need to function well.

If this makes the carrot sound like a miracle food—and some people think it is—be disabused. Almost any vegetable in the produce section has a cluster of food values, as we shall later see. In most cases, there is a good reason or two why the plant has been selected from the vast vegetable world for preservation, improvement and mass cultivation.

But we are losing the habit of vegetables—commonly using them as little more than a garnish. The day's food *feels* right without the half or two-thirds cup of vegetable which nutritionists consider a serving. And a tablespoon or two of vegetable—such as we are likely to see in the prepackaged meal at home or out—just isn't the same.

The vegetable decline and the mounting heap of fat on the national table are only examples of a broad trend toward distortion. And the children are being trained to carry that lamentable trend still further.

Are the children protected?

There is a tendency in this country to believe that our young are shielded from nutritional folly in a number of ways. In some respects, they are. Their milk, for example, covers a multitude of nutritive sins. And their breakfast cereal has been likened by more than one nutritionist to a multivitamin dose with sugar, which helps to sweeten that milk.

But what happens when milk-drinking stops with childhood, if they follow our example? What happens when the school lunch program stops protecting them? Our children become settled into the questionable nutrition rut we have plowed.

We spend over a billion dollars a year on school lunch programs in the belief that we may thus assure at least some portion of nutritive excellence to the young, regardless of errors at home. We are going to spend more. Breakfasts are being added, experimentally, to school programs, and in some poverty areas dinners are being tried.

It is a noble and impressive effort. Nineteen million children benefit. The Type A Lunch, as it is known, is a complete package aimed at supplying two-thirds of the food needs (as RDA) of the child for the day.

But recent random samplings have shown some nutritional gaps in the school lunches. Researchers from the Agriculture Research Service of the USDA literally took actual samples from the lunch counters of 300 test schools, randomly selected. By and large, the program offered good lunches, and yet:

Fifteen percent of the lunches were lacking in calcium, and a few lacked thiamin, from the B vitamin family. Two-thirds of the lunches were low in iron. A third fell below the goal for vitamin A. And more than a third of the schools had lunches that were well above desirable levels for fat.

In other words, even with some scientific control, the lunches tended to make nutritional errors along the national pattern. Still, they weren't bad—as they were put on the trays. Then the researchers, who had weighed the food going out on the plates, weighed the discards coming back in.

What was actually entering the young mouths? For the most part, youngsters ate the main dishes well, dishes planned to accommodate their tastes, such as spaghetti with meat sauce, smoked sausage and frankfurter with chili. (One can see where some of the extra fats came from.) But they left nearly half the vegetables and a third of the fruits, as well as "substantial amounts of other foods." Moreover, the vegetables they did eat, by weight, excluded certain leafy classes to a large extent. "Tossed salad," the report reads, "cabbage slaw and spinach went largely uneaten."

The lunches looked pretty good on paper, in other words. But the report tells us that the amounts of certain nutrients "actually received were drastically reduced."

Again, remember that the fat content, a serious concern to medicine, already tended to be high. With the omission of the rejected foods, one can deduce that the fat percentage of what was actually consumed went sky-high.

Why? Comments Dr. Ruth Leverton, who coordinates human nutrition research for USDA: "The school lunch is definitely a soft-sell program, and yet many of its customers believe that only things promoted by . . . hard-sell technique are worthy of their attention."

Other nutritionists point out that the children also bring with them food habits learned from the model and the experience of their own families. A great many, in fact, are not interested in a lunch which looks like a Type A Lunch; it is off their nutritional path. So they bring or buy luncheon-meat sandwiches instead.

(It should be added that the school lunch program is still a long way from reaching all children. We will, painfully, gloss over the grim, cold-blooded politics and parsimony with which the states deny millions of free lunches to poor children, to avoid contributing dollars. Hopefully, new plans forged at the White House Conference will be executed to feed our hungry youngsters. But even the middle-class child is commonly denied even the present benefits of the nutritive school lunch. This is especially true in the grade schools, which at this writing make up 90 percent of the schools which have no facilities to serve the lunches.)

Do we want to return to the good old days?

Myriads of cranks, quacks and faddists are now promoting the idea that our nutritional past was a glory of "natural" healthful eating to which we must return for food salvation. We will soon look at some of these ideas more closely. But in general, we must say that the "good old days" are a myth.

Just before World War I, for example, rickets, beriberi, pellagra and goiter—all extremely serious nutrition-deficiency diseases—were, according to American Medical Association conclusions, "common diseases in the United States." These are no longer even tabulated as causes of death in this country, but they were a couple of generations ago.

The fact is that in 1900, the infant death rate was over 162 per 1,000. Today it is less than 25 per 1,000. A better nutrition indicator, however, is the mortality rate between one and four years. In 1900 it was about 20 per 1,000. That rate has now been reduced by more than 95 percent! Moreover, children reach their mature height five years sooner than they did in 1900, and grow three to six inches taller.

Of course, much of the life saving is due to infectious-disease control and modern drugs. Faddists say that drugs would be less necessary if children ate better, but this is a specious idea.

Today we can see in less developed countries, with "natural" diets, how much less effective are all our drugs in the face of the "natural" deficiencies.

Other food cranks try to wave aside our greater longevity as having nothing to do with improved nutrition.

They say the figures are averages, and that they have been raised solely by the reduction in child deaths. But the fact is that since 1900 we have lengthened life by more than 20 years. Percentage-wise, our senior population is now some two and a half times greater than in 1900.

So experts unanimously agree that we do not want to go back. We have come far. The nutritional hazards and problems we face now are new barriers to still longer life, more useful years and the maximum realization of what we can be.

The question of what harm is being done by errors of eating today is a blurry and complex one in some respects. Doctors see little of the old kind of frank nutritional disease.

Even among our economically poor, the damage is more subtle, as Dr. Arnold Schaefer is finding in his Public Health Service surveys. The frank physical signs of vitamin D deficiency, among children who come mainly from homes with less than $3,000 of annual income, is less than four percent. A few of these children show protein-calorie malnutrition or goiter, and fewer show vitamin A lacks in physical symptoms.

Laboratory tests show more. They reveal some low vitamin levels in blood serum, some growth retardation and some anemia.

These problems are serious and urgent matters, and programs have been designed to meet them. For the most part, they tend to be vestiges of the past, holdovers from old injustices, which are being redressed.

What of the population mainstream, however? Are you likely to see medical signs of malnutrition in your own family?

Let us look quickly at what these signs may be.

The physical signs of poor nutrition

Putting matters in a positive light first, here is a recent AMA simplification of the physical signs of *good* nutrition:

1. A general appearance of vitality and well-being.

2. A sturdy, well-shaped skeletal frame.
3. Well-formed teeth and healthy gums.
4. A muscular structure which is strong, well developed and properly balanced so that posture is generally erect.
5. A well-rounded body contour suggestive of sufficient, but not excessive, subcutaneous fat which provides moderate padding for protection of the muscles and skeleton.
6. Adequate bodily functions, such as good appetite, digestion, elimination, physical endurance, nervous stability and prompt and adequate recovery from fatigue or other stress.
7. Clear, smooth skin and mucous membranes. . . .
8. Physical measurements of height, weight and body composition . . . [which meet] standards of growth and development. . . .

The trouble with virtually all these characteristics is that the absence of any of them is not necessarily the result of bad nutrition. With the exception of fatness and some body measurements, none of these nutrition indicators can stand alone. They are cited here to show how nearly impossible it is for the average American today to spot very much wrong with his nutrition by looking at his body. The signs are too vague, and when they do appear, they are such as might result from any of a hundred causes.

The price of nutritional error today is more hidden, less direct. Among the hidden results of less-than-adequate nutrition are anemias, especially among women. Typically, these are recognized only through blood tests, for the symptoms are the shadowy ones of weakness, fatigue, perhaps a little shortness of breath. The national deficiency of dietary iron makes us fairly certain that mild anemias are very common.

Some doctors refer to these marginal deficiency ailments as "hidden hungers." There is not enough wrong to raise a sense of alarm. One does not feel sprightly, perhaps, or seems to lack the energy to do all one would like, or to stay with a project as long as one would like. And under stress, from emotional strain or infection or a heart attack, one does not hold up well or recover easily.

The author is almost reluctant to suggest the problem of "hidden hunger." For a little neurosis, or even a little imagination, can seize upon the idea as all-explaining for minor discomfort or depression. And the quack element of nutrition has long exploited the concept. But the fact is, what we eat can have an important effect on our physical reserves. It can also keep us from hitting the top of our physical game. In the simplest terms, for example, numbers of studies have shown that both youngsters and adults feel better and perform better in the morning when they eat a reasonable sort of breakfast.

Doctors also see in our present nutrition errors the seeds of suffering later in life. Most believe that our excessive dietary distortion toward fats and sugars speeds up the narrowing and clogging of arteries, which is a plague of middle and late years. The results include peripheral vascular disease, which is the narrowing of small blood vessels in the extremities causing, among other things, varicose veins; the gradual shutdown of brain arteries which hastens senility and sets the stage for stroke; the failure of kidneys; high blood pressure; heart attacks; and even the fading of the senses.

Scientists now understand, as we shall explain, how eating patterns in the first years of life can condemn a child to a lifetime struggle with overweight, and this seems to be happening more and more. We will later look at our national fattening trend. As one indicator of how early obesity now begins, Dr. Charlotte Young of Cornell University found that of 325 college freshmen, 23 percent of the boys and 35 percent of the girls were medically overweight.

There are literally dozens of serious ailments associated with overweight—especially the triad of obesity-diabetes-heart disease. Our fatness is a plague. And our dietary proclivities make the plague almost incurable.

In aging, a key problem is osteoporosis, the absence of enough calcium in the bones. What causes this? Researchers are not sure. But they have suspicions involving dietary calcium deficiencies and lacks of the micronutrients which enable the body to use calcium.

The examples are many. But the defense against food failures is essentially simple. It is an understanding of how our food affects our lives.

Dr. Elmer V. McCollum, one of the great pioneers and vitamin discoverers of nutritional science, once pointed out that mankind had been on the earth for more than 300,000 years. "Yet for less than 50 years," he wrote, "has man possessed the knowledge that would permit him to provide and then select combinations of foods to nourish his body as it rightfully and properly should be nourished."

The practical basics of that knowledge should be yours.

SECTION II

How Food Becomes Life

CHAPTER 3

The creation of food

A balanced diet, contrary to popular belief, is *not* the ideal way to good nutrition. That concept belongs to the science and philosophy of the late 1800s.

Modern nutrition has quite a different view of how to select and combine foods so as to make the most of the human potential. That view, which this book is intended to explain, is the product of some of the most advanced and exciting research of our time—research which began to unlock the secrets of what food is and how life is created and maintained from food.

The new view of the relationship between man and his food provides some rather simple keys to good nutrition. They are keys with which anyone can easily follow a maximally healthful kind of eating, usually without any painful restrictions on taste, without supplements, much bother or unusual expense.

To describe this concept of food, the author has coined the phrase *biogenic diet*—meaning the food that creates and supports life. And to understand how to choose food biogenically, it helps to know how the old balanced-diet idea came to be and how a series of scientific breakthroughs made it obsolete.

By the end of the 1800s, scientists were fairly certain that they had found the secrets of how food nourishes. They had disproven the earlier idea that all foods contained a mysterious "nutrient factor" in varying amounts but with a single chemical property.

The late-Victorian biochemists (literally, researchers dealing with the chemicals of life) understood that there were three kinds of fuel, which the body combined with oxygen to provide the energy of life. These, of course, were fats, carbohydrates and proteins. The biochemists of the late 1800s also understood that each of these nutrient classes had special properties. For example, a number of German and American researchers believed that meat proteins made both animals and man combative and aggressive, if not vicious. The lion, to take one case, killed so enthusiastically and was so short-tempered because he ate meat.

German experimenters "proved" this idea by working with some surly bears, denying them meat and feeding them only breads and the like. Very quickly, the bears became quite docile, and a great number of European and American doctors accepted the conclusion that, for this among other reasons, it was a poor idea to eat too much protein, and that carbohydrate was the "natural" food for animals.

(It is not recorded what became of the bears. Plainly, they were weak with hunger, we now know, too feeble to cause anyone very much trouble.)

Actually, these early researchers were right to believe that all three types of nutrients were energy sources, that the body "burned" them, and that each was somehow different. But their understanding of both the differences and the processes of life erred. Convinced, however, that they had found the answer to an ideal diet, they measured what went into animals and what came out and decided that what was consumed in between was all that life required. The ideal diet, they concluded, could thus be computed as a perfect "balance" of fats, carbohydrates and proteins. They even fed the simplest forms of the nutrients, ideally balanced, to animals. Some of the animals in such experiments ate heartily, but after a time, sickened and began to die.

In the years that followed, one discovery after another began to explain why the balanced diets had failed—the vitamins, the function of minerals, then the mysterious workings of hormones and enzymes, the incredible chemical production of the cell. Finally science began to open up the submicroscopic world of the cell nucleus, with its mystery of heredity, which turned one cell into a laboratory for making stomach acid and another into part of a nerve receptor for light. From this took shape our insight into life beginning. In brief, we began to know how food *became* life.

It was from such understanding—still incomplete—that science began at last to comprehend that, though the body burned fuel, it was *not* a machine. Food, it was now known, was not merely fuel but the raw material from which life was made. The dietary was a complex warehouse which had to supply all of that material, in amounts sufficient to the demands of thousands upon thousands of different cell blueprints. It was not balance that mattered so much as sufficiency.

To furnish the material for the plan of life, one must know something of the links between man and all of nature, and how those links forge a chain of life which extends unbroken to the first living spark on this planet. For man exists only because he is a part of that chain, and only as long as he takes in the lifestuffs that serve a plan which was three billion years in the making.

The reader may have no fondness for chemistry. Yet food and health depend upon the chemistry of life. So the author is compelled to wander for a time among the atoms and molecules which make up both food and the body that uses it. He invokes the patience of the reader who has studied chemistry, perhaps extensively, who probably did much better at it than the author did and hence may be bored—and also of the reader who went to lengths to avoid chemistry (as the author did after his first year of it).

The chemistry of food and life

Back in the 1940s, a certain chemical company used to advertise that it made all sorts of things, such as nylon, from coal, air and water. Using the same ingredients, life performs some chemical tricks that make that company's achievement look like an exercise with a $2.95 chemistry set.

Let us begin by looking at the air. Omitting gasoline fumes, dust, pollen, shaving-lotion vapors and other minor components, today's atmosphere is chiefly one of nitrogen, oxygen and water vapor.

It was not always thus. Looking back two or three

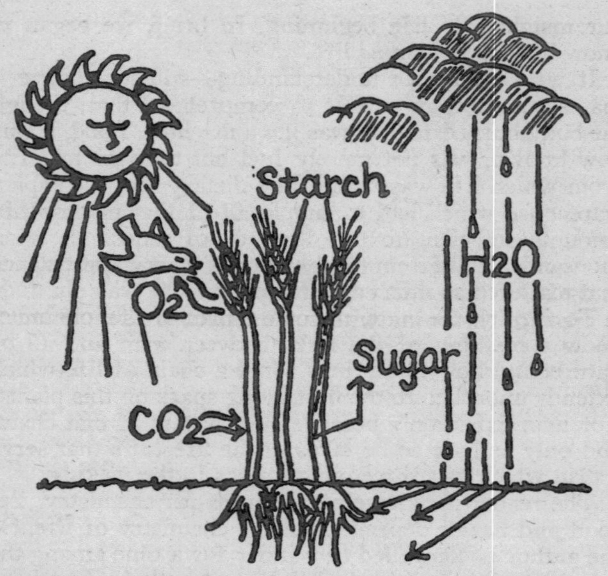

How a plant traps the energy of the sun to make food. The plant takes in water and carbon dioxide. Using solar energy, it combines the two chemicals into sugar and starch, releasing oxygen. The bird uses both the sugar and starch for energy and breathes oxygen to "burn" them. The waste products the bird produces in this reaction are carbon dioxide and water, which the plant can use to make sugar and starch, continuing the life cycle.

billion years, there is good evidence that earth's atmosphere was primarily one of nitrogen, carbon dioxide and water vapor. The key difference is that our oxygen seems to have replaced the old carbon dioxide part of the air.

The oxygen was not really missing, of course. Nothing much has been added to our planet since its birth. Instead, the oxygen was there, but combined with carbon (the same as the coal in the chemical company's nylon) in the form of gas, carbon dioxide (CO_2). The interesting question: how did the oxygen get free of the carbon so that animals (such as we) could breathe and live?

Victorian chemists had a good idea of the process.

They knew that man and other animals needed oxygen to burn their fuel and thus get energy. And they knew that when the fuel burned, one of the main products was carbon dioxide gas. They understood that body fuels were carbon compounds. And they had become aware that in plants the cycle was just reversed. The plants took in the carbon dioxide from the air, broke it down to get the carbon they needed and then disposed of oxygen as "waste."

The first illustration suggests how this happens, and at the same time tells something about the way our food is created, beginning with some extremely simple building blocks. The water, taken out of the atmosphere as rain, falls to earth and is picked up by the plant roots. Meanwhile, the leaves take carbon dioxide out of the air.

Now the sun, the chief energy source of the earth, and of all life, goes to work. Through a complex phenomenon, using the still cryptic plant substance chlorophyll, the sun energy is used to break up the carbon dioxide and water and reassemble their atoms as entirely new matter. Putting it simply, the process goes like this:

Carbon dioxide is made of two oxygen atoms bound to one carbon atom. (Each atom has a valence, or combining ability. Carbon, for example, has a valence of four—meaning it offers four links to other atoms. It tends to bond to other atoms until its links are all filled. Oxygen offers only two bonds. So to fill all four of its links, carbon takes up two oxygen atoms.)

Water, of course, has only one oxygen atom and two hydrogen atoms. For hydrogen has a valence of only one. It is the smallest atom and the most plentiful, by the way, comprising some 90 percent of the matter of the entire universe.

Now, if we add the energy of the sun, as trapped by chlorophyll and then put to work, the atoms all separate and then rejoin to make quite a new pattern.

The plant has taken in carbon dioxide, one gaseous waste product of fuel-burning in humans, and now gives off oxygen to the atmosphere to start that cycle again. But what is left over is interesting, too. It would be written HCHO, or formaldehyde. It is one of an almost infinite number of compounds which can be made by combining carbon with water molecules.

But let us suppose this HCHO takes a slightly different form. One hydrogen atom joins first with the oxygen atom, with one of the oxygen bonds unfilled. This is called a hydroxyl radical or OH. It has a valence of one. It now links its one bond to the carbon atom, which is also bound to the other hydrogen atom.

Our leftover atoms are now joined so that they have two open bonds. So the plant cells unite them with three other similar groups made from water and carbon dioxide. We will see that one of these is arranged differently, as a kind of mirror image. These rearrangements of the same atoms in the chemicals of life make possible much of their infinite variety.

To finish off the new molecule being made, the plant cells take a sixth HCHO and split it up a bit. One H goes to the top of the molecule, to satisfy a leftover bond sticking out from the topmost carbon atom. And the OH radical of the sixth HCHO separates so as to take up three bonds of the carbon atom, which then hooks onto the bottom of the chain.

This is *glucose,* which has been called "the universal sugar." In both plants and man, this is the basic form of food energy. All the most complex energy nutrients we eat must be broken down to glucose before we can use them.

Note that all the carbon atoms have been combined with water molecules, or *hydrated.* Thus the name of the family to which glucose belongs—*carbohydrate.*

Glucose is not the only *simple sugar. Fructose,* for example, is another. It has the same formula ($C_6H_{12}O_6$) but a different arrangement of atoms. We encounter the simple sugars in fruits and vegetables, primarily.

Often, simple sugars are not, for various reasons, practical forms for nature, so two of them join. Each simple sugar makes this combination in the form of a hexagon, which science, in its perversity, insists on calling a "ring." The carbon atoms make all the corners of the hexagon, except one, which is oxygen. In the combining process, if we wanted to go through all the tedium of arranging and showing the Os and Hs, we would see that, to free the necessary bonds, one O and two Hs fall out, as a molecule of water.

This last fact seems hardly worth knowing, if you are not planning to join any sugars together. But it is mentioned because it is another very common method of life chemistry—adding and dropping molecules of water to create change. We shall see it again.

Two simple sugars, glucose and fructose, link to make a double sugar, sucrose (table sugar). We have here used fructose and glucose, for two practical reasons. One is that we thus get *sucrose,* or ordinary table sugar, which is likely to be more useful for the reader than, say, *lactose* or *maltose,* which are also *double sugars.* The other reason is to show the practical use of all this chemistry.

For example, scarcely anyone has not heard the miracle claims for honey—and for special honeys at that, from orange blossom to clover and hymettus. You can pay astonishing prices for certain special miracle honeys at the health-food store. But they are *all* just fructose (fruit sugar) and glucose (sometimes called *dextrose*). Only certain flavor factors, which have no nutritive importance at all, differ. It is always the same Cs, Hs and Os in the same arrangement. As an amateur biochemist, you can now say with confidence, "Why pay more?" And you also know that, nutritively, honey and table sugar are the same.

Both the simple and the double sugars are ready for quite rapid use as energy. But the plant or animal may not want them just then. So they now go into storage forms. Several hundred sugar rings are linked together, merely by dropping water molecules.

What we have here is *starch.* Let's go back to our first illustration (p. 40) and take a look at the chain of life again. Atmospheric water and carbon dioxide go into the plant. The sun's energy is used by chlorophyll-containing cells to break up the water and carbon dioxide and recombine their atoms.

Free oxygen comes off, letting the bird in the picture breathe. The glucose made by adding water to carbon atoms travels up the plant stem in the sap. Gradually it changes to double sugars. Then it chains still more to become starch, which is stored as reserve energy in the seeds the bird is going to eat.

As the bird burns the starch to live, it exhales carbon dioxide, and some water vapor. These the plant needs for *its* life. If the bird were a turkey, we in our turn might eat it. We would now take the sun energy into ourselves in still another form.

(It is generally accepted that the life cycle of plants is the means by which earth's carbon dioxide-laden atmosphere became oxygen-rich. And this explains one of the concerns of today's ecologists. For by our rapid burning of carbon fuels—coal, gas, wood, etc.—we are speedily pouring carbon dioxide back into the atmosphere. At the same time, we strip the earth of thousands of acres of the green plants which "breathe in" carbon dioxide and pour out a "waste" of oxygen. It is as though we were renouncing the miracle of life which allowed man to exist.)

The second major form of our food is also entrapped solar energy. Let us look back to our seed-bearing plant to understand a little about that form.

As carbon dioxide and water are broken down and reassembled by the plant cells, using solar power, some of the building blocks can go into a form other than carbohydrate. The reader will recall that sugar was formed from six atomic groupings arranged as HCHO. Another major food family uses three of these groups together. A hydrogen atom is then tacked onto each end; it is taken from water, freeing more oxygen.

This looks like a kind of half-sugar. But it behaves very differently. It is a clear, viscous liquid, called *glycerol,* or sometimes, glycerin. And it is likely to be hooked up to some other carbon-hydrogen-oxygen arrangements. These look a lot like glycerol, or sugars, except for two things.

First, and very important, it looks as if the oxygen atoms have almost been omitted from their make-up. Second, they have at one end a somewhat odd little cluster, made of the same atoms, which is an acid.

This is a *fatty acid,* of great concern in questions of diet and heart disease. Usually, fatty acids are much longer than our example—with 15 or more carbons.

When fatty acids are joined to glycerol, the result is a fat, which when it is warm and liquid is known as an oil.

But why does the plant bother with all this when it has perfectly good food-energy in carbohydrates? The answer lies in the missing oxygen atoms. The less oxygen a fuel has, the more oxygen it can combine with. Since that process of combination is *burning*, the missing oxygens of fats allow them to burn more, and so yield more energy.

In general, carbohydrates have about 50 percent of their weight in oxygen—and fats have about ten percent. This makes the fats much more concentrated fuel. For example, one gram of carbohydrate yields about four calories; one gram of fat yields nine.

Here we must note that the body does not *burn* fuel in a literal fashion, as an automobile engine does. We will explain the process of human fuel use later, in chapter 6. For the moment, let us say only that it is an extremely complex process, which releases energy from food by the breaking and forming of chemical bonds between atoms. So when we speak of "fuel-burning," we are using a kind of shorthand.

This form of food-energy is more compact and longer-lasting, for storage. Plants do not tend to make a great deal of the stuff. Mainly they store energy by converting sugar to starch. (That conversion can be seen as the sweetness of young corn disappears when the the ear matures, and the kernels become less sweet and tender, more pithy. Old corn is starchy. The stored fuel of the potato, being starch for the most part, makes it dense, and unappealing to eat raw. But the carbohydrate of the strawberry, being sugar in the main, makes it seem to melt in the mouth.)

Conversely, human beings and other animals tend to store food fuel as fat. We do, however, make a form of carbohydrate in the liver. Called *glycogen,* it is a storage form of glucose.

Some biologists explain these storage differences in terms of the fact that plants do not have to spend energy moving around, and they are always in touch with their sources of food. Man must move and must carry his fuel with him. So he favors the more compact form.

This theory can be extended to a reason why most plant usage of fats is in connection with seeds and nuts. These have to be portable, after all, and to carry fuel for supporting the early life of the new young plant. So the germ of wheat, as one instance, is oily. Nuts are high in fats. The cooking oils you use are crushed from seeds and nuts.

Thus we see that all the endless forms of carbohydrates and fats, our two most important energy sources, are built from nothing but Cs, Os and Hs. This suggests that the pattern is a very primitive one. Scientists even wondered if it might not once have taken place outside life. And in checking this idea, they opened a path to some of the basic secrets of life's—and food's—beginnings.

In 1950, Melvin Calvin, of the University of California, put into a test chamber simple carbon dioxide and water vapor, which with nitrogen had made up the earth's primeval atmosphere. He exposed the two gases to radioactive particles, of which there were plenty a couple of billion years ago. When Calvin tested his chamber later, there were some new compounds in it. One was CH_2O, the formaldehyde we saw when we first looked at how plants caught and held sun energy. Another was formic acid (HCOOH); it contained the hydroxyl (OH) radical which is so important in the construction of sugars, starches and fats.

This experiment excited biochemists. For it proved the theory that an earth without life could build up food-like molecules. By 1962, Juan Oro, of the University of Houston, had gone several steps further. He started with the formaldehyde—which it was now known was very quickly and easily formed from carbon dioxide and water vapor. Oro switched energy sources to ultraviolet light (there had been enormously more ultraviolet reaching the earth from the sun before oxygen flooded the atmosphere and blocked most of the rays). Sure enough, sugars formed.

Some of the excitement attending such experiments was due to the understanding that all of life seemed to be made from these simple building blocks. Was such a process the origin of life?

At the University of Chicago, famed scientist Harold Urey gave an idea to one of his students, Stanley Miller. Into a glass container Miller put a sample of what is thought to be the still earlier atmosphere of earth—water vapor, methane and ammonia.

These are all gas combinations of hydrogen, the earth's most plentiful element, with each of the three elements next in quantity—oxygen, carbon and nitrogen. Miller applied energy. At the end of the first day, the colorless gas mixture turned pink, then day after day, it began to turn a darker and darker red. Miller analyzed the mix. And a whole host of life-associated combinations appeared.

One of those, which was made entirely of Cs, Hs and Os, resembles the fatty acid molecule. Indeed, this arrangement is also in the mold of a fatty acid, about as simple as such an acid can be. This one is the familiar *acetic acid,* which you know best as vinegar.

In Miller's experiment, some of the acetic acid was carried another step. The ammonia from the primitive atmosphere dropped one of its three Hs, to combine with the fatty acid.

The result is called *glycine*. It is an *amino acid*. As other researchers pushed the experimental idea further, more and more amino acids spontaneously appeared. Soon they began to hook together, in what are called peptide linkages. The primeval atmosphere, sparked by mild energy, had yielded *proteins,* which are just chains of amino acids.

With the emergence of proteins—possible once nitrogen enters the food picture in ammonia—the larder of energy foods is complete. We now have all three sources of fuel. And looking back, we can get a quick glimpse of how they came to be.

First, the plants take up the energy of the sun and trap it in simple sugars. These are made by breaking carbon dioxide and water into Cs, Hs and Os and recombining them. These simple sugars are now doubled and redoubled, to form the long sugar molecules which are starches, the main energy-storage for plants.

At the same time, the plant makes glycerol from the same atoms—a molecule that looks like half of a sugar. Similar atoms also go into the form of fatty acids—which look like sugars and starches from which most of the oxygen has been omitted. The glycerol and fatty acids join to make fats, the more compact form for storing sun energy.

Finally, ammonia enters, usually from the breakdown of living things and their wastes. Its nitrogen seizes the acids, too, to make amino acids. The aminos join, sometimes in chains of thousands, to give us protein.

If we look at these foods only as fuels, they are astonishingly the same. The body can use them almost interchangeably. The main differences are the speed and ease with which they can be broken down to free the sun energy.

But whether we start with fats, carbohydrates or proteins, we are dealing with much the same atoms. And the body must first break down the chains until all that is left is simple sugar.

This is the great chemical unity of nutrition, and the great fail-safe system of human eating. The body, in this context, might be compared to a car which could run on *any* fuel—wood, kerosene, gasoline, oil, coal. Of course, no car can. Chemical refineries must first reduce the car's fuel to one special compound. But the body is its own refinery. Give it any raw material in which the Cs, Hs and Os are available to it.

One of the great proofs of this fact is to analyze the waste products of energy production. Start with fat, carbohydrate or protein, and what is left after burning is always the same—carbon dioxide and water, the material with which we started in the first place. (The exception, of course, is the nitrogen of protein, which must be cast off—mostly in the urine—before the fatty acid portion can be burned.)

Other proofs of the units of food energy can be seen in the widely varying diets of man. Arctic explorers have lived well on virtually nothing but protein. Carbohydrate is the vast part of the diet of many Central and South Americans, as well as some people of the Orient. Some African tribes get almost no pure fat. The Japanese get very little. Some Eskimos eat ten times more.

Our first food need, then, is to take in trapped solar energy. The test of whether we get too much or not enough is also very simple. Are we losing weight or getting fat?

For if we are not getting enough energy (measured, of course, in calories) the body will begin to burn itself up, to keep going. Not to do so means death. If we are getting too much, the body stores the energy excess as fat, and we get bigger. From what we have seen, we have the general picture of how the body takes the simple sugars which have been broken down from food, disposes of most of the oxygen (to make it less bulky) and converts them to fat.

In this book's section on weight control, we will look closely at this energy storage. And we will see that, if we allow certain automatic controls to operate in the body, we will want to eat just about as much food as we need for energy. So under the right conditions, appetite can be a dependable signal for how much food to consume.

Doesn't it matter what proportion of our diet is carbohydrate, fat or protein? In terms of fuel alone, no. First, there are some practical limits to how much protein we can take in. Proteins are always found combined with large quantities of carbohydrate or fat in foods, even in meat, so that a diet which is 15 to 20 percent protein tends to be a practical upper limit, except in very special circumstances.

Almost all of the rest of the diet must now be divided between fats and carbohydrates. Again, in simple terms of energy it theoretically makes little difference how this is proportioned.

But food is far more than just fuel. Food is also the stuff of which the body and all its machinery are made. Does that mean that all the subtleties of life—the beating heart, the seeing eyes, the thinking brain—are all made from these same simple Cs, Hs, Os and Ns? Not entirely, but astonishingly, it is almost so. Take a look at the table to see what, in the eyes of the biochemist, a 152-pound man is really made of.

What is a man made of? Man is made mainly of a few simple atoms in many complex combinations. Below are shown the weights of these atoms in a 152-pound man. Only about three pounds of his weight are made of chemical elements other than carbon, oxygen, hydrogen and nitrogen. The latter four atoms make up perhaps 98 percent of the vast majority of all forms of life and food.

Oxygen	**111 pounds**
Carbon	**21 pounds**
Hydrogen	**14 pounds**
Nitrogen	**3 pounds**
Other elements	**3 pounds**

One curious fact is that the vast bulk of us is made up of elements which are usually found in the form of gas. The life process concentrates this gas amazingly. In gas form, the oxygen, hydrogen and nitrogen of which our 152-pound man is made would take up almost 4,000 cubic feet of space. That is, they would fill a corridor five feet wide, 100 feet long and with a ceiling eight feet high.

Most of the remainder is carbon, the same carbon which makes up the charcoal with which you barbecue and the "lead" in a pencil. If the carbon combined with oxygen to make carbon dioxide, and the rest of the oxygen joined the hydrogen and nitrogen in the simplest combinations, modern man would become a very large puff of the primeval atmosphere again—so many whiffs of ammonia, methane, water vapor and carbon dioxide.

Left over would be a packet of chemicals with not much more bulk than this book. And if we now removed the calcium and phosphorus, the remainder would be a sprinkle of ounces on the palm of the hand.

The chemicals remaining once the primeval gas is gone from the body were once the metals and salts of the earth's crust. Endless rains, scientists believe, washed them into the warm sea which was being born. In all probability, it was in tranquil, heated corners of that sea, radiated by the ultraviolet light of the sun, lashed by lightning bolts, that the dissolved gas from the atmosphere was reassembled into food.

Such a sea, in fact, still exists. It is kept within the envelope of our skin—where the body fluid is much the same as the ocean. There is one striking difference. The body's inner sea is only about one-third as salty as is the ocean. In recent years, geologists have been able to determine that the primeval ocean, the sea of the time when life was born, was about a third as salty as it is today.

In that sea, life was made from food. In our inner sea, the miracle happens again, constantly. Thus, to understand our food, and what it ought to be, we must understand much more than its role as fuel. To provide what the body needs for the miracles of its growth, its survival and reproduction, we must know how our food becomes our life.

CHAPTER 4

Protein and the secrets of life

Once we have followed the food chain to protein, we approach the threshold of life itself. For in many ways, it may be said that protein *is* life.

Indeed, much of life may be thought of as the building up, breaking down and rebuilding of proteins. And it is through this ceaseless taking-apart and putting-together that foods change into things that grow and reproduce, things that act and know and feel.

That miracle is happening every moment—and at dazzling speed—not only within us, but within all the life, plant and animal, around us. The move we understand the miracle, the better we can help it to continue, and the longer. The better and longer will be our own share of life.

So, having seen how the stuff of life is assembled from a few simple atoms, let us look at man when he has gone some hours without food, and is hungry. Primitive or civilized, he is now much the same, restless and irritable, perhaps even a little weak. His stomach growls and churns periodically. It contracts on its empty self. So he goes into the jungle or the supermarket—for our purposes, it does not matter very much which one—and he begins to search for food.

He takes the seeds of certain grasses (such as wheat), the muscles of animals and fishes, berries (such as the tomato), the fruits of trees, the tubers of vines (such as the yam), the eggs of birds, stems (perhaps asparagus or rhubarb), leaves (spinach or chard), or steals the milk of female mammals with young. When he has scavenged the earth for bits of almost every living thing —even, among more civilized men, the molds of cheeses and the microbes of soured cream, the fungi (mushrooms and truffles) and some flavorful blossoms for seasoning—he eats.

Having eaten, he feels much better, unless he has overdone it and winces with the bloat. He feels content, passive, the restlessness gone.

The ancient and powerful feeling that food and well-being are related encourage man to think that he is feeding one living unit, which he thinks of as Himself. I. Strong though it be, this concept is false and makes possible much of the common misunderstanding about food and health.

For only in a broad sense are we integral units of life —only in the same sense that a city or state or the population of the earth itself is a life unit.

Each of us is, instead, only a colony of many interdependent lives. But because these lives are arranged in a system of incomparable order and beauty, we can scarcely perceive of ourselves as other than One.

Cells: the lives within our life

The truth is that each of us is only a complex organization of life units, which live together in order to survive and reproduce. These life units, of course, are the cells.

To get some idea of how many and minuscule are these little lives of which we are made, we might look at a drop of blood. No, not even a drop. Let us take a cubic millimeter of it, a cube about one twenty-fifth of an inch on each side. If we fill that cube with blood from an average man, it will contain some five million red cells alone, plus other life.

In one human brain, the cells number *billions*. In all, scientists estimate that a typical human is a society of perhaps many *million* million individual cells, thousands of times the population of our entire planet.

To describe the cells as separate lives is no mere poetic license. It is simple fact. With just a few exceptions, each cell, within its own "skin," carries its complete hereditary plan and can reproduce itself. It has its own systems for taking in food. On the average, it produces some 300 complex chemicals—and some cells make thousands—to break that food down, rearrange its atoms and replace damaged or aging cell parts. It has its own system of waste and its ways to communicate with other cells. It has its specific work to do in supporting and controlling its fellow cells. It even breaks itself down into harmless chemical bits when death comes.

It is almost too much to believe—that these cells can conduct such lives when, in many cases, a million of them can fit onto the head of a pin. It is difficult to accept the concept that we have no life aside from these tiny lives, that all of life on earth, from insect to oak tree, is nothing more than such colonies.

But it is true. Take away the cells, and man is only a puddle of salty, chemical-laden water, with a little flotsam of grease, gelatine and fiber—which the cells have made.

Even for most biologists, the concept is a little unnerving. Yet now, for example, it does not seem so strange that tiny microbes (which are single cells) can strike down man with disease. They are really at war only with other cells which are their equals in size and strength. And much of our modern medicine could not exist until it was understood that the war was at this microscopic level. In fact, the vast bulk of modern pharmacology—from penicillin to the exotic drugs which combat leukemia, from sulfa to the birth control pill—is aimed at guarding, healing and controlling, not the vague entity of man, but the cell.

Thus we come also to the first principle of practical food choice. What we are feeding is not one large life, but trillions of miniature lives.

So it is the needs of the cells that we must know. And to learn them we must again enter the atomic jungle, with the core of life somewhere between the human cell and the shuffling, reshuffling atoms which trap the energy of the sun and become food.

Cells differ very widely in some respects. Some which circulate in the blood, for example, are extremely small. Others in the blood, such as the white cells called *phagocytes* (literally, "cell eaters"), are especially large and can actually swallow up and digest such things as strep germs.

Some cells can relax and contract, as the muscle cells. Some tend to stack themselves like stones in a wall, as do skin cells. Some have deep indentations, as do the goblet cells in glands. Some rapidly produce chemical reactions which send electric impulses along a chain, as nerve cells do.

But all human cells have certain attributes in common. A typical cell is drawn below, and the reader may want to refer back to it a few times to keep his bearings. A few key features of the cell are shown, but it should be pointed out that other features are found which simply do not concern us here.

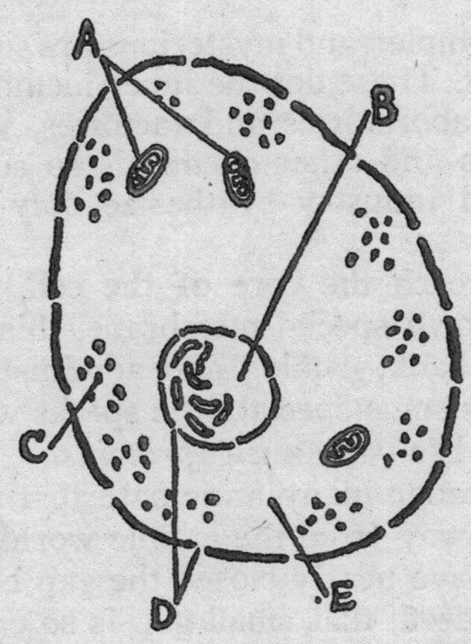

Inside a typical cell. (a) Two mitochondria, in the chambers of which energy is released from food. (b) The nucleus, where the hereditary pattern and the chemical keys of life are found. (c) Ribosomes, the tiny chemical factories of the cell. (d) Openings in the walls of the cell and its nucleus, through which foods, wastes and chemical messengers pass. (e) The cytoplasm, the body of the cell.

First, we might notice that the cell has an outer skin, known as its *membrane*. It is actually not a sealed envelope, but has tiny openings of special sizes, which allow certain chemicals to enter and not others. The extremely small size of a virus, for example, lets it enter into cells through such openings and then take over control of the cell to cause illness.

Inside the membrane lies the *cytoplasm,* the runny body of the cell. The cytoplasm has a very great many small bodies within it. Around these wash foods, wastes and chemicals, circulating without the special tubes or conducting systems common to larger organisms.

Some of the bodies in the cytoplasm are *mitochondria,* which are like the power centers of the cell. It is in these tiny bodies that the fuel foods are finally burned to free the energy we need to live. We shall see that they then convert this energy into other forms of power. To do this, they are divided into little chambers, each of which is for a special process in converting fuel to energy.

Even more complex and mysterious are smaller specks called *ribosomes.* These dot the inner membranes of the cell. They are laboratories and factories, which manufacture enzymes and other chemicals so subtle that all our science and industry synthesize only the simpler ones.

Finally, we reach the core of the cell, the *nucleus.* Isolated by its own special membrane, this is the computer, memory bank, catalog and administrator of the cell. For it holds some special little specks which are the quintessence of life—the *nucleoproteins.*

The astute reader many anticipate that we are now only a shadow away from the atomic world of the food chain, that we have nearly closed the gap between food and life. But indeed, that small gap is so crowded with meaning that in recent years many Nobel Prizes have gone to the men who are building the first bridges across.

Here chemistry, biology, physics and medicine merge like rising steam from pots on a busy stove. Here is the vague border between life and nonlife.

Perhaps the easiest path into this ultimacy of food is by way of the chemistry laboratory. Here in the chambers and retorts, the gas of the primeval atmosphere swirls in its chemical simplicity, an intermixing cloud of Cs, Hs, Os and Ns. Exposed to energy, the cloud has bred all three of the food factors. When we last looked, it had formed amino acids, and these had linked to make the chains which are proteins.

We had also seen the prehistoric sea, where simple mineral elements had washed from the rocks. One of these elements, one of the most plentiful of atoms, is phosphorus. It is an extremely active element, hungrily combining with others.

When the chemists added phosphorus to the primeval soup, something new began to appear. The phosphorus joined easily with hydrogen and oxygen, to make several forms of *phosphoric acid.*

Meanwhile, the researchers noted that a special sugar was appearing in the soup. It was only slightly different from glucose, the first food we saw formed. (Technically, the difference is a matter of one carbon atom and one molecule of water less. Glucose is $C_6H_{12}O_6$. The new sugar is $C_5H_{10}O_5$.)

This new sugar is called *ribose.* With it came another similar simple sugar, called *deoxyribose.*

There was a strong attraction between such sugars and the phosphoric acid which had just appeared in the "soup." The two quickly snapped together. And just as quickly, the new pair snapped up a third new chemical which had appeared.

This last new molecule is a kind of second cousin to amino acids. Like them, it is made of Cs, Hs, Os and Ns. But it is not an acid. In fact, it is quite opposite. It has an alkaline reaction, like lye. Chemists call it a base.

This chemical is known as a *nucleotide.* And with the first artificial making of nucleotides, a wave of excitement went through the scientific world.

For the nucleotide is the key to the creation and sustaining of life. Our understanding of its three-way molecule has revolutionized the life sciences.

And something even more. Remember that to make the nucleotide, we had only to add Ps (phosphorus atoms) to the familiar Cs, Hs, Os and Ns of our primeval soup, and add energy. The experiment has now been done again and again, and the result is always much the same.

In other words, scientists conclude that life will result eventually whenever these five elements come together under the right conditions. Such conditions are not generally present on earth today. But they do exist on some planets outside the solar system, and they have existed on others. In the universe are many true stars (suns such as ours) which shed warmth and ultraviolet rays on their planets. The five necessary elements are believed to be present on some of these worlds. So science is certain that life exists on islands scattered through the galaxies.

If we watch our new nucleotides, we see that they begin to join with one another in chains. Such chains have a curious tendency; each joins with one other chain. But the joining is not end to end, to make a longer chain. It is side to side. Their *bases* snap together.

The result is a kind of a chemical ladder. The sugar-phosphate parts of the nucleotides are now the sides of the ladder. The bases make the rungs. And now the ladder twists into a spiral.

This spiral is called DNA (*deoxyribonucleic acid*). And it is the master control of all life. To DNA is attributed the differentiation of all life's forms and processes. It makes the difference between a cell of heart muscles and that of an elbow, between a nose and a leaf, between a mosquito and a tiger.

How does DNA lead to this panoply of life? How does it control all the ways of life within our own bodies? How does it determine what our food must be and how that food shall be used?

First of all, this super molecule is made of many millions of nucleotides joined together. Linked with certain proteins, DNA makes up the largest of the dark specks we see in the nucleus of each cell, the *chromosomes,* the controls of heredity.

Just 23 pairs of chromosomes carry the design for every detail of a human being—the glands, nerves, organs, bones, hormones, enzymes, the family facial features, the hair color, the tendencies to hay fever or heart attacks or tooth decay. They are the blueprints of our selves and our biological destinies. More specifically, they are the plans and working instructions for each of our trillions of cells. And each cell carries such plans in its nucleus; that is, it holds the entire blueprint for making and running the whole human organism.

Human DNA is estimated to contain nearly two *billion* instructions in each tiny repository. If each of these instructions was just a single word, the words would add up to some 1,500 books like the one you are reading.

Each instruction is condensed to a code, the *genetic code.* And the recent breaking of much of that code is possibly the most important breakthrough in the whole history of science.

Within this code is the master plan for all our food need and use. If we understand the plan, the most troublesome questions of food and its effects on health become clear.

One researcher analyzed a part of the code by using ordinary playing cards. Biochemists had found that there were four kinds of nucleotides in DNA, repeating over and over again in a seemingly meaningless order. But they were sure that the order was somehow the coded plan of life.

The differences in the nucleotides were their bases, the "rungs" of the DNA spiral ladder. So let us focus for a moment on a tiny section of DNA.

One fact which struck the scientists was that the "rungs" of the "ladder," the bases, paired always in the same pattern. Only one certain base will join with one certain other base. An analogy would be clubs linking only with spades, and hearts linking only with diamonds.

Certainly, however, this slight variation could not account for all the endless forms of life. Scientists were blocked until another discovery was made. It was found that three links of the DNA chain, three rungs of the ladder, operated as one unit. This is called a *triplet,* and and the triplets provide 64 possible combinations.

Then another discovery: each triplet combination stands for an amino acid. It is the code signal for that amino acid.

Now the answer to the puzzle rapidly emerged. For by this code, the DNA in each cell can call for amino acids in a specific order and number. Such a chain of amino acids, as we have seen, is a protein. The DNA holds the plans for the body's proteins.

Those plans are spelled out by the arrangement of the triplets along the DNA spiral. The spiral is much like an extremely long computer tape, on which the names and arrangements of life's building blocks—the aminos—are imprinted. The genetic code, the plan of heredity, works by mustering up aminos and arranging them into proteins, much as a clever child makes anything he wants out of his small variety of blocks.

This may seem hard to believe when one realizes that only some 20 amino acids are used for all the variety of human life. But let us see how this is possible.

Suppose we consider one of the code triplets in DNA—say, a heart-club-diamond—as a "letter" in the alphabet of heredity. We know how our 26 English letters can be formed and reformed into all the subtle variation of language—from the ingredients on a package to the Gospel. We know that our alphabet can be made into millions of different words. And then we know that those words, by being put into different arrangements, have a variability beyond conceiving.

Remembering that in our analogy each amino acid stands for a letter, we can find some statistics. If we take just one each of the 20 aminos, and combine them without repeating any, we find that the possible number of different combinations is approximately *242,000,000,000,000,000!*

Yet in the language of heredity, even that awesome number is small enough to be thrown away and never missed. There are two reasons why. First, we know that in many of our English words, letters can be repeated in any combination, thus vastly increasing the possibilities. The genetic code repeats amino acids in its "words."

Secondly, the words with which we communicate are very small. A dozen letters make quite a large word—such as "carbohydrate." The words of the genetic language beggar ours in size. They are commonly *thousands* of letters (aminos) long. But let us look at a word (protein) of middling length.

One author has made some calculations based on hemoglobin, the medium-size protein of blood which carries our oxygen. Hemoglobin is made up of 539 amino acids. If we combine our 20 genetic-code amino acids in words 539 letters long, the possible variations total about 4,000,000,000,000,000,000,000,000,000,000, times a trillion, times a trillion, times a trillion, times a trillion, times a trillion, times a trillion, times a trillion, times a trillion, times a trillion, times a trillion, times a trillion, times a trillion, times a trillion, times a trillion, times a trillion—taken ten million times! Larger proteins, of course, would provide many more possible combinations.

Such a number is the edge of infinity. It represents the almost infinite variety of life.

Another scientist tried to compare the information-storing ability of DNA to a computer. In doing so, he pointed out that DNA becomes more complex with the increasing complexity of its life form. Thus, the DNA of a lowly bacterium such as *E. coli* is simple indeed compared with that of man.

Computers, of course, store astonishing amounts of data. One bank of them, for example—big enough to fill a fair-sized building—can store all the military records of Americans. A few regional banks store all the tax records of the land. So the scientist tried to envision a computer which could hold the DNA in a teaspoon of *E. coli* bacteria. He found that such a computer could be conceived—if it were a mile high (almost five times as tall as the Empire State Building), four miles wide and in length went completely around the earth at the equator.

No calculation, apparently, was made for the DNA of a man.

But let us get on to more practical matters. Let us see how our own DNA puts to work the food that our bodies take in. For our objective is to understand that food and how to make the most of it.

Let us watch a long thread of DNA in one of our cells, millions of code triplets long. We see its double strand "unzip" for a short length, letting the two strands separate.

We assume that the body has called for the production of a certain protein. And for clarity, we look at the *end* of the chain. But actually, the "unzipping" can happen anywhere along the line, depending on what instructions to the cell are needed to make whatever kind of protein is in short supply.

The length of the unzipping, of course, is governed by the length of the protein for which instructions are required. It has been found that the genetic code includes one triplet which stands for STOP.

To keep matters as simple as we can, we will now follow just one side of the unzipped double chain. And we will follow just one letter (triplet of nucleotides) in the code word, one amino acid in the chain for which the DNA is issuing instructions.

There are three main stages involved. First, the blueprint for the protein has to be reproduced. Then the reproduction has to be sent out from the nucleus to the main body of the cell, where the manufacture is conducted. Finally, the needed raw materials (amino acids) have to be brought together and assembled in a chain.

The reproduction of the blueprint is a fairly recent discovery. It begins with myriads of submicroscopic bits which float freely in the nucleus. These bits are nucleotides, but differ slightly from the nucleotides that make up the triplets in DNA. Some of the differences would lead us into needlessly technical discussion. However, one difference is in the sugar which joins with the phosphate and base to make up a nucleotide.

In DNA that sugar is deoxyribose. Hence the name

for which DNA is an abbreviation, *deoxyribonucleic acid.* In the loose bits floating in the nucleus the sugar is *ribose.* Thus the new material is called RNA, an abbreviation for *ribonucleic acid.*

Each of the new loose bits is much like a single heart, diamond and so on. And the moment that the DNA spiral unzips, the RNA bits rush in to seize the open places. A diamond snaps onto the heart of our triplet, a club onto the spade and a heart onto the diamond.

The RNA bits do not stay in position long, however. As soon as they lock onto their opposite numbers in the DNA spiral, they tend to snap tightly to one another, and begin to make their own chain. And at the same time, our new triplet snaps to the RNA triplets forming on either side of it. To put it another way, the triplet "letters" link up as a "word."

As soon as the word is formed, perhaps fifty letters long, perhaps a thousand, it breaks its bonds with the DNA spiral and pulls free.

The blueprint for a protein has been reproduced. But not exactly. The reproduction of heart-spade-diamond (DNA) is diamond-club-heart (RNA), a kind of reverse image in chemicals. One might compare it to the negative of a photograph.

Now, through some force which is still a mystery, the newly formed chain of RNA, having freed itself, begins to move. This is the second phase of the process. It heads for the wall of the nucleus, which has many small openings. It goes through one of the openings and, tapelike, floats out into the cytoplasm, the cell's main body. Here it seeks one of many tiny particles, *ribosomes.*

The ribosome is like a small factory in the heart of a wholesale raw-materials district. It floats freely in the cytoplasm, where all around it swirls a melting pot of chemicals. These have been supplied from the food.

It is here that our RNA instruction tape arrives, all its triplets still in perfect order of arrangement. Because of the function it performs, our wandering RNA tape is given a more specific name. It is called *RNA mes-*

senger. And it delivers its message by entering into a channel in the ribosome it finds.

To understand what happens now, it will help if we focus in on our triplet again, as the tape of which it is part begins to feed into the ribosome. As we move in closer, we begin to see some odd-looking particles.

At one end, these new particles look like the three nucleotides which make up our triplet. That is, the new particles each have their own triplet of hearts, clubs, spades or diamonds in some special combination.

At the other end, the new particles have a curious shape, which looks something like a piece from a jigsaw puzzle. It is a highly specific shape. For it is made so that one certain amino acid will just fit it.

(Remember that an amino acid is a *definite arrangement* of C, H, O and N atoms. These arrangements are used by the cells as an identification system.)

Thus, each of our new particles has two key qualities. First, it has a triplet code. Second, it has a jigsaw shape which singles out one special amino acid.

This particle is called *transfer RNA*. It, too, gets its name from its function, which is to attach to a certain amino acid and bring it to the ribosome. Something more is also implied in the name, however.

As each triplet on the tape of *RNA messenger* enters the channel of the ribosome, it calls for a complementary triplet. Going back to our model triplet on the messenger tape, we watch as it follows this process. Its diamond-club-heart triplet attracts one bit of *transfer RNA* with the sequence heart-spade-diamond.

If we think back to the start of all this, to the triplet we saw on the DNA spiral, it, too, was heart-spade-diamond. Remember, also, that this triplet is DNA's code for an amino acid. That amino acid, and no other, is now attached to the other end of the transfer RNA.

As all the triplets on our tape of RNA pass through the ribosome, each does the same job. Each singles out the right transfer RNA molecule, which in turn holds the right amino acid—until dozens, or hundreds, of amino acids are all lined up in the exact sequence called for originally by the DNA of the chromosome. The process looks like this in a very short section of the tape:

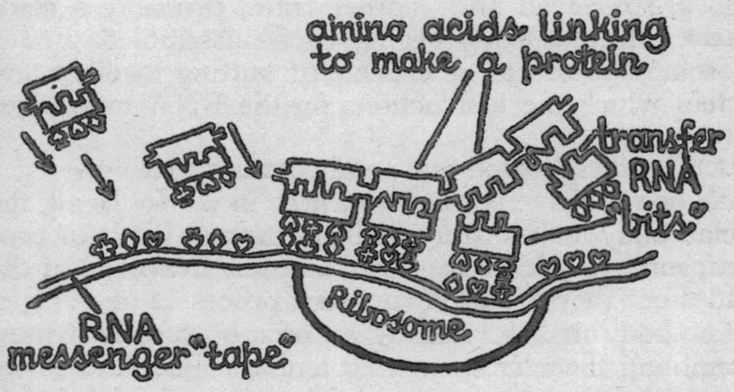

A simplified picture of the ribosome "assembly line" in action. Bits of transfer RNA arrive with amino acids in tow. These are lined up according to the instructions of the RNA messenger tape. The amino acids are held in proper order until they link with one another to form a protein, which then frees itself to be used in the life processes.

Now, as the aminos are lined up, they join with each other. And as they link into a long chain, the chain gradually breaks free. That chain, of course, is a new protein.

Let us recap briefly what has happened. In effect, the DNA in the nucleus has printed out a negative image of itself—more specifically, of one "word" in the library of instructions it contains. That print-out is the tape-like RNA messenger.

The tape is cut loose and travels to the ribosome. At the ribosome, each triplet "letter" of the word calls for a complementary triplet of transfer RNA.

Each bit of transfer RNA is marked with a corresponding letter, which is the code for an amino acid. It also has a shape which singles out and holds that amino acid. It rushes to the ribosome, bringing the amino acid called for.

That amino acid is snapped into sequence to make one link of a chain, which we know as a protein. It is as though the RNA messenger had the instructions for assembling a freight train. At the ribosome, which is like a marshaling yard, each type of car needed is summoned up and coupled in line. Once completed, the train is immediately released for its destination. Then new instructions are received and another train, probably a completely different sort, begins to be assembled. For a ribosome appears to be capable of putting together any protein which the instructions on the RNA messenger call for.

It is by this method that food becomes life.

For, as we have pointed out, protein *is* life. In all, the human body makes over 100,000 different kinds of proteins, some of which are constructed by nearly all of the cells, since they are used for basic processes of cell life.

The body makes virtually all of the proteins it uses, assembling them from just 20 amino acids. And so we can see clearly why our need for protein food is basic. We can also see that the true need is not for the proteins themselves, but for the amino acids they contain. (The practicalities of this fact are covered in the next chapter.)

While some proteins are common to more than one life form, by and large human proteins differ from those of plants and other animals. But amino acids are very few, and they tend to be almost universal. That is, all the life forms make their proteins from the same couple of dozen amino acids—from microbes to crocodiles, the building blocks are essentially the same. This, in turn, is why our food choice is so endlessly broad. Mouse protein would be just as useful to us as beef protein. We break both down into the amino acids which our cells require.

For example, in one experiment, a short length of human DNA was linked to a length of mouse DNA. Put into the proper biochemical situation, the half-breed DNA turned out an RNA message, which ordered up amino acids for a protein. And the protein was one which is common to both mouse and man.

In the human body, proteins make up some three-fourths of all the solid matter, from hair to the many glands, from muscle to bone, from brain and nerve cells to those of bone and teeth, from membranes to the secretions of reproduction and metabolism and digestion. All are custom-made by the cells, not only to the specifications for humans in general, but also to the specifications for the heredity of each individual human. For each word on each DNA spiral, the code for each protein made by the cells is a gene.

There are four basic kinds of proteins. There are *structural proteins,* which give form to the body and its parts. These include the proteins of skin, nails, bones, walls and the like. There are *contractile proteins,* which can actually change shape, lengthen and shorten. These enable the body to move about and make possible internal movements, from swallowing to the contractions of the stomach in hunger, from heartbeats to breaths. There are *transport proteins,* which serve to carry things about in the body and deliver needed materials to the cells. The most familiar example is the hemoglobin of blood, which takes the oxygen from the lungs to every smallest corner of the body, so that fuel can be converted to energy.

The fourth class are known as *process-activating proteins.* And they include two types which especially concern our food. For we have not yet explained how the body breaks down the food it takes in, for example, to provide the amino acids needed for construction. Part of the work is done by the large-scale processes of digestion, such as the mechanical churning and strong acid of the stomach. But most of the job is done by *enzymes,* which compose the greatest number of all the proteins we make.

Like other proteins, enzymes are pretty much specific to the plant or animal which makes them. Contrary to certain popular ideas, we generally do not use the enzymes made by other life forms. Thus, for the most part, we do not consider enzymes in thinking about our food. Many faddists raise cries of alarm about enzymes being lost in the making of white flour from wheat, for example, which suggests their ignorance of biochemistry.

In our section on overweight, as another example, we will find a myth which holds that grapefruit enzymes can work some special magic to break down the stored fat of humans. Grapefruit enzymes are certainly useful things—but only for grapefruit.

Each cell makes hundreds of enzymes. And each enzyme has unique characteristics called "active sites." These are small, specially shaped areas like the jigsaw patterns we saw in transfer RNA. Each such site fits to part of a specific protein linkage, at a weak point in the chain.

The protein and the active site of the enzyme fit together. By a method which is not fully understood, the enzyme snaps the link apart.

Thus are proteins broken down, perhaps two links at a time. It is easy to imagine how many steps can be involved in the full breakdown of a very long protein. And each individual kind of linkage can be broken by only one certain enzyme.

If one does not have a needed enzyme for a life process, the consequences can be dire. Missing enzymes are often the problem in serious hereditary illness. One example is *cystic fibrosis,* a hereditary childhood ailment which generally proves fatal and which afflicts thousands of youngsters. It has been traced to the absence of certain digestive enzymes in the pancreas. These enzymes are absent because of the absence of their genes—the appropriate "words" in the DNA spiral—which carry the blueprint for them. A single missing enzyme is the cause of mental retardation in many otherwise normal children. A number of such diseases are known, and more are being uncovered.

The enzyme's work in breaking up a protein is reversible. That is, an equally important function of enzymes is to put amino acids together as new proteins. The appropriate amino acids fit into the active sites on the enzyme. Held close together, they join.

Isn't protein-building the job of RNA? Yes, but it needs help. The chemistry involved gets subtle, but there some simple ways to get the picture.

For example, we have seen how nucleotides are attracted to unzipped sections of DNA, where they form into chains, making RNA messenger. Then why don't they link together while they are floating free in the cell in just any order at all?

It is, of course, a good thing that amino acids, nucleotides and other building blocks don't join up on their own. If they did, the results could bring all the body processes to a screaming halt.

So all of the millions of bodily chemical processes are

designed to take place only under precise control. In that control, the enzymes play a key role. For the reactions cannot take place unless the enzymes step in.

Some idea of the effectiveness of enzymes can be seen in their "turnover rates." These are the rates at which they foster a reaction, let go and then begin a new reaction. On the average, turnover rates of pulling chemicals apart or putting them together are hundreds per minute. Rates in the thousands are commonplaces, with each enzyme in a cell functioning at such speeds.

At the highest rates, the speed of reaction is almost beyond comprehension. To choose an enzyme display which most of us have seen, consider what happens when we put hydrogen peroxide on a cut or scrape to disinfect it. Immediately, we see a violent bubbling. That is caused by oxygen atoms being broken free, and it is they that do the disinfecting. Hydrogen peroxide does break down if it is simply left open to the air, or poured out, but much more slowly. The speedup is caused by a body enzyme called *catalase*. Each molecule of this protein breaks apart hydrogen peroxide molecules at a rate of *five million per minute*.

How does the DNA decide when to make one kind of protein or another, and how much of it? How does it determine, for example, to produce more enzymes?

The answer lies in messages received from its own and other cells. These messages are thought to take effect by causing the "unzipping" or "zipping up" of sections of the DNA spiral. The messages are sent in the form of other process-activating proteins—*hormones*.

Hormones, for example, may signal cells in the wall of the womb that conception has taken place, and that preparations must be made to foster the new life. Similarly, hormones are sent to cells in the breasts, announcing that birth is upcoming. The DNA of certain breast cells then unzips sections of instructions which may have gone unused for 25 to 30 years. These genes are the instructions for making milk proteins, and food is produced for the infant's arrival.

The variety of hormones is great. Their messages are widely different. Messages sent in case of injury might be: "More blood proteins are needed for clotting."

"More structural proteins must be made to mend the wound." "Foreign cells have entered with the wounding. Special proteins are needed to isolate the invaders." "Bacteria-consuming white cells are required to destroy infection and must be multiplied."

Each of the demands of the hormones is largely for protein manufacture or breakdown. Each calls for the building blocks of life—primarily amino acids—and for fuel to do the word needed. In other words, the demands require food.

Our food choices are, indirectly, responses to such demands. So let us see what we can do about our food to help our cells survive and function at their best—or at least to avoid sabotaging these tiny lives, the sum of which is health or illness, life or death for us.

CHAPTER 5

Choosing proteins

One of the more curious facts about proteins is that they are not really needed in human nutrition. We could get along very nicely without a single protein—*if* we consumed the amino acids that proteins hold.

It is actually quite possible to do so. Pure amino acids can be made and bought. But there are at least two things wrong with the idea. First, the dining table would become a dull place of flasks, white powders and clear liquids. And secondly, we would be quite a lot poorer. For those pure aminos would cost about thirty dollars a day for each of us.

The day may come when we move closer to eating in this way. As the earth's population grows, it is less and less practical to get our amino acids by the cumbersome method of raising feed crops to support animals, then eating animals to get the crude collection of proteins they make, and finally breaking down the proteins to get the amino acids we wanted in the first place.

Algae, for example, the one-celled animals which make green slime in ponds, are much more efficient paths than are ordinary food crops to the trapping of solar energy and the production of amino acids. And just a few technological improvements could probably make it far cheaper to assemble aminos in factories, out of common atoms. But so far, we are lucky. We are happily stuck with juicy beef roasts and broiling chops, with buttery filets of fish and dark creamy mousses, with big stuffed birds roasting brown and sweet yellow corn.

Such things beautify life, but they also make it a bit more complicated. Because we must think of these foods as chains of amino acids, strung together into proteins by other life forms, plant and animal. In our foods, these amino acids come to us quite diluted, more than half water and then some, and complicated by fats and carbohydrates. So while eating thus is more pleasurable, it demands more science of us to choose well for our cells the needed building blocks, fuels and chemical bits, which are hidden in food.

Aminos we can and cannot make

Our method of getting amino acids by taking apart complex protein foods is a little like demolishing four or five old houses to get the building blocks for one new one. It is as though the body had to dismantle the walls to get bricks, perhaps use the accompanying lumber as fuel for firewood, salvage a few usable odds and ends of pipe and fasteners and then dispose of quite a lot of remaining rubble.

But, to carry the image a bit further, not all the bricks have to be acquired ready-made. Let us suppose that the land under the houses offers fine clay and sand. The body can use these to make some of its own bricks, those which are of a simpler kind.

So it is with amino acids. There are two kinds. Some have chemical structures that the body cannot imitate. So these structures must be procured from food, from plants or animals which have the trick of making them and incorporating them in the proteins they build.

There are eight of these amino acids—building blocks that adults absolutely must have to live but cannot make themselves. They are known as the *essential amino acids,* meaning that it is essential to include them in the diet. (For young children, we shall see, two additional amino acids are regarded as dietary essentials.)

One or two other amino acids are thought of as marginally essential. The body can make them. But there is a problem of quantity. In certain phases of life, such as the years of growth, the limited amounts the body can make for itself may not be enough.

Ten of the amino acids are considered *nonessential.* This does not, as some people seem to believe, mean we can do without them. It means only that the body can build them out of the five simple kinds of atoms of which aminos consist. It can take the Cs, Hs and Os out of sugars, starches and fats, for example. The few necessary sulfurs are liberally sprinkled through the food world. And the Ns can come from any protein foodstuff, as well as from other food sources—even from the urea, which is the main waste product carried off by the kidneys. In planning out our food needs, however, nutritionists include enough extra proteins to serve as a dependable source of raw materials for making nonessential aminos.

What must you know about amino acids?

Since there are 20 amino acids from which human proteins are made, and since each is needed in different quantity, trying to choose foods which supply each in the right amount could be a nightmare. Fortunately, the practicalities are much simpler.

First, as a matter of curiosity for some readers, as a kind of reference for others, and as a key to the occasional use of the names, on labels and supplements, here are the names of 20 amino acids, and their usual abbreviations:

Essential Amino Acids

Arginine*	Arg
Histidine*	His
Isoleucine	Illeu
Leucine	Leu
Lysine	Lys
Methionine	Met
Phenylalanine	Phe
Threonine	Thr
Tryptophan	Try
Valine	Val

Nonessential Amino Acids

Alanine	Ala
Aspartic acid	Asp

(*Not essential for adults in good health.)

Cysteine	CySSCy
Cystine	CySH
Glutamic acid	Glu
Glycine	Gly
Hydroxyproline	Hypro
Proline	Pro
Serine	Ser
Tyrosine	Tyr

Occasionally, these rather obscure names do come up. For example, it is an inability to metabolize the amino acid phenylalanine that causes PKU—a much talked about infant flaw, which causes mental retardation. And MSG (monosodium glutamate), the flavor enhancer about which there has lately been much popular and legislative alarm, is actually a salt of glutamic acid, another amino acid. (Its chief raw materials are the gluten of wheat and casein, one of milk's proteins.) Thus, most nutritionists feel sure it is harmless in the amounts we use.

Having done his encyclopedic duty for the extra-inquiring mind, the author wishes to assure the reader that he may feel perfectly safe in ignoring all these names. So let us now see what we need to know about aminos and the proteins in which they are found—in order to choose the most healthful diet and to be protected from myths and deceptions.

The differences between proteins

Late in the last century, many scientists tended to look at protein as pretty much a single food factor, of which you got enough, too little or too much. And there were grim battles about whether men and animals did best with a lot of protein or a little. But as we have noted earlier, when researchers tried to reduce animal diets to a simple balance of fats, carbohydrates and proteins, the result was sometimes health and sometimes illness and even death. But why?

Quite a few years ago, Osborne and Mendel, two pioneer nutrition researchers, set out to find an answer. They put three groups of young rats on special diets, from which all proteins were carefully omitted save one. The one protein that was fed differed for each group.

The first batch of rats got only the protein *zein*, from corn. Gradually, though they ate heartily, they sickened. Eventually, they began to die off.

The second group of rats got only a protein of wheat, called *gliadin*. These animals did not sicken. They even kept their weight. But they did not grow.

The final group received the protein *casein*, from milk. They ate. They waxed healthy. And they grew.

The reader may well have guessed the secret in a general way. The answer lay in the amino acid composition of the three proteins.

Lacking in the zein of the first group were two amino acids, *lysine* and *tryptophan*, which are essential. Osborne labeled this protein and others like it as *incomplete*. It could not sustain life. We might say that it did not provide a *biogenic diet*.

The gliadin which the second group of rats ate was missing only one essential amino acid, lysine. And even though growth stopped in the young animals, life itself was not impossible. So the scientists cataloged gliadin and similar proteins as *partially incomplete*.

(Quite a few people still misunderstand this classification, including some self-styled popular experts. Just because lack of growth was the most obvious result of a diet without lysine does not mean that lysine is needed only by the young. An adult deprived of lysine would, in time, be unable to replace his dying cells. We may only say that the adult's need for an everyday supply of lysine does not seem to be as *urgent* as that of a child. With all nutrients, a growing body or a sick one is more vulnerable to food deficiencies and is likely to get into trouble faster; its demands are simply greater and more pressing.)

Finally, since the casein fed to the third group of rats supported both life and growth, it was classed as *complete*.

To test their theory, Osborne and Mendel continued

to feed the same diets to each group. But they added the missing amino acids, in pure form, to the corn and wheat proteins. Now all the rats lived and grew.

These experiments still left some scientific loopholes in the amino acid question, however. So at the University of Illinois, Dr. William Rose went a step further. He wanted to uncover the amino acid requirements of humans, and began tests on both a group of rats and a crew of young male student volunteers.

It was thought then that complete proteins contained 19 amino acids. So Rose fed both the rats and the students a diet in which there were no proteins at all, just the 19 pure amino acids which were then thought to be the only ones needed by man or other animals. But the rats would not grow. And the students showed laboratory signs of getting into trouble.

Something was missing, and Rose soon found what he thought was the missing factor—a twentieth amino acid called *threonine*. When all 20 amino acids were fed, both rats and students thrived.

Was this really nutritional bedrock? Rose now began to remove each amino acid from the diet, one at a time, and watch the results. Some removals were disastrous; others were harmless.

Thus did the concept of essential amino acids develop. And experiments since that time have changed the concept very little. If an adult human receives the eight essential amino acids—in sufficient quantity, of course—his protein needs are met.

Rose also learned what we have mentioned earlier—that two amino acids are produced by the body, but in such small amounts that they are on the borderline between essential and nonessential. In these early tests, the small amounts made by the body proved sufficient for the volunteer students. But Rose suspected—through the reactions of test rats—that such small quantities were too little for growing children.

One of these two amino acids, *arginine,* is still a bit of a question mark, but probably should be taken in ready-made from food during infancy and childhood. The other amino acid, *histidine,* is now definitely known to be in too short supply during early years, despite the fact that it is made not only by our cells but also by microbes which live in our intestines.

If a child gets *complete* proteins, however, there is no practical problem. Arginine and histidine come in the package.

By now it should be clear that complete proteins are complete because they contain all the essential amino acids. So let us explore the world of food to learn where those amino acids are, where they are conveniently grouped in bundles, what to do when they are not and how well your present diet protects you from the serious consequences of insufficiency.

Do you get the amino acids you need?

On the average, Americans get plenty of complete proteins, and hence an ample supply of essential amino acids. And if you take a look at the illustration you will see what a broad margin of safety there seems to be, *if* you belong in that hazy category of "average."

On this chart, we can see what typical men and women need in the way of essential amino acids, and what the national food supply provides. These averages show that most of us get not only what we need, but *multiples* of it. And the situation is usually even better than it looks here. For the "needs" shown are actually what nutritionists call "safe levels" of amino acids. These are *double* the minimum requirements—if we are adult, in good health and free of physical or emotional stress.

Then why talk about amino acids? Because averages in a nation of over 200 million people can include millions whose food is not fully life-supporting. The reason can be lack of money, lack of information or indifference.

For example, many fads can knock our neat averages into a dietary cocked hat. "High-carbohydrate" reducing diets cause serious trouble. (They are discussed in the overweight section of this book.) Fad "disease-curing" diets of fruit, liquids or a few vegetables can reduce amino-acid intake even more. Still-growing teenagers and others are turning to low-in-aminos "spiritual" diets. One lamentable example is the *Macrobiotic diet,*

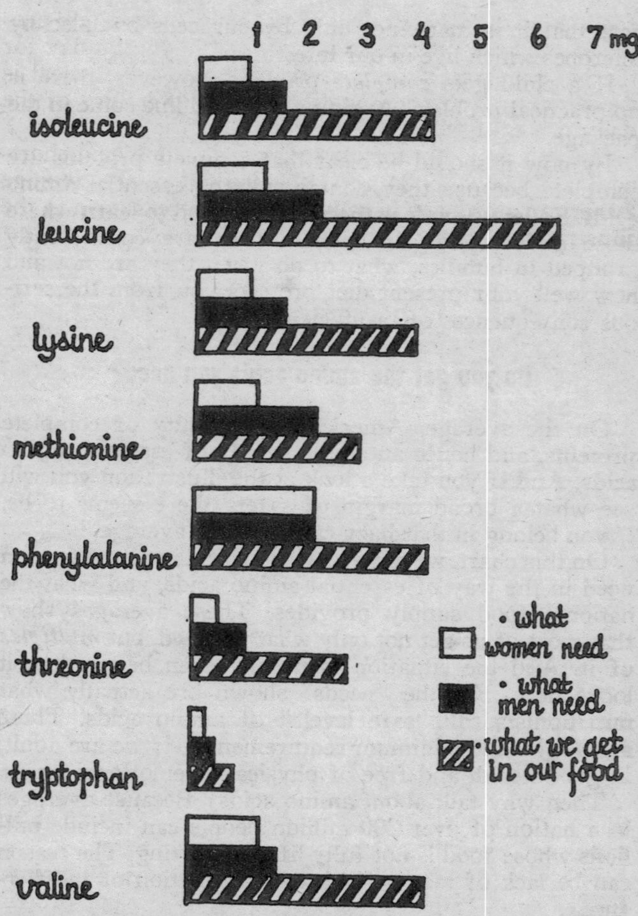

Essential amino acids: What we need and what we get. This chart makes it plain that the average American has a wide safety margin of surplus essential amino acids in his everyday food. The bar showing "what we get in our food" is an average of typical male and female daily intakes. The average of male intakes is much higher.

which may offer meals of nothing but rice and fruit, woefully lacking in amino acids.

Millions of the elderly, alone and disinterested in

food, seriously distort their diets. More than a few people who live alone depend largely on one meal a day for the bulk of their protein. And commonly, that meal is a prepackaged item designed to supply one-third of the daily protein need.

We can get a clearer idea of where amino acid shortages are likely to occur if we see where the average American's proteins usually come from, as shown in the illustration:

Where our proteins come from. Our sources of amino acids are widely varied, with no single group of foods supplying even as much as a third. This variety is a major reason why dietary shortages of essential amino acids are so rare in the U.S.

One can see here that the sources of amino acids in this country have a broad base. But unusual ideas about eating can chop away large chunks of this base.

For example, if the vegetarian disdains all animal foods, he eliminates well over half the usual protein source. Misguided efforts to control obesity commonly strike out nearly all grain and dairy products, or nearly half the typical supply. A self-prescribed antiheart-disease diet, in seeking to expunge animal fats, can erase a good half of the usual amino acids.

And suppose that fad or preference should make us choose only corn products for protein. The reader will recall that two essential amino acids are missing from corn. And he may also remember that when rats were given only corn protein, they sickened and died.

Of course, such extremes are very rare in the United States. But the idea suggests a basic nutritional truth—that if one is going to depart very far from the average American dietary, he really should consult his family doctor to avoid leaving serious food gaps. For while our typical dietary has some problems, in the main amino acids are not among them. Contrary to what many people believe, that typical dietary—complete with all the hot dogs, hamburgers, TV dinners and other processed and prepared foods—gives us a plenitude of our primary food need, the amino-acid building blocks from which our cells make the key structures and chemicals of life.

Which are the high-quality proteins?

In general, the proteins of animal products tend to be complete, while those of vegetable products tend to be incomplete. Animal sources also are likely to have higher concentrations of protein.

These differences in protein quality and quantity are not small. To demonstrate the protein value of fruits and certain vegetables, for example, two Utah nutritionists, Elna Miller and Elfriede Brown, planned a fruit-vegetable diet with adequate protein quantity for one day. Prepared for the Utah State Nutrition Council, each of its portions is about half to two-thirds of a cup of each food. It goes like this:

Just consume about three and a half ounces each of apples, apricots, bananas, blackberries, cantaloupe, cherries, cranberry sauce, dates, canned figs, canned fruit cocktail, grapefruit, grapes, grape juice, oranges, raw or canned peaches, pears, pineapple, plums, raspberries, rhubarb, strawberries and watermelon, from among the fruits. But also remember to eat the same amount each of asparagus, cooked or canned green snap beans, cooked beets, cooked broccoli, raw or cooked cabbage, cooked carrots, chard and cauliflower, canned corn, cucumbers, eggplant, raw or cooked kohlrabi, lettuce, canned mushrooms, okra, cooked onions, peppers, potatoes, pumpkin, radishes, rutabagas, cooked spinach, squash, baked sweet potatoes, tomatoes and cooked turnips.

What you have eaten is not really a good diet as far as protein quality goes; only the quantity is supplied—unless, of course, you are a man, in which case you need about 20 percent more of the same.

One problem with the diet is that it totals about 13 pounds of food, which you may find a little filling. And if you could eat this diet, and stay on it for a few days, you would notice another problem. It totals almost 6,000 calories a day. That means that the average woman will gain a little weight while eating it—about 350 pounds a year is a good, conservative guess.

There are easier ways to get one's protein, fortunately. We can, for example, take advantage of the greater protein density of nuts, grains and legumes. This way we can approximately match the protein value of the above large menu with a day's food like this:

Nine slices of bread, two half-cup servings of baked beans, a quarter-cup of peanut butter, two servings of spaghetti (each a half-cup to two-thirds), and a quarter cup of chopped English walnuts. This is closer to adequate protein quality. The calories total 1,650, which leaves room for other foods.

Finally, we can take a simple shortcut. We can get the same protein, with better quality (more complete), from seven ounces of meat and two glasses of skim milk. If the meat is lean hamburger, the caloric total is about 540, leaving lots of room for anything else we want to eat, being less than a fourth the calories consumed by an average woman in a day.

The reasoning behind these food differences is simple. In talking about man, we have noted that some three-fourths of the solid matter of his body is protein. The same is approximately true for all animals (including fishes and birds—and reptiles, too, if you happen to fancy iguanas or rattlesnake meat, as many people do). So when we eat animals (which are any living things that are not plants) the protein content is very much the highest, and the quality or completeness in amino acids the best. If we remember that the human produces over 100,000 different proteins, we can see why animal meats offer such good amino acid packages.

As a general principle, nature makes up its choicest amino groupings for the processes of reproduction and the care of the very young. The most obvious example of this is the egg, which must carry all the nutrients to make an entire little organism. So it is not surprising that the egg comes nearest to perfection as an amino acid food.

Among mammals, of course, eggs are almost hopelessly small. The human female, as the reader may know, is born with all the eggs (some 500,000) she will ever produce, and they are single cells. So in mammals, the eggs are not the best practical food source associated with new life. Milk is. For obviously, it must contain all of the nutrients necessary for the survival and rapid growth of the young. So milk scores almost as high as the egg in protein completeness and concentration.

The plant world has characteristics that sharply limit protein value. One is that plants do not have muscle to move them around, and muscle is the main meat source in animals. Another is that much of the structure of plants is not protein structure but cellulose, of which bark and wood are good examples.

Cellulose, made as one more step in the sugar-to-starch chain in plants, is nothing more than very long molecules of hundreds of sugars. That is how termites can live on lumber (mainly cellulose). And it is how cows can live on grass (mainly cellulose). We would starve on either. The cow, for example, has a stomach-like organ called a rumen, where cellulose-rich plant matter can sit as in a big fermentation vat, with microbes breaking down the hay into digestible sugars.

Such plant matter does have proteins, but they are in what might be called extreme dilution. For example, we eat certain stems, such as celery, asparagus and rhubarb, but not for their protein primarily. To get his recommended protein from celery, an average man would have to consume about 80 servings of it a day, and then he would get a very incomplete assortment of amino acids. We have much the same problem with leaves. To get his protein from lettuce, our average man would require 150 servings a day. If you have any doubts about these numbers, watch the damage that a rabbit does to a garden in one outing.

Roots are really not much better as protein sources. But tubers (such as potatoes) mark a strong step upward. A potato, for example, offers four or five times as much protein as does a carrot. Why? Think about how a potato is reproduced. The tuber (what we eat—the rest of the plant is actually poisonous) is cut up, and each eye is a potential source of a new plant. Nature packs the stuff of reproduction into the potato. Even so, a potato can really be thought of mainly as supplemental protein, with no more than a twenty-fifth of daily protein as recommended for a typical adult.

This pattern suggests that we should look to the reproductive factors of a plant, as well as for an animal, to find the best, most nearly complete, protein source among botanicals. The seed is our best bet, as in wheat, corn, rice or barley. Of course, nuts are also in this group. So are the peas, beans and soybeans of the legume family. But because of completeness problems, no plant seed is recommended as a sole amino acid source by itself. It takes a combination of them to do the job.

As for fruits, they are biologically designed to attract plants and animals with sugar, aroma and moisture, to spread, plant and fertilize the seed they contain. In general, they are watery, dilute protein sources.

How much protein in each food?

Let's look at some numbers that illustrate the protein concentration of food groups. First, remember that our own bodies are largely water. So are those of other animals. Thus, the protein content of meat, fish and poultry (*after* cooking) is no more than 20 to 30 percent. Lean meat cuts, such as those of beef round or of young animals (veal, lamb), fowls or non-oily fish, have more protein weight per pound. Fatter meats, such as porterhouse steak or fatty pork cuts, have less. Ironically, finer grades of meat, such as "prime," offer less concentrated protein than do tougher, cheaper grades

How much protein in foods?

Most fruit	½–2%
Most deep green vegetables, corn, rice	2–3%
Milk	3.5%
Most cake	3–5%
Legumes	5–8%
Breads	8–10%
Eggs	13%
Most nuts	15–17%
Most fish, meat, cheese	20–28%

such as "good." The differences in cut and quality can add up to 20 percent more or less protein in a food.

In most cheeses, the protein is pretty concentrated. And in general, harder, more compact cheeses tend to be more protein-rich, while softer, fluffier, or runnier cheeses are usually more protein dilute. Cheddar, for example, is about 25 percent protein by weight. Cottage cheese may have only half as much. And processed cheeses are somewhere in between. The protein source, being milk, is of course top quality.

While the quality of eggs, in terms of the wide range of amino acids in their protein, is unsurpassed, their protein density is not extraordinary. It is about 13 percent, about the same as the lowest-protein cottage cheese. But this is high enough when it is *the whole diet* of the developing chick.

In the vegetable world, nuts are at the top in protein concentration. They average about 15 to 16 percent. The quality is good, but limited. Grain products, such as bread, are next down the line, at between eight and nine percent, and with somewhat less amino-acid sufficiency. Most breakfast cereals, made from grains, are in this range, from five to 12 percent protein, but one or two can go as high as 19 percent. And the protein of such foods is incomplete unless the grains are mixed and supplemented.

With most fruits and vegetables, there is another downward fall in protein, to a level between one-half and one percent, with few reaching one percent. Peas and beans, of course, are the exceptions, for reasons we have mentioned above. Their protein concentration is between four and six percent.

Some denser fruits and vegetables can have a little more protein. For example, the avocado (2 percent), cauliflower (2.5 percent), dates (2 percent), potatoes (2.5 percent), black raspberries (2 percent), spinach (3 percent), turnip greens (2 percent—or more than three times as much as the turnip itself, oddly), mustard greens (2 percent), kale (2.5 percent), brussels sprouts and broccoli (3 percent), and asparagus (2 percent).

It is worth noting that these fruits and vegetables (to which we can also add such fungi as mushrooms) are of about the same protein concentration as most breakfast cereals, hot or cold, though the amino range of the latter is likely to be better.

How much protein do you need?

It is quite easy to check out the amount of protein you are getting by looking at the food-composition table in Appendix A of this book. But how much do you need for the continuing processes of life? How can you be sure of getting proteins made up of a proper and adequate variety of amino acids? And how do changes in life-style, activity and age affect these needs?

In general, nutritionists have come up with a simple, basic rule for adequate protein at "safe levels." It is about *one gram of protein, daily, for each kilogram of body weight.*

Because food-composition tables give protein in grams, we will keep that measure. Then, following the recommendations of the Food and Nutrition Board, we get a formula of .424 grams of protein needed for each pound you weigh. To know pretty accurately what is your safe level of daily protein, you can multiply your weight in pounds by .424.

The table below shows figures for some weights. The requirement is essentially the same whether you are male or female.

Your Weight (in pounds)	Daily Protein (in grams)
100	42
112	47
125	53
137	59
150	64
167	70
175	75
187	80
200	85
212	91
225	96

These figures remain remarkably constant for adults. That is, protein need is directly related to weight from about the age of 14 years. There are two principal exceptions. The pregnant or nursing mother needs more. So does the patient in certain illnesses—for example, when growing tissue after an injury, or after the shock and stress of surgery, severe infection, and sometimes when under emotional duress. These situations will be discussed somewhat more in the appropriate sections of the book, as will the special protein needs of the growing years.

By and large, repeated experiments have shown that people can get by on much less protein than the amounts recommended above, probably half as much. But these minimums, most nutritionists believe, are a little too close to the knuckle. They leave no room for stress or error. For example, when protein levels are at a bare minimum, one must be quite concerned about the proportions of the essential amino acids contained in the proteins. A comfortable cushion is the wiser way.

Will such a cushion surely guarantee that you get an adequate number and quantity of essential amino acids? The answer must be made with some reservations.

If we look back to our needs for essential amino acids, we see that the total "safe level" requirement is some 12 grams a day for a man of average weight (about 150 pounds) and less, of course, for most women. The rest of the daily need can be met by any proteins, theoretically.

But in practical terms, an even larger safety cushion is probably desirable. That is, it is probably wiser to consume a larger percentage of one's protein as complete protein. For in theory, our 150-pound man would be safe if less than 20 percent of his protein were complete.

This is really quite a small amount. The 12-gram, "safe-level" total is less than half an ounce. And the amino acid tryptophan at that level, for example, is about one fifty-sixth of an ounce. Practical nutritionists tend to back away from such narrow margins. Most recommend that we choose complete proteins for at least half the daily total. And the author has, over the years, noticed that when nutritionists are at the table themselves, they are likely to consume complete proteins as a substantial majority of their total protein intake. To do so is quite consistent with our national fondness for meats, fish, poultry and dairy products.

We should keep in mind, too, what a small part of protein food is actually pure protein. Three ounces of cheddar cheese, for example, has about three-fourths of an ounce of protein. The same would be true of most chicken or lean beef. With choice but fatter cuts of meat, such as a rib roast, only a fifth of the weight is protein, even after cooking. Curiously, two-fifths of the weight is fat. In lima beans, only 7.5 percent of the weight is protein. A full 20 percent of the bean is carbohydrate.

So in practical terms, even if we ate nothing but complete protein foods, we would have to consume at least five or six times the weight of the protein requirement in actual food. Using conventional foods and trying to get the needed amino acids from vegetable sources (including grains) we must take in much more bulk still—at least 12 to 15 times the protein need.

Of course, the total protein need for the average man is only about 2.25 ounces. The average American, with a typical mixed diet, probably eats well over a pound a day of good protein sources to meet this need. And when the source is a fluid (as milk), its high water content sends the weight of food eaten much higher. Half a pound of milk (an eight-ounce glass) has only a little more than a quarter ounce of protein.

Some of these facts may help to give the reader a better feel for his protein requirement. After all, he does not want the pleasure of eating to become a grim mathematical exercise. The best way to avoid having to think very hard about protein needs—and, in fact, most other food needs—is simply to choose a widely varied diet.

The fact is that many proteins have what are known as "limiting factors." That is, even if the amino acids are all there, one or two of them may be in short supply. So experts have concluded that mixed proteins make for the highest safety.

Of course, whenever we are eating the cells of plants or other animals, we are getting mixed proteins. We know there are hundreds of kinds of proteins in every animal cell and quite a few in plant cells. Even so, there can be shortages. If we eat many different kinds of cells, the strengths of one tend to balance the weaknesses of others.

The narrower the diet, the greater the chance of omission. Poor protein sources and narrow food choice are the central problems of most nations where malnutrition is a concern. But United Nations food experts have salvaged much health and life in such nations—where a few grains and vegetables are the main protein sources—by adding tiny amounts of animal foods. One team has found that adding legumes (such as peas and beans) to diets based on grains (such as corn or rice) relieves much suffering. While neither protein source is complete, together they tend to close one another's amino acid gaps.

What do you know about protein?

Here are some common beliefs about protein needs. See if you can separate the truth from the false ideas:

QUESTION: *Athletes need unusally high amounts of protein at the training table. True or False?*
ANSWER: *False.* Like every other adult, the athlete needs

just a little less than a gram for each 2.2 pounds he weighs. Protein in extra amounts does not confer strength or health, even though less protein than is needed can make for weakness.

QUESTION: *If you are going to be working hard, as a farmer does, or playing hard, as on a mountain-climbing or skiing weekend, you should have extra protein. True or False?*
ANSWER: *False.* Again, no matter what your activity, or lack of it, an adult's body-repair processes and chemical manufacture proceed at a pretty constant rate. Excess protein will merely be broken down into glucose and nitrogen waste and be used for energy food (the most expensive sort) or stored as fat.

QUESTION: *Protein content should be balanced against the rest of the diet (the fats and carbohydrates). The protein content should be about ten to 17 percent of the calories one consumes. True or False?*
ANSWER: *False.* This percentage is often cited. But it is the *result* of good nutrition under ordinary conditions.

If one becomes more active, one has a larger appetite. That appetite, as we shall see in detail, is the result of a demand for more energy fuel. But the protein need rises little, and so becomes a smaller percent of total food.

One might compare the body to an automobile. If a car is driven at 60 miles an hour instead of 40, it may well burn more fuel. But this will not make the seat covers or windows wear out faster. An increased demand for fuel does not also mean a greater demand for repair or replacement, which is the special job of protein.

QUESTION: *Older people need less protein, because they are slowing down, and their bodies are not renewing themselves as quickly. True or False?*
ANSWER: *False.* It has been found that while calorie-consumption (the energy value of the diet) is gradually reduced as one ages, the protein need is just as great. Some doctors think it may be proportionally somewhat greater, because of the growing inefficiency of the older person's body.

QUESTION: *The protein content of a food is equally available to the body, no matter what the source. True or False?*

ANSWER: *False.* The availability of protein differs somewhat in different sources. About 97 percent of the protein in food from animal sources (including fish and fowl) can be used by the body. But when the proteins are contained in vegetable matter, some of the tough, starchy membranes that enclose the food substance are not broken down by the digestive process. The result is that most fruits, vegetables and grains actually let us use only about 83 to 85 percent of their protein. Peas, beans, lentils and the like give up less than 80 percent. (They are still among the best protein sources of the vegetable family.) This is especially a problem for a vegetarian, whose entire diet is of vegetable origin and whose meals, therefore, must be very bulky. The true vegetarian should probably increase his protein quantities by about 20 percent. Those who are willing to use milk, eggs, and cheeses as protein sources are getting foods from which the protein is more completely absorbed, but should probably enlarge their safety cushion of proteins somewhat.

QUESTION: *Cooking, especially to the point of "well-done," destroys the protein value of foods. True or False?*

ANSWER: Generally, the statement is false. Rare meat is no more nutritive than well-cooked meat. The protein in many vegetable foods, moreover, becomes much more available after cooking. This is especially true of the pea-and-bean family. There are exceptions, however. One is the family of cereal grains. When these are toasted at high heat, some of the amino acids, notably lysine, are lost. They combine chemically with carbohydrates and become unavailable to us. This reaction is what produces browning. Protein value is also lost when grains are puffed, as in breakfast food. The protein is still there, but its structure is slightly changed, making it difficult for enzymes to break down the protein. The heat of some milk-canning processes also has a similar effect. But the heat of pasteurization, it should be said emphatically, does *not* reduce protein availability.

QUESTION: *It doesn't matter when you get your protein, or which amino acids you get at any meal. The only need is to take in adequate amino acids every day. True or False?*

ANSWER: This statement must be labeled false for one important reason. Understanding how the cells assemble amino acids into the scores of thousands of human proteins, by combining and recombining them, we can see the necessity for giving thought to timing. For obviously, all of the amino acids must be available to the cells at the same time. If a needed amino is missing, the protein simply cannot be made.

Protein is absorbed almost entirely from the small intestine, after the food leaves the stomach and before it reaches the large intestine. Passage through the small intestine (about 15 to 16 feet) takes approximately 12 hours. The stomach has been emptied of most meals within two to three hours. So while digestive processes can vary quite a lot in the time they take, we can draw some broad conclusions about when proteins ought to be consumed.

Let us assume that Henry has dinner at 6 P.M. every night. Between 8 and 9 P.M. proteins are starting to be absorbed from his small intestine. Most of that absorption is over by dawn. At 8 A.M. he has a breakfast of orange juice, toast and black coffee, with jam. His toast gives him only a small part of his daily protein need (perhaps 5 to 6 percent) and that protein is not complete. The orange juice and jam add some aminos, but small amounts and also incomplete.

Henry lunches at one. He has a ham-and-cheese sandwich, with one slice of cheese (an ounce) and one of ham (a little more than another ounce). With the bread, lettuce, tomato slice, lemonade and four ounces of French fries, his total lunch protein is not bad. The sandwich has about 20 grams of protein. The lemonade has almost none. The French fries offer a little over four grams. The total is just under 25 grams, better than a third of Henry's daily safe requirement. Sixteen grams (the meat and the cheese) are in complete protein.

But it will be 4 P.M. before that protein is being absorbed. Thus there is a kind of "protein gap" from dawn to late afternoon, perhaps ten hours. This, nutritionists consider, is probably not wise. And only five hours later, Henry will consume more than half his protein need at dinner.

Henry is not in great danger. The body has what are known as "labile stores" of protein, which provide a small bank account against protein starvation. But most doctors agree that Henry stresses his body needlessly by continuing this pattern, and that he would feel better if he divided his protein consumption into more even parcels, making sure that he had complete proteins at every meal.

What if Henry runs short of needed amino acids? For a short time, his body can rely on some emergency procedures which are quite complex. But it will soon begin to break down its own protein structures to provide the amino acids for essential processes. If starved, Henry would literally consume himself—which is why doctors warn against self-imposed fasting for any reason.

Of high protein and health

In recent years, partly due to our national weight-consciousness, many Americans have come to associate the "high-protein" diet with good health. The concept holds something of truth and quite a lot of fantasy.

It is true that those nations with diets rich in complete proteins tend to have populations with long lives. For example, the United States, Russia, France, Australia and Japan all have average life expectancies of about 70 years. And these nations top the list of major protein consumers.

Conversely, where a population eats less protein, and more of it incomplete, people die younger. Some Latin American countries—with perhaps two-thirds of our protein per capita, and much less of it animal—have average death ages of 50 or less. In lands with still less quantity and quality of proteins, matters are even worse.

Life expectancies in lands such as India and Haiti fall off into the 40s and even the low 30s.

Such figures are often cited. But their meaning can be deceptive. For while nutritionists agree that lack of protein is the primary food problem of underdeveloped nations, there are other factors involved. Protein foods are expensive, especially animal proteins. Where much protein is eaten, there also we generally find money and education for good medical care, immunizations, proper sanitation, better housing and all of the other things which give people long, healthy lives. The poor die young. And contrary to what so many "nature-faddists" say, so usually do the primitive.

The simple fact is: protein is a basic necessity of life and health, but it is *not* a fountain of youth and beauty, as some promoters would have us believe. When we have adequate protein with adequate amounts of essential amino acids, and perhaps with a very ample safety cushion to boot, additional amounts have no further biologic value. And for some people, very large amounts of protein can actually be harmful.

The high-protein picture really looks like this to the physiologist: as long as the cells have all the amino acids they need, more will not be put to work. Making more amino acids available will not make cells multiply or renew at a faster rate. To pour excess amino acids into the body is no different from delivering to a mason more bricks than he needs to build a house.

Some of the same people who call for floods of protein have also begun to promote diets rich in enzymes, RNA and DNA. Their claim is that our chromosomes will be renewed, for example, in such a way that old people's cells will manufacture young skin. But these proteins are broken down like any others, and become so many building materials of a common and plentiful kind. Taking gobs of ready-made nucleotides or enzymes into our bodies will not make our cells reproduce any faster, or more youthfully. These big molecules will never reach our cells intact.

But some promoters imply that we can use ingested RNA and DNA to replace that which is already in our cells, or to add more instructions for making more proteins. This, if true, would be a disturbing idea. For consider. We know that each bit of RNA and DNA carries instructions for making the organism in whose cells it was born. Some of the RNA and DNA being promoted as a reprieve from aging is from yeast. Some is from the meats of animals. So if the promoters are right, the author is concerned about the possibility of people rising to much greater size if left in a warm place overnight. He is also alarmed at the possibility that those receiving animal DNA may begin to grow wool, hooves or horns—and perhaps be inclined to moo in public places.

Fortunately, while biology does still deny us rejuvenation, it does also protect us from such embarrassing conversion. This protection is evidenced by the fact that we already consume so many plant and animal cells in our meals, that each of those cells, of course, contains RNA and DNA, and that so far no one has grown roots, leaves or a tail.

This newest fad is cited to suggest that we cannot eat proteins of any kind or amount to change our physical potential or plan. For most of us, it is harmless to eat lots of extra protein foods, if we enjoy them. When the cells have taken all the amino acid building blocks they can use, however, the excess aminos cannot be stored as such. They are broken down. One part of the molecule goes into the energy cycles of the body, the reader will recall, being converted into simple sugars. If this fuel is needed, it is burned, and our extra protein is no more than expensive energy.

But the other part of the excess amino molecule, the nitrogen-bearing part, becomes urea. The kidneys must work to remove this chemical in the urine. There is no harm for the healthy person. But excess urea can cause real problems for those with certain ailments involving the kidneys.

There is another important area of consideration for excess protein foods. As we have seen (and as will be covered more thoroughly in the discussion of weight-control) proteins are always found wedded to other food factors. In complete-protein foods (such as meats, milk, eggs and the like) that union is commonly with animal fats.

Suppose an average man is getting one of his servings of complete protein in rib roast; suppose four ounces of this tender meat gives him about a third of his day's recommended protein. And assume he met the other two-thirds of his protein need at other meals. However, like most American men, our friend disdains a small serving. Instead, he knifes out a 12-ounce slice for himself. It's protein, isn't it—and good for you?

True, but it is also fat, and a lot of it. In the extra half-pound of meat there are about 45 grams of pure protein. Associated with it, however, are some 90 grams of animal fat. That is quite a lot of fat, and the reader may wish to read about human fat and food fats before he decides how to slice his own roast. For fats, being concentrated food, have so many more calories per ounce.

The pure protein in that extra half-pound of rib meat has a value of 180 calories, not a big chunk of our average man's daily food. But the caloric bill for the fat comes to an impressive *810 calories more.*

So don't be deceived by overenthusiasm about so-called high-protein diets. It is quite hard for us to get our diets much above about 17 percent protein. And the rest must be divided between fats and carbohydrates.

We will see that this principle—that once bodily needs are met and a safety margin added, large extras are useless and may even be harmful—is true for *all* nutrients. For each and every nutrient has what might be called its *biogenic range.* This is a range of quantity within which a nutrient tends to foster the life processes.

Below that range there is not enough of the nutrient to supply the needs of the cells. Some body processes will suffer.

Once a life-supporting quantity of the nutrient is reached, the quantity that can be tolerated by the body is fairly great. But excesses simply offer no benefit.

Eventually, with any substance, the biogenic range can be exceeded. There is an amount the body will not tolerate. Depending on the nutrient, and the degree of excess, the result can be mild discomfort or a threat to life. Nothing can be consumed limitlessly. Even table salt or water can be toxic. And any quantity between safe sufficiency and toxicity is waste.

Nutritionists agree that a great many of us do quite a lot of this sort of wasting—out of misguided fear or hope—and that a great many others suffer, needlessly and often unaware, the consequences of not knowing the healthful ranges of nutrients. Let us see what these nutrients and their ranges are.

CHAPTER 6

Choosing foods for life

As important as proteins are, they really make up very little of the diet—perhaps 50 pounds a year of our half-ton of food. Let us see what else is essential to the best possible nutritional support of life and health.

It seems appropriate to begin with the body's most urgent need, which is not protein, fat or carbohydrate, but water. Moreover, of all the nutrients, water occupies the largest part of both food's weight and volume.

Man is a watery animal

People have lived without food of any kind for months. These, of course, have usually been very large people, who simply consumed their own bodies in the process. But the longest recorded water-fast, and it is extremely unusual, was 17 days and ended in death.

Ordinarily, life would fail much faster. And in the sun and low humidity of the desert, the survival time might be only 12 hours, or less.

There are many reasons for the extreme urgency of water need. But, in general, they may be summed up by remembering that our cells still require a kind of sea in which to live, just as did the first cells.

So each of us is about two-thirds water. But beyond this, water is the medium and participant in nearly all of life's chemistry. We have seen before how the hydrogen and oxygen of water enter into the building of foods by plants. With carbon, these elements make up the only constituents of sugars, starches and fats.

The evaporation of water is the body's main technique of getting rid of the heat produced as fuel is burned; without this cooling we would literally cook ourselves to death. Moreover, water is essential for flushing away the body's chemical wastes. For example, the use of proteins by the cells leaves a waste of poisonous *urea*. The kidneys dispose of this and other toxins by mixing them with water and excreting the resulting solution as urine.

We get a great deal of the flood of water we need from food. Fruits and vegetables are an average of about 85 percent water. Meat is usually at least half water. Even such seemingly dry stuff as bread is actually heavy with moisture. An ordinary small loaf of bread holds about a third of a pound of water.

In all, adults need about three ounces of water for every 100 calories of food consumed. An average man, consuming perhaps 2,500 calories daily, needs about 75 ounces of water each day, which is well over two quarts.

Because of the high water-content of foods, we do not have to drink all this water. But the American Medical Association concludes that a quart of liquid a day is an absolute minimum, and that a safe level of liquids is two quarts.

Contrary to the beliefs of many, this water can be taken in any form—as coffee, tea, soft drinks, fruit juices and the like. With hot weather, heavy exercise, fever, vomiting or diarrhea the need for liquid zooms, and the penalty for failing to satisfy the need can be severe. What is often taken to be "heat stroke" or "heat collapse" is commonly just dehydration, as the body seeks to cool itself and runs out of enough water to do the job.

Myths that bar water drinking during exertion are often dangerous. Water drinking will not lead to weakness or cramps if it is kept to reasonable amounts. A vigorous game of football or basketball, for example, can cost a grown man three to five quarts of water. The U.S. Army, in experiments at Yuma, Arizona, found that a working day in the desert could commonly cost a soldier eight quarts of water. At losses of three quarts, weakness and mental confusion occur in a person of average size. Smaller people can stand to lose less; larger people can lose more.

How much water in foods? The water content of some typical foods—shown as percentages of total weight.

Dry cereals	4%
Breads	35%
Cheese, cheese spreads	35–50%
Most meat	45–55%
Eggs, fish	65–75%
Potatoes	80%
Most fruits	85%
Peas, beans, other vegetables	75–90%
Most leafy vegetables, milk, fruit juices	90%

There is a valid warning signal for those exercising heavily or in the heat. It is thirst. And it should be responded to promptly. The Army found, by the way, that the temperature of the liquid drunk is unimportant. Whether ice water or hot coffee, it is likely to be a moderate temperature by the time it reaches the stomach.

The more protein we eat, and the more sodium incorporated in our food, the more water we need. For the kidneys demand more water to flush away both. The protein of a big steak will certainly make us thirst, as will the high sodium content of shellfish. For the kidneys must have wastes and sodium diluted to a certain level in order to excrete them. This is the reason, for example, that sea water is of no use to a parched man. Sea water has salt (a sodium compound) at a concentration of about 3.5 percent. The kidneys can handle salt only up to about two percent. If salt exceeds two percent, extra water is needed to dilute it to a level of kidneys can manage. An ounce of sea water contains so much salt that the kidneys need an ounce and three-quarters of water to dispose of it. So, ironically, drinking sea water actually makes the body lose still more of its water and become dehydrated faster.

Alcohol is another chemical that can cause dehydration. One estimate is that the body must use eight ounces of water to manage every ounce of alcohol consumed. (One does not actually lose this amount, since some of the alcohol we drink is evaporated from the lungs and does not enter into the body's food-use systems.) This eight-to-one rule is useful to remember at cocktail parties. It can save much discomfort the morning after. (Since a typical ounce of whiskey has less than half an ounce of pure alcohol, less than four ounces of water are needed to metabolize an ounce of liquor.)

The rule suggests some principles of social drinking in the heat as well. For in hot weather, the body may have less water available to deal with alcohol. So a gin-and-tonic really is a wiser choice than a martini. And beer, which has a still higher ratio of water-to-alcohol, is less apt to cause after-effects than a highball.

In the heat, after heavy exercise or at high altitudes (where the air holds less water and reduced atmospheric pressure hastens evaporation from the skin and lungs), alcohol can carry quite a lot more kick. For one thing, the effect of alcohol increases as it becomes a larger percentage of the blood. (The percentage of alcohol in the blood is commonly used as an intoxication measure in drunk-driving tests.) When we are low on water, the volume of blood circulating in our bodies is less, for the blood also loses water content. So every ounce of alcohol we drink is a bigger percentage of the blood, and rather little can make us a lot more fuzzy.

Thus, after a tennis match in the sun, have a glass of water before sitting down at the club bar. On a hot day of boating or fishing, choose watery highballs. And on a passenger jet, you might want to follow the same rules —for despite pressurization, the effect is of an altitude of six or seven thousand feet.

The best protection against excessive water loss remains thirst. For scientists believe there is a water-control center in the brain, similar to the center that controls the body's reactions to heat and cold. And this center is thought to direct the dryness of the mouth as a dehydration warning. It is an error to say, "I'm not really thirsty; it's just the salty appetizers and fish." You really do need extra water to take care of the extra sodium you have taken in. If, after a very salty meal on a hot day, for example, you seem to have an endless thirst, drink slowly. For taking in all the water you need to deal with a great amount of salt, protein or alcohol may indeed end in a bloated feeling, if you gulp it all at once.

One good idea is to drink water or other liquids along with eating a lot of protein-rich or sodium-rich food. Moderate amounts of water, soda pop or milk will have no bad effect on digestion if drunk at meals—even three or four large glasses. But there is one reservation. As we shall see later, digestion begins in the mouth, where foods are broken up into small particles by chewing, and where enzymes in the saliva start to break down the carbohydrates we eat. So don't allow liquid-drinking to replace chewing.

In general the belief that the mineral content of the water we drink has much effect on health is false. Similarly—except for germs—changes of water supply for the traveler are unlikely to have much impact on his well-being.

Some people believe that drinking water before a meal is harmful. But doctors say no. By its volume, liquid before any meal may produce some sensations of satisfaction and lessen our desire for food; however, for most of us this is not such a bad thing. In fact, low-calorie soup or fruit juice before a meal is helpful to reducers. In any case, the liquid goes to the stomach very rapidly, where it tends to start gastric secretions flowing, usually an aid to the digestion of the solid food which follows.

Don't worry if children seem to consume more fluid than you do, in proportion to their small size. The younger they are, the larger proportion they need. In hot weather, or under other water-stress conditions, it's a good idea to offer fluids often to very small children, because they are sometimes slow to recognize their thirst.

As a final note on water, some commercial "sports drinks" have come in to the market recently, advertised to deal with thirst more effectively and claimed to replace lost fluids faster. Because these have racked up big sales, especially in warmer climates, we might note that very little scientific research has been done on them, and that most of the claims appear to be based on the testimonials of athletes and coaches.

Medicine has found that testimonials are poor evidence. Impressions of thirst, hunger and general well-being are easily suggested to many people.

Comments a publication of the AMA: " 'Sports drinks' are dilute solutions of glucose [a simple sugar], sodium chloride [table salt] and other salts, citric acid and an artificial sweetener. One of the few objective research studies suggests that water absorption is increased when glucose and sodium chloride are present in proper amounts. Whether the *slightly* [author's italics] increased rate of water absorption credited to the drinks is of physiological significance is not clear."

At 35 to 40 cents a quart for a "sports drink"—much more than whole milk—one may wonder if the possibility of a little faster water absorption is worth the price. One also wonders if the coaches who have adopted the drinks include the many who falsely believe that athletes should be restricted to just a swallow or two of water during long periods of energetic work. For sensible gradual water intake can eliminate any problem.

Which fuel should you use?

Aside from the large amount of water and the small amount of protein (little more than two ounces a day), the usable food of humans is almost entirely made up of just two basic nutrients—fats and carbohydrates, which serve mainly as fuels for the operation of the human machine, but are also important sources of chemical building materials.

What about all the other things in food, which crowd cereal boxes and advertising and the minds of faddists? It is worth noting that the term for most of these items —"*micro*nutrients"—is very accurate. To make this point, one nutritionist used a photograph of the amount of vitamin B_{12} which would be enough to control pernicious anemia in a patient for two years. (This anemia is the primary result of a deficiency of B_{12}.) The photo is of a single clear crystal. It is passing through the eye of a needle.

So the vast bulk of our food is fuel and must be some combination of fats and carbohydrates. Yet so little is this simple fact understood that the author has actually heard and read recommendations from "experts" which said that to be healthful, or to lose weight, one should "avoid foods which are sugary, starchy or fatty."

Yet we have seen that even if one confines one's diet solely to high-protein foods, large quantities of fats and carbohydrates are automatically consumed. So the real dietary question is, how ought we to divide the great majority of our food between the fats and carbohydrates? And how do we recognize these two fuels?

In fuel terms, it seems scarcely to matter whether fats or carbohydrates predominate, provided there is at least a little of the other being consumed—perhaps two ounces of fat a day, and about seven ounces of carbohydrate. (The exact amount of fat or carbohydrate which is essential varies with the individual. The Food and Nutrition Board finds that the carbohydrate need is less clear-cut than that for fats, however. About 60 grams [a little over 2 ounces] of carbohydrate seems to be a bare minimum for the average person, who usually eats about 200 grams of this nutrient [7 ounces] and who may get a toxic effect if he eats less than 100 grams [3.5 ounces]. These amounts are for pure carbohydrate, such as sugar. It would take much more weight of fruit or vegetable to provide these amounts of the nutrient.)

Both fats and carbohydrates are made of the same three kinds of atoms—carbon, hydrogen and oxygen. To be used as fuel by the body, both must be broken down to the same simple chemicals. And when they have been used by the body, the waste is exactly the same—carbon dioxide and water. The primary difference, in terms of fuel, is that fat is more concentrated. An ounce of fat yields more than twice as much energy (calories) as does an ounce of sugar.

Certain differences between fats and carbohydrates will be discussed later. These areas are:

1. In weight control. (See chapters 7 through 11.)
2. In diseases of the heart and blood vessels. (See chapter 18.)
3. In the problems of digestion. (See chapter 17.)

These special problems can involve either controversy or complexity. At present we will deal with what is agreed upon and basic, the facts which can guide the reader in his personal food decisions.

The secret of human energy

It is common to talk about the human engine as if it were like that of an automobile or a vacuum cleaner. But the similarities, luckily for us, are very limited.

In the engine of a car, a carbon-hydrogen fuel is mixed with oxygen from the air. An electric spark touches off the mixture, and it burns, with such violence that we describe the event as an explosion.

Human fuel releases energy differently. For if we were designed along the lines of sedans, life would be much more difficult. We would have to eat every time we wanted to move, or we would have to have a fuel-storage tank. We would get terribly hot when we walked and awfully cold when we sat still. And we would have a nagging fear of running out of fuel and being helpless.

As it is, we can keep going when we take in far less fuel than we use. We stay at a remarkably even internal temperature. All our parts work instantly, on command. And in emergencies, all our tiny cell "engines" can work even without oxygen. In sum, we can get energy from our fuel in a carefully controlled way, at any time, yet delay the spending of the resulting energy as long as we choose.

The system which lets us do these things is complex. The core of this system is known as the *Krebs cycle,* and it happens in every cell. Before the cycle begins, each kind of fuel has been broken down to simple chemicals in many steps, each step having its own enzyme or enzymes.

The cycle itself has some 20 more steps, each again with special enzymes, which continually reshuffle the C,

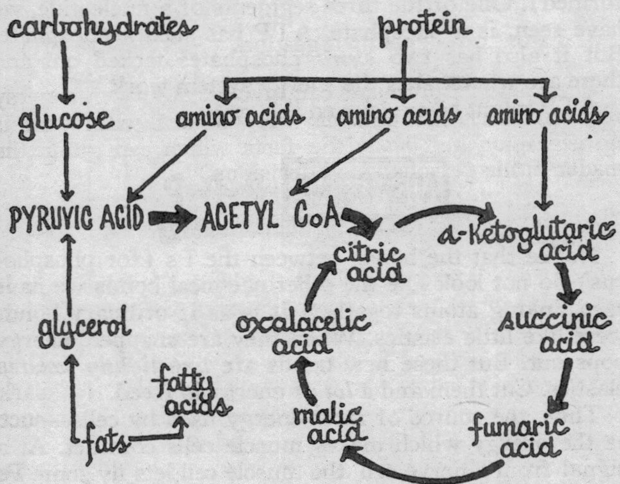

The secret of human energy—the Krebs cycle. This is the process of chemical change by which each cell takes its energy from food. It is shown here in highly simplified form. The steps shown include as many as 20 sub-steps, each of which is controlled by a special enzyme. Moreover, the steps tend to be reversible, suggesting how the body can synthesize so many of the materials it needs.

H and O atoms of which all the fuel substances are made. The object of the whole thing is really to break off individual H atoms and combine two of them with one O atom to form water. This is what releases the needed energy. That energy is in the bonds which hold atoms together, such as those which link two hydrogens and one oxygen in a relationship that makes the combination into ordinary water. In fact, in the energy-yielding Krebs cycle, it is the breaking off and bonding of hydrogen and oxygen that frees energy in each cell.

The energy released does not leave the cell. Instead, it is trapped by a very curious chemical called ATP, which is the secret of human energy.

ATP looks a lot like a *nucleotide* (one of those three-way bits from which the chains of DNA and RNA were formed). One of the three segments of a nucleotide, we have seen, is a phosphate. ATP has such a phosphate. But it also has two *extra* phosphates tacked on, and these are what makes the energy system work.

ATP might be envisioned this way:

ADENOSINE -P~P~P

Notice that the bonds between the Ps (for phosphorus) do not look like the other chemical bonds we have seen linking atoms together. It is as if ordinary bonds were like little elastics. When they are snapped, energy pops out. But these new bonds are like *tightly twisted* elastics. Cut them and a *lot* of energy is freed.

Thus, the source of most energy used by cells—such as the energy which makes muscle cells contract. At a signal from a nerve cell, the muscle cell lets fly some Ps from its ATP, and there is action.

The process is similar to letting go an arrow from a bow. The P atom is the arrow. The high-energy bond holding onto the P is like the drawn bow.

With a regular bow, of course, the string can be drawn over and over again. All you have to do is get another arrow and use some energy to pull. So it is with ATP. The energy released from food-fuel—that which finally comes out of the Krebs cycle—is used to put the third P atom back onto the ATP with a high-energy bond. In effect, it fits another arrow to the bow and pulls. In the cycle, every time two Hs are taken out and linked to one O, another ATP molecule is restored to its energy state and ready to fire.

This, then, is the final step in the conversion of our food to physical energy. But the Krebs cycle is also something more. For partway through the cycle, all the foods have been reduced to very small C-H-O clusters. And it is these that form a kind of supply pool of atomic parts for tissues and chemicals the cells need to make.

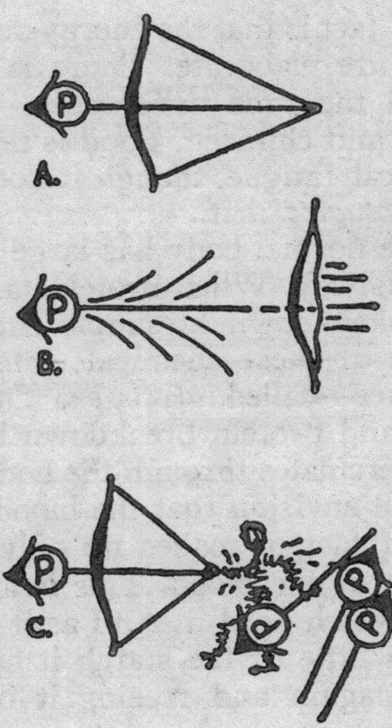

Where our energy comes from. (a) The ATP molecule may be seen as a drawn bow. The last phosphorus atom in the molecule is like the arrow, held to the bow with a high-energy bond. (b) When a cell needs energy for work, the bond is snapped and the energy released, the phosphorus "arrow" flying off. When the cell takes energy from food, that energy is used to restore a phosphorus atom to the impoverished molecule. In effect (c) another "arrow" is fitted to the "bow," which is now drawn and ready to fire again. Each cell employs this process for all its energy needs, from protein-building to the contraction of a muscle fiber.

How the body stocks up on energy

From the explanation above, we can see that there is many a step between food and energy. This suggests some facts about claims for foods that supply "quick energy," "instant go-power" and the like.

Plainly, the simple sugars, such as glucose, maltose and the like, can be made available as energy a little bit faster. But the fact is that the energy-releasing processes for *any* food are elaborate. There is not really much significance in the time differences—at least, not for healthy adults and children. Food is not an instant cure for true physical fatigue, though it does provide an immediate *psychological* lift.

Actually, the normal body has large stores of energy. They work this way. When proteins and carbohydrates have been broken down to simple chemicals, the liver converts some of these chemicals into the only starch the body makes—called *glycogen*. Other products of carbohydrate and protein breakdown become the *blood sugar*, which circulates through the body.

Many people envision that the blood sugar is a large supply. But in fact, it makes up only about one-tenth of one percent of the blood. This is a source of ready fuel for cells which need it. And as it is used, the liver breaks down a little of the starch it has made, turning it into sugars again and freeing it into the blood as blood sugar.

Ordinarily, the body has fine controls over the amount of this free sugar. When there is too much, the cause is usually *diabetes*. When there is too little, we speak of "low blood sugar," *hypoglycemia*.

Recently, a fad has arisen for self-diagnosing low blood sugar. One claim is that ten million Americans suffer from it. Medical authorities, however, are unaware of what would be a serious national problem. If it exists, they say, the victims are indeed well hidden.

The truth is that logic is against the existence of serious low blood sugar in otherwise healthy people. The average person, for example, can get along very vigorously for half a day just on the glycogen stored in his liver. And this is just one of the energy reserves of the body.

The order of these reserves goes something like this: some of the free blood sugar is picked up by each cell. It may be used right away, or go through atom rearrangement to become fat. This fat may be found in tiny reserve droplets within individual cells.

Meanwhile, the liver is busy making glycogen. It does not keep all of the glycogen, but sends some of it out to muscle and other cells, which hold body starch as a fast source of fuel for sudden bursts of effort.

When the glycogen levels are well up, the body makes extra sugars into fats. These are held by cells designed as living silos. We will look closely at these *adipose storage cells* when we talk about overweight. For they make up the body fat most of us worry about.

When the individual cells perform work, they take their fuel from themselves and from the blood sugar flowing by. This lowers the blood-sugar level, so the liver breaks down glycogen and frees it to the blood as sugar. If more fuel is needed, the adipose storage cells break down some of their fat stores to simple chemicals which can enter into the energy-yielding processes. Thus, there is no question that the average adult would not run out of fuel sources within his body for weeks.

How much energy, that is, how much food fuel, each of us uses will be covered shortly. But first, let us fill in some facts about which foods are sources of that energy, so that we can choose from among them.

Understanding and using carbohydrates

Each group of people has its own pattern of fuel sources, usually according to what is most easily available. For the Central American it may be corn and beans. For some South Sea Islanders it is the sugary substance of manioc. But taken in world sum, man's chief sources of fuel are the carbohydrates.

Carbohydrates are almost entirely the products of plants. Meats are almost totally devoid of carbohydrate —except for liver, which makes and stores glycogen. Some shellfish also build carbohydrates, to the extent of perhaps five percent of their food value. But the only important animal-made carbohydrate in man's food supply is *lactose*. This is a simple sugar which provides much of the food value of milks, including human mother's milk.

How much carbohydrate in foods? The carbohydrate content of some typical foods—shown as percentages of total weight.

Leafy vegetables	2–5%
Fresh fruits	12%
Legumes, beans, peas	16–20%
Grains, noodles, potatoes	20–30%
Bread	50%
Dried fruits, jam	70%
Flour, cookies, crackers	70–75%
Most dry cereals	80%
Sugar, honey	99%

The table above suggests what foods are our main sources of carbohydrate.

The carbohydrates we eat are mainly sugars or starches. (The reader will recall that starches are only chains of many sugars, assembled for storage purposes.) We do consume quantities of another carbohydrate, *cellulose*. But as we have pointed out, man does not have the ability to use cellulose, though grazing animals do. The only way we can get the food value of cellulose is to eat the animals which have digested the cellulose for us.

High cellulose content is the reason that foods such as lettuce and celery have so little caloric value and are so much the refuge of those who would reduce. For the most part, leaves and stems have rather little sugar or starch.

Cellulose itself does have value for the eater. That value is mechanical, rather than chemical. For cellulose makes up much of the bulk and fiber necessary to keep our intestines working well. Otherwise, the contracting muscles of our intestines would have little to push against. The passage of food through the alimentary canal would be poorly controlled. Being quite liquid, the digesting food would move too fast to be well absorbed through the intestinal wall, or so slowly as to lead to constipation.

Starchy foods also have a tendency to resist digestion and assimilation. For when plants store fuel as starch, they usually pack it together in microscopic granules, which they coat with a stuff closely related to cellulose. You can easily recognize the characteristic texture of such granules. Just think of such starchy, crunchy foods as potatoes, carrots, beets or turnips.

It is to help break down the starch granules that we cook starchy foods. And this suggests the poor logic of the view that we would be healthier if we ate everything raw. For it takes moist heat to make starch granules absorb water, swell up and finally burst. Once this happens, the starch disperses evenly through water, in what is known as a colloidal form. In this dispersion of tiny particles our digestive juices can get at the sugar chains and break them down for use. This also happens when we eat the same foods raw, but the digestion is much less complete.

The dispersion mostly stays within the form of the vegetable. But anyone who has ever cooked soups and stews knows that if we cook, say, potatoes beyond the ready-to-eat stage, their starches begin to disperse through the cooking water, too, until the original form of the vegetable can vanish. This phenomenon is desirable, and delicious in potato soup. But it is lamentable if our ultimate aim is to get mashed potatoes. Because we will be throwing away the cooking water, and the valuable starches will escape us, along with other food values. Thus we cook in a minimum of water for a minimum of time if we want to get the most out of our starchy foods.

We might also mention a food class which is partway between starches and sugars. This is the group of *dextrins*. One often sees them on food labels.

Dextrins are starches which are partly broken down. In digestion, for example, starches are broken down two molecules of sugar at a time. Each of these broken-off pairs of simple sugar is a molecule of *maltose*, a name we also see on labels. Maltose is simply a double sugar, similar to common table sugar. The chain left over at each stage of breaking off maltoses is a dextrin. The cleaving continues, of course, until the whole long chain is snapped into a lot of maltoses. The maltoses are then broken in half to make molecules of glucose, which we can use for energy. So when you see dextrin or maltose on a label, you know that you are getting carbohydrates.

It is dextrins, for example, that are removed from beer to make the so-called "light" or "low-calorie" beers. The removal is effective, and the calorie claims are true.

Also, from the breaking-down process described above, we can understand what is meant by the *malting* of barley, a happy phenomenon which leads not only to malted milks, but to Scotch whisky. Centuries ago, barley was an important food. But it lacks the gluten which would let it become breads, as some other grains do. So its main use in the world now is for malt. The barley is allowed to ferment. The bacterial enzymes break off maltoses, just as human enzymes do. We use the maltoses to make flavorings and for beers and whiskies.

(Just as a curiosity, beer does taste a bit malty. Scotch does not because the whisky makers keep the barley in a fermenting state by warming it with peat fires—and the smoky peat gives the resulting whisky its dominating smoky flavor.)

Sugars, of course, are the simplest carbohydrates. And their forms in our food can vary. But it is well to keep in mind that table sugar does not vary much because of its slightly different sources. For example, whether sugar is from beets or cane it is exactly the same. It is almost pure sucrose, as has been noted before, a molecule of the simple sugar fructose and one of simple glucose. So is honey. So is maple syrup. So look for no food miracles in these different forms.

Sucrose is an important food in the United States—perhaps a little too important, we shall see. The typical American consumes some 100 pounds of it a year, amounting to something less than 400 calories a day.

Nutritionists do *not* see sucrose as an unabashed villain. The problem with it is that it is so pure that it carries almost nothing but pure energy. So it can take up the place of other more complex foods in the diet.

Brown sugar and raw sugar, we might add, are also sucrose. Brown sugar retains a little of the molasses from which table sugar is extracted. This gives it a brown color, or perhaps tan, depending on the amount of molasses. Raw sugar is not raw, but has simply not been cleaned up as much as white or brown sugars. It has no special health value, though many people think it does.

Speaking of health and sugars, we might as well deal now with a very popular concern, which is partly correct and partly incorrect.

Sugars, starches and the dentist

As a nation, we worry quite a little about the kinds of foods we eat and the effect they have on the cavities which plague our teeth. The fact is that the kind or amount of carbohydrate which goes into our metabolisms is not known to affect our teeth. The common belief that sugar, especially, or other carbohydrates somehow interfere with the body's use of calcium is absolutely not established by any research. Experts are quite certain that neither sugars nor starches prevent the body from making good teeth or bones. In fact, brown sugar *provides* some calcium, from the molasses which colors it.

On the other hand, carbohydrates do become involved in our dental problems. The reason is that many bacteria find these foods as useful and energy-productive as we do.

We tend to accumulate quite a few bacteria in our mouths. They find good, sheltered places to live, and they get to choose first from the best foods we ourselves consume. So, distasteful as it may be to think about, the coating on our teeth when we wake in the morning is thick with fast-growing microbes. These do not eat our teeth, or injure the body as a whole. But the waste products associated with their metabolisms are quite acid.

Since fermentation is the life-style of these mouth bacteria, any fermentable carbohydrate feeds them—the more fermentable, the better. The acid produced in this process eats into the tooth enamel and the structures below it, and we get cavities.

But we can't go without carbohydrate just to starve

out our bacterial companions. So it is wiser to keep removing their colonies, and to keep their food away from them. This is best done by simply cleaning our teeth, especially if we must eat sticky food—such as caramel or other candies—which clings to the teeth. Brushing after every meal is intended to clean up at the time of greatest danger, when there is lots of food for the bacteria.

Tooth-brushing is not always practicable, however. So the American Dental Association recommends at least rinsing the mouth with water after eating—even after drinking soft drinks, or sweetened ones, such as coffee with sugar. Mouthwashes, by the way, will not kill the offending bacteria in great numbers, only serve as liquid to rinse them away, and water is a good deal cheaper.

Understanding and using fats

The second great source of food energy is a somewhat more complex family, the fats. These, as we have seen before, are made by both plants and animals, for extra-compact fuel storage. The table suggests where fats are found, and in what quantity.

How much fat in foods? The fat content of some typical foods—shown as percentages of total weight.

Most bread, fruit, vegetables	under 1%
Milk, shellfish, plain rolls	2–4%
Most fish, lean lamb	6–8%
Lean pork, ice cream, cakes, pies	12–13%
Lunch meats, franks	25–30%
Cheese, beef roasts	30–35%
Peanut butter, bacon, donuts	50%
Most nuts	60%
Butter, margarine	80%
Oils, shortenings	100%

Generally speaking, fats from animals tend to be hard

—what are sometimes called plastic fats. And fats from vegetable sources are likely to be in liquid form, and known as oils. There is a basic chemical difference which causes this difference of physical form.

Hard fats tend to be *saturated.* The bonds, the atomic linkages, are satisfied by having hydrogen atoms hooked onto them. Thus the term *saturated fat.*

Oils do not have all their atomic linkages filled. Thus the oil looks like an incomplete fat. It has vacancies where hydrogen atoms ought to be. So it is called an *unsaturated* or *polyunsaturated* fat.

Actually, all fats have two parts. One is always glycerol. The other is always a fatty acid. It is actually the fatty acid which is saturated or unsaturated, making for a lot of discussion and confusion. Below, these two kinds of fats are shown.

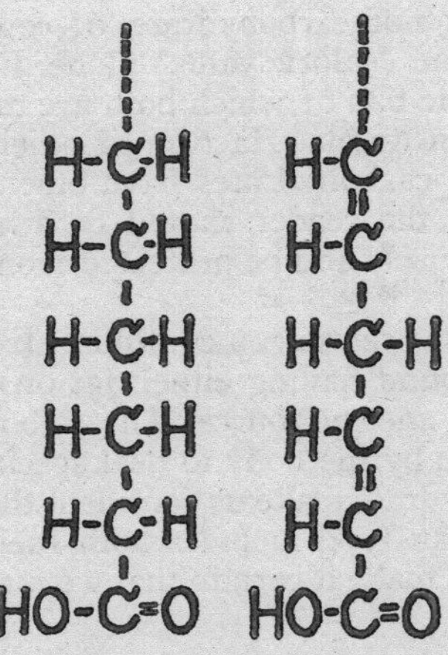

Two kinds of fatty acids. On the left, part of a saturated fatty acid, with all its possible hydrogen bonds filled. On the right, part of an unsaturated fatty acid, with a number of possible hydrogen positions open.

Modern food technology does many complex things with fats and oils to provide such in-between consistencies as those of soft margarine. Sometimes, in such processes, missing hydrogen atoms are added to unsaturated fats. And this is where the familiar label term "hydrogenated" comes from.

As we said earlier in this chapter, some of the health implications of fats will be dealt with separately. In general, fats as a fuel food are more concentrated, slower to leave the stomach, somewhat more difficult for the body to break down, and in excess can coat other foods to make digestion slower or less complete. Yet a healthy body can tolerate a diet very, very high in fat. The upper limits of fat intake are described by its very high calorie values. By weight, fat foods can be ten times as caloric as equivalent weights of many carbohydrate foods, which tend to have most of their weight as water. An ounce of butter, for example, can yield 200 calories. An ounce of watermelon provides fewer than eight calories.

Neither fat nor carbohydrate, of course, is a source of energy value (caloric value) alone. For we have seen how the atomic bits of which both are made can be used by the body in its manufacture of other chemicals. But both fats and carbohydrates have other essential qualities of which the reader should be aware, in order to choose food wisely and be protected from dangerous fad ideas.

For at least a century, a continual stream of fads has been built around hailing either fat or carbohydrate as *the* "natural" energy source. The elaborate systems of enzymes made by the body to deal specifically with only fat or carbohydrate make us confident that the "natural" plan for human food includes both fuels. But two specific essentials make it certain that we *must* have the two.

The biogenic range of fats

While our bodies can use a great deal of fat, it cannot be the *only* energy food. For unless there are carbohydrates to take part in the fuel chemistry, the huge amounts of fat needed for energy are incompletely broken down. In this incomplete metabolism of fat, substances called *ketones* are formed. The body cannot eliminate them fast enough, and as they accumulate, they reach a level which is toxic—a body state called *ketosis.*

Ketosis often results in coma, and even death. This is the state which most urgently threatens diabetics; for the diabetics (untreated) cannot handle carbohydrates. So almost the only energy source becomes the fat in the diet. Reducing carbohydrates to less than a little over two ounces per day risks ketosis. Self-prescribed starvation produces the same threat, because the body is forced to use only its own stored fats for energy. It is like being on an all protein-fat diet.

There are lower limits, too, to the range of fats. These arise from the fact that the body cannot build its own polyunsaturated fatty acids of a certain kind. These are necessary for growth and health. That is, they are used for certain body chemicals which cannot be made without them. This has proven true in careful studies, not only of animals, but of human infants, especially when the babies were on formulas made from evaporated milk that did not have the necessary additions.

The needed fats are known as *essential fatty acids.* And the body's requirement for them makes self-prescribed fat-free or very-low-fat diets dangerous.

The fatty-acid essentials are *linoleic, linolenic* and *arachadonic acids.* But we needn't worry about all three. For if the body has *linoleic acid,* it can make the other two from it.

How much linoleic acid do we need? The figure is between one and two percent of our daily calories. In other words, a man who needed 2,500 calories a day of food would need only 25 to 50 calories' worth of linoleic acid. (To get which, of course, would demand much more total fat.) But since a typical American dietary includes at least that much linoleic acid, most of us need not be concerned.

Just in case the reader would like to get an idea of where that much essential fatty acid would come from, here are some food portions with their approximate content of linoleic acid:

Where Linoleic Acid Is

Food	Linoleic Acid (grams)
Corn, cottonseed or soy oil, one tablespoon	7.0
Peanut oil, one tablespoon	4.5
Pork, 3 oz., lean and fat of pork loin	2.8
Beef roast, 3 oz., average cut	2.7
Pork, 3 oz., lean and fat of broiled pork chop	2.4
Lamb chop, 3 oz., broiled loin	.9
"Polyunsaturate-rich" margarines, one pat, about ⅓ oz.	.6 to 2.5
Lamb leg, 3 oz., lean and fat	.6
Butter, one pat, about ⅓ oz.	.3
Average standard margarine, one pat, about ⅓ oz.	.3

Linoleic acids occur in many foods other than these. But this list suggests the pattern. Animal fats are more limited in essential fatty acids than are vegetable fats. Of the animal fats, beef and pork are rather higher in their EFA content. But note that we must eat the lean *and* fat on the meat to get it. Vegetable oils are the best sources, and these are contained in a number of commonly eaten prepared foods—such as mayonnaise made from corn oil, or salad dressing made from soy or cottonseed oil. Some baked products also contain oils. In general, essential fatty acids tend to appear with other polyunsaturated fatty acids. And we will discuss the sources of the latter in the chapter on food and heart disease.

One can see, also, that while an ample mixed diet does supply all the essential fat we need, arbitrarily cutting out all the fat we can may produce a deficiency of the essential fats. For the essentials are often only small percentages of the total fat.

The practical conclusion we must draw is that it is

sensible to include both fats and carbohydrates in our daily food, and to treat neither as villainous.

How much fat do you eat?

Whenever we look at fats or carbohydrates, we are looking at a food seesaw. However we adjust one of them in the diet almost automatically adjusts the other.

As we saw earlier, we are tending to eat more fat and less carbohydrate as a nation. This is a pattern which is typical of increasing wealth. Fats are generally more expensive food, more usually associated with costly protein, and often closely involved with what is flavorful, such as chocolate.

There are quite a few estimates of how much fat Americans eat, but the average is probably about 45 percent of the diet. (This percentage is not of the weight of the food consumed, but of the caloric value of the food.) Individuals vary in their fat-carbohydrate mix, of course, and experts believe that many American diets are now more than 50 percent fat.

High-fat diets seem to lead to a variety of troubles, as we shall see. So most nutritionists now suggest that dietary fats be not more than about a third of the calories you take in, and perhaps as low as 25 percent. That gives us an eating pattern with about 15 percent protein, 25 to 33 percent fat and 52 to 60 percent carbohydrate.

If pure fat, protein and pure carbohydrate were all we needed, we could just stir up some amino acids, sugar and oil and wax healthy. The fact is that almost every important nutrient carries some traces of micronutrients with it—such as vitamins and minerals. For most Americans, these tend to muddy the nutritional waters. And just a little knowledge can help to clear things up.

Plain, practical truths about vitamins

The subject of vitamins can be made as confusing as astrophysics and as frightening as a Sunday preacher on the theological warpath. Conversely, it can be as gloriously promising as the pearly gates.

But in practical terms, neither the complexity, the terror nor the promise has much real meaning for the typical American eater. True, vitamins are a tricky technical matter for the biochemist. For example, most people think there is vitamin A in carrots. Actually, there is none in carrots or any other vegetable—only alpha, beta and gamma carotene. But don't worry. The body uses these to make vitamin A. Don't even worry about the fact that actually this vitamin includes a group of active substances—such as axerophthol, retinene, vitamin A acid, 3-dehydroretinol and retinene-2. Eat your carrot and relax.

Did you know that vitamin C may not really be a vitamin at all, but a missing substance believed by some experts to be needed in food because the human body suffers from an inborn metabolic error? Other animals, except for monkeys and guinea pigs, make their own.

The list of vitamin-deficiency disorders is a litany of physical threats. Blindness, scaly, deteriorating skin, hemorrhages, nerves failing, paralysis, swellings and bleeding sores are just a few of the less frightening results. Such deficiencies are known, tragically, in other lands, but scarcely ever among ordinary Americans. The kids are *not* going to get beriberi because they won't drink their milk, or scurvy because they hate orange juice.

On the other side of the coin, listening to faddists or to the claims of commerce, we might almost begin to think that vitamins alone *equaled* food, and that the more vitamins we got, the healthier we would be. Alas, it is not so. True, were we without vitamin A our vision would be impaired. But once we have enough, more will not improve our sight one whit beyond what heredity has given us. Crushing bunches of carrots every day and drinking the juice will only tint our skin a little yellow—and if we carry it far enough, make us quite ill. In fact, most of us store in our livers a supply of vitamin A which can keep us for months, or even a year. The cells can have all they want.

Much is made of the fortified breakfast cereals, some of which incorporate all our daily needs of all the major vitamins. One recent ad even implied clearly that this fortification could relieve a mother's mind, if, for example, her children missed lunch. Yet the cereal had only a tiny fraction of the day's protein need, and that in incomplete protein. And it supplied only one twenty-fifth of the day's energy food for an average man.

Vitamins are not magical. True, some people consume low levels of some vitamins. And it is important to remedy these lacks, because they may deny optimal health or growth and protection against illness or weakness. But the job can be done quite simply. No elaborate system, no super-high-potency formula, no special single food is necessary. We can see the truth of this if we merely apply a little biology and common sense.

The first and hardest question is, what is a vitamin? There is no simple answer. Generally, it is a compound made, like proteins, mainly of Cs, Hs, Os, Ns, and maybe an atom or two of sulfur. But it does not become either energy or structure for the body. It is necessary in only very tiny amounts. It seems to work mostly like an enzyme, often to be a kind of enzyme helper (coenzyme) or to be used by the body as part of a coenzyme. It might be said that a vitamin helps out around the chemistry laboratories of the cells, and it is usually indispensable.

Vitamins have been known, in a general sense, for two hundred years, through trouble caused by their absence. But they were not named until Casimir Funk dubbed them, in 1911, "as vita-amines." (Unfortunately, Funk's chemistry was wrong; they are not amines, which is why nutritionists removed the "e" at the end of the word.) Until quite recently, we knew vitamins only by the symptoms of deficiency. Their real role in body chemistry is only now being understood, along with the extent of our real needs for them.

The most typical role of the vitamin might be understood in a general way by analogy. The reader will recall how an enzyme worked—by fitting the shape of its active sites to chains of amino acids and either breaking them apart or putting them together. Keeping this in mind, we might think of the enzyme as a kind of chemical tool, perhaps like a wrench.

Sometimes the enzyme, like the wrench, works fine by itself—just as a wrench does when we use it on the nuts of an automobile wheel to change a tire, or on a plumbing fixture securely mounted to a wall. But suppose our amino chain is sometimes more like a few lengths of loose pipe joined together. One wrench does us no good. Each thrust only turns the whole pipe chain. We need another wrench to pull in the opposite direction in order to take the pipes apart. The co-enzyme functions much like that second wrench.

Without the second wrench, the first is useless. In some cases, the body can build *part* of its second wrench, but it does not know how to make some essential segment, a handle, for example. The vitamin may supply that missing part of the co-enzyme.

We can carry the analogy further. Once we have the second wrench, or the needed part of it, a third or fourth wrench won't get the job done a bit better. Of course, if we have a whole work crew (many cells) all needing second wrenches, we must have enough to go around. Otherwise, either workmen will have to wait their turns or some will just have to remain idle. Either way, the job goes more slowly. So, with too few vitamins, necessary body processes slow down, and the cumulative effect of a long slowdown may be disastrous.

On the other hand, if we supply a great number more wrenches than are needed, they are either thrown away because we have no way to store them (as generally happens with an excess of the water-soluble vitamins) or some will just have to remain idle. Either way, the they become a serious handicap (as is likely to happen with the fat-soluble vitamins).

With vitamins, we need enough to do the job, with some spares in case of trouble. But overconsumption is either pointlessly wasteful or actually destructive. More than we can use obviously has no value.

Vitamins, moreover, are not food factors which must usually be ferreted out of obscure hiding places. They are usually plentiful. Thinking biologically, it is not reasonable to assme that nutrients essential for survival would have been unavailable to evolving man. Were they so, we would think that man should have been phased out by natural selection as a bad design, just as some of the prehistoric monsters evidently got into nutritional trouble.

Remember, too, that man has flourished in many climates amid quite varying food sources. The Adams of the world did not have supplements available or fortified breakfast food. Some may have had oranges each day, but not many. Their neighborhood grains, fruits, roots, leaves and animal quarry differed widely. They could not count on a continuing supply of anything. Vegetation changed with the turning season. There were not always the same seeds or leaves. Meat supplies were a question of luck and cunning.

Man probably survived well just *because* he could adjust to differing nutritional environments. He could eat just about anything and get along, at least for a while. He developed biochemical systems for managing almost any safe eatable—protein, fat or carbohydrate in many forms. Obviously, the trace nutrients necessary for handling these foods had to come in the package.

It is still so. When we choose foods intelligently, we are likely to get all the little nutritional bits and pieces needed to use them and get along. It is as though any tools we can't make ourselves tend to come with the raw materials. Generally it is only when our dietary becomes highly monotonous and narrowed—through poverty, as in underdeveloped lands, through fads and pseudoscience, through narrow tastes and commercially inspired diversion—that we are endangered by distortions of normal eating.

Good food, all of science agrees, is the simplest and best way to assure ourselves of the best health nutrition can provide. Let us see, then, what micronutrients we need, as a way of learning which sources of protein, fat and carbohydrate provide most completely for life.

One fact to keep in mind as you read about these nutrients is that trying to set down nutrient problems and sources is today a bit like trying to take a snapshot of a snowbank. It is constantly changing. Rapid changes in our food industry are taking place every day, with a broad effort to plug the nutritional gaps. All the author can do is to present the latest snapshot he could take, knowing that tomorrow it will be a picture of yesterday's snowbank. On the other hand, the main features are likely to stay much the same. Certainly human beings continue to be made much in the old model.

Shortcuts to the B vitamins

Although there are usually considered to be nine vitamins in what is spoken of as the "B complex," three of them are much better known than the rest. These three are *thiamine* (B_1), *riboflavin* (B_2) and *niacin*. Despite some of the confusion caused by the letter-symbol tradition for vitamins—which began when researchers thought there were very few of the micronutrients—each of the nine Bs is a separate entity, with different work to do and found in quite different proportions in different foods. Today the B designation for a vitamin really means very little—except that it can be dissolved in water and that it contains nitrogen. Vitamin C would be classed with the B group, except it has no nitrogen and so stands alone.

Deficiencies of B vitamins produce such dread diseases as beriberi, pellagra and pernicious anemia. But though these diseases—and those of other vitamin deficiencies—are dramatic, as are the stories of vitamin discovery, an examination of them does not serve our practical purposes.

The symptoms of any serious deficiency would send any reasonable person rushing to his doctor. Suppose, for example, you were badly deficient in thiamine. You would find your feet going numb. There would be cramping pains in your legs. You would stumble when you tried to walk and finally become paralyzed. Meanwhile, you would have signs of deadly heart failure and might notice that you were swelling up with fluid. It seems likely to the author that you would not ignore these signs even if you did not read this book, and that you would be a good deal less likely to say to yourself, "Well now—I think I'll just eat a few thiamine-rich foods and see if this goes away."

All major deficiencies of all vitamins are similarly striking. As for minor signs of dietary deficiencies, they are usually far too vague for self-diagnosis. So in either case, diagnosis and treatment are a medical matter, not a do-it-yourself project. For example, diagnostic signs of deficiencies include such shadowy matters as irritability, sleepiness or sleeplessness, loss of appetite, indigestion, fatigue, itchy skin, poor color or unmanageable hair. No wonder that promoters and faddists have such a field day waking hypochondria in the hearts of their readers and thus selling them on secret systems and supplements.

All major studies on the nutritive status of Americans agree that extreme cases of deficiency are now very rare. So we shall omit the terror campaign which has so often been the hallmark of promoters of healthful eating. Similarly, we will not make promises about curing anything. *Nutrients will cure nothing but the lack of nutrients.*

So we will simply see what our bodies need and how to get it—in vitamins as we did in the other nutrients.

Among other things, *thiamine* is needed as a co-enzyme in the processes of getting oxygen to the body tissues, in the using of carbohydrates and in the building of ribose, the sugar which is such an important part of RNA.

Riboflavin is part of several enzymes and co-enzymes, entering into many body chemistry processes, especially as a carrier of hydrogen. This work is so basic that riboflavin can be found in almost any tissue of the body.

Niacin is also an essential of reactions within almost every cell. It is involved in the very basic shuffling about of H and O atoms. In other words, it, like the other two principal B vitamins, helps to provide some of the key tools of the body for taking molecules apart and putting them together. These tools can be likened to the hammer, saw and crowbar of the carpenter. The cells' work of dismantling foods and putting them to use cannot be done without these vitamin tools. Chemically, they enter into so many processes, directly and indirectly, that it is hopeless to try and describe them here. The body's work without them is about as handicapped as would be that of a housewife without any soaps, detergents or cleaners.

Small amounts of these vitamins are almost unavoidable if you eat at all. On the other hand, some fairly meaningful B vitamin omissions are occurring in the diets of certain population groups—in terms of the recommended daily allowances, which of course include ample safety margins.

In USDA and other studies, thiamine is below the RDA levels (a small percentage) in boys 12 to 14 years old. All other males seem to be getting enough. But females from the age of nine seem to get a little less than the RDA for thiamine. In girls 15 to 17, and in women over 65, the lack is between ten and 20 percent. So take cautious note if you or someone in your family fits one of these groups.

Riboflavin is also below desired levels in some groups. There is a lack up to ten percent in women from 20 to 34 and from 55 to 64. The lack is worse (up to 20 percent) in women 35 to 54 and also in those who are between 65 and 74. Elderly women (over 75) show a still greater omission of up to 30 percent.

There is not considered to be a national dietary deficiency of niacin of any importance, for several reasons. One is that niacin is so plentiful in foods Americans eat a lot. For example, less than a quarter-pound of meat provides about a third of the day's need. Grains and nuts and beans are other excellent sources. But another reason niacin deficiency is less likely is that, unlike most B vitamins, niacin can be stored to some extent in the liver. The other B vitamins are stored little or not at all, and any excess is removed in the urine.

But possibly the biggest guarantee against dietary lacks of niacin is the fact that the body can make the vitamin. All that is needed is the amino acid *tryptophan*. So a diet rich in proteins is likely to be niacin-safe. For example, a quart of milk contains only one milligram of niacin, perhaps a fifteenth of the average adult RDA. But it also has 480 milligrams of tryptophan—enough to yield eight milligrams of niacin. So the tryptophan in a quart of milk can provide 60 percent of an adult's daily niacin requirement.

Let us now see what we need of thiamine and riboflavin and where we can get it in our food. The needs—and the sources from which they can be met—are shown in the accompanying table.

The "Big Three" of Vitamin B

Food	Thiamine (mg.) (RDA 1.0)	Riboflavin (mg.) (RDA 1.6)	Niacin (mg.) (RDA 17)
Asparagus, fresh cooked, ½ cup	.16	.18	1.4
Bacon, broiled, 3 strips	.13	.09	1.3
Banana, medium	.06	.08	0.9
Beans, lima, ½ cup	.14	.08	1.0
Beef, lean ground, 3 ounces	.08	.20	5.1
Beef, rib roast, 3½ ounces	.05	.15	3.6
Blueberries, fresh, ⅔ cup	.03	.06	0.5
Bread, whole wheat, slice	.06	.03	0.7
Broccoli, boiled, ⅔ cup	.09	.20	0.8
Brussels sprouts, 5–6, cooked	.06	.10	0.6
Butter, tablespoon	—	—	—
Cabbage, raw, 3½ ounces	.05	.05	0.3
Cereals, dry	(Vary according to enrichment)		
Cheddar cheese, 1 ounce	.01	.14	trace
Chicken breast, half, fried	.05	.22	14.7
Corn, fresh, small ear	.12	.10	1.4
Cottage cheese, ¼ cup	.02	.14	trace
Crabmeat, cooked, 3½ ounces	.08	.08	1.9
Egg, one large	.06	.15	0.1
Fish, halibut, broiled, 3½ ounces	.05	.07	8.3
Fish, tuna, canned, 3½ ounces	.05	.12	13.3
Flour, white, enriched, ½ cup	.24	.15	1.9
Ham, 3½ ounces	.47	.18	3.6
Honey, tablespoon	trace	.01	0.1
Ice cream, 3½ ounces	.04	.19	0.1

Food	Thiamine (mg.) (RDA 1.0)	Riboflavin (mg.) (RDA 1.6)	Niacin (mg.) (RDA 17)
Kale, ½ cup	.06	.10	0.9
Lamb, one average chop	.12	.23	5.0
Lettuce, loose-leaf, 4 small leaves	.03	.04	0.2
Liver, beef, two small slices, fried	.20	3.14	12.4
Milk, one cup	.07	.41	0.2
Molasses, average, tablespoon	trace	.02	0.2
Mushrooms, raw, 3½ ounces	.10	.46	4.2
Nuts, mixed, ½ ounce	.09	.02	0.6
Okra, boiled, 3½ ounces	.13	.18	0.9
Orange, medium, raw	.15	.06	0.6
Peanut butter, two tablespoons	.04	.04	4.8
Pear, medium, raw	.04	.07	0.2
Peas, green, fresh or frozen, ½ cup	.22	.09	1.8
Pineapple, canned, two small slices	.10	.02	0.2
Pork loin, 3 ounces	.45	.21	4.4
Potatoes, one medium, baked	.10	.04	1.7
Prunes, 8–9 medium, cooked	.04	.09	0.9
Raspberries, fresh, ⅔ cup	.03	.09	0.9
Rice, white, enriched, cooked, ⅔ cup	.11	—	1.0
Roll, one hamburger type	.11	.07	0.8
Sausage, frankfurter, average	.08	.10	1.3
Sausage, pork, 3 links	.47	.20	2.2
Spinach, cooked, ½ cup	.06	.13	0.5
Squash, summer, boiled, ½ cup	.05	.08	0.8
Strawberries, fresh, ⅔ cup	.03	.07	0.6
Sweet potato, small, baked	.09	.07	0.7
Tomato, fresh, medium	.09	.06	1.1
Tomato juice, canned, 6 ounces	.09	.05	1.4
Turkey, light meat, 3½ ounces	.05	.14	11.1
Turnip greens, cooked, ½ cup	.11	.18	0.5
Waffle, one from mix	.11	.17	0.7
Wheat germ, rounded tablespoon	.20	.07	0.4

While it is hard to draw sure conclusions, the riboflavin lacks in the food of women may possibly be explained by the great concern with overweight and popular concepts about "fattening" foods. Women, we shall see, are doing a better job of weight control than men are. But this may well be at the price of good nutrition.

The explanation for feminine lacks of thiamine may be similar. Check the foods richest in thiamine and riboflavin—such as pork, beans and peas, enriched and whole-grain flours (meaning "fattening" breads, rolls and the like), milk, cheese, ice cream and eggs. These are often needlessly feared as fat-makers. Women who think they may be low in B vitamins, and who worry about "fattening" foods, will do well to read the weight-control chapter and learn how to maintain or lose weight without sacrificing needed food factors.

The small lack of thiamine in the food of 12-to-14-year-old boys is not clearly explained. However, the answer may be that they are consuming too many "empty" and "luxury" calories, pushing other foods out of their diets. They are old enough to have pocket money and some free choice, yet young enough to have little information about food and to consume much less than do older teenage boys, whose caloric consumption is so great that it is hard for them to lack in any nutrient.

One protection against dietary deficiencies of the B-vitamin big three is the enrichment of flours. Probably 90 percent of the white bread sold in America now is made with enriched flour. This enrichment alone is estimated to provide the following daily percentages of the major B vitamins needed in the diet: thiamine, 16 percent; niacin, 13 percent; and riboflavin, three percent. But not all bread is enriched, and many other grain products needlessly lack enrichment, among them cakes, pastries, cookies and such. However, it looks as if that enrichment will soon be boosted, and will be taken advantage of in more and more prepared foods, especially breads.

It is well worthwhile to read the labels of all flour products to watch for the adjective "enriched" in the contents. The same caution is a good idea in buying cornmeal, grits, rice and baking mixes of all kinds. A more detailed comparison of the food values of enriched, unenriched and whole-grain eatables is made in the following chapter. Nutritionists see no excuse for omitting enrichment. It is a cheap and simple safety measure, acceptable in every way.

The other B vitamins

As far as nutritionists know—and they have gone to a lot of trouble to find out—the other B vitamins are plentifully consumed by most Americans. Later, however, we shall see that special stress states can make it wise to seek out some of them in slightly greater amounts than usual. Most of these states are such, by the way, that medical supervision is in order—pregnancy is one example—and the doctor is aware of the greater need and will prescribe accordingly.

Vitamin B_6

This vitamin was isolated in the late 1930s, and it really occurs as three different chemicals. *Pyridoxine* is probably the form you see most on labels, and it is largely of vegetable origin. *Pyridoxal* and *pyridoxamine* are the other two B_6 chemicals, and they occur mainly in animal products. Any one of these serves as the vitamin. For whichever type is consumed, the body uses it as the raw material for making a chemical called *pyridoxal phosphate*. This is a co-enzyme (like our aforementioned "extra wrench") and is a basic body tool. It is involved in the cells' ability to make amino acids, to shuffle carbon dioxide around, to produce certain hormones, to convert essential fatty acids to different forms and more. So far, some two dozen amino-acid reactions are known to require B_6. Obviously, without this vitamin, we do not operate well.

How much do we need? No RDA has yet been set, except tentatively, using a wide margin of safety. For example, B_6 needs change with the amount of food, especially protein, we eat, which figures, considering its job seems largely to be handling body building blocks. And of course, the more we eat, the more B_6 we are likely to get. (That figures, too. Evolution does not usually lead to unworkable systems, but tends to take advantage of what is handiest in creating basic chemistry procedures.)

Careful studies indicate that about three-fourths of a milligram of B_6 is needed to manage up to 2,900 calories a day, with 100 grams of protein. That is a high-protein diet for a big man. The amount of the vitamin is less than a thousandth part of a twenty-eighth of an ounce.

The Food and Nutrition Board (which sets RDAs) tentatively suggests we play safe by taking about two and one-half times the amount that seems to be needed for that big man eating lots of protein. The suggestion: about 1.75 to two milligrams of B_6.

How much do Americans get? Diets classified as "very poor" overall—and there aren't too many of those around—have about one milligram of the vitamin B_6. That's about a third more than the *minimum* need for our large high-protein eater. "Average" American diets provide *at least* twice to three times that much, between two and 2.7 milligrams daily.

One can see that there is no problem if one looks at the B_6 content of some foods. For example, here are the B_6 contents for typical servings of:

Food	B_6 (milligrams)
Liver	1.42
Ham	.70
Lima beans	.60
Corn	.39
Popcorn	.37
Banana, small	.32
Canned salmon	.28
Milk	.22
Carrot	.21
Frankfurter	.16
Frozen peas	.11
Egg noodles	.09

This is just a suggestion of the spectrum of foods with substantial amounts of B_6. Even unenriched flour has about .1 mg. of the stuff, and there is talk of adding B_6 to flours in still greater amount. Meat is such a good source that meat-eating people are usually safe by a nice margin. Even vegetarians who are wise enough to eat plenty of legumes and whole grains can't miss. For example, in Burma, a nation with nutrition problems, the B_6 content of the diet appears to be above minimum need.

Pantothenic acid

When they named this B vitamin *pantothenic acid,* they scratched their heads for some suitable Greek and finally came up with words meaning something like "from everything." The reason is just what you might expect. Pantothenic acid is found in all living cells, plant and animal, and that is where our food comes from. The effects of having too little pantothenic acid were difficult to learn, for a naturally occurring deficiency had not been recorded in a human being. Nutritionists finally got a look at a deficiency by designing an odd diet—and finding a chemical which blocked pantothenic acid from working in the body. In other words, unless you are willing to go to a great deal of trouble, you are simply going to have to go without a pantothenic acid deficiency.

This vitamin, you see, is part of *co-enzyme A,* the pivot point of the whole Krebs cycle, the process by which every cell gets its energy and some of its most basic building blocks of Cs, Hs and Os. Nutritionally, it is hard to get more basic than that. And it seems reasonable that, since all foods ultimately require pantothenic acid to become energy, this vitamin is virtually universal.

If the reader is curious, the foods with the most pantothenic acid include eggs, liver, peanuts, peas, the germs and bran of wheat and rice, milk, meats and poultry. Fruits and vegetables generally have less, but the amounts are meaningful. So don't worry about pantothenic acid.

Vitamin B_{12}

This is another vitamin which poses no problems for most of us. Known as *cobalamin,* it is another very basic chemical of cell survival. It gets involved in the making of nucleic acids (RNA and DNA), in the making of amino acids, the workings of the nervous system and digestive tract, and especially in keeping up the number of red blood cells.

Faddists make some curious statements about this vitamin, and their ideas often seem to be related to *pernicious anemia.* Some of the uneducated confuse the latter with more common forms of anemia, which is, of course, a lack of red blood cells. But pernicious anemia is something special and quite rare. It most commonly results from a hereditary inability to take up vitamin B_{12} from the intestines. You can imagine that such inability can play havoc, and does. But when B_{12} preparations are injected, all is well. It is a clean and simple story.

You don't need much B_{12}. About five micrograms or less a day does the job very nicely. That is .00000017 ounces. The Food and Nutrition Board finds that average American diets meet these requirements quite adequately. Even low-cost diets are found to contain three to five times this need. Moreover, B_{12}, unlike most other B vitamins, *is* stored in the kidneys and liver, and in no small amounts. The normal adult could get by for two or three years, probably, without getting a speck of cobalamin.

There is a possible exception, however, to unconcern about B_{12}. It is the group of vegetarians who do not eat milk, eggs, cheese or fish. Plant products do not seem to contain B_{12}, whereas it is most plentiful in meats, fishes, eggs and milk.

Pernicious anemia is common in countries where animal products are avoided for religious reasons or tend to be out of economic reach. It is mainly seen in infants. Though plants do not really develop any B_{12}, it can sometimes be picked up by their roots, casually, by crude absorption from the soil. Certain soil bacteria make the stuff. Even when this absorption takes place, the amounts are described as "traces." Yet this may be enough to let some adults scrape by.

Folic acid

Sometimes known as *folate,* this B vitamin is another intimately involved with basic human chemistry—such as the breakdown of amino acids and some processes of the blood and reproductive system. The compound (really a group of compounds, each of which can serve as the chemical raw material needed by the cells) gets its name from the Latin word for leaf. So our situation here is almost the reverse of that in B_{12}. Meats are poor sources of folic acid; leaves are best. One can begin to see the predominant pattern of biogenic eating—that man eats optimally when he eats some of everything, at least something of every broad class of plants and animals. *Omnivorous* (eating all) is not a casual term for man.

Other good sources of folic acid are green vegetables, dried legumes, nuts, whole wheat, liver and yeast. But we need not worry much. Deficiencies are rarely known to occur—except in pregnancy. So obstetricians are now careful to caution expectant mothers not to omit leafy and green vegetables. However, only tiny amounts seem to be needed to protect even pregnant women. One serving a day of the folic-acid-rich vegetables should do the trick, when eaten with an ordinary, varied diet.

No matter what supplement promoters say, it is easy to get enough folic acid, and excesses accomplish nothing. Folic acid substances do not effect other anemias, such as those due to lack of iron. They are used only for certain specific anemias which occur at times in pregnant women and very young children. They do not cure nervous disorders. And above all, they will neither prevent nor cure dread *leukemia.* Folic acid derivatives have been used experimentally in leukemia, but served only a special medical purpose and that for only a limited time.

Biotin

We have two solid protections against biotin deficiency. One is the fact that there is plenty of this B vitamin in the foods we eat that also provide the other B vitamins. The second protection, even more soothing, is that we have bacteria living in our intestines which make at least enough biotin to supply our requirements, and usually some extra.

So, as interesting as biotin is to biochemists, it need not worry anyone in a practical way. Of course, there is always the possible exception. When heavy doses of antibiotics are used, it is possible to kill off some of the friendly microbial biotin-makers. In most cases, however, our second line of defense, the ease of getting biotin, in ordinary food, still protects us.

Biotin, like all the vitamins, is important to our chemistry. It gets concerned with the making of fatty acids, with the food-energy cycles, amino acid building and the making of glycogen to store energy in the liver. But the Food and Nutrition Board is quite sure that we get plenty. No worry here.

Choline

This vitamin in the B group is still a bit of a puzzle. It may not even be a vitamin. A vitamin is partly defined, and its needs generally measured, by finding or producing a deficiency. Alas, no one has yet been able to find a person suffering from choline deficiency. In fact, the best efforts to produce one in man have been doomed to failure so far.

This biochemical frustration is nevertheless soothing to us eaters. In fact, the Food and Nutrition Board has seen no point in suggesting even a tentative RDA for choline.

The vitamin—it probably really is one—is mentioned here as a defense against any nonsense about deficiencies of it. It is known to be used in metabolizing fats, as a component of one of the most important chemicals that make the nervous system function, and as a participant in the body's synthesis of proteins.

Interestingly, choline is used in larger quantities than any other vitamin substance. It comes in fat-like substances called *phospholipids,* such as *lecithin,* and is very plentiful in egg yolk, beef liver, all meats, whole grains, legumes, milk and vegetables. This, of course, is academic. Ignore fanciful claims which are being made for choline-rich foods and chemicals. Lecithin, for example, has been the hero of some promoters' spurious tales about heart-disease prevention and nerve-soothing. These result from the ignorant distortion of research reports on phospholipids. Beware. If any of these reports had really said anything about success in curing or preventing blood-vessel or nerve diseases with lecithin, you can bet your egg yolk that you would have read the headlines.

Inositol

Let us be quick to note that inositol is not a vitamin. For a time, researchers thought it might be a B vitamin, and some ill-informed writers describe it so still. But this idea seems now to have been an error. Even if it should some day turn out to be a vitamin after all, we need not worry. Inositol does get involved in body chemicals, but our own cells make all we need. To top it off, inositol is available in many foods. We bring it up because once in a while, a faddist or promoter rediscovers inositol. Ignore him.

Common sense about vitamin C

The way is which vitamin C is being added to foods lately, practically to anything which tastes a little sour, suggests some misleading ideas about this important vitamin. Advertising has further confused matters with direct, questionable statements and false implications.

First of all, if we look at the Department of Agriculture and other surveys of American nutrition, we find only one significant sign of a lack of vitamin C. It occurs among males of more than seventy-five years, and is less than ten percent drop below RDA levels.

Of course, we have all heard the story of scurvy on ancient ships and the British discovery that lime juice would prevent or cure this serious deficiency disease. But if there is any scurvy in the United States, doctors do not seem to notice it. Nor are minor signs of small vitamin C lacks observed to any extent. With the flood of *ascorbic acid* (the chemical name for the vitamin) pouring into our food, one can hardly envision a shortage.

Ascorbic acid helps maintain blood-vessel strength, carries hydrogen here and there in body chemistry, gets into the formation of hemoglobin, the absorption and depositing of iron and is associated with the development of connective tissues. There are a number of other roles, too, from wound-healing to infection resistance.

Many millions of dollars have been spent to establish vitamin C as the "orange-juice vitamin." Orange juice is certainly a fine source of vitamin C, a good source of other nutrients and one of the author's favorite beverages. But there are lots of ascorbic acid sources around, and the reader is urged to look carefully through the following list of them.

Before that look, bear in mind the RDA levels for vitamin C. They are: 35 mg. for infants, 40 mg. for children, between 45 and 55 mg. for teenagers, 55 mg. for women, 60 mg. for both adult men and pregnant or breast-feeding women. These levels are quite a lot higher than the USFDA's minimum daily requirements. Now let's see how our ordinary diets can supply ascorbic acid:

Food	Vitamin C or Ascorbic Acid (milligrams)
Orange juice, 6 oz.	93
Broccoli, ⅔ cup, cooked	90
Pepper, one medium shell, cooked	83
Grapefruit juice, 6 oz.	61
Brussels sprouts, six average	61
Strawberries, ⅔ cup	59
Cauliflower, ¾ cup, cooked	55

Food	Vitamin C or Ascorbic Acid (milligrams)
Turnip greens, half cup, cooked	52
Mustard greens, ⅔ cup, cooked	48
Tomato, one medium, raw	35
Cantaloupe, half a 4½-inch melon	33
Watermelon, two cups	28
Asparagus, six stalks, cooked	26
Spinach, half cup, cooked	25
Sweet potato, medium, baked	22
Blackberries, ⅔ cup	21
Tomato juice, half cup, canned	20
Pineapple, ⅔ cup, raw	17
Potato, one medium, boiled in skin	16
Green peas, half cup, cooked	16
Avocado, half of 4-inch fruit	14
Lima beans, half cup, cooked	14
Banana, medium	12
String beans, ¾ cup	12
Cherries, 15 large	10
Apricots, raw, 2–3 medium	10
Squash, half cup, cooked	10
Radishes, four small	10
Corn, medium ear	9
Lettuce, two large green leaves	9
Peaches, one medium	8
Onions, half cup, cooked	7
Cucumber, half a medium	6
Carrots, ⅔ cup, cooked, cubed	6

An almost endless list of fruits and vegetables have vitamin C at levels of 4 to 10 mg. And by looking down the appropriate column of the food-composition tables in the appendix, you can see how one can easily put together recommended amounts of this vitamin.

Remember, too, that though the need is said to be daily, it is not urgently so. A little more or less will probably make no difference. Minimum requirements are possibly half the RDA levels. One advertiser, for example, sells orange juice in bottled form by saying that it has *double* the minimum daily requirement. This amount is about the RDA. Such games are typical among vitamin-C purveyors.

Many experiments with human volunteers indicate that the body has wide tolerances for vitamin C lacks and excesses. British studies showed that it took some five months for scurvy to appear when the vitamin was sharply reduced or entirely eliminated.

One of the signs of deficient vitamin C is a greater susceptibility to infection. This is one of the sources of a belief in vitamin C as a curative or preventive for colds and other assorted illnesses. Sadly, these beliefs have proven unfounded. That is, if adequate body levels of vitamin C exist, the maximum protection against infection is secured. More means only a lot of pointless pill-taking and wasted money.

Nevertheless, someone is always "rediscovering" a value of vitamin C for preventing or curing colds. One of the latest is chemist Linus Pauling, who has written a tiny book on the subject. He recommends taking one or two *grams* of ascorbic acid a day to prevent colds. That is 100 to 200 times the amount needed to prevent scurvy and 20 to 40 times the average adult need. Then he urges that you raise this to four grams a day if you catch cold.

Pauling's personal research in the matter is quoted by *Newsweek*, to the effect that when he and his wife started to take these giant doses, they "immediately noticed an increased feeling of well-being, and especially a striking decrease in the number of colds that [they] caught." The magazine further quotes Pauling, "I do not know how effective the regimen really is." Then why, one wonders, did he write a book?

Well might Pauling doubt the subjective feeling of well-being, a classically deceptive sensation, which many people can get from swallowing anything they think will provide it. As for the fewer number of colds, what sort of meaningful numbers can he possibly be talking about? Yet an enormous segment of the public is now gulping a month's supply of C every day.

Comments Dr. Frederick Stare: "Linus Pauling is a man of peace and chemistry, not of nutrition. I think it's absolutely ridiculous to recommend huge doses of vitamin C since most of it will be eliminated in the urine in two or three hours."

Summing up the studies of vitamin C as a cold cure, the American Medical Association statement reads: *"No specific vitamin or vitamins will prevent or cure a cold. There is also no evidence to support the contention that vitamin C is any more beneficial than any of the other vitamins."*

According to a growing literature of myths, the list of illnesses which vitamin C is supposed to prevent or manage is becoming very long. Millions of Americans are dosing themselves with extra—usually in amounts of 100 mg. or more a day, almost twice the daily need if they were getting *none* in food. The practice is not known to be dangerous. It just doesn't make any sense.

Vitamin C is certainly used in clinical medicine. For example, it seems to relieve purpura, a blood-vessel problem which can result from the use of certain medicines. But if you should develop purpura, big purple splotches on your skin, perhaps almost covering your legs, you are likely to show the condition to your doctor.

The principal use of vitamin C, medically, is to relieve a lack of vitamin C. Dentists sometimes suggest vitamin C for gum disorders. It will work if the cause is a lack of ascorbic acid. Otherwise, it will not. Chances are you do not have an ascorbic acid deficiency. If you think you are the least bit low in this vitamin, all you have to do is eat more vitamin-C-rich foods. From the chart above, you can see how easy this is to do. Even if you don't need the C, the foods you will eat to get it are good foods with many other benefits. You don't need pills unless the doctor orders them.

P, the non-vitamin

This little section is summed up by its title. For a while, some chemists thought they had a "new" vitamin, which was found in certain citrus and other fruits. It was sometimes referred to as *citrin.* Claims were made. They did not prove true. They are still being made. They are still not true.

This error took place in the 1930s. Anyone who tries to impress you with needs for vitamin P, or miracles to be wrought by it, is a little out of date.

By 1950, the Joint Committee on Biochemical Nomenclature of the American Society of Biological Chemists and the American Institute of Nutrition resolved that the term *vitamin P* be abandoned. The stuff, now called *bioflavenoids,* mostly, and including substances called *hesperidin* and *rutin,* may have uses in the pharmaceutical industry. They are described commonly as nutrients. But there is as yet no evidence that they are required by man, or that they can lessen the need for vitamin C, as was once supposed by a few researchers. Don't be impressed by these names on the label of any supplement. In fact, finding such names on a label might well inspire one to question how reliable is any nutrition information given to him by the seller.

The vitamins in fats

The many fads and fancies about the water-soluble vitamins create mainly a waste of money, effort and disappointed hope. Quite massive doses of these vitamins, while not recommended unless ordered by a physician, are not likely to cause much trouble. For the most part, excesses just flow away. Unhappily, such is not the case with the next group of vitamins, those which dissolve in fats. They might well be stamped HANDLE WITH CARE, for excesses are truly dangerous here.

There are four groups of fat-soluble vitamins. As we saw earlier in this chapter, the A vitamin group has a number of chemicals under its banner, all of which are capable of being turned into true vitamin A by the body. Such is the case with the other fat-soluble vitamins we shall look at—D, E and K.

The chemistry of these vitamins is closely associated with fatty foods and with their pathways in the body. For example, when illness interferes with the absorption of such foods from the intestine, the stores of related vitamins may become depleted, too. Also, self-imposed fat restrictions in the diet, as in weight control, can carry with them a risk of restricting the fat-soluble vitamins as well.

Again, as with the water-soluble vitamins, there are some easy shortcuts through the maze of technicalities and many myths. Let us see how simply the practical problems can be dealt with.

Vitamin A

Vitamin A is probably the only vitamin value one can actually see in many of its food sources—and not only see, but see in relative quantity. This handy phenomenon results from the fact that three of the chemicals from which the body makes vitamin A, called *carotenes,* are yellow, or orange-yellow. So when one sees these colors in food, one can easily spot the vitamin A potential.

Carotene yellow provides the characteristic colors of carrots, pumpkins, apricots, nectarines and corn. Butter, Cheddar cheese and egg yolk are other examples. Usually, the deeper the color, the more vitamin. For example, milk from some breeds of cows has a golden quality, like guernsey milk. Such milks have more vitamin A potential.

Carotene must be split in half to make true vitamin A, and so is known as a *provitamin.* The true vitamin is colorless, as in, for example, fish liver oil.

Many people recognize this yellow sign. But they do not realize how often it is camouflaged by the chlorophyll green of such good vitamin A sources as spinach, broccoli, asparagus and dark green lettuce. Nor do they know that the red of the tomato includes the carotene color. The depth of greenness is as good an indicator of provitamin A as is the yellowness. And one can even see the differences in vegetables of the same kind; a pale carrot has less A than a bright one. Outer green leaves of lettuce are more vitamin-rich than are the less colored inner leaves. Sweet potatoes when deep yellow can have *five times* as much provitamin as when they are light.

Carotene pigments can accumulate under the skin and tint it. More than one alarmed new mother has rushed her infant to the doctor fearing yellow jaundice, only to be told to serve fewer yellow vegetables. A lot of this pigment is normal in Orientals, of course; but in other races it is a warning sign to ease off on foods heavy with the yellow vitamin.

It seems ironic that this most noticeable vitamin is one of the most pressing vitamin problems in world nutrition. And even in the United States, nutritionists are concerned about less-than-desirable levels of vitamin A in the diets of elderly men and women, and teenage girls. The reason for this is apparently a matter of poor food choice. For on the average, there is more than enough vitamin A available in the food supply for everyone.

Vitamin A's different food forms yield different amounts of the actual vitamin. For example, only 25 percent of *beta-carotene* actually becomes vitamin A in the body. So scientists have developed a system by which one can judge what might be called the "vitamin A potential" of a food, which takes these variances into account. This measure of potential is the *International Unit,* or I.U. And this is why the A content of a food is expressed differently from the measures of other vitamins, which are usually indicated by weight, as in milligrams or micrograms.

Vitamin A requirements do not vary much with the size of the individual. RDA levels are set at 5,000 I.U. for everyone over the age of 12. (Children's needs are discussed in a later chapter.)

The following table shows how easy it is to reach

such levels of the vitamin. Note that some single foods quickly provide excess. And bear in mind that this excess is stored, so that if we normally get enough vitamin A, with a little extra, we need not be concerned about even severe lacks for days or weeks. In fact, many people carry a year's supply and more in their livers.

Food	Vitamin A (I.U.)
Lamb liver, less than 3 oz., broiled	55,880
Beef liver, two slices, less than three oz., fried	40,050
Deep yellow carrots, ⅔ cup, cooked	10,500
Sweet potato, one small, baked	8,100
Spinach, half cup, cooked	7,290
Mustard greens, ⅔ cup, cooked	5,800
Collards, half cup, cooked	5,400
Swiss chard, half cup, cooked	5,400
Kale, half cup, cooked	4,570
Pumpkin pie, slice	3,710
Cantaloupe, half a 4½-inch melon	3,400
Apricots, 2–3 medium, fresh	2,700
Broccoli, ⅔ cup, cooked	2,500
Swordfish, 3½ oz., cooked in butter	2,050
Tomato, one medium, raw	1,350
Peaches, one medium-large yellow	1,330
Omelet, two small eggs, with milk	1,080
Asparagus, cooked, 6–7 spears	900
Butter, two pats	600
Margarine, two pats fortified	600
Ice cream, vanilla, ⅙ pint	520

There are numerous foods in the 300 to 600 I.U. range, such as prunes, unmentioned yellow and green vegetables (which, if deeper in color, may have much more A), watermelon, an ounce of cheese or cream cheese, a glass of milk. Nutritionists recommend an occasional serving of super-rich A foods for storage purposes. One serving of beef liver, for example, can allow you to get by for over two weeks with only half the RDA of the vitamin. In general, it seems prudent to build up one's storage supply as a simple safety measure.

Vitamin A is another all-around chemical in the body, closely related to the formation and maintenance of skin, linings, hormones such as cortisone, to the splitting of proteins needed to restructure cartilage into bone, and to the chemistry of vision. But as with all vitamins, no degree of excess A intake will improve any function beyond your hereditary potential. If you don't see well at night and are getting 5,000 I.U. of vitamin A daily, massive doses of A will leave you with exactly the same vision—plus a yellowish skin.

Similarly, there are many myths about extra vitamin A improving resistance to infection. True, if we exhaust our stores of the vitamin and consume too little, we seem to be more prone to infection. But once we have our 5,000 daily I.U. in good food, no additional amount will keep us from catching cold.

How much vitamin A is toxic? The American Medical Association cautions that daily doses in excess of 50,000 I.U. can cause serious illness. In general, supplements of this vitamin should be unnecessary. A daily diet brightened by living carotene color is the best way to meet vitamin A needs for adults.

D, the vitamin we need not swallow

Vitamin D is curious stuff, about which there remain many puzzles. It is the one vitamin which one is not likely to get enough of in ordinary foods—unless those foods are artificially fortified. On the other hand, just a moderate exposure to the sun seems to meet the needs of most healthy adults. The Food and Nutrition Board sums up informed opinion about vitamin D this way:

"The adult requirement of vitamin D in adult life is not known, yet the existence of deficiency states (though very rare) indicates that a need exists. Probably the amounts needed are so low that the requirement can be met by the average diet and exposure to sunlight.

For persons working at night and for nuns and others whose habits shield them from sunlight, the ingestion of small amounts of vitamin D is desirable."

The light which triggers the production of vitamin D is ultraviolet, the potent radiation which is most available between the hours of 10 A.M. and 2 P.M. This can be blocked by smoke, dust, smog and all the pollutants which ecologists are concerned about. Of course, those people who live in parts of the world where it is warmer, and who wear less clothing more of the year, have an advantage over those who live in cold climates, who stay indoors a lot and bundle up. To sum up, the California nudist has a definite edge here.

In humans, a relative of cholesterol (known as provitamin D_3, one of ten vitamin D factors) is the precursor of vitamin D. This substance is on the surface of the skin in an oily lubricating (sebaceous) secretion. But there is no way of measuring how much D the sunlight makes this way, one of the scientific problems with these vitamins.

As a very educated guess, informed nutritionists set the D need for infants, pregnant and lactating mothers at 400 International Units. (D vitamins are measured this way for the same reason that A vitamins are.) Thus milk in its liquid forms is fortified to the tune of 400 I.U. per quart. This 400 I.U. level is recommended from birth to 20 years of age. (We shall see later that this includes breast-fed infants and why.)

The food sources of vitamin D are predominantly animal, and they include egg yolk, liver, fish with considerable fat, and butter fat. But a medium egg has only 27 I.U. Three pats of butter total only 28 I.U. of the needed 400. A little less than a quarter-pound of liver contains from 15 to 45 I.U. And so on. Milk is the only truly rich source of the vitamin, and this is because of the intervention of science. The vitamin is not there naturally.

If you don't like milk and can't get into the sun, some margarines and breakfast foods also are fortified with D. But nutritionists caution that if you drink much milk (say, a quart a day), you should be cautious about these other fortified sources, especially fortifications of milk flavorings, which can go as high as 150 I.U. for the amount needed in one glass. For *excess* vitamin D is dangerous. It builds up in the liver, to cause serious illness. So if you are a milk drinker or have a child, D-fortified fruit drinks, cereals and even candy should be used in moderation. For the American Academy of Pediatrics has found that it would not be difficult for a child to get *five times* the RDA of vitamin D, and this amount can be hazardous; even three or four times the RDA might be hazardous.

In looking at labels for vitamin D fortification, you may notice the word "irradiated." This does not refer, as some people seem to believe, to atomic radiation. It simply means that a food substance has been exposed to ultraviolet light and thus been converted to usable vitamin D. *Ergosterol,* a vitamin D precursor from plants, is one such substance. Ultraviolet-radiated yeast yields a D substance called *calciferol,* which is sometimes dissolved in natural oil and then called *viosterol.*

The functions of vitamin D are closely associated with the use of calcium and phosphorus by the cells. This explains some of the importance of the vitamin for youngsters, whose bones and teeth are forming. D is sometimes known as the *antirachitic* vitamin, for its ability to prevent or relieve rickets (a lack of calcium or phosphorus deposition in body structures). Some scientists believe that a lack of D vitamins may be involved in some cases of softening or weakness of bones in the aging. Other subtle functions of D are still vaguely understood. But a little milk and sunshine are thought to be good things for almost everyone.

E, the new fad vitamin

Let us make it clear that deficiencies of vitamin E are thought to be practically nonexistent in the United States. Doctors simply do not see them. And let us quickly remind ourselves that once adequacy is attained with any vitamin, and a safety margin established, no additional amount can possibly be used by the body.

Certainly vitamin E is an essential nutrient and an important one, about which there is much to learn. A few deficiencies of E are seen in impoverished lands. On the other hand, there have recently been many threats and promises about this vitamin which seem absurd to nutritionists—especially in view of the fact that dietary adequacies of E are the rule in the United States by any scientific standard.

Nevertheless, enthusiasts—generally people without scientific credentials of any kind in nutrition—have been hailing this vitamin as the solution to problems of the heart and blood vessels, the answer to sterility and sexual impotence, disorders of pregnancy, rheumatic fever and muscular dystrophy. They usually say that vitamin E deficiencies are commonplace, and that larger doses of the vitamin bring the sex and circulatory organs to a peak of strength and performance. The AMA reports there is no basis for such claims.

Of course, when rats are *entirely deprived* of vitamin E, they show heart symptoms and reproductive problems. So if promoters have sold you vitamin E supplements with their claims, all is not necessarily lost. Someone you know may have a pet rat.

If your pet is a cat, do not be misled by the vitamin E often added to oily, fishy cat foods. The primary function of E (which actually has four different forms) is to prevent the oxidation of fats, particularly of unsaturated fatty acids, such as those in fish or vegetable oils. This makes E a good antirancidity additive for oily food, and that is why it is used in cat food; it prevents spoilage.

One of the reasons E deficiencies are almost unknown is that the vitamin tends to appear naturally in foods that carry unsaturated fats. Thus the food "package" is complete. E is also widely distributed in the food world —in such items as vegetable oils, green leafy vegetables, legumes, nuts, meats and eggs. Wheat germ oil, the favorite E source for many faddists, does have plenty of the vitamin. But it is a waste of money to buy the oil, or any other form of E supplementation, in the hope that amounts beyond the body's need will work cardiovascular, sexual or other miracles.

K, the coagulation vitamin

The name vitamin K is an initial for the German spelling, *Koagulation*. For the chief work of the vitamin seems to be assisting liver cells to form *prothrombin,* a complex factor in the clotting of blood. Deficiencies are almost unknown in normal adults.

K is plentiful in such foods as all green leafy vegetables, liver, soy oil, egg yolk, cauliflower, cabbage and lettuce. There are quite a few myths about K, some of which originated in the supplemental use of the vitamin in poultry farming, a use related only to special problems of birds and their feeding. These problems have no bearing on human health, however, for the human intestinal tract holds bacteria which make lots of K. Tiny amounts are often given to infants, who have not yet developed these bacterial colonies. Otherwise, the layman need give vitamin K no thought.

The minerals of animals and vegetables

Much that has been said about vitamins may also be said about minerals. They occur in tiny amounts in foods, but evidently in sufficient quantity so that nearly all minerals needed by the body can be found in an ordinary, varied diet, with a few possible exceptions. Once the minuscule requirements are met, excess is useless, and carried far enough can be toxic. Fantastic claims for extensive deficiencies are generally just that—products of imagination or of ignorant fanatics misinterpreting scientific research, for ego and profit.

Unlike vitamins, minerals tend to be incorporated into the actual structures and working chemicals of the body. That is, the vitamins seem to function mainly in a catalytic way—promoting chemical processes without actually becoming part of the products of the reactions. But minerals do also become involved in the building of enzymes which then work as catalysts, and in the building of actual tissue structures.

For example, we have already met two minerals, sulfur and phosphorus. We have seen that they are atoms, chemical elements. (There is a slight difference of connotation between minerals spoken of by the nutritionist and by the geologist. For the latter, the term implies the whole range of naturally occurring, complex chemicals, such as ores. The nutritionist usually thinks of minerals as the pure atomic elements.) We have seen that *sulfur* is part of the structure of some amino acids. We have seen *phosphorus* used to make RNA, DNA and the key chemical for energy use, ATP. These examples suggest the pattern of mineral use in the body.

The healthy human animal need not be concerned about most mineral needs. For the most part, those foods which supply our other nutrients adequately give us ample minerals, too. Again, one may reason that evolution would not have produced a system in which any essential factor would be obtainable only through elaborate manipulations of the diet or through rare, special foodstuffs.

Calcium

Calcium is the most plentiful of the body's minerals, and though some 99 percent of it goes into the bones and teeth, the remaining one percent plays a crucial role in body chemistry. For example, without calcium, nerves would go out of control and send out repeating impulses. Only in fairly unusual circumstances, however, is the nervous system affected by lack of calcium in the blood. For the teeth and bones act not only as structures, but as dynamic body supply depots for calcium.

In chemical terms, there is plenty of calicum action going on continually at the ends of the bones, the *epiphyses*. When cells need calcium, certain parts of these bone ends, called *trabeculae,* can give up calcium salts for other uses.

The bones are about two-thirds mineral compounds and one-third protein substances. They are very much alive, not at all like the skeleton of a skyscraper. If they were not, they could not do the wondrous self-mending they routinely do.

Faddists claim that large-scale supplementation of calcium will benefit nervous disorders. Yet the huge bone reserves and the small calcium chemical needs of humans (less than one percent) make all such claims quite ridiculous, in such matters as nerve remedies and similar functions. Still, inadequate dietary calcium is one of the nation's primary nutritional concerns.

As usual, the problem is most serious in women. Girls from nine to 14 are, on the average, getting from 21 to 29 percent less calcium than is recommended. The same lack is true for young women from 18 to 34. And in girls from 15 to 17, and in women over the age of 35, the calcium lack is over 30 percent.

The only males getting adequate calcium are small children, and the 18 to 34 age group. The lack of calcium is less than ten percent at ages nine to 11 and 15 to 17. It is the same between 35 and 54. But it rises to 11 to 20 percent at ages 12 to 14 and after 55. In quite elderly men the lack is as high as 30 percent.

The most serious aspects of this problem are among the growing adolescents, pregnant women (whose bodies give up calcium to the forming infant), breast-feeding women (whose infants depend on the breast for bone materials) and among the elderly, whose bones tend to become brittle as calcium is lost with aging.

While exact reasons for calcium lacks are unknown, it looks to most experts as if two cultural patterns are mainly responsible. One pattern is a tendency to reject "fattening" foods, such as milk products, or to refuse these same foods out of concern for the cholesterol-heart-disease question. Other good calcium sources, such as nuts and legumes, are also being cut back out of fear of overweight. (We shall see that there is no good reason to eliminate any good food from a weight-control program. And we shall see that even if one is concerned about animal fats and their effect on the circulatory system, one can still use milk.) The other cultural pattern is a growing decline in the use of vegetables. (Green leaves are exceptionally good calcium sources.) One can see this in almost any restaurant, where meals are generally limited to meat and a starchy vegetable, but no green vegetable is served. The sole leafy exception is the lettuce salad, which for practicality's sake is usually made from pale lettuces, such as the iceberg compac head. Greenness, we have seen, is a good indicator o micronutrient content, and restaurant salads are rarel very green.

Let us see where calcium comes from. But first not the recommended allowance of 800 milligrams a day along with the opinion of many nutritionists that this i quite a generous number, and that 500 milligrams a da is adequate for the healthy individual who is not unde any unusual stress, such as growth.

This suggests the pattern of calcium distribution. W can see that, if we eliminate milk products and flui milk, 800 mg. of calcium can be troublesome to find Suppose we set up a calcium program, for the day, o two servings of green, leafy vegetables (280 mg.), ar orange (62), a serving of string beans (50), two egg

Food	Calcium (milligram
Milk, one cup, regardless of type	28
Cheddar cheese, 1 oz.	22
Green, leafy vegetables, average serving	80 to 15
Artichokes, average serving	10
Broccoli, ⅔ cup	8
Cottage cheese, 3 heaping tablespoons	7
Orange, one medium	6
Eggs, two large	5
String beans, ⅔ cup, cooked	5
Lima beans, half cup, cooked	3
Salad greens, average serving	20 to 4
Raisins, ¼ cup	2
Bread, one slice, whole wheat	2
Dates, 3–4	2
Dried apricots, four halves	2
Orange juice, 6 oz.	2
Bread, one slice, white, enriched or not	1
Peas, fresh or frozen, ⅔ cup, cooked	1
Prunes, 4–5 medium, cooked	1
Peanut butter, one tablespoon	1

(52), two slices of bread (38), two tablespoons of peanut butter (22). We now have just over 500 milligrams, a minimal calcium ration.

To be realistic, it is doubtful that most adults will eat all these calcium-rich foods in one day. For example, national averages indicate only a fraction of a daily serving of green, leafy vegetables is typical.

With a pint of milk, however, the diet instantly leaps to almost 600 mg. of calcium. Throw in a cheese sandwich and you are over the 800 mg. mark.

Our sample milk-free calcium menu does not take into account casual additions of small amounts from other typical foods, which do contribute. But even so, without milk and its derivative foods, calcium is a dietary headache.

(Among our casual additions, mentioned above, could be margarine or butter, 2 or 3 mg. per pat; tomato catsup, 4 mg.; hamburger bun, 28 mg.; mayonnaise, 3 mg.; cherry pie, 22 mg., or mince, 45 mg.; a serving of French fries, 15 mg.; cookies, 9 mg.; a serving of fish, perhaps 25 mg. There are also some other uniquely good sources, such as small fish, when one eats the bones. A 3-oz. portion of sardines at 371 mg. will outdo even milk. A little more salmon, canned, is the equal of milk. Molasses used in baking is a booster. Ice cream is a good milk-calcium source at 123 mg., and ice milk is even better at 156 mg. a serving. Onion is a good vegetable source. And oysters give better than 100 mg. per serving. Puddings, pies, and other recipes which use milk can be big contributors.)

The gentle tyranny of milk

The calcium picture pushes many nutritionists into a corner that they do not like very much. In order to keep dietary needs simple enough to be easily managed we are forced to an inflexible everyday use of the milk family. This seems reasonable for infants, but not for adults.

Moreover, some cardiologists are genuinely concerned about what they feel is an overuse of milk because of the possible hazards of the animal fat it contains.

In general, the watchword of good nutrition is variety, we know. But variety helps little with the calcium problem. (At this writing, it seems very likely indeed that calcium will be added to other common foods, particularly flours and breads. Good label reading will let you take advantage of such changes.)

How did we get into this corner—in which adults need to drink a daily glass or two of nature's food for infants? Is this consistent with what we have said about the evolution of man's dietary needs, that a complete dietary should be widely and easily available?

The problem seems to be that man has changed habit much faster than he can evolve. Even a century ago, caloric intake was much higher because we expended much more energy. We are now down to a bare minimum of movement and physical work. So our diets are *much smaller*. The calcium requirement, like many mineral needs and much like the need for protein, is largely a function of body size. If we ate a lot more food, we would be likely to get a lot more calcium from fair or middling sources.

Moreover, it is speculated that primitive man ate more small bones. We saw the benefit of this in the sardine example. He also is believed to have cracked bones and chewed on them.

We shall look at some other implications of man's habit changes shortly. But the gentle tyranny of milk appears to be a unique example of its kind. We have even compounded the problem by choosing to add to milk our main vitamin D enrichment (probably also made necessary by habit changes, which keep us away from the sun). The reasoning, of course, is the need for D to help us use calcium. Still, the reader can escape the dairy tyranny. He can eat more green stuffs, which he should do anyway. And he can count milligrams, eat small fishes now and then and certain shellfish, and think quite a lot about calcium. A judicious use of cheese, low-fat milk desserts and puddings can avoid using fluid milk. Or he can just relax, gulp a glass or two a day and learn to tolerate it with all or some of the fat taken out.

Skim milk is seen as an ideal solution to this problem. A glass is only 85 calories, yet provides almost 300 mg. of calcium, and is less caloric than the serving of cereal to which it might be added. With one serving of green, leafy vegetable, it makes up a comfortable MDR of calcium for an adult. Even whole milk, at 165 calories per cup, is not objectionable for one who is trying to control weight. Consider that both milk and green vegetables offer other short-supply nutrients, too, such as A, B and C vitamins and iron. For this reason, nutritionists do not recommend getting calcium in pill form. To do so may lead to unwise avoidance of basic foods, with a false sense of security. If you *should* choose to use a calcium supplement, do remember two things. First, it replaces neither milk nor green vegetables. Second, massive doses can cause problems for some people—such as those who may, unaware, be prone to kidney stones. Aim only at RDA levels of calcium. More, as usual, is *not* better.

Not to consume RDA levels of calcium is to risk problems of teeth and bones. It does not seem mere accident that the wear-and-tear types of arthritis take their toll at the bone ends, the sites where calcium is surrendered for other body uses. And it seems reasonable to arrive at middle years, when joint problems become more common, with one's bone density high and one's bone ends at maximum strength.

Once joint problems have begun, calcium generally does not help. And conversely, there is no truth to the fear that dietary calcium *causes* joint problems; in all, it takes quite a lot of calcium to cause trouble.

Phosphorus

This second most abundant body mineral is found mainly in teeth and bones, closely associated with calcium in the building of these tough structures. Eighty percent of phosphorus goes to this kind of use. As we have seen earlier, the other 20 percent plays a broad and absolutely essential role in the heredity, control and energy use of every single cell.

Happily, phosphorus is so little a problem in the United States that authorities do not even bother with an official RDA. The requirement is generally thought to be about that of calcium. And in practice it is found that we tend to get about 50 percent more phosphorus than we do calcium. In a general way, almost every good source of calcium is also a good source of phosphorus. But in addition, many calcium-poor foods are phosphorus-rich—for example, meat and cereal. So while nutritionists find that it is important to get enough phosphorus with one's calcium, this is rarely a matter of practical concern for us.

An ordinary hamburger gives 165 mg. of phosphorus; a fish serving is likely to be about 200 mg.; one shredded wheat biscuit provides 102 mg.; two eggs are endowed with over 200 mg.; a serving of liver has 311 mg.; beans and peas and corn have good amounts; milk offers 227 mg. in a glass. As a general rule, take care of your calcium need and the phosphorus will take care of itself, especially if you eat meat. A vegetarian who disdains products such as eggs, milk and seafood has a nip-and-tuck tangle with the calcium-phosphorus-vitamin D triad, unless he informs himself well and carefully.

Sodium, potassium, magnesium

These three are the other "macrominerals," that is, mineral elements which occur in the body in some relative quantity. Other minerals are involved in the diet and body chemistry, but in very, very small amounts, and so are known as "microminerals," or sometimes "trace" minerals.

In healthy people, deficiencies of these other macrominerals are either unknown or extremely rare. These atoms are all very plentiful in foods. And within reasonable limits, the body even handles excesses quite nicely. So except for a few oddments, in the healthy person data on the macrominerals is an academic matter.

About half the magnesium is deposited in bony structures, along with calcium and phosphorus. The other half is involved in very basic cell processes, such as energy use and the handling of glucose and other nutrients in such a way that they are readied for energy reactions. Knowledge of magnesium is of little or no use in planning your food, except as a defense against some pretty silly claims made by faddists.

Sodium and potassium salts are the main *body electrolytes.* This brings us to an extremely important concept in physiology, in fact, to a whole catalog of concepts which the author will make every attempt to avoid. These subjects are depressingly technical, though fascinating, and the practical knowledge involved for the layman is pleasantly limited. So we will mention only the practical things.

Sodium and potassium are so omnipresent in the average diet that in healthy people the problem tends to be one of excess (at least of sodium)—if there is any problem at all. People get along very nicely on 500 mg. of sodium a day, a typical restricted diet. But the average American consumes 2,000 to 4,000 mg. in his table salt alone, which is 39 percent sodium. Because there may be a relationship between sodium in the body and high blood pressure, most doctors think we might go just a little easier on the salt shaker. As a principle, they suggest tasting before salting, without fear but with the question: is this shake necessary?

Sodium and potassium salts are the main preservers of our bodily inner-sea. Their importance leads many people to fear excessive salt loss with sweating. Actually, the body gradually decreases the salt concentration of sweat and thus protects itself from becoming badly salt-depleted. One does not need salt tablets in summer or with sweaty work. An extra shake or two at table is all we need, if that much.

In the main, sodium and potassium depletion occur only in disease states, such as dehydration from vomiting or diarrhea. We will discuss the practicalities of this problem in our look at indigestion, where knowing when and how to replace lost electrolytes can save you much discomfort.

A number of people are concerned about the sodium

added to water in water-softening processes. This is of no concern to healthy folk. At most it adds 35 to 45 mg. to a quart of water, one or two percent of what most of us get from the salt shaker.

Iron

One of the many ancient folk sayings about food is, "Pale foods cannot make red blood." The adage is noteworthy because it is among the few about food that happen to be true. It is true because the redness of blood is so dependent on iron. And iron, like the carotene of vitamin A, is a food colorant.

Among the best sources of iron are such dark foods as red meats (especially organ meats), dark whole grains, prunes, raisins, molasses and all the green, leafy vegetables. This makes it sound as if iron is such a commonplace in plentiful foods that it could not possibly be in short supply among Americans. Yet iron shortages are among the chief concerns of today's food scientists.

Recent surveys such as those of the U.S. Department of Agriculture have turned up gloomy figures on iron consumption, *numbers more depressing than those for any other nutrient.* For the shortages are substantial, and they seem to occur in just those population segments most likely to be injured by them. Again this problem is not being ignored. It should soon be eased by greater additions of enriching iron to such foods as breads and grains.

Mother's milk is lacking in iron. The infant is normally protected by being born with a three-month supply of iron—*if* his mother has been properly fed during pregnancy. But today, chances are she has not been getting enough iron to provide that three months of protection.

In the USDA study, infants from the first few months of life to the third year were more than 30 percent short of iron. From three to five, they were between 11 and 20 percent lacking in this element. Again, the males are largely protected after the first five years—except for a 21 to 29 percent shortage during the twelfth through fourteenth years, and a very slight shortage that continues until age 18.

But for women, the diet deficiencies become rather disturbing. The American female, from age nine to age 55, is *at least* one-third deficient in iron. After that time, shortages among women, even among the elderly, who usually get nutritional short shrift, are very minor or nonexistent.

The reasons for these deficiencies, and the varied consequences, involve some pretty complex reasoning and science. Once again, let us confine ourselves to that knowledge which has practical value.

Growth, menstruation and childbearing make the biggest dents in iron supplies. The iron is needed for its ability to seize and release oxygen. Two-thirds of the element is found in the blood, in molecules of hemoglobin, which give blood its color. The hemoglobin in each red blood cell picks up oxygen from the lungs and carries it throughout the body, supplying it to each tissue cell for its energy processes. When oxygenated, the blood is red. When the hemoglobin has given up its oxygen to a cell, it turns a bluish color. Thus, arterial blood leaving the heart is red. Venous blood, returning to the heart, is bluish.

So also, people who have enough hemoglobin have a pinkish skin color. Those who have too little, and are *anemic,* have a pale color, sometimes bluish or even a bit greenish. The small blood vessels under the skin produce the coloration.

Anemia can result from a lack of hemoglobin, or a lack of red blood cells, or both. In either case, a deficiency of iron can be the cause.

Since the oxygen carried by hemoglobin is needed to burn fuel in the cells, one can easily see why the person who is anemic feels a lack of energy and vitality, may sleep overmuch, fatigue halfway through the day, perhaps be emotionally depressed, and also be short of breath, easily winded by games or climbing stairs.

No one really knows how many children and women are anemic because of insufficient iron. But indications are that there are a great many cases of at least a marginal kind. Recent studies have led the Food and Nutrition Board to raise its recommendations for dietary iron. They now look like this:

		Iron (milligrams per day)
Infants	0–2 months	6
	2–6 months	10
	6–12 months	15
Children	1–3 years	15
	3–10 years	10
Males	10–12 years	10
	12–18 years	18
	18 on	10
Females	10–55 years	18
	55 on	10

These requirements fit rather nicely into the picture of the iron insufficiencies in the American diet. That is, in general, when the iron need is high, deficiencies tend to occur.

For all adults, iron *consumption* appears to be relatively the same. For men that consumption level is adequate; for women it is quite inadequate. (Note that men, whose iron requirement in adulthood is about 10 mg. per day, get that much and more. Women, whose iron need is 18 mg. daily, are one-third or more *lacking.* At a one-third deficiency, a woman would be getting about 11 or 12 mg. a day, roughly the male need.)

We will look at children's requirements in more detail later. But among adults, it seems safe to conclude that the concern is for women to consume iron in excess of what a typical American dietary is likely to provide. This can be done with supplementation with pills. But nutritionists would prefer to see the lack made up by iron-rich food. Let us see how this may be done by looking at some typical iron-rich foods on the next page.

Detailed facts about different foods as iron sources can be found in the food-composition table in the appendix. Our list suggests the iron content of several food groups, and why it is not easy to get 18 mg. of iron a day. Suppose, for example, that a woman has two eggs and two slices of toast for breakfast, a hamburger on a bun as the main lunch dish—perhaps with milk—a slice of roast beef for dinner, potatoes, a serving of iron-rich vegetable and lemon meringue pie. Various meal oddments are omitted, of course, but her basic iron intake for the day would be about 12.2 mg. She is about one-third short on iron.

Food	Iron (milligrams)
Beef liver, 4 oz. serving	10.0
Oysters, sardines, shrimp, 3 oz. serving	2.5–5.5
Hamburger patty, 3 oz.	3.0
Prunes, raisins, dates, 3 oz.	2.0–4.0
Most meats, 3 oz. serving	2.0–3.0
Dried beans, half cup	2.5
Pork chop, medium, 3 oz.	2.5
Green leafy vegetables, average serving	.8–2.0
Most nuts, ¼ cup	1.2
Molasses, one tablespoon	1.2
Egg, one	1.0
Sweet potato, medium, baked	1.0
Broccoli or brussels sprouts, average serving	.8
White potato, medium, baked	.7
Enriched macaroni products, ½ cup	.7
Oat or wheat flakes, average serving	.6–.7
Enriched white or whole wheat bread, one slice	.6
Carrots or string beans, average serving	.6
Fresh fruits, average serving	.3–.6
Milk, one cup	.1

Of course, she could increase the iron dietarily. Eight or nine prunes for breakfast would add 2.4 mg. A bran muffin substituted for one slice of toast would bring the addition to 3.1 mg. A few cocktail nuts would make the total 3.5 mg. A lettuce salad, quite green, with dressing, could add 1.1 mg. for lunch to make it 4.6 mg. Three strips of bacon with her morning eggs add .8 mg. for a total of 5.4 mg. A snack of an apple could give .5 mg. more, and a medium stalk of celery could give another .1 mg. to top out the day. But unless the lady had a good knowledge of iron values, and watched her food fairly carefully, she would be likely to run short. For example, if she had swordfish for dinner (instead of beef) she would lose about 1.5 mg. of her iron, and if she chose other vegetables or salad, she might lose a milligram more. Certainly, if she is reducing, matters get more difficult. It takes a fair total amount of food to get 18 mg. of iron without puzzling or straining.

So, many nutritionists are suggesting that women add supplemental iron pills to their daily food until such time as the iron fortification of certain foods is increased.

There are hidden minus and plus factors affecting iron intake, too. For example, spinach is well known to be rich in iron, about 2 mg. to a serving. The problem is, this iron is to a large extent not in an available form. On the plus side, cooking in an iron pot can work wonders for foods. Cooking acid foods in iron can add 100 to 400 percent to the iron content of the finished product. Iron skillets are not only good cookware, but good iron sources for the family. So are those old iron pots in which one can simmer stews and pot roasts and the like. Long, slow cooking, of course, adds more. But it is hard to say just how much is really added in each instance, and so hard to know exactly what that iron cookware means for one's daily iron supply.

You may read that iron is very incompletely used, and this is true. Only perhaps a tenth of ingested iron is actually used by the body. The iron RDAs are established with this in mind. A woman would need only 1.8 mg. in food if she could use it all, against her 18 mg. RDA. This does not mean she should take a lot extra, no matter what promoters say.

Copper

Copper is also involved in the chemistry of hemoglobin and the blood. But its requirement seems to be much smaller than that of iron—perhaps two milligrams daily—and the average American gets that much and quite a lot more from his food. Copper cooking utensils contribute to this amount, as do copper rollers and other vessels and utensils used in the food industry. Pay no attention to faddist talk about copper needs, some of which is based on the distortion of studies on sheep, goats and cows. Their food is quite a lot different from ours and so is their body chemistry. Nothing to worry about here unless you get your food by grazing.

Cobalt

Cobalt is a dietary essential of man, but in extremely small amounts. It is impossible for vitamin B_{12} to be formed without a few atoms of this trace element. And since, as we have seen, B_{12} is widely and amply distributed in our food, so is cobalt.

No cobalt deficiency has ever been observed in man. However, grazing animals have been known to have problems. This, of course, has absolutely nothing to do with us. A few faddists have leaped unreasonably to the conclusion that, if we eat the meat of such animals, we will then be cobalt-deficient, too. First of all, we are not very likely to, since in such a state the animals become terribly wasted. And even if we did, we would get plenty of cobalt anyway.

On the other hand, *excess* amounts of cobalt are quite hazardous for man and many other animals. It can seriously interfere with the normal levels of red blood cells and of hemoglobin. Your greatest safety in the matter of cobalt is certainly just to forget about it.

Other trace minerals to forget (and one to remember)

There are quite a number of other trace elements in our food which seem to be used by the body—selenium, manganese, zinc, molybdenum, silicon, chromium, cadmium and iodine are all present in minute amounts. Only one of these is known to be absent from the American dietary in any significant way. That is iodine.

Only between 50 and 75 millionths of a gram of iodine is needed by humans. But that bit is essential to the normal function of the important thyroid gland and the production of key thyroid hormones. When we do not get enough iodine for this job, the result is goiter, a swelling of the thyroid, which lies in the neck.

Goiter used to be quite a problem in certain states of the United States until about the time of World War I. *Washington, Oregon, Montana, Idaho,* Nevada, *Utah, Wyoming,* Colorado, North Dakota, Minnesota, Iowa, *Wisconsin, Michigan,* Illinois, Indiana, Ohio and West Virginia were the trouble spots. The states which are italicized here were the worst offenders and still have the greatest risk of iodine lack. But there are spotty problem areas scattered about in addition to these.

The problem was solved simply by adding a little iodine to table salt. However, so nearly forgotten is the old iodine question that the use of iodized salt has been declining, a source of concern to doctors and scientific nutritionists. There is absolutely no harm possible from the amounts of iodine in table salt. The American Medical Association urges that Americans use *only* iodized salt. Buying salt which has not been iodized accomplishes nothing and carries a possible risk.

All other trace minerals are adequately supplied by almost any dietary that even approximates the average for Americans. Concerns to the contrary are wrong and needless, as far as any authoritative body can determine. Only in grazing animals has a lack of trace minerals been found. The questions about trace minerals in humans have been asked in the laboratories and in the field, and the answers are very reassuring indeed.

On the other hand, do-it-yourself mineral supplementation, which has sometimes been recommended by faddists and irresponsible promoters at very high levels, does carry a real and substantial danger. A good example is the element *selenium.*

Says Dr. W. H. Allaway, an authority on trace minerals for the U.S. Department of Agriculture: "Even though selenium is essenial to animal life—in very small amounts—it is more poisonous than arsenic and is less abundant in the earth's crust than gold."

Here is an excellent example of the *biogenic range* for nutrients. In selenium and some other trace minerals, that range is not very wide. When we satisfy our needs from ordinary food, we are generally quite protected from excess. But if we tamper, we can do ourselves harm. In the case of selenium, the amount needed by cows and sheep is less than one-fifth of an ounce for a ton of hay. Below this level, the animals become patently ill. When the selenium goes slightly higher than one-fifth an ounce per ton of feed, sheep and cattle can die.

Current medical research has produced some new data on metals—such as chromium and cadmium—and their influence on human health. These data are still cloudy. But certainly, doctors do not believe that individuals should conduct experiments on their own bodies by manipulating their intake of such elements, especially not by large supplements without a physician's advice. And doctors in practice are not using trace mineral supplementation, other than iron or iodine.

Even if some trace elements later prove useful in therapy, as drugs, the layman should not self-prescribe. Drugs are often given with conscious risk. For example, the earth's crust still contains quite a lot of radioactive material. Minuscule amounts of this can be picked up by plants from the soil, so radioactive minerals are "natural." And they are used in medicine to treat cancer and other disease. So radioactive elements can be "good" for people. But because these chemicals are "good," "natural" and normally in our food does not mean that people ought to supplement their diets with capsules of radioactive carbon or cobalt or uranium. Anyone who did so to any extent would suffer. So beware of the salesman who would have you buy mineral supplements, such as the quite popular "sea salts." Chances are that they will not really make you ill; but chances are even better that they will not make you one bit healthier.

Some practical conclusions

We have now reviewed the nutrients that support and become life. And we have found some general principles which, if followed, could improve the nutritional status of many millions of Americans. Here are some of the salient points and major issues:

1. *Protein.* As a nation, we get plenty of complete protein. If we make any error, it is failing to provide complete proteins at every meal, with breakfast probably the worst offender.

2. *Carbohydrates.* Our consumption of "empty" carbohydrates seems to be a little too high, omitting valuable carbohydrate foods (such as vegetables and fruits) which provide micronutrients, some of which are commonly less in our dietaries than they ought to be. Carbohydrates should never be eliminated from the diet, nor taken below about four ounces per day as an average *minimum.*

3. *Fats.* Our consumption of fats is believed to be too big a part of our food. In the mix of carbohydrates and fats as the bulk of our food, fats should have the lesser role. Fats, of course, must not be wholly eliminated from the normal diet, or we will exclude essential fatty acids and fat-soluble vitamins, as well as other minor food factors found along with the fats. On the other hand, "empty" fat foods (the pure or nearly pure fats) probably cheat us of important nutrients which come in the package with some fat-rich foods. For example, it would be wiser to get the same calories from peanuts than from peanut oil, from cheese than from shortening.

4. *Vitamins.* The decline in consumption of fruits and vegetables, especially of deep green and yellow foods, is apparently causing some dietary shortages in the B vitamins. It is easy to get the "big three" B vitamins from many foods, and when we do, we certainly have no need to worry about other members of the B complex. Supplementation *should* be unnecessary.

In general, the belief that *extra* vitamins confer strength, health or happiness is a myth.

Vitamin C is important and deserves attention, but we can easily get what we need from ordinary food. Most people do not realize what plentiful sources are all about us other than citrus fruits and juices.

There are some very small shortages of A vitamins, which would be eliminated quickly if fruits and vegetables were more widely consumed. On the other hand, overdosing with this and other fat-soluble vitamins confers no benefit and is even quite unsafe.

Sunshine and the wide use of fortified milk products should keep vitamin D insufficiencies very rare. The adult requirement, especially, seems to be small enough to cause few practical problems.

5. *Trace elements, and other minerals.* Calcium is the only important macromineral shortage. Iron needs are high enough so that care or supplementation is needed by girls, women and very young children, and some older boys as well. Iodine should be supplied in safe amounts through the use of iodized table salt.

As we have seen, there may be some refinements of the above principles under stress of growth, pregnancy or ill health. These matters will be covered in special sections. By and large, however, most Americans can correct their diets to an optimal quality simply, easily, and probably with no additional food expense.

The author urges the reader now to return to the second chapter and the diet-evaluation which he met there. There is a good chance that this simple outline of a biogenic diet will have extra meaning now. And the implications of any omissions will be clearer.

But many people are raising questions about the popular and ordinary foods of an optimal diet. Some are genuinely alarmed and threatened by what they find on the supermarket shelves. Is all this processed, refined, precooked, prepackaged, fortified, restored, enriched, synthesized, preserved, freshened stuff really able to support life at its very best? Or have we tampered with our foods and soils until we are in danger? The questions have been studied expertly. Let us look at the best available answers.

SECTION III

The Nutritionist On The Scales

CHAPTER 7

Were you born to be fat?

Once upon a much simpler, and in many ways happier, time, fat was beautiful.

The reasons were many. Partly, Americans were closer to the farm, where plump animals won the blue ribbons and tilted the scales to bring home more money. Partly, fat meant affluence; the poor ate badly, and were further thinned by long days of toil. Partly, there were still many emaciating plagues of childhood, such as diphtheria, and fatter babies seemed to survive best.

Now all is changed. By the early 1950s the old attitudes had reversed. Almost everyone knew that fat was dangerous. Moreover, it was completely unfashionable. The burgeoning belly was a public accusation of sloth and gluttony, and our Puritan origins made us quick to feel the shame. We were a soft, pudgy nation, and the knowledge made us guilty and afraid. Our culture was flooded with an awareness of fat, and with schemes and devices for disposing of it.

For some twenty years our fat-consciousness has grown steadily. We spend at least $100 million a year on weight-reducing plans and remedies. We read millions upon millions of books to tell us what to do about fat. We think and talk about it endlessly. The adult who enters an ice-cream parlor does so with feelings akin to those once associated with the speakeasy.

The result? A losing battle. In 1955, about one child in seven was overweight. The newest research adjusts that number to one child in *five*. In our cities, about one-third to one-half of all adults are found to be obese. The United States is the only member country of the World Health Organization which has seen no increase in the life of its men in twenty years, and this fact is considered obesity-related.

The majority of seriously overweight Americans are in their 40s and 50s. For it takes most people time to build up big fat deposits, and after they do, they do not tend to survive very long. The death rate is half again as great among the obese. They are far more likely to develop heart disease, high blood pressure, diabetes, arthritis, kidney disease and other problems. Overweight women have more trouble during pregnancy and bear fewer healthy babies. And they have more difficulty in conceiving at all.

Most people have at least an inkling of these facts. If they become fat, they fear the risks and they despise and blame themselves. Nutritionists are generally agreed that the majority make real, painful efforts to reduce. Yet studies show that only a small proportion of those who try to lose weight succeed in doing so and keeping it off; at best it would seem that no more than one or two of every ten dieters really accomplish very much. Most seem to enter into what Dr. Jean Mayer has sadly described as "The Rhythm Method of Girth Control"—a grim cycle of lose-a-little, gain-a-little-more. And we shall see that many people among even those who appear to be holding their own, or even losing a little according to the scales, are actually getting fatter.

This much of the truth about overweight in America is grim. But there is another side to the coin, and it is brighter indeed. It is summarized by two simple, scientific facts.

1. If you are overweight, you need feel neither gluttonous nor sinful. You are probably only a victim of a family destiny—and of a changing culture, which has unleashed some powerful physiological forces.

2. With scientific information, and common sense, you can rather easily balance those forces, as nature seems to have intended that they be balanced, and get certain body mechanisms to work for you instead of against you. Even family tendencies to fatness can be controlled, and usually without radical life changes or painful deprivations.

As one obesity expert puts it: "Americans generally need only forget most of the complicated nonsense they have been told about eating and overweight and be given some simple facts."

The great fat frustration

The time is not at all long ago—perhaps as recent as yesterday. The scene is a medical office. The atmosphere is melancholy. Mrs. Whyte is standing on the professional scale, and her doctor is shaking his head.

"Three pounds over last year's check-up," says the doctor. "And we were going to *lose.* According to our charts, you are now thirty-eight pounds over your ideal weight."

"I've tried," says a shamefaced Mrs. Whyte. "Really I've tried. All year. I don't even eat breakfast—just coffee. I skimp on lunch. I don't eat sweets or butter or—"

"Now, Mrs. Whyte, I know you may think you are eating less. But the scales don't lie. And if you are eating less," he chides smilingly, "then you ought to be losing."

"But I feel hungry all the time," protests Mrs. Whyte.

"Ah, but you may still be getting too many calories," says the doctor. "Better food choice, that's the thing. Do you know the number of calories in a single cashew nut?"

"Yes," says Mrs. Whyte. "I haven't eaten a nut in a long time. I count and count the calories, and it doesn't seem to work." A tear of frustration trembles on her lower eyelid. "Can't you give me pills or something? George, my husband, can eat anything, and he doesn't gain. But sometimes I'm sure I was just *born* to be fat."

"Not possible, Mrs. Whyte. This impression is a common illusion. Perhaps we're not counting those high-calorie snacks we have at night. Now, did I give you one of our sensible diet plans last year? Habit, that's the thing. We must form new habit patterns of eating."

"I followed the diet plan, but it didn't work," says Mrs. Whyte.

"Well, maybe there were a few little departures from the plan? Keeping careful track, that's the thing. Those little extra bites are very understandable, but—"

Mrs. Whyte leaves, barely controlling the anger that has grown out of her frustration. She knows that if she virtually starves herself, she can slowly lose weight. But then the fat rolls right back again, always a little more than before, no matter how cautious she tries to be. She remains in a perpetual state of self-denial just to hold her own.

She dreams of chocolate cakes and fresh rolls slathered in butter, of pork sausages and fried potatoes. She dreams, but does not eat. She knows that her husband eats far more. He has a desk job, yet eats ice cream and pastries almost with impunity. His weight seems almost fixed. It is more than a vexing puzzle for her; it is a very real threat to her self-image, to her emotional balance. She feels ugly and guilty, gluttonous and undisciplined. She feels doomed, a self-deluder, a weak-willed food addict.

Mrs. Whyte goes home. There, in the privacy of her kitchen, hating herself, peeling the potatoes she will not eat tonight, she weeps.

Are the overweight innocent?

In recent years, science has developed a new understanding of overweight which sees heavy people as victims, not villains. The grounds of innocence are varied, as are the causes of obesity. Experts now tend to view overweight as a symptom—like a fever or a headache—rather than a disease. And the old presumption of gluttony, either conscious or unconscious, is no longer made.

The information is not yet tied in neat and absolute little packages. The phenomenon of overweight appears to be far more subtle than was formerly believed. And so the newer knowledge of overweight has been slow to percolate through even medical circles. There is a tendency to cling to the older, simpler ideas which better suit some commercial purposes and a sensation-minded popular press. But the rising tide of fatness suggests how misleading many of the old simple answers tend to be.

Among the most basic of the new concepts is the question of obesity and heredity. Until recently, scientists were quite sure that obesity was not inherited. But this point of view is now changing—leading millions to a new understanding of their condition, and of what they can and cannot expect of their bodies. And research in this area has been explaining why people grow fat, how the tendency can be prevented and the damage undone.

One of the first clues in the new story of obesity appeared early in the 1950s in the work of Doctors Jean Mayer and R. Beaudoin, at Harvard University's Department of Nutrition. It had long been assumed by many experts that a major cause of fatness was that the fatter people consumed foods especially high in calories. But the Harvard study showed this to be untrue to a large extent. Three groups of women—one group obese, one of normal weight, and one underweight—were studied. No pattern of food choice appeared. The groups selected their foods from among fats, proteins and carbohydrates in quite a similar way.

In some observations, fatter people did not seem to eat vastly more food. Yet, generally speaking, there appeared to be no important glandular or other body-function differences between fat people and thin.

How then to answer the painful questions of people like our Mrs. Whyte—who insist that they fatten on less food than the dietaries of many skinny folk?

Some studies suggest possible answers in secret, unconscious or night eating. We shall see later that such patterns do exist. But often this extra eating appears to be a reaction to efforts to stay on too stringent a dietary, along the lines of Mrs. Whyte's valiant attempts.

The mystery of the fattening hands

In the next few years, other bits and pieces of the puzzle began falling into place. One clue came from a curious phenomenon among certain veterans of World

War II. These men had one thing in common. They had suffered hand burns in battle. Skin grafts had been necessary. These grafts seemed to succeed. But then, 15 or 20 years later, as the men became fortyish, many complained. For the grafts—usually taken from the skin of the abdomen—were growing fat.

Why? Surgeons were puzzled. Of course, it was well known that, with approaching middle age, many people experienced a thickening about the middle. The belly was the notorious accumulation area for the fat of middle years. No one really bothered to ask the reason. It was often assumed to have something to do with the sedentary life, especially with the limited use of abdominal muscles.

This subcutaneous (beneath the skin) fat generally makes up about half the body's stored fuel and is responsible for the roly-poly cosmetic effect which is so unwanted. Cut into it, and it looks much like the fat one sees on a steak or roast. It is a soft, thick, yellowish mass.

The other half of human fat is less visible. Some of it occurs in masses similar to those of subcutaneous fat, except that it is deeper in the body, around the kidneys for example. And some of the less-visible fat is intracellular; that is, it is found within the billions of body cells of all types. Here it makes up tiny reservoirs of energy. Under the microscope, these appear as little specks scattered through the cytoplasm of the cell. When the muscle cell, for example, has an emergency job to do, it can summon fuel rapidly from within itself.

Later we shall see how this internal fat deceives us about our weight, and about our total physical condition, as years pass. But let us look again for the moment at the subcutaneous fat growing on the hands of the burn patients. Did it not suggest that the fuel-storage tissue of the abdomen was somehow different from that of the hands?

Differences under the skin

The current explanation emerged from the work of Dr. Jules Hirsch, at Rockefeller University in New

York City. Dr. Hirsch was checking the similarities between rodent fat and human fat. His need to know was simple. Most research on obesity was done on laboratory mice or rats, on the assumption that, in essence, fatty tissue was simply fatty tissue, whatever the skin under which it grew.

To test this view, Dr. Hirsch used a special needle to take tiny samples of fat tissue from obese human volunteers. Under the microscope, he compared these samples with those from experimental rodents.

The cells themselves were generally similar. Microscopically, animal cells look like little grey blobs enclosed in thin sheaths. The grey is full of tiny specks, and the heart of the cell is a darker grey blob (the nucleus), also in a thin sheath. In most cases, a thousand such cells, lined up, would just cross the head of a pin.

Fat cells, like other cells, may be said to be very much alive, which helps explain why an excess can be quite a burden. Fat cells share in all the basic body processes, demanding oxygen, blood circulation, fuel and protein building blocks.

But these living cells are also storage tanks. The fat to be stored is taken into the center of the cell. The grey cytoplasm, and all the working parts of the cell, are pushed out to the rim in what is called a "signet-ring" shape, with the nucleus in the signet part. The yellow fat becomes the core of the cell.

Dr. Hirsch noted two differences in mouse and human fat cells. The cells from the obese humans were larger and more numerous. This finding led him to take another step.

He now took fatty tissue samples from volunteers of normal weight. Again there were differences between this fat and that of the obese people. They were much the same as the differences between mouse and man. The cells of the obese were bigger and there were more of them. Fat people had a greater density of the adipose-storage (fat) cells; each cubic millimeter of their fat tissue held more storage tanks.

The implications of this one simple fact are still being examined. But some important questions arose at once.

For example, was the tendency of some tissue to have more storage cells hereditary? Was this why the skin from the abdomen grew fat even when it was moved to the hand?

This idea was, of course, counter to the old beliefs about obesity. But Harvard's Dr. Mayer—searching for causes of fatness—had been accumulating some evidence for the hereditary view. He knew, for example, that at least four kinds of obesity were inherited among laboratory mice. Why should humans be different?

A survey in Vienna had shown that, among a thousand fat people, 73 percent had at least one fat parent. Similar studies had been made in Chicago, Pennsylvania and Scotland. In these, the percentages were even higher. Another study showed that, when one examined those children born of two normal-weight parents, the chance of fatness was only nine percent.

But the traditionalists tended to reject these studies, believing that people grew fat because they had learned to eat heavily, or to eat high-calorie foods. If parents were fat because of bad habit, it was reasonable to believe that their children would have the same problem.

Then this familiar argument was controverted by more research. A German scientist concentrated on identical twins, twins with much the same genes. He found that when the twins stayed with their parents, or left the parents but remained with one another, both tended to be fat or thin. But what if they were separated from parents and from each other?

The researcher found separated identical twins and checked their weights. Theoretically, their weights should have followed the eating habits each had learned. But they did not. They were nearly as identical in weight as if they had been raised together.

Then, in London, Dr. R. F. J. Withers asked similar questions about habit and heredity in a different way. Withers looked at youngsters who were adopted versus those who grew up with their natural parents. Again, both should have followed the weights of the adoptive parents. Again, they did not. An adopted child might grow up fat in a thin household, or thin in a fat family.

Neither of these reports received very wide attention. But Dr. Mayer was aware of them as he launched an intensive study to learn what made adolescent girls fat. With a small task force of experts he descended on a summer camp for obese teenagers. His tests and measurements on these subjects were to be compared with those made on normal-weight girls at the Adolescent Unit of Children's Hospital, in Boston.

The importance of body styles

The girls went through batteries of tests and measurements. They were weighed underwater—a technique for finding what percent of the total body is fat and what percent lean. Their food choices and emotions were assayed. Time-lapse movies of their play were taken with a special camera, which at brief intervals exposed one frame of film.

There were several important differences between the obese and the normal girls, but one stood out most strikingly. It was the difference in somatotype—the general style or build of the body—which is definitely a hereditary factor. Fat girls tended to fall into certain body styles, and thin girls tended to belong to others.

A typical case is that of a girl. Dr. Mayer calls Florence. She was 16. She stood just over five feet, five inches tall and weighed 171 pounds. She did not have a pudgy-soft look; rather, she was broad-shouldered, thick-muscled and firm looking. Her hands were short and broad. Her hips were thickish and rounded, as was her abdomen. By the best available charts—figuring the heaviest skeleton—Florence should have weighed no more than 135 pounds, with 125 pounds being average weight. She was considered to be between 36 and 46 pounds overweight.

Florence was a blend of two somatotypes, representing the predominant style of each parent. The girl's father had been a football lineman in school—a burly, powerful man, broad and stocky, with bunched muscles.

In top shape, he had weighed 225 and was now much heavier. He exemplified the *mesomorph,* the human powerhouse.

Florence's mother had been a pretty woman in school, just a little overweight according to the charts, but pleasing. Her shoulders were sloped, and her muscles were rounded, with a general coating of fat. Her hands were rather short and soft, tapering in a stubby flame shape. Her abdomen and hips tended to be wide and soft, as did her upper thighs. While pregnant with Florence, she became rather fat, gaining over 25 pounds, which she then slowly added to. She was an *endomorph.*

Dr. Carl Seltzer, an anthropologist on Dr. Mayer's team, and an expert in body type, described Florence as an *endomesomorph.* Athletic and physically able, she was destined to be heavy. She could never hope to meet "ideal" measurements or weight. She could never have a wasp waist. Her broad back would always give her a large bust measurement. Her wide hips and waist would always take a dress size which sounded like "fat." Her burly legs and arms could never assume the Hollywood-slimness women hope for.

When these facts were explained to Florence, at first she was a little crestfallen; then tears of relief appeared. She was at last free from a self-hate and self-accusation which had burdened her from rather early childhood. She no longer had to be repelled by herself.

The understanding of her condition relieved Florence in a more practical way, too. The doctors told her that the original goals for her weight reduction had been overly ambitious. By allowing for her greater than average weight of muscle and breadth of frame, her weight-loss goal could be dropped from 40 pounds to 20.

This understanding is important to anyone who believes himself to be obese. For there is a difference between overweight and obesity. Being overweight means only that one weighs more than the average for one's size; being obese means that too much of one's body is made up of fat. The obese person is always overweight. But the overweight person is not necessarily obese and need not always reduce.

Dr. Mayer is fond of illustrating this point by citing the patriotism of a group of Green Bay Packers football players when Pearl Harbor was attacked. A number of these huge and husky men, all in superb physical condition, rushed to enlist in the armed forces. They were turned down for medical reasons. They were overweight. Not until they were weighed underwater, which showed that their above-average poundage was bone and muscle, were they accepted.

Fortunately, not everyone has to be weighed underwater to know when he is too fat. The Harvard researchers found a shortcut. Once they had weighed many girls and women underwater, they took endless measurements to find a fat spot on the body which would correlate well with the total proportion of fat. They found several.

Unhappily the two best fat-indicator areas are difficult to reach by oneself. The most accurate indicator is called the *triceps skinfold.* This is a point at the back of the upper arm. One bends the elbow and then finds the halfway point between the elbow and the bony prominence which protrudes farthest from the shoulder.

To measure the thickness of fat, one lets the arm hang and pinches. This is best done with two hands, so you need help. With two fingers of one hand, pull the skin and fat back, away from the bone and muscle underneath. With two fingers of the other hand, using light pressure, measure the thickness of the fold, which is largely fat.

Another pinch measure which is nearly as accurate is the *subscapular.* This is an area about an inch below the diagonal of the shoulder blade, on the back.

There is a third pinching area which, though not quite as accurate an indicator, is a good one and has the virtue of being a do-it-yourself operation. From the middle of your side, measure in about two inches, toward the front. Then find your lowest rib. Pinch just below it.

Doctors now use special calipers to give them the exact thickness of a fat fold, with a precise pressure. But you can not only get a good idea of the fat fold with your fingers; you can also learn to recognize slight changes in it with practice. Watching this fold is the best way to know when you need weight control, and to assess how well that control is going. For we shall see that the scales can be very deceptive.

How fat is too fat?

Body build, which is inherited, seems to have a definite relationship to the degree of fatness which might be considered normal and reasonable to sustain. Some 15 percent of the population are true ectomorphs. Their bodies tend to be long and narrow. The ratio of the hand's (or foot's) length to its width is great; fingers are long and tapering; musculature tends to be stringy or rope-like; fat covering tends to be thin.

It is difficult indeed for the real ectomorph to grow fat. For one thing, under the microscope, his subcutaneous tissue has relatively few fat cells, so he does not have room to store much fat. A pinch of about a half-inch thickness would indicate that the ectomorph was getting a bit fat and might use a few simple controls.

On the other hand, the mesomorph is likely to have a general fat coating, which under the microscope shows far more fat-storage space available. And the endomorph probably has still more fat cells. These two styles would not usually be considered obese until a pinch was over an inch thick—though measurements close to an inch suggest that they are close to the borderline.

There is a good chance that you are some combination of these styles. One way to test for just what sort of slimness you can expect of yourself is see where fat tends to be deposited on the body. By pinching up these areas, you can get an idea of how much is fat, which might be lost by reducing. (Remember that with tendencies to endomorphy or mesomorphy, it is realistic to allow for reasonable fat thickness, because of the larger number of fat-storage cells which are probably present.)

For example, if you feel your legs are too heavy, check the fat layer. You may well find that bone and muscle account for most of the thickness, and that, being mesomorphic, you will never have slim legs. Only starvation can make mesomorphic people thinnish; bone and muscle make them wide. By understanding your body type, you can develop reasonable expectations of your figure.

Weight charts have their limits

Today's nutritionists and physicians are beginning to rely less and less on the old weight charts. More and more, the tendency is to make the judgment, "If you *look* fat, you *are* fat." But this judgment should be made with a realistic idea of body type in mind. The wrestler's child is unlikely to look like the bony Paris model. And the model is unlikely to become the curvy sex idol.

The hereditary aspects of fatness are becoming clearer, but this does not mean that a tendency to fatness should make one give up. On the contrary. Dr. Mayer and other researchers have found that real understanding can lead to greater success in weight control.

For one thing, the emotions do come into play in obesity, and can make the problem far worse. Because our culture is now so fat-disapproving, it has been shown that heavy people begin to disapprove of themselves. When overweight teenage girls were shown pictures and asked to comment on them, this attitude showed up clearly. One picture was of a group of girls, with one girl to the side. Normal-weight girls tended to explain that the lone girl was about to join the group. Obese girls explained that the loner was being rejected by the group.

Such self-disapproval is, of course, psychologically unhealthy. Moreover, it tends to produce depression which may be met by more eating. (Researchers do find that eating helps to relieve depression in people who are upset.)

Obese people tend also to regard themselves as gluttonous and undisciplined. Eating a piece of pie feels like a cardinal sin.

Yet, Dr. Mayer and other researchers have found that most obese people are not gluttonous, especially while they are growing up. (This is not true of *all* the obese, some of whom have been found to gorge incredibly, with meals or night-eating of 4,000 calories and even more.) In many cases, obese boys and girls actually eat less than their slim counterparts. Fat teenagers are often outeaten by skinny ones. Fat babies have commonly been observed to consume less than thin.

Does this mean that people like Mrs. Whyte, with whom this chapter began, may be right when they say that they eat little but stay fat? Evidently, this can be so.

Eating little, staying heavy

Newer research by Rockefeller University's Dr. Hirsch—confirmed by scientists at Cambridge University, and by Dr. Jerome Knittle of Mt. Sinai Hospital in New York—explains one way this works. Recall how the fatty tissue of the obese proved to have a greater density of fat-storage cells. In tests with rats, reducing diets were used for the animals. They lost weight. But under the microscope it was seen that the excess fat cells did not disappear; they simply gave up their fat, shriveled and remained empty. As soon as the rats were free to eat again, the waiting cells seemed to gobble up food, store it as fat and renew plumpness.

Dr. Knittle, who has been treating unusually fat children, reports seeing great extremes of fat-cell density among these youngsters. In some cases, the number of cells is actually double that of normal. One six-year-old was estimated to have as many as an adult.

Knittle is not dealing with heredity as much as with another phenomenon, the increasing of fat-cell numbers by early overeating, which we shall discuss in another chapter. But his work adds to the inheritance theories. It helps to suggest, for example, why some people say, "I can eat whatever I want without getting fat." Such people, it is theorized, have so few fat cells that, when the cells are filled up, the people are still thin. The person with more cells, however, at the same degree of fatness, has his fat storage cells rather empty and eagerly waiting to be filled. He can never hope to sustain a wiry look without great self-deprivation. And it is probably wiser for him to accept a reasonable fat coating.

In addition to fat-cell numbers, which seem to go with inherited body types, there appear also to be other factors. One is the matter of appetite cut-off. Among adolescents, it has been found that the skinny ectomorph will eat just so much and then suddenly be unable to eat more. The mesomorphs or endomorphs experience no such clear-cut stop or sense of satiety. They tend always to be able to eat a little bit more, and may become quite uncomfortable before they feel they *must* stop.

Another factor was suggested by the stop-action movies of obese girls at play. Whether in the swimming pool or on the tennis court, the heavier girls tended to be standing still far more often—perhaps 50 percent of the time—when the camera clicked. The thin girls tended to be in motion perhaps 85 percent of the time. Some researchers, and experienced observers such as coaches and physical education teachers, have long noted varieties of action habits among body types.

Moving or standing still

In general, the wiry ectomorph seems to be a mover. He is physically busy, a little restless even when sitting in a chair. He fidgets and hustles. As this body type shades toward the blockiness of mesomorphy, many note a tendency to hard bursts of activity, such as the charges of a football player, with rest in between. And among the roundish endomorphs, indolence seems to be more common, with slower motions and a greater tendency to be completely at rest for long intervals.

Dr. Mayer and his staffers have made such observations in infants. They note that the fat baby tends to be placid and inactive. The thin baby, on the other hand, cries much more, and his movement, as much as three times as great, looks almost like continuous motion.

These phenomena are seen at all ages, in fact. The vigor of activity, too, is a notable difference. And it can change caloric expenditure considerably. A leisurely stroll may burn half the calories of a bustly, energetic hike.

Today the inheritance of such body characteristics is quite well accepted, though uniform predictions cannot be made. Dr. Mayer has estimated that if both parents are obese, 80 percent of the children will follow suit. If one parent is fat, the risk of obesity in the children is 40 percent. If both parents are of normal weight, the chance of fatness, he feels, is only seven percent. In other words, what seems to be important is the *tendency* to fatness.

Body type, as we have seen, is destiny. But fatness or slimness within the limitations of that type can be a matter of choice. And we shall see how science is making that choice a much easier one to carry out.

The choice is evidenced in certain facts. Poorer people are much more likely to be fat than the rich. Once this might have been explained by the high-protein diets that only the rich could afford. But today this factor is much less important. What seems to count is education to the importance of not being fat, and the greater social pressure on those who wish to be fashionable. Even more telling is the report that an overweight condition among women in their 30s is only half as prevalent as it is among men in the same age group. This is the reverse of expected inheritance, because women tend to have 20 percent *more* body fat than men, simply by sex differences in anatomy. Motivation seems to account for the better weight control by women.

To put it very simply, whatever our body heredity in terms of fat, we can make the most of it. Careful studies have shown that the very vast majority of people at almost any age can be taught to do so without great suffering. Studies have also shown that the failure to gain reasonable control over our weight, in a consistent way, is a menace to health and to survival.

To sum up, we should first understand our individual body style and what we can expect of it. We should also understand the important implications of that style, in terms of tendencies to store fat, to have appetite work as an automatic control or as a constant enemy, to move or to sit. We should then accept the tendencies, but learn to deal with them. The person who would learn to live with and manage his body style might well consider the ancient prayer which asks for the abilities to change what he can, accept what he cannot change and tell the difference between the two.

The reader is advised by the experts to begin by confronting himself unclothed before a full-length mirror. He should note what he can about body type, taking a good look at hands and feet especially, perhaps checking dimensions by pinching up the subcutaneous fat. Such self-examination should suggest the tendency to fatness or thinness, and what are realistic goals for change. It should also make his present status clear.

The chances are very good indeed that most of us, after such an examination, will want to know what science knows about preventing fat gain—even if things are bad, they can get a lot worse—and about remedying the damage which has already been done.

CHAPTER 8

How and when we grow fat

By 1963, it was clear to doctors that the national plague of fatness was not responding to treatment. Their efforts to cure obesity, by the best estimates, did not succeed nearly as well as did their treatment of cancer, not even by half.

Fatness, the experts were saying, was probably the country's number one public health problem. Attempts to reduce met with perhaps ten percent success. And even after dieters won their battles, most started right back up the poundage trail, to fatten again with about the same speed at which they had grown thinner.

In March of 1963, the American Medical Association called a meeting of specialists to try and answer the question: "If obesity is so hard to cure, is there a chance that we can *prevent* it?"

The answer then was a cautious yes. And a growing body of knowledge has reaffirmed that answer.

One key to preventing overweight is an understanding that there are certain crucial times of life when we are especially vulnerable to an increase in fatness. These periods are scattered from infancy through middle age.

For about the first 25 years of life in both sexes, weight increases tend to come step-fashion, in spurts. Then begin a rather steady, slow climb. In women, that climb may be boosted by two more rapid-gain spurts, the last of which may occur as late as the 50s.

If we can anticipate these danger times and take action—with both ourselves and our children—it appears that we can break even hereditary tendencies to grow really fat. Many experts believe we may actually be able to prevent not only the upward spurts themselves, but to some extent also prevent lifetime struggles which are likely to follow once we have allowed ourselves to blossom subcutaneously.

How fatness changes us

Most people, like the scientists of some years ago, tend to think of weight gain as a kind of thickening of the body surface, like so many coats of paint on an old wall. But weight gain is a more subtle matter. The fat body behaves differently from the thin. It is different in a total way, not just in its flabby shell.

Many of these differences not only complicate the business of reducing; they make it easier to re-gain. It appears almost that the body develops a fondness for the fat state and tends to preserve and restore it.

Some 30 important bodily changes are associated with fatness, leading to scientific controversies along the lines of, "Which came first, the chicken or the egg?" Reduced to extreme simplicity the question becomes: does fatness make the body change, or does the change happen first, to foster adiposity?

The answers are not always clear. But in general it is believed that if we can resist the danger periods, we can avoid much subsequent fat-proneness.

Among these changes is an increase in the number of fat-storage cells, which then seem almost to lie in wait for a chance at filling up with fat. The kidneys do not function as well, are slower to dispose of fluids, and the body begins to retain more of them. (We shall see that this creates problem deceptions for the would-be reducer.) Some researchers find that the fatter person becomes less efficient at burning starches and sugars and may convert more of them to stored fat. The fatter person begins to be less active, and his automatic appetite controls—which we shall explain—begin to malfunction. These and other changes tend to perpetuate a vicious circle of weight increase and make fat-prevention an important matter indeed. For the fat, alas, grow fatter.

The first threat: is it the worst?

It is possible that one kind of fatness takes shape in the first months of life. And for a glimpse into what happens, we must go again to the fat rats of Dr. Jules Hirsch of Rockefeller University, and his colleague, Dr. Jerome Knittle of the Mt. Sinai School of Medicine.

It was Dr. Hirsch who first observed the increased numbers of fat cells in the obese. When, he and Dr. Knittle wanted to know, did these cells appear? To answer the question, the researchers juggled a quantity of rat mothers and their new babies. Some mothers were given as many as 22 infants to breastfeed. Others got as few as four. The latter, one might say, grew up eating high on the rat. The former had to scramble and scrounge. It is no surprise that the pampered little ones grew plump, and their deprived cousins were lean.

At five-week intervals (equivalents of much longer times in a human life) fat samples were studied under the microscope. The rats had now been weaned and were allowed to eat all they wanted. But curiously, the lean rats did not rush to feast.

Why? Under the microscope, the high-living babies proved to have grown far more fat cells. And for months afterward—equal to human years—they continued to produce still more cells. The deprived rats, however, made far fewer cells all along, and stopped increasing the number as they matured.

The fat young rats became fat adults. The lean rats stayed lean. Now the scientists put the fat animals on reducing diets. Sure enough, they could lose weight. Their fat cells shrank toward emptiness, but their number was unchanged. And the moment the diet was stopped, the formerly obese animals fed until the cells were full again, and they were just as fat as ever, or perhaps even fatter.

In other words, the heavily fed rats had stepped onto the obesity merry-go-round, and it was going to be a constant effort to get off. There is now sufficient evidence to show that their human counterparts can expect the same results from similar food experiences early in life.

The opinion of most experts is that both heredity and early feeding play their roles in obesity patterns which are set in infancy and childhood. They can apparently operate together or separately, and one can influence the other. For example, the true ectomorphic child (narrow body build) is probably rather resistant to overfeeding. But if, as is likely, he also has some endomorphic or mesomorphic genes, heavy feeding tends to exaggerate his style. The slim-armed, slim-legged person with narrow chest may nevertheless carry a substantial pot belly in adulthood.

Conversely, an inheritance of the stocky or rounded body styles may possibly dispose to more fat cells. Heavy feeding will be likely to exaggerate the problem.

Looking back at what we know of fat and heredity and adding the new knowledge of what stuffing can do to a child, we can conclude that any wise parent will take certain physical and psychological precautions, but that heavyweight parents will be especially cautious and watchful.

In general, authorities tend to describe the infant danger period as beginning with weaning from the breast. (It is too tricky to try and exercise much control over breastfeeding intake.) And they see this danger period as extending until the age of about 36 months.

As proof of this concept, they cite studies of fat adolescents. It appears that most obese teenagers were fat by the age of three—in fact, usually by the ages of 12 to 18 months. These teenagers, in turn, tend to become obese adults.

The second age of fat

According to some studies, there is a second childhood time when children often fatten—between the ages of seven and 11. But what is happening here is less clearly explained.

Perhaps the best clue to the obesity which seems to emerge in this period is suggested by a seasonal study of youngsters. Most often, they fatten in winter, implying to experts that lack of activity is the main change. What looks like the most reasonable theory goes something like this: the fatter child is less active. His hereditary tendency, or overfeeding which early builds up an overload of fat cells, may make him plump, but may not be marked enough to stamp him as obese. Then school begins.

Now for six or seven hours of the day there is enforced inactivity. The balance of calorie intake versus calorie output is tipped. And a slow buildup of caloric excess begins. In one, two or perhaps three years the child's appearance gradually changes, until he is no longer just plump, but fat.

This insidious development of fat is well known at all ages. One cannot easily see it happening because it can occur with almost unbelievably small changes in eating or exercise.

Let us suppose we have a child who weighs 50 pounds. Assume that school reduces his active play by 30 minutes a day. (Not his free time, but the actual number of minutes daily when he is moving fairly vigorously.)

Roughly, this reduction in activity amounts to 50 or 60 calories each day. In a little over two months, the child will have gained over five pounds. In two years, he will have taken on 11 pounds of extra fat.

Put a little differently, in terms of food intake, this change would equal the unexpended energy of half an ounce of chocolate per day. It would amount to one small pat of butter, an extra slice of bread, or two and one-half cashew nuts.

The very delicate energy balance

In a child with a hereditary proclivity toward fatness, or one who has been slightly overfed as an infant, the edge of obesity may be honed even finer. It may take much less to do the job.

Chances are, such a child is by age six a little plumpish, perhaps ten percent over his ideal weight. One really would not call him fat. The rapid changes of size and shape in childhood confuse the issue still more, as the youngster goes through various phases of maturation.

Probably half the energy imbalance described above will push this child over the brink of frank fatness. A

15-minute daily reduction in exercise will do it, as will half the extra food amounts mentioned above.

If the pattern continues until age ten, half of even these few calories will make him obese. Seven and a half minutes less of exercise is now all it takes each day —or an extra tiny bite of meat, half a marshmallow daily, perhaps one three-inch cookie every nine days.

Here we come upon the appallingly delicate energy balance which operates in teenagers and adults just as in children. For adults, in fact, the balance is even finer, more tricky to control.

For example, in our last formulation, for the fattening child, the damage done is slightly over an extra pound of fat a year. That may sound unimpressive— until you realize that it can make an adult 25 pounds heavier at 40 than he was at 20! A daily activity decline of two and a half minutes of swimming, stair-climbing or dancing is theoretically enough to have this effect on an average man.

Seen in these terms, the problem of energy balance looks almost impossible. One gets the impression that one would have to clock every step, to weigh each food to the gram and keep a computer in the kitchen to hold one's weight. This, happily, is not necessary. There are some simple ways to solve the problem—and in fact, to use the phenomenon advantageously, to adjust weight up or down. They will be explained.

Childhood's second danger period for fatness may be seen as a time for the open emergence of the results of small errors in energy output or intake. That emergence is important because it is likely to be a predictor of a lifetime pattern. It is a warning signal which should not go unrecognized. The child who becomes fat by age 11, and especially by age nine, can face a lifelong struggle against obesity.

As a girl becomes a woman

The next danger period is for females only. It comes with the onset of menstruation, usually at about age 13, though in recent years this time of puberty is earlier for many girls.

Again, the reason for weight gain seems to be twofold. First, the 13-year-old girl stops climbing trees and racing the boy next door. Her interests turn to lingerie and lipstick. This is partly a cultural change. But it is also a physical shift.

With the production of feminine hormones, the girl tends to develop greater fatness as a sexual characteristic. The shaping breasts and hips and legs develop their soft curves primarily by an increase of fat. (When these same hormones are given to men for various medical purposes, similar things happen to them, such as enlarging breasts. In fact, some promising tests with estrogens in the control of heart and other important diseases had to be given up partly because of the unacceptable figure changes they produced in the males being tested.)

What happens to the girl entering adolescence resembles the pattern of the fattening child—an activity shift which reduces energy output. But this is compounded by the addition of fat as a sexual characteristic. Fat gain in the girl continues slowly until the age of 16 or 17.

Somewhat ironically, the boy goes into a happy reverse of this process as he enters adolescence. Male hormones, coupled with such factors as increasing physical strength, generally cause his activity to rise. In the next few years, his bodily pattern swings toward leanness, toward replacing fat with a higher and higher proportion of muscle.

When bone growth stops

Until the human skeleton has reached its mature size and weight, and for a short time afterward, there is a heavy demand on the food supply for the building materials of growth. When bone growth stops, food consumption may continue at much the same level as for growing, and the unused nutrients are stored as fat.

For reasons which scientists cannot clearly explain, this phenomenon is more troublesome for men than for women. The female skeleton is usually at full size by about the age of 16, while male bone growth continues until about 22. And this may be the most important reason why women are less affected. For their growth stops in a time of physical activity, while male growth stops at just about the time the man gets his diploma and turns in his football pads, his track shoes or his sweatshirt for a three-button suit and a desk.

For both sexes, the early 20s are the time when the adult styles of living are set. And these styles become critical determinants of how grim will be the adult war with fat, of whether one's hereditary fattening tendencies will be controlled or allowed to run wild.

Dr. Mayer comments on the old saw about the football player who leaves *alma mater* behind and goes on eating in his former way to become tubby. Actually, Dr. Mayer points out, this man is certainly eating much less. But the drop in activity makes him fat, partly because his burly mesomorphic build makes him tend to do so anyway. It is worth noting, the Harvard nutritionist suggests, that the rangy long-distance runner, usually a more spindly ectomorph, can give up just as much activity, go on eating and yet is likely to stay quite slim. The wise young man or woman with mesomorphic or endomorphic tendencies will take action in his early 20s to develop a fat-preventive style of living, which we shall discuss. And he or she will take particular note of a striking bodily phenomenon of which few Americans are aware.

The threat of secret fatness

One of the most important discoveries in the newer knowledge of obesity and health is that we can become fat without knowing that it is happening or has happened. For the truth is that we can become fatter without seeing an extra ounce on the scales!

This insidious factor tends to begin in men at about the age of 25, and in women a little earlier, at about 22.

It depends on a simple physical characteristic—that muscle weighs more than fat.

Consider Mr. Jones, whose case is based on experimental fact. When he leaves college, at 22, he weighs 160 pounds. He is in the typical good shape of an active young man who enjoys sports, though he is not a letter-winning athlete. About 12 percent of his weight is fat, or just under 20 pounds.

(Experimentally, this has been determined by weighing underwater, by x-ray shadow patterns of subcutaneous fat, by tracer tests using a special form of potassium which shows researchers the lean body mass, by bone measurements and by measuring skinfolds with special calipers. So the phenomenon we discuss here is well documented.)

But now Mr. Jones begins to get less exercise. His muscle cells become fewer and are replaced by fat cells.

Let us look at Mr. Jones 35 years later, at the age of 57. He is proud indeed of his physical condition. He is fond of pointing out that he weighs no more than he did when he left school, 160 pounds. But when fat researchers check, they find his body composition is radically different. Instead of 12 percent fat, it is now 24 percent. Some 40 pounds!

True, Mr. Jones's dimensions have changed slightly in a few areas where fat is deposited. His silhouette is a little less shapely. But he would be dismayed indeed to learn that he is now *twice* as fat, with the usual health effects.

And what if Mr. Jones follows a more characteristic pattern? Suppose he gains 20 pounds in those 35 years, a record which would not seem at all bad in terms of suit sizes and even general appearance. First, that 20 pounds is fat. Second, it means a gain of only about nine ounces a year—the energy value of little more than a minute a day of vigorous exercise, or less than the caloric worth of an extra daily peanut.

Mr. Jones now carries about 60 pounds of fat, out of a total of about 180 pounds. He is one-third fat—three times as corpulent as he was in his youth. It is easy to see how health implications may arise from this very substantial change in the composition of Mr. Jones's body.

The perils of pregnancy, menopause and middle age

It is no secret that women tend to gain weight during pregnancy, far beyond the weight of the growing baby and the fluids which protect it. Nor is it any secret that commonly this weight never leaves. But scientists caution women about two particular fattening dangers which have been connected with pregnancy.

One is that the greatest chance of fattening comes with the *first* baby. Though there is speculation, no one really knows exactly why. But the risk is by far greater than it is with subsequent births. A few experts hazard that those women who are susceptible to pregnancy gain—perhaps through heredity—fall prey to the danger at once. But then, why shouldn't *every* pregnancy produce similar gains? Could it be because partially empty fat cells become filled up?

The second fact is that the age of the mother at her first pregnancy has a great deal to do with the extent of the risk. Only about 11 percent of pregnant teenagers become obese. But at the age of 35, the obesity risk with pregnancy has grown until *four out of ten* first-time mothers become genuinely fat.

Again, the reason is a matter for speculation. But the meaning is that pregnancy should be taken as a warning sign, especially for those women with fat-prone body styles.

The final hazard for women is menopause. When menstruation stops, women tend to gain weight. Experts say this may be caused in a number of ways. Menopause comes at a time when activity is decreasing. It often brings on depression, and heavier eating and physical lassitude are common ways of dealing with depressed states. Hormonal factors may be at work, also; at least, there seems to be evidence that when female hormones are given to menopausal women, one of the many desirable effects is a reduced chance of fattening.

Finally, the slow gaining pattern of men seems to become accelerated about age 40. Reduced activity is seen as the primary cause, with the added hazard of greater wealth, which makes the luxuries of the table more accessible.

The decline and fall of food need

Making the entire problem of slow, steady weight gain still more difficult is one more vexing body phenomenon. This is the decline of basal metabolism, the rate at which the resting body burns food in order to perform necessary life functions such as digestion, temperature balancing and the normal levels of breathing and blood circulation while at rest.

From late adolescence, the total amount of food needed just to keep the bodily engine idling goes down steadily. The age at which the down slope takes form is usually given as 25. The rate at which total food need thins out is usually between five and seven percent for each decade of life.

For example, a woman whose weight ideally is 121 pounds needs about 2,000 calories a day in all, if she leads a moderately active physical existence. This need is at age 25. At 45, if our woman keeps up her level of activity, food need is down to 1,800 calories per day. At 65, still assuming moderate activity, she needs only 1,550 daily calories, and the food requirement continues to drop still more.

If our 25-year-old woman continues to eat at the same rate, while her needs drop, by age 45 she will be gaining about 20 pounds a year. In the process of continuing her 25-year-old's food consumption during her middle years, she will gain more rapidly each year, with astonishing results.

Mathematically, at 26 she will gain one pound, at 27 she will gain two pounds, at 28 three pounds, and so on. This does not sound like much. But the progression would give her a weight, on her 46th birthday, of about 331 pounds!

Fortunately, this is just mathematics. The body is

How Your Food Needs Decline
(food calories needed)
Women

Weight	At 25	At 45	At 65
88	1600	1450	1200
99	1750	1600	1300
110	1900	1700	1450
121	2000	1800	1550
128	2100	1900	1600
132	2150	1950	1650
143	2300	2050	1750
154	2400	2200	1850

Men

Weight	At 25	At 45	At 65
110	2300	2050	1750
121	2450	2200	1850
132	2600	2350	1950
143	2750	2500	2100
154	2900	2600	2200
165	3050	2750	2300
176	3200	2900	2450
187	3350	3050	2550

wiser than that. As food need declines, so does appetite. But researchers find that appetite rarely diminishes as fast as food need does. The resulting difference between fuel used and fuel eaten is small. Typically, it might be on the order of 20 excess calories a day, causing our poor young lady, by the time she is 46, to weigh 160 pounds.

It may be worth taking a look at the table on this page (from the Food and Nutrition Board of the National Research Council) to get an idea of how much less food you are likely to need as time passes. The weight shown in the left-hand column is "ideal" weight, without any clothing. Moderate physical activity is assumed.

At this point, the reader may feel that in the battle against corpulence the cards are heavily stacked against him—unless he is among about one in seven people who seem born to be thin. But he should also see that if he is a little pudgy—or even quite a lot—it is not because he is an unbridled glutton. And most experts agree that when we eliminate the undeserved gilt and shame which are so typical of fatness, we are far more likely to overcome the handicap.

Plainly, the accumulation of fat is a problem for most of us from birth until late middle age. So bursts of battle against obesity—no matter how ardent, no matter how gallantly self-denying—are likely to give us only temporary victories. Steady, inexorable life processes tend to defeat us in what is not only a struggle for pride, but for health and survival.

To overcome fat, our understanding must be basic, and so must our changes in life style. But these changes, happily, need not be great. For just as weight gain tends to be a slow evolution rather than a violent change, so our ways of meeting it usually require no very grand gestures or sacrifices—*if we know the techniques of fat prevention.*

These techniques have double value. For they let us roll back our present fatness and also give us a guarantee that the adipose enemy will not rise to plague us again. They teach us to use bodily phenomena to keep us slim instead of making us fat.

CHAPTER 9

How to prevent fatness

Possibly the most important key to preventing fatness is understanding how to put to work your body's controls over the desire for eating.

Science's knowledge of hunger and the subtle satisfactions of feeding is yet imperfect. But enough is known to make obesity-prevention fairly simple for that majority of us who tend to grow ever fatter.

On the surface, appetite appears to be a personal thing. For example, let us look at a study of hunger patterns among 800 men, women and adolescent boys and girls.

This research showed interesting difference between sex and age groups. Hunger seemed to hit different people at different times of the day. For some 80 percent of adults, the most longed for meal was dinner, with lunch and breakfast each getting the most attention from only about ten percent of the grownups.

Twice as many teenagers as adults were hungriest for breakfast, and three times as many were hungriest for lunch. Teenage girls favored lunch four times as often as adults did, a total of 40 percent giving first place to the noon meal. (This may have had to do with the fact that the same number of the girls skipped breakfast —against only 15 percent of grown women.)

Women seemed to be the steadiest eaters through the day. And evidently this was not because of the proximity of the refrigerator, since these women were all Boston-area schoolteachers. Not only did the women have the smallest number of breakfast-skippers, but the smallest total of lunch-skippers, 14 percent. And only a few more of them went without between-meal snacks.

Virtually none of the teenagers went without lunch or snacks, the girls averaging better than two snacks a day and the boys three. But, to the surprise of many scientists, about half the men did without lunch or snacks, making adult males the largest group to do so.

There were differences, too, in how and when people perceived that they were hungry. They generally had some sort of stomach signal when very hungry—it might be tenseness, rumbling, a feeling of emptiness, ache, pain or nausea, or some combination.

Men had more mouth sensations—from salivation to dryness and bad taste—than did women. And adults had more mouth sensations than youngsters. The same was true of throat feelings.

Men and women had an average of twice as many head sensations of hunger as did the adolescents. They also had a third more feelings of general weakness, sleepiness, fatigue, restlessness, and so on, and up to twice as many moods of irritability and nervousness.

Women and girls had far more preoccupation with thoughts of food long before the meal than did the males.

The teenagers reported, in general, stronger urges to eat than did the adults.

Whatever the differences, all the subjects were agreed on one thing: they knew when they were hungry. This will hardly surprise the reader. But what may give him pause, as it has the nation's nutritionists, is the fact that the subjects had great difficulty describing what happened when they were sated. The very vast majority, when asked what made them stop eating, said they were "satisfied," but had trouble saying *how they knew* they were satisfied. Nearly all of the others said they stopped sooner because they were trying to control their weight.

Stomach or abdominal discomfort was one satiety sign mentioned, but by only about one subject in four—though in teenage boys, as might be guessed by experienced parents, and even more so among girls, a "full stomach" was given as the sign of stopping. And, of course, there was also a change of mood, after eating, toward contentment.

One would think that there might be some pronounced differences in the hunger sensations and feeding habits of the obese. The habit differences, however, tend to be such factors as skipping more meals, eating desserts less often, more commonly cleaning up whatever is on their plates and eating fewer large meals. It seems that the fatter people differed primarily in that they were trying to grow thin.

What of the hunger sensations of the obese? "No important differences," was the thrust of the research report. In fact, in some categories, their sensations were actually fewer. They thought a little more about food two hours before a meal. And their urge to eat, half an hour before a meal, was curiously less.

As for the satiety feelings of the heavy folk, they had rather typical ones, though oddly they more often reported discomfort, such as distention and nausea, after eating. Most importantly, more of the obese said that they needed more will power to stop eating, and that they thought more about food half an hour after eating; this, of course, could be explained by their wish to reduce.

Such studies further belie the old view of the stouter people among us. Rarely do they experience ravening appetite, it would appear, or unconscionable self-indulgence.

One nutritionist has suggested that the truth of this concept—that only the very most unusual of the overweight are the gobblers of comic literature—is easily checked. Suppose, he offers, that we have a woman who merely eats one two-inch slice of chocolate layer cake, or its equivalent, *beyond the needs of her body*. The Department of Agriculture estimates that slice at about 450 calories. If she does this daily, she would gain almost 50 pounds a year. If she started at the age of 25, at a weight of 125 pounds, by age 30 she would weigh 375 pounds. At age 40 she would weigh 875 pounds. By 43, she would be over half a ton!

Of course this is absurd, though medicine knows of 400-pound people and larger. And really, that modest slice of extra layer cake can hardly be seen as an orgy.

Four and one-half extra tablespoons of butter would have the same effect. So would about four ounces of broiled steak.

Understanding these simple facts should convince the most fat-shamed reader that he is simply not a glutton. His appetite does not run wild. He is not out of control. Only a modest sort of change is needed to stop the heartbreaking accumulation of fat and prevent further gain. For appetite is running just a little out of kilter with need.

Here we have what may look like a paradox. For if only a small change is needed, then why have the genuine efforts of so many millions to stop weight gain and reduce failed?

That small change is attainable, experimental evidence has shown. It is attainable at any age, though the strategies may differ in detail. The millions of failures rarely need to happen.

Let us look more closely at what science had learned about how the difference between need and food appears. To do so, we must go back to our friends, the rats.

Quite a few years ago, scientists began to realize that somewhere in the body there had to be a delicate and amazingly efficient control for food intake. The story of the search is complex, but it neared its end as researchers carefully destroyed two tiny centers in the brains of rats.

These areas are in the most primitive part of the brain, at the bottom-central portion, called the *hypothalamus*. In this region are controls for such biologic essentials as sex and temperature regulation, so physiologists believe that it had to develop first. (Language, for example, appears to use areas of the brain's cortex, its uppermost layer.)

The two destroyed areas (one for each of the brain's halves) proved to have the hoped-for effect on feeding. The rats began eating beyond their food need and tended to become obese.

Then experimenters, using other rats, destroyed cells

in the same general area of the brain, but farther out to the sides. The rats simply stopped eating.

Today, while it is far from complete, the knowledge of these eating-control centers of the brain is considerable. Each brain half apparently has two centers, one which triggers feelings of hunger and another which produces feelings of satiety.

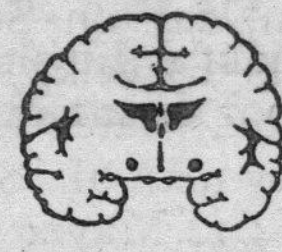
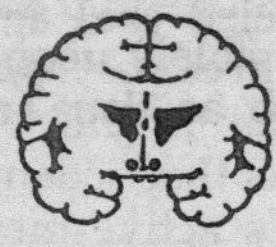

The "on-off switches" for appetite. A cut-away view of the human brain, showing the four nerve centers which some researchers call the "appestat." The two centers on the left, one on each side of the brain, appear to be the originating points for appetite. The two shown in the drawing on the right seem to be the limiting centers which turn appetite off.

Satiety mechanisms seem to be largely unconscious. (The full stomach is just a mechanical feeling, and has little to do with essential appetite.) The feeling of contentment is usually vague and often appears slowly, after about half an hour.

Nutrition researchers are now quite sure that the satiety centers of the brain operate primarily by somehow measuring the quantity of glucose, the sugar form to which the body converts much of its fuel. They also find subtle brain controls involving fats, complex proteins and oxygen. But for our purposes, it is probably enough to know that there is a way by which the brain considers our food supply and signals hunger feelings or stops them. This mechanism is sometimes called the *appestat.*

Why, scientists wanted to know, did the appestat fail to keep people from eating more than they needed? Researchers began to look at the habit changes which seemed to be associated with fattening.

The reader has surely read to the point of tedium how push-bottons and machines have reduced our energy output. But Dr. Jean Mayer summed it all up in a news interview. He was speaking of the classifications of energy use and how these have changed since 1890.

"The sedentary type," said Dr. Mayer, "was a clerk —somebody who got up, split wood or shoveled coal for an hour, walked to work for close to an hour, worked ten hours a day, six days a week, at a stand-up desk, walked back home again another hour, then split wood or shoveled coal again, and on Sunday took his family for a three- or four-hour walk. Now there isn't any city dweller in the United States who expends as much energy as that sedentary man of 1890."

Even today's active men, Dr. Mayer points out, are not nearly so active as they used to be, because machines do much of their work, too. The only comparison to the "active" man of 1890 is our vigorous athlete.

But if our energy output was down, scientists asked, why did not the appestat simply allow for this? To find the answer, they kept some rats idle and forced other groups to exercise for different periods, from one to eight hours a day. The rats were all allowed to eat as much as they wanted.

The results were dramatic. The rats who ran for an hour a day seemed to consume just as much food as they needed. But as their exercise was reduced below that point, their food consumption did not go down; it went up!

So the idle rats grew fat. Evidently, their appestats simply did not function effectively below a certain level of activity.

What of the rats who went on to higher levels of activity, and eventually to exhaustion? The additional exercise did not make them lose weight. Their appestats seemed to function beautifully, providing them with almost exactly enough food to match their energy output. Between one and six hours of daily vigorous exercise (beyond which exhaustion destroyed appetite) made the rats hold their starting weight exactly.

What does this mean for humans? Dr. Mayer—who had directed this research—was able to match the rat test to human performance in a significant way. Studying different occupational groups in India, where machines are often scarce, he found that human and rat responses were very much the same.

His conclusion: *"In the U.S. most of us are down in the sedentary range, where the regulators (in the brain) don't work very well for most people."*

Certainly, this is not the only reason for the fatness of Americans. But making use of this information appears to be the simplest and most effective means of breaking the vicious circle of fattening and preventing obesity.

At present, the person who is in that circle is like a man on an escalator. He is moved toward fat by a constant upward pressure, a tendency to eat a little too much and gain. So even if he reaches a desired weight by dieting, to hold that weight he must eat less than he wishes. His body simply has not evolved to accept a life of sitting down.

Ironically, after devoting so much creative and scientific effort in the 20th century to freeing ourselves from the necessity of physical work, we must now restore some of that energy output to maintain a healthful state. Obesity is not the only effect of cutting down physical activity, of course. The sedentary pattern is a threat to health in many ways.

Moderate exercise is an excellent control for blood pressure—and rising blood pressure is the precursor of the blood-vessel abnormalities which yield heart attacks, strokes, peripheral vascular disease (such as varicose veins) and early senility. Exercise helps to strengthen, and even multiply, blood vessels around the heart, so that in case of a heart attack, the chance of survival and recovery is much greater; it helps to protect against lung disease, such as emphysema; it keeps us emotionally more stable, by being a wholesome outlet for tension; and it has even been shown to help the brain function more efficiently.

But activity is only one side of the energy balance. Food intake is the other. And even with added exercise, Americans have developed eating habits and choices which help confound the body's natural weight control. Let us look more closely at how obesity can be prevented in practical ways.

Insuring the baby against obesity

The growing evidence is that with a few precautions parents can bring up babies with a maximum of protection against the lifelong battle with obesity.

In practical terms, there is little that parents can do while the baby is being breast-fed, or while breast-feeding would be taking place. By weaning time, however, some judgments about body style can usually be made by a well-informed physician. Also, by this time the parents have a good idea whether the child is restless and active or plump and placid.

What if the initial assessments by doctor or parents are wrong? It probably doesn't matter. The defensive strategies recommended here are safe and desirable for any child.

Food, of course, is not denied to the infant. Both the physical and emotional hazards would be far too great. Efforts at food reduction with children at all ages have been known to interfere with growth and development. In fact, until recent years, attempts to control weight by any means were usually unsuccessful until after the age of 15.

But some things can be done. Consider Mrs. Newmother. She watches her new baby with a clinical eye, with the feeling that her job is to make him grow, a bit as if he were a rose bush or an elm tree.

The baby has recently taken to bottle-feeding. Mrs. Newmother is anxious: will he live separated from her breast? Mrs. Newmother measures the formula with precision. The baby nurses, but turns his head away while there is an ounce left in the bottle. He may starve! "Please," she cozens, trying to keep her composure. "A little more, just another sip, for Mama's sake."

After a long struggle, Mrs. Newmother wins, and the baby nurses a little more. He is rewarded with all the affection that a relieved mother can lavish, which is plenty. He has also begun to learn a lesson: "Eating earns me love."

Mrs. Newmother has signed up her baby for what the American Medical Association's Dr. Philip White calls the "Empty Bottle Club." Nature's controls over caloric intake have been thwarted, and as the game continues, the fat cells multiply.

Nutritionists find that fat babies are often the end-product of motherly fears and/or motherly pride. But what if the baby is thin? Probably it is because he is destined to be thin. Remember, if underweight in an infant *is* a medical problem, it had better be handled by a professional. Coaxing and rewarding are rarely the answer. Ask the doctor, if you are afraid that a child is underfed.

On the other side of the coin, Mrs. Thirdtime is just delighted by her six-month-old boy. "He sleeps," says Mrs. Thirdtime. "I mean, I can do my housework. I can telephone. What a wonderful baby!"

But while the baby sleeps, he is also getting fat. Mrs. Thirdtime lets him stay in his crib as long as he chooses. But here, the experts say, perhaps she should be interfering with a natural bent. The "good baby" should not be encouraged to vegetate. He should be played with, when he is awake, so as to encourage movement. Energy and activity should win approval.

Studies suggest that physical activity is rather habit-forming. If we are in the habit of being active, we are restless when inactive. If we are used to being indolent, we feel more comfortable that way.

So unless there is a contravening medical problem—and the baby should be under medical surveillance which would spot such a problem—two fat-prevention rules obtain.

Rule One: Do not stuff the baby. Do not reward eating with love. Let his inner appetite controls operate.

Rule Two: Do not encourage inactivity or reward a placid acceptance of confinement with loving approval. Encourage activity and physical curiosity.

Continuing to protect the preschooler

Dr. White's "Empty Bottle Club" is the training ground for the "Clean Plate Club" which follows in the preschool years, and often throughout life. The reasons for membership are several, but the keys are in this little drama:

"Where are you going, Albert?" says Mrs. Moralbite, as her four-year-old starts to slip away from the table. "Look at that plate." Albert's lower lip quivers. "Don't you know that there are children in India who would give anything to have those nice instant mashed potatoes? And that piece of hamburger? It is a sin to waste food. And finish your milk, too."

Most Americans regard the food on a dinner plate as possessing some mystical significance. They eat the food before them because they have been made to feel guilty if they do not. Their mothers, like Albert's, may have reminded them constantly of starving children in other countries—who would never see the food even if Albert agreed to pass up dinner entirely. Other mothers will protest they have slaved for hours over a meat leaf, making it just the way the child likes it. Isn't the child going to show his appreciation by eating it?

Of course he is. For the rest of his life, he will eat it, all. Guilt pangs will do their work.

"I'll just have to throw it out," is an urgent call from Ameircan mothers to their children to get food down, somehow. Better the food should load another few ounces of handicap to breathing and circulation than end up in the garbage can.

Thus the Clean Plate Club, which may well be one of the nation's most subversive organizations. For it unwittingly seeks the overthrow of bodily appetite controls.

The Clean Plate Club has some subsidiary groups, too, which teach destructive food attitudes. One of these might be called the "Just Desserts Society." "What did you say to Mother? I heard you! No chocolate ice cream for you, young man."

Food used as a punishment can easily condition an inability to say no to eating. Conversely, food used as a reward—or a bribe, might often be more accurate—is equally dangerous. "Come with Daddy to the dentist like a brave little man, and afterward we'll get a strawberry malted with whipped cream on top."

These attitudes can all be confused, too, in a really telling way. "So you're ready for the banana cream pie, eh? Well, you haven't finished your lamb chop yet, or the peas, and what's that half slice of bread and butter doing on your plate? You're not ready for dessert yet."

Also, in the preschool years, the docile, indolent child continues to be less troublesome and so may be rewarded for his inactivity instead of being placed in active situations.

Shaping the child's energy choices

Every family's energy style has a powerful influence on the children, shaping their preferences for activity for years to come. For example, what does a family do with leisure time? Is Sunday spent with Father watching football on television and Mother reading quietly, and the two running the eight-yard snack relay to the kitchen all day? Expect Junior to emulate them.

Especially if a family tends to be heavy, the effort should be made to spend Sunday in the country or at the beach, perhaps walking to a picnic site, or perhaps ice-skating, swimming, skiing, horseback riding or bicycling. Obviously, there will be health benefits for all. Parents may not be willing to do it for themselves, but they benefit just as much as the child for whom they make the "sacrifice." It's the rare small child who doesn't enjoy sharing such activities with the parents.

Food choice, moreover, can be handled in a similar way. If the parents eat intelligently, the child will copy. If Dad wrinkles his nose when there is fruit for dessert, but grins when pecan pie appears, Junior will learn. Anyone who doubts this need only look at food choices from culture to culture. There are societies where insects and worms are delicacies, where seal blubber is a lip-smacker, where a sheep eye is the choicest morsel of all.

The author once wrote an article on a cardiologist who wanted to teach his family a way of life which would protect them against heart disease. Both because of weight hazard, and because of certain beliefs about fats which we shall examine later, the doctor and his wife established an unusual eating pattern for the family.

The youngsters were always fed fat-free milk, for example. Result? They wouldn't drink milk in restaurants; it tasted too rich. In fact, most of the high-fat food choices of Americans were distasteful to these children. They preferred ice milk to ice cream. Beefsteaks were only occasional choices for them; they liked fish better. They enjoyed potatoes more without butter added.

Their existence was not nutritionally bleak. It was full of good things to eat. But they simply had little taste for *intense* sweetness or fat. Such tastes are well demonstrated to be matters of custom and repeated experience.

"The interesting thing to me," the cardiologist said one evening as we talked about the story, "is that *I* no longer like these things so much. Fat-rich sauces and desserts taste good. But I really don't want a lot of them."

The point is, as nutritionists have long been able to demonstrate, we can shape our food tastes to serve our purposes, not defeat them. When we do so, our children tend to follow suit.

The narrowing chance

With each passing year, from birth, the possibilities for fat prevention decline. By the time a child starts school, many of the most basic attitudes toward food are rather firmly set, though not immutable.

A recent study of over 3,400 preschoolers, from 2,000 families, showed that unhealthy food attitudes were being instilled. Better than three out of four mothers were concerned about their children eating too little at meals. About one of five mothers feared the children were not getting enough meat or milk. Fewer than three percent worried about the little ones' eating too much.

One in four mothers admitted using food as a reward, though experts suggest this number is probably much, much higher than the mothers recognize. Of these women, 75 percent used desserts to reward.

Attitudes toward receiving food treats as a sign of love or an inducement to good behavior seem to be firmly entrenched by the time school begins. Similarly, the threat of food held back as punishment becomes ingrained early. These two factors encourage people to turn to food when they feel unloved, afraid of loss, or deprived.

Some basic aspects of taste seem also to be inculcated during this period—for example, a demand that milk taste rich and that sweets follow meals. The older the child gets, the harder it is for him to accept changes in taste. Styles of activity or inactivity appear to have taken form in the first six years, too, as part of a total general life style.

In other words, by the time the child is a preadolescent (seven to 11), it is a little late for some defensive measures. For one thing, the child may already have stepped into the vicious circle—many fat-storage cells, slight overweight making him less inclined to active play, and so on.

By now, added exercise and the correction of food habit are the remaining defense line, and remain so through life. Doctors do not recommend trying to reduce children through adult-type diets. They do recommend cutting down on sweets and pure fats, to a large extent, for they have little else but fuel value, and also cutting down on extremely high-calorie foods and snacks, such as nuts. (In a later chapter, the reader will find some quick ways to identify these foods easily and limit their intake.)

For four years, Harvard nutritionists worked with several hundred obese children who had not been able to reduce; they employed only food education, high-calorie-food reduction and physical exercise. The exercise pattern was one hour a day on school days, and three hours on each weekend day. Ninety percent stopped gaining fat (not weight, necessarily, for they were growing) and reduced fat to some extent.

Similar strategies are used for girls who begin to fatten at the onset of menstruation, another danger period. Exercise is especially important here, for the cause of fat again is twofold now—the development of sexual characteristics and the end of tomboy-like child play. The girl needs more mature kinds of physical activity.

Preventing adolescent fatness

It seems fairly clear that most fatness in adolescence is usually a result of continued eating-exercise habits of childhood. So more activity makes for especially effective weight control. And limiting food, without medical supervision, risks interfering with growth.

All adolescents should be guided a little in the kinds of exercise they get. It is wise for parents to take a look at how all that energy is being burned.

One would not think, for example, that there was need to worry about the football or basketball star. But remember, for such team members, rigorous training is the price of staying on the team. Once school is over, it will not be so easy to get 21 other men and a football field every time one wants a little exercise. So it is wise to help teenagers find pleasurable activities they can continue as adults.

Research has shown that hardly anyone will stay on a program of make-work exercise, such as calisthenics, unless he has a fairly short-range goal or lots of company. Most people are consistent about exercise only when it gives them pleasure. So such more individual sports as tennis, swimming, hiking or golf, and such active recreations as folk-dancing or camping, become indispensable in our save-the-muscle society. Why start so early? Partly to form the habit and partly to become good at the game, for skill makes any activity more alluring.

Adult girth control

The preventive techniques for adolescents also apply to young adults, whose growth is ending or just ended. The object, nutritionists now believe, is to arrive at age 25 near ideal weight and fatness.

For from this time, it is thought, one should be able to hold the line, despite the steady fall in food need. If one is not fat at 25, fat prevention can usually be managed with the simplest kinds of nutritional knowledge and effort, plus the added exercise which keeps one's automatic food controls in efficient operation.

How much exercise does one need for the appestat to function well? The answer is not absolutely clear. But authorities believe that for most people, the extra energy outlay needed is something like that required to walk two miles a day—perhaps 40 minutes daily of moderate activity beyond our sedentary habits.

There are many other tricks to hold the fat line. But for probably 40 million adults or more, a little reduction is also needed. So we are going to look at what science has learned about curing fatness, facts some 85 percent of us can use to help us look and feel more the way we would like.

But first, let us get a clearer idea of what that dream of self-image ought realistically to be. For the new knowledge about body weight and shape probably holds some surprises for us all.

CHAPTER 10

How much should you weigh—and eat?

Almost any modern reducing program begins with finding out how much you ought to weigh and how many calories a day you ought to consume. These numbers are very simple to arrive at. You merely look up your ideal weight on a chart, and then use a simple calculation to learn how many daily calories you need to hold your present weight or to lose weight.

The idea is a very reasonable one. The only trouble, scientists now believe, is that all the numbers are probably quite wrong.

The height-weight chart is the worst offender. The idea began in 1912, when insurance companies got the idea that body weight had something to do with how long their policyholders were likely to live.

How height-weight charts were made

The numbers for the first height-weight charts were taken from averages of men and women who had bought life insurance between 1885 and 1908. These people had been weighed with their clothes on. Their height was either measured—or estimated—with the subject in his or her shoes. The averages were divided according to age and sex, with an implication that the older one got, the more one was supposed to weigh.

Some more numbers of this kind were looked at in 1929. They were close enough to the originals so that the chart was not revised.

During World War II, however, a somewhat more sophisticated approach was used, introduced by the Metropolitan Life Insurance Company. The insurance men recognized the important principle that older people did tend to be fatter, but that this was undesirable. So averages were now taken only from younger adults. It was also seen that body frame affected desirable weight, so the tables were divided into small, medium and large frame. But the different body styles were never defined.

From this vague table, the two most modern charts are descended. The weights and heights were revised, averaged from several million insured people from the United States and Canada, in a study made in 1959. The authors of the charts assumed men's clothes to weigh from seven to nine pounds, and women's from four to six. They allowed two inches for women's shoes and one inch for men's. Body build was taken solely from chest and hip width, though even these misleading measurements were not actually specified.

The result was an average of the inaccurate weights and heights of people in three different body styles, with the builds judged by standards which scientists have pronounced of "extremely limited" significance. Ignored completely was the fact that a great number of the subjects were too fat, possibly a third of them markedly so.

It was from this data that the Metropolitan deduced the table of "desirable" weights which so many of us starve to match. How could the insurance company decide which weights were desirable?

Finding the magic age of ideal weight

"Desirable" weight was taken to be the average of what people weighed at 25, according to the 1959 study. Why 25? Because the death rate appeared to be lower among men and women who kept the weight of their 25th year.

It is from this questionable scale that the numbers come which deny some people insurance except at premium rates, which are given to patients as reducing goals, and which are actually conditions of employment for millions of servicemen, policemen, firemen, airline pilots and stewardesses and the like.

To begin with, it looks as if not even the averages of height and weight are right. Checked against a U.S. Public Health Service national survey, the numbers seem to be from nine to ten pounds too low for men, and from three to four pounds too low for the average woman.

If you are trying to arrive at your own ideal weight, the process is a statistical farce. First, how tall are you? "Two-inch" or "one-inch" heels vary considerably. Is it winter or summer when you are checked? Are you wearing wool tweed or thin silk? Are your shoes, if you are a man, heavy brogues or deerskin loafers? What is in your pockets? What jewelry are you wearing?

And your body build. So you have wide hips and chest. But is that width fat or bone? Mesomorphs and endomorphs may have the same widths, but the more solid mesomorph will weigh far more.

And what about the magic age? Are you a professional athlete, who at 25 still keeps in perfect trim? Or did you take a sit-down job at 17?

And what time of the day is it when you weigh? What is the state of your digestion? What have you been eating in the last 24 or 48 hours? We shall see that anyone's weight can easily vary five or six pounds from one day to the next, meaninglessly.

So you are a five-foot, three-inch female. Your height, with shoes, may have been classed as five feet four, or as five feet five. Take a hypothetical look at the "desirable" chart.

Are you somewhere between large and medium frame? Medium frame might mean you should weigh 116 or 130. On the large side, 125 would be the lightest, and 142 the heaviest. If, actually, ideal weight for you is 120, at 144 you are medically *obese*. (20 percent over ideal weight). At 131, you would be ordered by the doctor to start reducing. (You would be ten percent over the ideal.)

Yet what are your chances of guessing the 120-pound *actual* ideal? Very small. Even if you get the right frame category, the range is 116 to 130.

You can see, too, that the cards can fall so that a

woman in this weight division who was deceptively small-boned, yet rather square-shouldered and perhaps full-busted, could actually appear to be medically *under-weight*!

For a large male, the tables get even more inaccurate, with ranges for a six-footer from 156 to 194—*if* his height comes out right, *if* we ignore a probable ten-pound or maybe even 15-pound error in the averages themselves, and *if* he happens to be wearing the right weight of clothing. It is easy to understand why a physician who understands the problem smiles sadly when this man asks him: "I figure I need to lose just eleven pounds; is that right?"

The physician smiles even if his patient is using a more accurate height-weight table, such as the table developed by the U.S. Department of Agriculture. In this table, heights are without shoes. Weights are without clothing, and so they are less variable.

One must still guess at frame. But the table is intended to be used only to determine a range. If you feel you have a small frame, you use the "average" poundage for your height as an *upper* limit. If you think you are average, you can assume your weight ought to be somewhere around that "average" number. If you believe yourself to be large-framed, you use the "high" number as an upper limit.

This table is reproduced, and interpreted on p. 221. It is developed from a federal survey of people across the country, with averages of weights between the ages of 20 and 30.

You can't even trust the scales

Sadly, however, even if you arrive at a magic number for your weight which satisfies you as a goal, this can only approximate what you read on the scale. Not that the scales are wrong, for most bathroom scales are really surprisingly accurate, considering the difficulties in producing them cheaply. The trouble is that human weight is such a flexible thing that it is useful to watch it only as a guide, and over a long period of time.

Generally, some of the variable factors include: how much food is in the digestive tract at the moment you weigh; how much water is retained by your body; how well your kidneys are disposing of fluid; how much salt you have eaten in the preceding day or two; the weather; how much you have exercised in recent hours; constipation or diarrhea; the menstrual cycle; what medicines you may be taking. And none of these factors has anything to do with how much fat you are carrying.

Can you tell what you should weigh?

All of this does not mean that we should discard our scales, only that we should not be tyrannized by them. We must keep in mind that what counts is fatness.

An approximate reference point for what you should weigh as an adult is your weight at 25, if you were then in fairly good shape. If a woman goes to college, her weight at graduation may also be a good indicator, as it is for a man if he did not leave school too long before he had physically matured. Weight during military service is a fair indicator, but might actually be a little high due to physical conditioning, since muscle is so heavy.

Check back on old driver's licenses, job applications, insurance forms, military discharges and the like. You will get a reasonable idea of your lean, youthful weight. But be honest about whether you were then in fairly good shape. If you were always rather pudgy, be hard on yourself. And be kind if you are of heavy build.

The most accurate answer lies in the skinfold pinch, of course, since your degree of fatness is what you really want to know. What would it take to bring that little fat roll down to half an inch or less? That is the more realistic question. The scales then provide checkpoints which can tell you generally in which direction you are moving.

Isn't skinfold measurement likely to be quite vague? Not really. "If you pinch in the right place," says a spokesman for the Council on Foods and Nutrition, "the thumb and forefinger make fairly good calipers,

Approximate Desirable Weights*

Height (without shoes)	Weight in pounds (without clothing)		
	Low	Average	High**
	Men		
5′ 3″	118	129	141
5′ 4″	122	133	145
5′ 5″	126	137	149
5′ 6″	130	142	155
5′ 7″	134	147	161
5′ 8″	139	151	166
5′ 9″	143	155	170
5′10″	147	159	174
5′11″	150	163	178
6′ 0″	154	167	183
6′ 1″	158	171	188
6′ 2″	162	175	192
6′ 3″	165	178	195
	Women		
5′ 0″	100	109	118
5′ 1″	104	112	121
5′ 2″	107	115	125
5′ 3″	110	118	128
5′ 4″	113	122	132
5′ 5″	116	125	135
5′ 6″	120	129	139
5′ 7″	123	132	142
5′ 8″	126	136	146
5′ 9″	130	140	151
5′10″	133	144	156
5′11″	137	148	161
6′ 0″	141	152	166

*From U.S. Department of Agriculture.

**See text for meaning of these categories, which correspond roughly to small, medium and large frame.

and you can't beat them for price." (Medical calipers are usually about sixty dollars or more.)

What about ideal weights for children?

Because of individual differences in growth patterns, the weight charts are even trickier. If a child looks fat, ask a pediatrician to make a judgment about how fat he is. Arbitrary numbers on the scale are really unimportant. Moreover, growth spurts make the scales almost useless indicators of changing fatness.

Weight charts for children are included in this book. But they are to be found in the child-nutrition chapter, where they are used to suggest typical growth patterns.

Should "ideal" weight be ignored?

Many nutritionists and doctors have still another argument against making a great fuss over determining ideal weights. And often, they actually try to avoid discussing the subject with people who need to reduce.

"Look at it this way," says one doctor who is expert in weight reduction. "A middle-aged patient comes in here, and I can see that he probably needs to lose, say, 35 to 45 pounds. Actually, even with an experienced eye, I can't really tell exactly how much.

"For one thing," he continues, "it's really a little hard to get a clean-cut picture of his frame until some of the fat is off. For another, I'm going to start this person on a program of getting some exercise. When he begins walking more, and maybe climbing stairs at the office, his leg muscles are going to build up. If he swims, his arms and back will develop a lot more muscle. In other words, his body ratio of lean-to-fat will change. His dimensions will be smaller in key areas, and yet he will be putting on some muscle weight.

"I might discourage this patient needlessly with a bad guess. It's an awful thing to face, the amount of going hungry it can take to dispose of, say, 40 pounds. I want to help this person find a comfortable way to control his weight. So I begin by giving him a goal he can work with. I may say something like, 'You know, Mr. Smith, you'd be quite a bit healthier and feel much better if you could lose a little weight. I'd like to set up a program which will let you lose ten pounds without suffering too much.'

"Mr. Smith goes home and says, 'The doctor wants me to lose ten pounds and then come back in three months. I guess I can do that.'

"I'm not trying to kid the man. When he himself sees that he can meet that realistic goal, I really don't have to ask him to lose more. He comes in proudly and says, 'Well, I did it, Doc. And my wife says I look great. But you know, I've still got a little pot. I think I'd feel a lot better if I dropped ten more. What do you think?' "

Experts agree that the most powerful motivation for weight control is success. They advise the would-be dieter to set a small goal and prove to himself that it can be reached.

Says one doctor, "When we start learning to bowl, for example, we don't insist on perfection, with every game a 300 score. We don't demand, if we want to know French, to master every single word in the dictionary before we feel satisfaction. The ideal-weight concept sets a rigid standard of perfection as the only acceptability. And we can't even really say what that perfection would be with much accuracy, certainly not until the patient approaches it."

The ideal-weight-or-bust attitude appears to be destructive. And in practical experience, a less self-demanding attitude bears far more fruit.

How to calculate your food need

Just as ideal weight is something of a popular illusion, so also is the cultish mathematical game of counting calories. While it certainly has many real values for any adult, the knowledge of the caloric worth of food and of body need has some delusive and self-defeating aspects. One cannot follow tight equations for eating and exercise which will assure weight-control.

Most readers have probably seen formulas for calculating how much food they need to lose or gain weight. These formulas are useful. But let us see what their practical limitations are.

A typical rule of thumb for calculating how many calories a day you actually burn—and consequently, how much you can eat without gaining—is this:

Multiply your "desirable" weight by 16. The answer is an approximation of your daily calorie burn.

For example, Mrs. Brown is five feet, five inches tall. She believes she has an average body frame. So using the more reliable Department of Agriculture weight table, she should weigh in the vicinity of 125 pounds. Multiplying by 16, she finds she uses about 2,000 calories a day.

The knowledge is a useful guide, but nothing more. For let us see how one finds true energy consumption. What follows may seem a little technical. And the reader is warned that, while we will come up with a formula, the answer is doomed to be hazy. Yet the reason for the haziness can teach us much about weight control. And thus it can help us toward practical success.

Basal metabolism—the heart of hunger

Almost everyone understands that the body is, in one view, a fuel-burning machine, similar to the family car. But most of us tend to think that the bulk of that fuel is burned by our working activity. In fact, this is the lesser part of fuel need for the vast majority of Americans.

For, unlike the automobile, the body can never be shut down. It must idle until it dies. Basal metabolism is that idling, the energy use of the body when it is as close as possible to full rest.

That idling rate is a bit stunning the first time you look at it. To get an idea of the output, consider that it is usually expressed in terms of heat. For the physicist, the basic unit of heat is the calorie. The nutrition calorie is *not* this amount of heat, but 1,000 times as much. It is actually the *kilocalorie,* or Kcal. One Kcal.

(the calorie we talk about in foods) is enough energy to raise four pounds of water one degree Fahrenheit in temperature.

The basal metabolism of a young man, five feet, ten inches tall and weighing 150 pounds, typically consumes about 1,800 calories in a day. If you want to see that much energy at work, measure a quart of cool tap water into a pan, put it on the stove and bring it to a full boil. (If you don't think this takes a lot of heat, try building an open fire that does the job.) Yet this is the basal energy expended by our young man in less than an hour of sleeping.

If he were to sleep for 24 hours, his basal energy output would be enough to bring 25 quarts of tap water to a boil. If he is a moderately active person, doing a job such as carpentry, this waking activity would add 1,400 calories more burn, enough to boil another 19 to 20 quarts. In all, his day's energy could boil 11 *gallons*.

What goes into basal metabolism?

To get an idea of where all that energy goes, consider first such obvious needs as the beating heart and the bellows-action of the lungs. Then think of more subtle expenditure—such as the contracting and relaxing of the intestines, as they slowly move digesting food along. Most major muscles are kept in a state of partially contracted readiness called tonus.

In addition to slight resting body movements—from the swallowing of saliva to stirrings in sleep—chemical energy is burned by every cell in the body. The kidneys and liver are especially active. But the supreme example of chemical energy being used is the human brain. It demands a full fifth of resting energy. In a day for our young man, it consumes about 360 calories, as much as his muscles would demand in 40 minutes of active football, enough heat to boil nine quarts of tap water.

(An interesting aside is that the brain's energy use is constant. It scarcely varies whether you are sleeping or working a problem in nuclear physics.)

Figuring your own basal rate

If you want to know approximately your own body's energy use in an idling state, here are some average examples:

Body Weight (pounds)	Basal Metabolism (calories per day)
Men	
132	1440
154	1680
176	1920
Women	
110	1080
132	1296
154	1510

If you want to be more precise, normal basal metabolism is about one calorie burned per hour for each kilogram of body weight. To simplify that, if you multiply your weight in pounds by 11, you will get a close idea of basal metabolism for a man. Women's basal rate is about ten percent less; so deduct ten percent from the answer if you are female.

That ten percent difference between men and women is instructive. It results from the fact that men have more muscle and less fat than do women. Muscle burns more energy. Thus, a person in good physical condition, who does not let the fatness of his body increase, can handle much more food without gaining weight. If you like to eat, getting into shape can let you enjoy more food. Or, if you eat the same amount, conditioning can automatically help you reduce.

How age reduces basal metabolism

The basal energy we are talking about is for the young adult. It is much higher for children. For example, a baby one week old has a basal rate of almost 23 calories per pound of body weight. So an eight-pound infant needs some 180 calories a day to cover resting needs. If an adult had a similar rate, he would use twice as much food to sustain his resting requirements, the equivalent of an extra half-gallon of milk a day with a hamburger thrown in.

Basal rate declines rapidly from infancy. At five, the child is down ten percent in his need; at 15, he is down 20 percent from babyhood. From about the age of 20 on, the basal requirement declines about one percent a year. For our 150-pound man again, the pattern looks like this:

Age	Basal Calories
20	1800
30	1730
60	1600

So if you want to calculate your food needs, you must adjust them for age. Then you are ready to add the calories you burn in more active living. And now the picture blurs.

How activity burns calories

Since World War II, scientists have been measuring the energy consumed by different human activities. These measurements are charted for you here.

Type of Activity	Calories per hour
Sedentary activities, such as: Reading; writing; eating; watching television or movies; listening to the radio; sewing; playing cards; and typing, miscellaneous officework, and other activities done while sitting that require little or no arm movement.	80 to 100

Type of Activity	Calories per hour
Light activities, such as: Preparing and cooking food; doing dishes; dusting; handwashing small articles of clothing; ironing; walking slowly; personal care; miscellaneous officework and other activities done while standing that require some arm movement; and rapid typing and other activities done while sitting that are more strenuous.	110 to 160
Moderate activities, such as: Making beds; mopping and scrubbing; sweeping; light polishing and waxing; laundering by machine; light gardening and carpentry work; walking moderately fast; other activities done while standing that require moderate arm movement; and activities done while sitting that require more vigorous arm movement.	170 to 240
Vigorous activities, such as: Heavy scrubbing and waxing; handwashing large articles of clothing; hanging out clothes; stripping beds; other heavy work; walking fast; bowling; golfing; and gardening.	250 to 350
Strenuous activities, such as: Swimming; playing tennis; running; bicycling; dancing; skiing; and playing football.	350 and more

We will see how an understanding of activity and calorie burning can help you control weight. But meanwhile, let us take a look at some of the factors that complicate these numbers and make them only a general guide to the relative energy cost of different tasks.

Foremost is the fact that our activities can be seen in terms of moving weight around, mostly our own. The simplest example is that, if you are a 110-pound woman, an hour's walk burns about 100 calories. But if you are a 190-pound man, the same walk will burn 173 calories.

Climbing up 15 steps, our 110-pound woman spends 2.2 calories. Our 190-pound man burns 4.1.

And so it goes. The heavier you are, the more each activity costs you. Because the man's arm is heavier, even typing would make him spend more energy. So would sewing on a button.

But because weight-moving is the critical point, there are other modifications. If it is winter, our 110-pound lady has a heavy coat on, perhaps wears boots and is possibly carrying two pounds of loaded purse. She may very well now be a 120-pound lady in caloric terms, and burns nine more calories on her walk.

Outside factors also change the burn rate. Here are just a few. If the air temperature is high, calorie consumption goes up a half percent for each 1.8 degrees over 86. But if the air is cold, the body will burn more calories just to keep itself warm. If things get really chilly, the body will resort to jerky muscle spasms to produce still more heat; we call this shivering.

If you are taking a walk and the grade is uphill at ten percent, you will burn nearly twice as many calories as on level ground. More, but not so many more, may be burned going *down*hill. And the rate on beach sand is higher than that on sidewalk.

Just our style of moving can change the whole picture. Dr. Herbert Pollack, who led the way in considering the importance of activity patterns in weight control, made this interesting calculation about two men who are standing. This is not an estimate; it is the result of actual measurements of oxygen consumption, an excellent indicator of fuel-burning.

Says Dr. Pollack: "Individual 'A' was the relaxed type. He never remained standing if there was a chair available. When he sat down, he leaned back and relaxed. When he was standing, he would lean against the nearest support. 'B' was a man who never stood still. He paced back and forth and he used his hands to gesticulate. When he sat down, he leaned forward, sat on the edge of his chair and was up on his feet at the slightest excuse."

Dr. Pollack found that, while standing, Mr. A burned 90 calories an hour. Mr. B burned 138 calories.

Dr. Pollack comments: "There is a . . . difference of 48 calories per hour between them. In a ten-hour day, this is 480 calories. In the course of a week, the difference may be as much as 3360 calories . . . in the course of a year is approximately 40 pounds in body weight equivalent."

How weight is affected by energy use

These figures are dramatic, and they are real. But here we come to an extremely important physiologic point. Mr. A is not gaining 40 pounds a year. And Mr. B is not losing 40 pounds. Because the body's appetite controls demand more food for Mr. B and less for Mr. A.

This, obviously, is why there are limits to the practical ways in which activity can be used for weight reduction. Activity is certainly a critical factor. Mr. B can eat more, without gaining weight, than Mr. A can. And from what we have seen earlier, we can guess that Mr. B gets enough exercise to activate his body's controls over appetite, so that he is not likely to gain.

Recently there have been overenthusiastic claims for "painless" weight reduction through exercise. An hour a day of exercise is a wonderful *preventive* for *weight gain.* But one cannot say that because one walks a daily hour, burning 110 calories, one *will lose* a pound a month. The arithmetic is right—*but only as long as one eats no more.* If one takes extra exercise beyond the point of intake-output balance, one's appetite is that much greater. Weight reduction, alas, requires hunger.

A second look at your calorie needs

Dr. Pollack's example of the two men standing, taken with the other variables we have seen, suggests how nearly impossible it is to tell accurately from looking at a chart or table how many calories you use. This is an individual matter, varying from person to person, from life to life, from day to day.

At this point, you may suspect that calorie needs can be understood in only a general way, except under laboratory conditions. But although they cannot be determined exactly by the layman, there are ways to arrive at an approximation which is better than the rule of thumb proposed earlier. Using the simple height-weight chart from the Department of Agriculture, find the desirable weight average for your height and frame. Now fit that weight into the following tabulation.

Average Calorie Allowances

"Desirable Weight" (pounds)	At 25	At 45	At 65
Men			
110	2500	2350	1950
121	2700	2550	2150
132	2850	2700	2250
143	3000	2800	2350
154	3200	3000	2550
165	3400	3200	2700
176	3550	3350	2800
187	3700	3500	2900
Women			
88	1750	1650	1400
99	1900	1800	1500
110	2050	1950	1600
121	2200	2050	1750
128	2300	2150	1800
132	2350	2200	1850
143	2500	2350	2000
154	2600	2450	2050
165	2750	2600	2150

This chart is composed of realistic averages. It assumes a U.S. average temperature of 68 degrees, and it takes into account a range of activities which would be summed up as "moderate." The allowances are stated to the nearest 50 calories, because cutting them any finer would imply an accuracy for the individual which is not possible.

A final adjustment should be made, however. Most people who live in cities, for example, cannot be said to have a moderate activity level, unless their jobs call for physical effort. A man or woman in sedentary work must reduce the calorie allowance by about 25 percent.

A housewife may or may not have a moderate activity level. Mopping, scrubbing or making beds is moderate. But cooking and dusting are *light*. Talking on the telephone, sewing or having a cup of coffee with a neighbor is *sedentary*. So the housewife, typically, might reduce her calorie allowance by only half the 25 percent reduction; ten percent might work pretty well.

The reader should keep in mind any special activities, if they are out of the usual line of effort, but regularly engaged in. For example, a man who jogs when he gets home from an office job might halve the reduction for his occupation. But one who bowls one night a week is indulging in a sport which burns substantial energy only in bursts of a few seconds. The same may be said of the weekend golfer who wheels about in a cart. The snack or drink after the game probably restores more calories than he actually used.

If the reader has once-a-week activities, for example a couple of sets of tennis, these are meaningful. But he will do best to set his allowance at the sedentary level, if this is right for his occupation, and then consult the activity chart for the calories-per-hour burned in tennis. Spreading this extra burn over the week will show him how significant his weekend sport or hobby really is.

Someone who does genuinely *heavy* work regularly needs to adjust his allowance upward 25 percent. Bear in mind that heavy work is something like that done by an active farmer. In our society, heavy work usually occurs only in brief spurts—as with the plumber who occasionally wrestles heavy pipe, carries a fixture for a few minutes or who briefly digs into the soil. One must make his own approximation of how much time is spent doing what and try to err on the conservative side.

More accurate ways to find calorie need

One possibility for getting closer to your true calorie need also begins with your ideal weight. Multiply this weight in pounds by 21, if you are male, and by 18 if you are female. This is your caloric need at age 25 with *moderate* activity.

The number must now be age-corrected. This can be done as follows, *before* you correct for activity:

If you are a woman, and your desired weight is under 130 pounds, deduct 100 calories a day for age 45, and deduct a total of 400 calories a day for age 65. To be still more accurate, you can cut five calories for each year over 25, up to the age of 45. Then cut 15 calories more for each year over 45.

If you are a woman with a desired weight over 130 pounds, trim 150 calories for age 45 and 350 for 65. Yearly reductions are fairly close to proportionate to these numbers.

If you are a man under 140 pounds at desired weight, take off 150 calories for age 45 and 400 calories for age 65. If your desired weight exceeds 140 pounds, subtract 200 calories for age 45 and 450 calories for age 65. Again, the decline of calorie need may be figured as proportionate for each year. For example, with 200 calories cut for age 45, you may take ten calories off for each year over 25.

Now you must correct the result for activity, as we explained before.

A nutritionist's method of finding calorie need

Perhaps still more accurate, because it omits finding ideal weight, is this method:

First find your basal metabolic rate. (Your actual poundage times 11, if you are male. If you are female, subtract ten percent of the total.)

Again, this basal rate is for the young adult; you must correct it for age, by the method we used earlier.

Now take the corrected total and add on one of the following activity factors. For sedentary activity, add 30 percent. For light activity, add 50 percent. Add 75 percent for moderate activity. And double the total for strenuous activity.

Scarcely anyone can be strenuously active through a

full work day. The other categories can serve as averages, or you can divide up your active day and make estimates as detailed as you like.

Can you tell how many calories you eat?

Now let's see how hard, or easy, it is to match your food consumption to your calorie need, or to choose food that will give you less than your need, as in reducing. Most people believe this is just simple arithmetic, but sadly, this is not really true.

As a guess, most nutritionists say that they have great difficulty assessing the calorie value of a subject's daily food within 50 to 100 calories. And even this assumes that the subject can recall exactly what he has eaten, omitting nothing and accurately measuring that which is included.

The reader might find it interesting to try answering the following little quiz. The object is to learn some of the hidden pitfalls of the calorie-counting game.

QUESTION: *Many experienced reducing-dieters claim they can judge to the last bean how many calories they eat. Are they likely to be right?*
ANSWER: Not likely at all. Obese people are especially likely to be wrong, often because they deceive themselves. In one study, the histories given by obese patients showed intakes of less than 2,000 calories a day. Dietitians then got friendly with the subjects and did more detailed histories. The actual intakes ranged from 3,000 to 5,000 calories for some subjects.

Even the absolutely honest and scientifically informed dieter misses his true caloric total, for reasons which should soon be clear.

QUESTION: *How large was the last meat serving you ate? And given a good caloric table, could you find its caloric value?*
ANSWER: Few people can answer the first part of this

of this question, especially if they ate in a restaurant, or if the meat was in a sandwich. A one-ounce error in, say, a broiled steak is a difference of about 110 calories. And did you trim some visible fat off your meat? What did that fat weigh? Was there a bone, or some gristle? If so, what did it weigh?

It is doubtful, moreover, that you could accurately determine the caloric value, even if you knew the basic weight of the serving. For one thing, the quantity of fat in meat varies widely with the grade. You trim off the fat, you say? No matter. The fat that remains *within the lean portion of meat* may very well be as high a caloric value as the protein. Meat is generally a rather high-in-fat food. And just one gram (one twenty-eighth of an ounce) of fat yields some nine calories.

If the meat was not broiled or roasted, the puzzle can get much worse. If it was fried, with oil or butter as the frying medium, how much was used for your meat? A quarter teaspoon will cost over ten calories.

Sauce on the meat? Or a meat loaf? You may begin to need a computer to find the nutritional composition. Sure, there is a meat loaf in the calorie table. But what was it made from? And if the meat was a factory-made sausage of some kind, you'll need a crystal ball.

The calorie game with meat is no place for amateurs. At best, you can hope for a relative understanding of which kinds of meat and preparation mean fewer calories. And if a table offers you the number of calories in a "serving" of meat, beware. For some strange reason, that "serving" is traditionally three ounces, rather less than most American adults eat at a sitting. Remember that restaurants offering a "small" or "ladies' " steak are serving you approximately ten ounces. If you look quickly at the calorie table, a steak serving is likely to show as 330 calories. Your "small" ten-ounce portion comes equipped with 1,100 calories, and even if you trim the visible fat, it's still quite a food chunk. And you'll probably be happier if you don't even think about that nice *thick* restaurant cut of prime rib. It can actually offer almost 2,000 calories all by itself.

QUESTION: *So meat is tricky. Fruits and vegetables are nice and simple, aren't they? Can you figure their value accurately?*
ANSWER: Even with a calorie table in your hand, the experts think you will miss, possibly with dietary significance. We have the old problem of how many cups, ounces or what have you. But then we have more difficulty still.

Try lettuce. Were there 16 or 20 small leaves in your salad bowl? The difference is ten calories? Not much compared to meat, it's true. But it may be half your *excess* consumption of the day. And what's a *small* leaf? And what's in that dressing you added to it?

Care for an apple? Exactly 70 calories for a medium apple, it says in the chart, adding that "medium" means two and one-half inches in diameter, or about a third of a pound. But the apple is not a sphere, and can you judge two and one-half inches with precision? And notice how sweet the apple is. That sweet is extra sugar. How much—half a teaspoon, maybe? That could cost you nine calories. Hybrids and different varieties of apples can also differ calorically.

QUESTION: *Which calorie values in the tables can you really depend upon?*
ANSWER: Very few. As Dr. Philip White wisely points out: "The values for food energy are estimates at best." He adds that these values depend for accuracy on the constancy of food composition, as we have seen, and also "on the exactness of the laboratory determinations."

The caloric values of food are estimated in two basic ways. One way is to burn a sample of the food in an airtight furnace which contains pure oxygen. The little furnace, called a *calorimeter,* is jacketed with a known quantity of water. The rise in temperature of that water indicates the caloric value of the food being burned. This method can allow some errors. For example, not all that burns with oxygen can really be used by the body as fuel. Some of the energy of protein, especially, is wasted into the urine and lost in other body processes.

An alternate method is to identify the quantities of

protein, carbohydrate and fat in the food. Standard values are then used to calculate how many calories they will yield to the body. This method, too, has potential small weaknesses.

The only really accurate caloric counts are those for foods which chemically are always almost identical. For example: sugar is always almost pure crystals of known energy potential. Fats are also quite constant. Whether lard or vegetable oil, a tablespoon yields 125 calories.

Some manufactured foods, such as dry cereals, are also fairly constant in calories. But though the statement of caloric value on the box is an honest effort, it is also an average, with slight variations possible.

"Calorie tables," concludes Dr. White, "can be useful but they must be used intelligently."

QUESTION: *Are some of these variables the reason why certain diet plans and reducing clubs call for careful weighing and measuring of portions? Does this help?*
ANSWER: This is one reason. But there is a misleading implication that the calorie value of one's dietary can be determined accurately. An exact measure of a variable item does not yield exact knowledge. Moreover, while scales are quite accurate in the main, measuring containers sold in this country are not. The Bureau of Weights and Measures find errors of up to 50 percent in measuring spoons, measuring cups and the like.

If there is worth in carefully weighing and measuring, it is educational. Practice gives one a feel for the quantities of foods, a familiarity with the look of certain size portions.

QUESTION: *If we do get a close idea of how many calories we take in, even then can we say precisely whether we are getting too much or too little food?*
ANSWER: No, not quite. The primary problem here is the phenomenon known as SDA, or *specific dynamic action.* Food has the effect of a stimulant on the body. As it goes through the processes of digestion, it appears to trigger additional body-heat production (burning

some calories) in ways which are not yet fully understood, or exactly measured.

So much for our quiz. Clearly, none of the factors in the numbers game of weight control—"ideal" weight, calorie need or the caloric content of the dietary—will stand still long enough to be counted accurately, except in a general way.

This does not mean that one's attempts to understand his caloric economy are wasted. The imprecise figures at which one can arrive are a useful guide.

But it becomes evident that a bookkeeper's preoccupation with these numbers is likely to be unavailing, and that those weight-control programs which demand such overconcern are likely to be flawed. They tend to rouse the hope of a tidy, machine-like management of food and weight, and that hope is unrealistic. When it fails, the dieter is likely to doubt the main scientific principles of food use and fat gain. Mistrusting science, his body and his character, he may well join the frustrated, shamefaced and heavy-hipped throng which turns to the hucksters—both literary and scientific—in search of caloric "miracles." There are plenty waiting.

CHAPTER 11

Curing overfat

For more than a generation now, one wistful bit of gallows humor has been very big in the fourth grade. Little Mary Alice confronts her mother in the kitchen.

"Hey, Mom," she says, "want to know how you can lose ten pounds of ugly fat?"

Mom braces for the worst. "All right, how?"

Mary Alice sputters. "Cut off . . ." she giggles, "cut off your head!"

Mary Alice's reducing plan has much in common with most weight-loss schemes which have captured the public imagination during the last few decades. For it is not physiologic; that is, it does not take into consideration the natural laws which govern the function and survival of the human body. Still, Mary Alice's plan is superior to most schemes in that, at least, it will indeed produce a loss of weight.

The plan is also similar to the more reasonable reducing ideas advocated by so many current books and magazines. It is that while Mary Alice's idea does induce a loss of pounds, very little of the weight is fat. And as we have seen, fat is the problem.

Thus can one gain a true understanding of the real facts of fat-reduction by first considering the nonsensical diet promotions. The nonsense, the plague of misinformation, is one of the chief reasons why America remains the land of the pudgy. For it is clear that few of those who are overfat accept their state. They try. They struggle. They suffer. And yet the pointer on the scale keeps climbing.

The object of this chapter is to show how, with a few simple scientific principles and a few practical commonsense tricks, one can ease the suffering while the effort actually pays off in a slimmer and healthier body.

The magic pill

There really is a pill that will make you lose weight. In a few days, without dieting, you can see the pointer on the scale begin to fall two pounds, four, six, even more. It is a heartwarming experience for the frustrated reducer. The only trouble is that what you see on the scales has nothing to do with losing fat. Physiologically, you can accomplish just as much by setting the scale five or six pounds lower and then standing on it.

How come? Because the pill is a *diuretic* (probably of the thiazide family, or ammonium chloride). This means it works by doing nothing more than stimulating the kidneys to take more water out of the body and excrete it as urine.

So you have actually lost pounds, all right. But if you stop the pill and take in any water, they come right back. You are as fat as ever. The truth is that the body of an average man cointains over ten gallons of water—in tissues, blood, lymph, secretions, and so on. Following the old rule of a pint-to-a-pound, that's more than 80 pounds. The body can give up about ten percent, or eight pounds of it, before it starts to get into trouble. (And that trouble becomes serious. For our average man, a fluid loss of 12 to 16 pounds can be fatal.)

"The use of [diuretics] in a weight-reducing regimen," says an American Medical Association statement, "is irrational."

Internal water sports

The water-pill deception is referred to first of all because it leads us into some very important principles of fat loss which can spell success or failure in reducing. They also help us to understand the lamentable popularity of certain questionable reducing plans and can help the dieter to spare himself much waste of money and effort.

A few years ago, Dr. S. K. Fineberg of Harlem Hospital in New York wrote in a medical journal that the body's mysteries of water (and of salt, which is related) "may be the greatest single cause of failure in the treatment of obesity."

These mysteries are not yet fully understood, but the practical aspects are well known to doctors. Among other things, they concern the way in which our bodily water content can go up and down like the tides in the Bay of Fundy, but much, much faster and more whimsically. This cycling can easily deceive the reducer who relies only on his scale. It creates the impression that fat can come and go with incredible speed.

Consider the effect of just air temperature and exercise. Water loss is one of our two chief ways to cool ourselves—to dispose of the heat created, for example, by our burning of fuel. The body machine works at about 20 percent efficiency, about the same as an automobile engine. Generally speaking, the fuel which does not produce work must go off as heat, and the body must get rid of that heat, for body temperature can vary only a few degrees with safety. Much of the heat goes off through sweating, about half of which is so fine that it is called "insensible perspiration." You are unaware of it. More water vapor is evaporated from the lungs for cooling. (This is the dog's chief cooling device and the reason why he pants. He can't sweat.)

With exercise in high heat, that evaporative cooling of the body has been recorded as eight quarts a day—16 pounds. The boxer who is trying to make a certain weight before a bout heads for the steam room. He does lose. But once he is off the scale, his thirst makes him drink copiously, and he is just as heavy as before.

So if you think sweating will make you lose fat—you are doomed to disappointment. Of course, if the sweat comes from exercise, the exercise is burning calories. But let us look realistically at what can be expected.

"I lost five pounds yesterday"

"Boy, I wish I could control my appetite," says Tom Green to a colleague at the office. "Joe and I played slambang tennis last Sunday for three hours in that sun. We even skipped lunch and took a sunbath. Then we hit the sauna and stayed there until I thought I'd drop. Sure enough, I'd lost five pounds. But then, you know what? We went crazy over this huge prime-rib roast Betty cooked, and had some drinks with a lot of appetizers. And when I got on the scale before I went to bed, it broke my heart. All that work, and then that night I ate my way up seven pounds! Two pounds more than I weighed the day before! What a pig I am."

Such things happen all the time. They are real. But let us see what the body is actually doing. To gain a pound, one must eat 3,500 calories worth of food more than we expend. For Tom to have eaten and drunk his weight to a seven-pound gain would mean an extra 24,500 calories at least. What could he have consumed in an evening to produce such an effect?

Booze? He could have done it with a mere 200 daiquiris, at the usual 3.5 ounce size. Even 175 Scotch-and-sodas would have served. Theoretically, at least. In practice, he might have had to take in, say, 20 percent more than these amounts, for alcohol has peculiarities.

The prime rib? It would have required quite a few seconds, totaling 36 pounds of the meat—perhaps 50 pounds of raw roast.

Let's see what really happened to Tom's body. His three hours of tennis is rated as costing about 1,000 calories. His sunbathing and sauna spent virtually no calories beyond his basal metabolic need, except for a little stirring and sitting. That 1,000 calories is impressive (and actually untrue, since Tom and his partner rested ten minutes between each set and spent some 20 to 30 minutes changing courts and arguing scores). Eight hundred calories is closer to his true caloric burn. That is less than a quarter of a pound of body fat.

But the sweat was considerable, and Tom refused to drink, in the old superstition that water prevents fat from being lost and may make an exerciser weak. But with the tennis, the sun-bake and the sauna, five pints of perspiration were lost, equaling five pounds.

Weak after the sauna, Tom drank two glasses of water (20 ounces). At home, he drank a beer (12 ounces) to help his thirst, and changed for dinner. When the guests arrived, cocktails began. In the next two hours, Tom had three highballs (30 ounces). He ate a pound of meat, of which 80 percent was water (13 ounces). He had two glasses of wine and another glass of water (18 ounces). His total intake of liquid: 93 ounces.

Of course, his body lost a little more water during the evening, but the weight of the other foods consumed added another pound. The balance? Seven pounds up from the post-exercise weight.

What actually happened to Tom's body fat? It declined a little less than a quarter of a pound. But since he skipped lunch, had a 600-calorie breakfast, 1,200 calories in beef, 600 in drinks and 900 calories in other foods, his caloric consumption for the day was 3,300 calories.

His normal sedentary needs, age-corrected, are 2,400 calories. So he had an excess of 900 calories intake and 800 excess calories burned. The score? Tom Green picked up 100 calories for the day, one thirty-fifth of a pound. As usual, need and appetite stayed pretty close together. But shifts in body fluid made his experience seem much more dramatic. And the apparent witchcraft of the scales leaves Tom vulnerable to outrageous claims and superstitions about weight loss.

Tom may be a potential customer for sweat rooms and devices. He may don a sweatshirt to exercise in, believing this will make the work more impactful on his weight. He may buy a special plastic belt to wear around his middle to make his rubber tire go away. And always he will lose the water game.

It should also be easy to sell Tom on salt-cutting myths as he tries to reduce. True, additional dietary salt does make one retain more fluid. (The medical understanding of salt and health is discussed in other chapters.) But in terms of weight reduction, we may say that eliminating salt from the diet is ultimately a fruitless way to reduce. It has little to do with fat.

Many other factors can make water retention shift a few pounds and mislead the reducer. Several pounds of water are commonly retained by a woman before her menstrual period. Alcohol requires large volumes of water for its metabolism. The quantity of sodium in the food one chooses for the day can make water content go up and down a matter of pounds—by causing more thirst. In general, a couple of pounds of water accumulate in tissues during the day. Some of this goes off as evaporation during sleep, when one does not replace it, and also as urine which is extracted by the kidneys and is disposed of on arising. This is why doctors urge using the scales at the same time every day, preferably soon after waking in the morning.

Still we have not finished with water effects. But let us go on to some popular new plans for fat-reduction, in which internal water sports play a role.

A quick loss of what?

Most people, when they become ashamed of or worried about fat, are impatient to do something about it. Winter comes, and last year's clothes don't fit. Vacation is at hand, and you can't wear a bathing suit looking like *that.* A chubby business acquaintance is hit by a heart attack at 48. "Well," says your Aunt Mathilda, "it's nice to see you looking so plump and healthy; you were always such a thin child."

We are stung or scared or disgusted, and we want that fat to be gone. *Now.*

Alas, it is not to be, science tells us. But then comes that new magazine issue or book-club offer, waving a magic wand. "What can I lose?" we say. "Whatever it is," replies the nutritionist, "it is not likely to be much fat."

One of the speediest weight losses offered in recent years is the "Doctor's Quick Weight Loss Diet." It is widely enough heralded in itself to justify inspection. But there are two additional reasons for a look at what makes the diet tick. One is that it will demonstrate some basic scientific principles. The other reason is that, at heart, it is essentially designed with *some* of the same reasoning as the Low-Gram Diet, the Drinking Man's Diet, an "Air Force Academy" plan (which the Air Force disavows) and even the once stellar Calories-Don't-Count diet. We might as well take these and others on, *en masse,* and get it over with.

Those quick case histories

One similarity among highly publicized diets of all kinds is that they begin with spectacular examples of reducing, plus promises that they really do not hurt much at all. Samm Sinclair Baker and Dr. Irwin Stillman follow this mold in their book, *The Doctor's Quick Weight Loss Diet.*

One of the exemplary patients in their book, for example, is said to have lost 25 pounds in the first week. This was a very obese patient, but the loss is nevertheless remarkable. To lose 25 pounds of *fat* in a week requires eating fewer calories than normal need to the tune of 87,500! That is a daily shortage of 12,500 calories.

Let us assume the patient is really enormous, perhaps 300 pounds, and so requires the huge total of 5,000 calories a day to maintain the same weight. We can then say that if the patient ate not one bite of food all week, it is conceivable that 35,000 calories, or ten pounds, could be lost.

We must still account for 7,500 more calories a day to trim off that 25 pounds. Perhaps a little extra exercise? It is hard to estimate for the very obese, but with walking this patient might lose 270 calories per hour. At that rate, 7,500 calories could be burned in just under 28 hours. We need more vigorous activities to get the patient's exercise into 24 hours and allow a little sleep besides. We find that only 11 hours of constantly playing football or running hard would do it.

But, we are told, this patient is eating freely of proteins and the fats that go with them. He abstains mainly from carbohydrates. So we must assume the running will have to go on a few hours more, daily.

Then it all works. The subject can probably lose 25 pounds of fat in a week quite painlessly by omitting most carbohydrate foods and running less than 100 miles a day. Thus, in a week, the subject can not only slim down. He can also get from Coney Island, where Dr. Stillman practices, to somewhere in Indiana. (A person of average weight who wants to accomplish the same loss should probably take along a heavy sweater. For he is going to end up in the Rocky Mountains.)

Since the *Quick Weight Loss* authors do not mention extreme exercise, or food deprivation, it is fair to assume that while the patient's weight declined, fat was not the total loss. Nor do the authors specify what was lost. But we can make some deductions.

About "high-protein" diets

The aim of the Stillman diet is avowedly to create a regimen very high in protein, but very low in carbohydrate. This means concentrating upon eating lean meats, eggs and cheeses and eliminating breads, cereals, potatoes and the like. This plan is worth examining, since so many popular diets are similar.

First, it it really high in protein? Yes, it is. On the other hand, there is some limit to the practical extent of protein eating, even though Stillman tells his readers they may eat all they wish of the permissible foods.

Why protein? Stillman says it is because the effects of specific dynamic action will then make the reducer burn an extra 275 calories a day, because the consumption of protein makes the body release extra heat. This principle was enunciated 50 years ago. Today nutritionists know that it does not work unless *pure* protein is fed, with no fat or carbohydrate. When a mixed diet is fed, specific dynamic action is a minor consideration.

No eat-all-the-protein-you-want diet can be anything like pure protein, outside the laboratory. Suppose our "unlimited protein" dieter eats a hamburger (no bun), three eggs and some cottage cheese for lunch. The hamburger, of average market grind, weighs six ounces. It will contain 164 calories in protein—but also 306 calories of fat. The eggs, even if boiled, offer 78 calories of protein—but also 162 calories of fat. The cottage cheese comes closest to what is suggested. If creamed, a quarter cup contains 30 calories in protein, 18 calories in fat. Uncreamed, the same cup has 38 calories of protein and only 1.8 calories of fat. But cottage cheese is almost a unique food. *The fact is: where there is protein, there is either fat or carbohydrate.*

If the protein source is animal, fat is the major companion. If it is vegetable, it is mainly carbohydrate that rides along.

Commenting on the Stillman diet in *The All-in-One Diet Annual,* Harvard's Dr. Fredrick Stare sums up: "This is a different type of physiology than we learn or teach and it doesn't make sense."

If the Stillman and other "high-protein" diets are really high-fat diets, too, is there any way they might promote weight loss? And if so, does that effect make these diets desirable for reducers?

Why cutting carbohydrates seems to work

Any diet which cuts carbohydrates way down usually results in the quick loss of just a few pounds. One reason is explained in a monograph in *Medical Progress.* Dr. Jean Mayer points out: "A carbohydrate-free, high fat diet does cause an immediate weight loss . . . but this is due to partial dehydration and is of no lasting significance in a program designed to reduce adiposity."

In other words, for complex reasons, such diets have water-depleting effects, and we have seen how these can deceive.

Another reason for such losses is suggested by Dr. Stare: "You *will* lose weight if you follow such diets to the letter, because the sheer monotony of the diet dulls your appetite and you eat less."

We shall soon see why such "monotony reducing" is,

in the long run, fruitless. All nutrition authorities reject reducing plans which seriously distort one's dietary. But to summarize medical opinion of the Stillman book, and others like it, Dr. Philip White speaks for the American Medical Association:

"This diet is an intentional nutritional imbalance. Anyone with kidney trouble, or with a proclivity for gout, diabetes, or any medical problem in which urea nitrogen, ketone bodies, or electrolyte balance are poorly handled, could be a candidate for sensational trouble."

Are these conditions rare? Indeed not. Kidney problems of one kind or another are said to affect over two million adults in any year, and many experts think that most of the victims are unaware of their ailments and go untreated. Certainly not fewer than three million Americans, conservatively speaking, can be said to have a "proclivity for diabetes," with at least two million active cases, most of them undetected and untreated. The hazard would extend also to those with heart failure and many other illnesses.

A final word about "high-protein" reducing in the name of specific dynamic action. Dr. Stillman says that 275 calories a day is the expected loss from SDA. Even if this were accepted medical principle, which it is not, it would still require over two weeks to trim away a pound of fat.

About frank "high-fat" diets

The "Du Pont," "Pennington," "Mayo," and "Drinking Man's" diets all advocate high-fat consumption. They have the weaknesses and dangers of any other low-carbohydrate diets. Most claim that the idea works in part because fat stays in the stomach longest, preventing hunger contractions, so that it has the highest "satiety value" of any food.

It is true that fat remains in the stomach longer than other foods. But we have seen earlier that the brain sends its hunger signals in response to the fall of glucose in the blood, and that it appears to respond also to protein intake. "Fat," says Dr. Mayer, "does have satiety value, but so do other foods."

Weight loss with these diets will continue only as long as the dieter meticulously sustains the monotony of the diet. And in practical experience, doctors have consistently found one truth about narrow, distorted "crash" diets of any kind. It is a rule which should be branded into the mind of anyone who has to watch his weight. It is this: *When weight is lost by means of a seriously distorted dietary, the pounds tend to be regained, usually at essentially the same rate at which they were lost.*

What is meant by a distorted dietary? It might be said to be a *non-biogenic* dietary—that is, one which would not be adequate to support life and health, or one which would support the body in a marginal way. It could also be called a *deprivation* dietary, in the psychological sense of making the patient deny himself reasonable, accustomed food choices, so that he constantly feels deprived.

The only deprivation a reducer should feel is one of quantity. *There is no food which must be totally excluded from any reducing plan.*

One useful, positive fact about fat in reducing diets is that it should not be eliminated entirely. A certain amount is necessary for health—without it, you cannot handle A and D vitamins for example—and it does enhance the satisfying qualities of reducing meals. But because it yields more than twice as many calories per ounce of food as do proteins and carbohydrates, it is a concentrated food source, and anyone who wants to reduce should keep his eye on fat content.

Truth about high-carbohydrate diets

High-carbohydrate diets became popular in the earlier days of fat-consciousness, and they still return periodically. The first celebrity among these was probably the so-called "Rockefeller," or rice diet.

This is the outgrowth of a medical diet of World War II, the Kempner diet. Its chief object was not weight-reduction but the control of high blood pressure and kidney disease, mainly by the cutting down of sodium. Doctors today do tend to limit sodium intake in such cases, but new drugs and other knowledge have made such severe dietary changes obsolete.

The Kempner diet was mainly rice, sugar and fruit, with no salt or fat and much less than today's recommended amount of protein. The "modern" reducing diets developed from this usually add such factors as low-fat milk (for protein) and butter (for fat).

Despite these additions, such high-carbohydrate diets cannot be life-supporting for very long. They lack protein, iron, niacin, and in most cases, vitamin A. So the low-calorie habits which would be learned by following this regimen cannot be recommended as a healthful way of life. For example, protein levels in such diets are commonly half of the recommended amounts, a deficiency which can make it impossible for the body to rebuild itself. Moreover, such proteins as *are* present in rice are lacking in essential amino acids.

Why do the high-carbohydrate diets gain any credence at all? Again, water is a key explanation. By depleting the body of sodium, the diet causes an increased secretion of urine. Water is lost, and the scale shows fewer pounds. So the dieter gets some quick satisfaction. But what is lost rapidly is not fat. And even the water loss does not go on for long.

This does not mean that one cannot lose fatness on a high-carbohydrate plan. Typical diets of this kind have been calculated at from 1,300 to 2,000 calories daily, and so almost any of them will produce a true loss of body fat. But rather few people seem able to adhere to such eating programs for many days—undoubtedly a good thing for the sake of health.

One of the most recent *high*-carbohydrate plans, ironically, was introduced by Dr. Stillman and Samm Baker—*The Doctor's Quick Inches-Off Diet.* The irony is that this "new" diet is generally a nutritional about-face from their *Quick Weight Loss* idea of *low* carbohydrate as the solution to the fat problem.

The biogenic limitations of the *Inches-Off* scheme are

admitted to some extent by the authors' warning that it should not be tried by growing children, pregnant women or nursing mothers. "Even a normal, healthy adult on this regimen for any length of time would suffer," concludes Dr. Fredrick Stare. "If you stay on a low-protein diet like this for long," he adds, "you become anemic."

The *Inches-Off* plan involves another basic popular concern about which there is great confusion—the question of controlling extra inches of the figure. So let us look a bit more closely at body dimensions and the techniques for changing them.

Of pounds, inches and figures that lie

One of the main motivations for weight reduction is certainly a physical pride. As we have seen earlier, fat pads tend to burgeon in a common pattern, and fattening hips, thighs, bellies and arms are at war with our conceptions of beauty and create problems with clothing. So naturally, the reducer often thinks of his fatness in an on-the-spot way: "I'd love to get rid of this pot belly," "I wish I could wear slacks," "I can't buy sleeveless dresses."

Thus the appeal of a number of reducing plans. In his *Inches-Off* concept, Dr. Stillman offers the hope, with the help of certain exercises, that one can remove "about six to eight inches around your waist, buttocks and hips." He also says one can hope to reduce thigh and shoulder measurements by four inches, calves about two inches, and achieve "extra trimming of ankles, arms and wrists."

How realistic are such expectations? First of all, it is true that if one loses weight, subcutaneous fat will go away to make one smaller. There are individual tendencies to develop a high density of fat-storage cells in different body areas, as can be seen in women's figure differences with one woman accumulating fat at the breasts while another will build it up at the waist or on the hips The areas from which fat is first lost are similarly whimsical and individual. But by and large, if you have thick wrists and ankles, fat is not likely to be the primary cause; hips, thighs, waists and abdomens, on the other hand, do tend toward enlargement with fat and usually change with weight reduction.

How muscles affect fatness

Body measurements can be changed by the toning up of muscles with exercise. But what happens to the muscle which underlies fat does not necessarily change the thickness of the coating. The thickness may appear to change, but what is really happening is that the fat is being pulled in by the muscle, which stays in a firmer, more contracted state.

The plainest example is the pot belly. You can decrease it markedly by standing up straight and sucking in your breath. If you exercise these abdominal muscles, they pull up flatter and tighter and tend to stay this way even when you are not making a deliberate effort.

With exercise, therefore, we do lose inches, but not fat, except for the extra calories burned by the exercise. And most body-toning exercises do not have much caloric impact. Says Dr. Herbert Pollack, a pioneer researcher into the caloric cost of exercise: "Half an hour of special arm and leg exercises, for example, might be very tiring, but this would burn very few calories, perhaps those in a teaspoon or two of sugar. You could lose far more weight by spending that half hour in a . . . walk."

Spot reducing is a myth

If spot-reducing does not result from food reduction or active exercise, it is easy to see that passive methods are not likely to succeed either. Yet, despite public exposure that began with a congressional committee in 1957, consumers are offered the rental or purchase of a wide variety of gadgets which promise to trim down selected measurements.

Some exercise machines move your body for you. Now, it may be vaguely beneficial to have your joints moved. But if a machine is pulling your leg up and down, *it* is doing the work, not you. And work, we know, is what burns our body fuel.

Another category of machine supposedly makes muscles contract involuntarily through small electric charges. The muscle movements are too small to consume much energy. And doctors believe certain of these machines may be dangerous to the heart and other organs which can respond to electrical stimuli.

A third type of spot-reducing machine introduces the whole question of pummeling fat from the body, with methods which range from massage to jiggling mechanical belts. In one test of such machines both upper legs were measured. Then the machine was applied to one thigh regularly during a ten-week experiment. At the end of that time, both thighs were still the same size. *Fat simply cannot be beaten, shaken, tickled or stroked from the body.*

The late obesity expert Dr. Norman Jolliffe, of the New York City Health Department, carefully explored such devices and concluded: "As far as I know, there is no machine which can cause a patient to lose weight. It is true that reducing salons have helped some people to reduce. But this is accomplished largely by the diet given. . . . The machines employed have little or no effect."

Do some foods make you lose?

Just as there are no machines that will cause you to lose fat, there are also no foods which can cause you to lose fat. Yet the belief that such foods do exist is so great that the term "catabolic" food is a common one. A "catabolic" food, if it existed, would be one which made the body break down and dispose of stored fat.

The grapefruit has such a reputation; some people believe it simply dissolves fat, others that it *oxidizes* stored fat, so that the fat is flushed out of the body. Neither of these ideas is true. Yet one major airline has been known to advise its employees that grapefruit should be used in a reducing diet to break down fat.

Some diets make grapefruit a key food in the reducing plan. Since half a grapefruit averages about 55 calories, it is easy to see that one could eat many without gaining weight. But one would be very hungry, and would have seriously distorted one's food intake.

A few mistaken souls say that grapefruit, and certain other vegetable foods, contain enzymes which can digest body fat. But, as has been noted, plant enzymes are designed for plant nutrition, not human. They generally have, according to the AMA's Dr. White, "no importance in human nutrition."

Other reducing plans promulgated in the press offer the idea that special foods make you lose fat because these items "take more energy to digest than the calories they provide." Celery commonly has this reputation. Certainly it is not a high-calorie nutriment (about ten calories in two eight-inch stalks), but the calories it provides are *added,* not subtracted. In many minds, apples have the miracle property of not adding calories. Nutritionists agree, however, that the whole proposition is nothing more than a charming, wishful thought.

Which foods really make you fat?

On the other side of the coin are the "forbidden" foods. And most American dieters seem to believe that beginning a reducing plan means giving up "fattening" foodstuffs.

The truth is that *all* foods are fattening, in the sense that they have energy value, or they would not be foods. If you ate enough of any food that you consumed more fuel than you used, you would grow fat.

But for silly reasons, a number of foods have been labeled as caloric villains. One of the best examples is the poor potato. It is widely considered to be "just a lot of fattening starch," and thus, anathema on a reducing diet.

The truth is, however, that an ounce of potato has no more calories than an ounce of apple, and fewer than an ounce of bran flakes or rice. While it tastes satisfying, the potato is some 80 percent water.

Nor is the "pure starch" label justified. For the potato is a complex food, so much so that the Agricultural Research Service of the USDA comments, "A diet of whole milk and potatoes would supply almost all the food elements necessary for the maintenance of the human body."

Yet because of caloric prejudice, weight-conscious Americans almost halved their potato consumption between 1910 and the 1950s. Thus they needlessly deprived themselves of a food which is not only popular but, as has earlier been shown, unusually nutritive.

Similar name-blackening has blighted cream, butter, bread, avocados, rice, corn, beans, and a whole host of other edibles. True, these have more calorie value than, say, lettuce. But one would not stay on a lettuce diet very long, and certainly could not survive on it.

It is far wiser to forget your prejudices and, in checking out the caloric values of foods, to keep in mind that the most appetite-satisfying and nutritively important ones tend to be somewhat concentrated. You must learn to live in peaceful moderation with our staple, nutrient-rich foods, or you can never hope to sustain a slim waist once you achieve it. Besides, a reducing diet which does not cheat you of familiar, loved tastes and textures is one which is most likely to succeed.

By offering food choices to test panels, Harvard experimenters have demonstrated nicely that most dieters have erroneous ideas about where the calories are. In one choice they placed side by side a small, six-ounce steak and a one-cup pile of spaghetti with tomato sauce. Virtually all the subjects chose the steak as reducing food. Yet it was rated at 700 calories; the spaghetti measured up at 200 calories!

So when you try to reduce, explore the calorie charts, but remember not to make choices on the basis of calories alone. Says Dr. White: "Foods should never be evaluated strictly on the basis of their caloric value. The inclination of the dieter is to exclude foods . . . of high caloric value and to choose only those which are low. The result is frequently a 'low-calorie diet' which is limited in important nutrients."

"A proper [reducing] diet," says Dr. Jean Mayer,

". . . must be palatable and easily available from the points of view of economics and convenience."

Calorie charts are commonly seen to be dull nuisances for the reducer. But they can help you break up the narrow and rigid food choices which most people think are necessary for weight loss. On the other hand, you can't really carry a chart wherever you go. So here is a surprisingly simple and useful rule of thumb for judging foods, especially helpful when you are dining out. It was compiled by noted nutritionist Dr. Ruth Leverton, of the U.S. Department of Agriculture.

Food is probably relatively high in calories when

1. Thick, oily or greasy-crisp
2. Slick, smooth or gooey
3. Sweet or sticky
4. Compact or concentrated
5. Alcoholic.

Food is probably relatively low in calories when

1. Thin, watery or dilute
2. Bulky or with lots of fiber or coarseness
3. Watery-crisp instead of greasy crisp.

The custom-tailored diet

Nutritionists have long known that diets for reducing work best when they are custom-tailored for the individual, taking into account his tastes, his habits of work and play, his cultural background and other personal details. For a crude example, what are the chances of success for you if your diet calls for one fish meal a day and you can barely choke fish down? It is unrealistic to say that fish is good for you. You won't stay on that diet. By the same token, if you have eaten ice cream for dessert every night of your life, or if you feel feeble and ill-fed without meat for breakfast, a practical diet *must* enable you to have these things, at least part of the time.

A practical reducing diet is, first of all, as comfortable as possible. For, let's face it, if you need to make the effort, it is going to take time for you to slim down, time during which you are going to be getting less food than you would normally elect to eat. Using some tricks of the experts, you can be less discomfited than you might think (but don't count on complete contentment). If the diet is to work, it will have to allow for *some* of every food you want, and for some human falls from dietary grace now and then.

Since you know yourself best, only you can really make a reducing plan you can live with. So the following rough blueprint is offered, together with scientifically proven devices which will help you stick to your plan.

How to analyze your caloric habits

A reducing diet plan represents a change. And before we can change, we must understand what is the usual in our caloric life. Moreover, since small increments of food above our needs are what make most of us fat, we might as well begin our diet plan with some changes that can become permanent.

These long-term changes are most easily made in the trimming down or elimination of what might be called "luxury" calories, foods such as sugar (white, brown, raw or even honey), which offer largely fuel of the most plentiful type, accompanied by little or nothing else in the way of nutrients.

For most Americans, the reduction of "luxury" foods would probably be enough to eliminate the gaining trend as well. For example, let us look at coffee. In itself coffee has almost no caloric value, about five calories per cup. But four cups a day, not an uncommon amount, means 20 extra daily calories, or about two pounds of weight a year when *added* to our food need.

Most of us, of course, do not want to give up our coffee. But could we cut it down? More important, do we add sugar and/or cream to it?

Four cups of coffee a day with a teaspoon of sugar add up to a pound of weight every 50 days. Two teaspoons of sugar extra could mean 14 pounds a year! A teaspoon of sugar with cream would make even more needless poundage.

What happens if we put this system in reverse? Suppose we begin by drinking just one cup a day without sugar and cream? Conservatively, we would expect a caloric reduction of 35 to 40 calories a day, or about three and a half pounds a year.

Where should you look for luxury calories? First, check to see how much fat you are getting in your diet, for fats are far more concentrated calorically than other nutrients.

An ounce of protein is	115 calories;
an ounce of carbohydrate is	115 calories;
an ounce of fat is	255 calories.

Make a fat-finding expedition

We have seen that fats are important nutrients and we would not eliminate them if we could. But a concentration of fats lets us spend our calorie allowance in a hurry.

For example, one pat of butter is 70 to 80 calories. Suppose you use two pats on a pair of toast slices at breakfast, a pat on a lunch sandwich and a pat on a dinner muffin. That totals 300 calories—or almost an eighth of the total calorie budget for a day in the life of an average woman.

What else could be done with the caloric value of that butter? Have you ever skipped breakfast to hold down your food intake, or made it just a cup of coffee? Those 300 calories could have provided the following breakfast menu:

Six ounces of orange juice	(80 C)
A large boiled egg	(80 C)
A strip of broiled bacon	(50 C)
A slice of toast	(60 C)
A teaspoon of jam	(18 C)
Two cups of coffee (black)	(10 C)
Total	298 calories

It is worth looking also at what nutrients these two uses of 300 calories provide. Let us compare:

The butter offers just a trace of protein; our small breakfast has 5.7 grams or about ten percent of RDA. The butter has 32 grams of fat; the breakfast 5.4 grams. The butter has a trace of carbohydrate; the breakfast has 36.3 grams. A much better nutrient distribution characterizes the breakfast.

In micronutrients, the comparison looks like this:

	Calcium (mg)	Iron (mg)	Vit. A (I.U.)	Thiamine (mg)	Riboflavin (mg)	Vit. C (mg)	Niacin (mg)
Butter	8	0	1320	—	—	0	—
Breakfast	41.6	1.1	370	.27	.14	93	1.7

The breakfast calcium is a small but meaningful amount. Its iron is the same. The vitamin A of butter is about a fourth of daily average need. The butter lacks B and C vitamins. The breakfast supplies more than the daily need of C and meaningful amounts of the Bs up to about ten percent.

In other words, the breakfast looks like a much better cross-section of one's daily food than does the butter. But please note. The object of this demonstration is not to make a villain of butter. It is to show how an *excessive* use of fats is poor caloric economy.

For example, the snack with your coffee break is very likely to be a pastry which is rather high in calories because of its fat content, and the same is probably true of a packaged cookie or cake. One cake doughnut is 120 calories, more with frosting. A medium cupcake is 185 calories—and they come two to the commercial package, or 370 calories. A two-inch square of gingerbread is 150 calories or more.

A slice of raisin toast with half a pat of butter is 95 to 100 calories. A three-inch cookie is 40 calories.

If you eat a better breakfast, you can go easier on the fatty baked goods when 10 A.M. rolls around.

Fats are plentiful in America's in-between foods. Ten two-inch potato chips cost you 115 calories. But the potato portion (the carbohydrate and protein) is only

44 of those calories. The frying adds more than 70. Much the same is true of fried onion rings or corn chips or shrimp.

Nuts are commonly used fat sources. Fifteen peanuts will cost you 90 calories, 72 of them in fat; so will a tablespoon of peanut butter. That cocktail-party handful of nuts can be 200 to 300 calories.

Chocolate is a favorite American food, and a fat one. A six-ounce cup of hot chocolate is 210 calories, and only a little more than half of that caloric value is from the milk.

Careless carving of meat is another fat mistake. The watchful use of your dinner knife can whittle away many, many calories. A medium-thick pork chop, for example, is 245 calories. But if you trim away all but the lean meat, it is only 110 calories.

Carelessness, indeed, is a key reason why so many desirable foods become known as villains of adiposity. Much of the meat of pork has very little fat if you trim what you see. Dairy products need not be forbidden. Soften butter before using it, then spread *thinly* on warm or toasted bread. Take it easy on cream and try low-fat or skim instead of whole milk. Skim milk is no more caloric than most carbonated drinks and actually less than drinks like root beer.

Those soft drinks are very common "luxury" foods. And the "diet" word on the label does not necessarily mean they are noncaloric. Some of the diet soda pop has half the calories of the all-sugar stuff. Read the label.

The point of all this is that a fat-hunt through your normal diet is a good place to begin planning a reducing diet, along with a careful combing through for other luxury or empty calories. This does not mean these foods should be entirely eliminated. It does mean you should be aware of their cost. Total elimination may make you feel that you are doing penance for gluttony as you reduce. Nothing could be further from the truth. You are merely correcting a small, but cumulative, error in the balance between intake and outgo of energy. You will profit doubly if you do not think of a weight-reducing plan as a hair shirt, and penitentially eliminate all the things you love.

Have a *little* gravy. Drink one cup of coffee white and sweet. Eat *half* of the doughnut, and save the other half for afternoon snacking. Don't punish yourself; you are not guilty of anything. Be kind to yourself. Be a little indulgent. But think.

Making small habit adjustments

The best way to be comfortable while losing weight is to examine and understand your own food habits. Then, by making small adjustments in them, you can start the scale downward, without feeling the sense of barren loss that one feels when one gives up any long-accustomed food use. That depressing feeling, psychiatrists say, is actually akin to mourning, and it can be so upsetting that it can make you give up the whole noble project.

Suppose, for example, that a workingman always has two beers as he leaves work each day. Instead of cutting out beer altogether, he promises himself that one day each week, he will have only *one* of the two beers, sipping it very slowly, so that he will not feel left out while his companions drink two. The rest of the week, he follows his usual practice. His theoretical reward? Two and one-half pounds lost in a year.

Or let us assume that the lady of the house has two eggs every morning, scrambled. One morning a week, she takes only one egg. In a year's time, this adds up calories enough to dispose of one and one-half pounds.

No one else can know your regular eating habits, or judge so well what you can trim down, *not out*. Can you bear to leave a quarter of a slice of toast on the plate every morning? That makes 105 calories a week, perhaps 120 if you use butter. In 30 weeks, you should lose a pound.

By making a number of these small adjustments, you can lose considerable fat. Once you have reached the weight you want, moreover, some of these new habits can be maintained in part to give you lifetime weight control.

Using Habits to Trim Your Weight

Food	Mow Much to Omit	How Often	Loss per Yea
Butter or margarine	one pat	daily	5 pound
Average layer cake	half of one slice	weekly	1½ pound
Breakfast ham	half a serving	weekly	2½ pound
Mashed potatoes	half a serving	twice weekly	2 pound
French fries	half a serving	twice weekly	3 pound
Medium-fried bacon	two slices	weekly	1½ pound
Ice cream soda	one	weekly	5 pound
Saltines	two instead of four	twice weekly	1 pound
Whipped cream	two tablespoons	weekly	1 pound
Oil-and-vinegar salad dressing	one tablespoon instead of two	twice weekly	1½ pound
Mayonnaise	one tablespoon	weekly	1 pound
Baking-powder biscuit (2½–in. diameter)	one	weekly	2½ pounds
Bread or toast	one slice	daily	6 pounds
Doughnut	one	weekly	2 pounds
Pie	half a slice	twice weekly	3½ pounds
Jam or jelly	one tablespoon	twice weekly	1½ pounds
Scrambled egg	one	weekly	1½ pounds
Sugar	one teaspoon	daily	2 pounds
Rice	half a serving	weekly	1 pound
Canned fruit in syrup	half a serving	twice weekly	1½ pounds
Pork and beans	half a serving	weekly	2½ pounds
Beer	12-ounce can	weekly	2½ pounds
Carbonated drinks	8-ounce glass	weekly	1 pound
Whiskey	1½-ounce glass	weekly	2 pounds
Wine	three ounces	weekly	1 pound
Most candies	one ounce	weekly	1½ pounds
Most cheese	one ounce	weekly	1½ pounds
Boiled or poached egg	one	weekly	1 pound
Potato chips	10 medium-size	weekly	1½ pounds
Bread stuffing	half a serving	weekly	1 pound

To suggest some relatively painless ways to get that calorie control, p. 262 is a table of small partial omissions which the author prepared for *Better Homes and Gardens* a few years ago. With them is the impressive theoretical loss for a year.

Using habits to trim your weight

You can easily calculate more of these reductions yourself. Simply go through a calorie chart, choosing foods you regularly eat. Try to choose those in which you can make a reduction, rather than an omission, so as not to disturb your eating habits overmuch. Cutting a serving in half is a good plan.

Then simply divide the number of calories for the item you choose into 3,500—the number of calories to equal a pound of stored body fat. The answer you get is the number of times you must make the reduction to get a pound. Then you can decide how frequently you can cut down on that item without developing unusual hunger for it or a feeling of deprivation. The frequency will tell you how long you must continue in order to lose a pound. For example, a 100-calorie cut, made once a week, will trim a pound in 35 weeks.

Habit adjustment is a good way to become acquainted with the weight-gain impact of various foods. And it can also give the dieter a headstart on his reducing. In fact, an entire reducing plan can be constructed in this way. For it is really only a dramatic and controlled device for following the nutrition axiom: *The surest way to reduce is simply to eat less.*

What should food reductions accomplish?

Most people find it useful to get the big picture of what they must give up, and for how long, to reach the weight they hope for. This gives the reducer a clearcut idea of what to expect for his effort, and a way to check on the effectiveness of his plan.

The reader will recall that in an earlier chapter, ways

were shown to estimate his food need. Even though such an estimate must be rough, it provides a good general guide for the planning which follows.

Knowing about how many calories a day you need, it is interesting to estimate how many you usually consume. Try taking a typical day and analyzing it like this:

On a sheet of paper mark off a space for each meal and each snack you ate. As a reminder, write down each food you ate at each meal and snack under the following general headings: MILK GROUP: milks, cheeses, ice creams; MEAT GROUP: meats, poultry, eggs, fish, shellfish, and other protein foods such as beans, peas, nuts, nut butters; VEGETABLE-FRUIT GROUP: including juices, preserved fruits, salads; BREAD-CEREAL GROUP: including rice, noodles, and baked goods; EXTRAS GROUP: sugar for your coffee, candy, soda pop and anything else which doesn't seem to fit under the other headings.

Now look up the caloric values of these foods and add them up. This gives you an idea of what you are now eating and where some trimming could easily be done. Don't be puzzled if what you eat totals less than what you figured you needed. Any overfat you have now is the result of the past, remember.

Now check out what you would have to omit to make this a reducing diet. This involves deciding how fast you want to lose weight.

Most experts set some limits on the speed of weight loss. Realistically, they believe that *few people are able to function effectively while losing more than two pounds per week.* In fact, they recognize that anyone who can lose half that much is doing a good job, and they find that people who get overambitious about weight loss generally fail.

To see why, consider that two pounds a week means going without 1,000 calories a day. With your typical day's dietary before you, trim the total by 1,000 calories. Even if you are quite a large person, your diet is going to look pretty skimpy with a 1,000-calorie chunk out of it.

Now try the same exercise with 500 calories. This

will let you lose a pound in a week. Most authorities agree that this is a desirable level of weight loss. It does not require either desperate hunger or such careful planning. It is fast enough to be rewarding, yet is not nutritionally hazardous.

If 500 calories cut from the day looks appalling to you, consider some fraction of it. One hundred daily calories, after all, will make you 12 pounds lighter in a year. And the more slowly you lose, the more likely it is that you will stay slim afterward.

The trouble with a slow-motion diet of perhaps 100 to 200 calories' deficit is that with the variations of food composition and the like, it is hard to be sure you are actually achieving it. The only check you can make is the scale. And a one- or two-pound difference in a month may be difficult to discern.

What about a crash diet? Under a doctor's supervision, this can be done safely, but not on your own. One reason that a 1,000-calorie-daily-trim diet is used as a maximum is that, beyond this, it may be difficult to get a diet which is adequate nutritionally. Healthy humans can withstand starvation nicely—some research suggests that the fatter you are, the better you can take it—but profound physical changes can occur. And there are risks such as fainting which make self-starvation an absolute medical taboo.

What is a nutritionally sound reducing diet?

A losing diet should probably have some of the following nutritional characteristics:

1. No less than 12 to 14 percent protein, preferably more.
2. No more than about one-third fats, with some regard for keeping down the saturated-fat content (which will be discussed in a later chapter).
3. The remainder, about 50 percent, in carbohydrates with sucrose (refined sugars, including raw sugar) held to a low level.
4. The whole should meet the requirements for a biogenic diet described earlier in this book.

Or to put it in another, equally simplified way, your diet should include the following food categories, with the percentages being in calories:

1. Protein-*rich* foods (meats, peas, beans, eggs and the like)—25 percent.
2. Milk and milk products—20 percent.
3. Fruits and vegetables—35 percent.
4. Cereals and bread, pure sugars and fats (as butter and oil)—20 percent.

This plan is quite an effective one for preventing nutritional deficits which might occur on a reduced intake, even if the planned diet gets down into the 1,000-calorie range.

That range is about the bottom which nutritionists recommend. Comments Dr. Mayer: "It is generally true that in ambulatory, busy patients, an intake of less than 1,500 calories for men and 1,000 for women is poorly tolerated over long periods."

Can medicines help control appetite?

Since any reducing plan supplies less food than the body demands, the reducer is going to feel somewhat hungry. There are ways to deal with this hunger, but there is no magic which can truly dispel it. If the dieter is well motivated and does not get overambitious, he should be able to get used to some feeling of dissatisfaction. Remember, much of the world lives with a little less food than it would like.

A good deal of the hullabaloo about wonder diets revolves about reducing hunger pangs. In the year following the autumn of 1956—when weight-reduction really entrenched itself as a national indoor sport—the U.S. Post Office was forced to file over 70 fraud orders against patent medicines which were claimed to stop that hunger. There were television advertising scandals, loud court battles and congressional hearings. The representatives in Congress concluded in their report: "The advertising of so-called obesity remedies or weight-reducing products is an area fraught with deception and outright fraud. . . . As a result, the American consumer is being bilked out of approximately $100,000,000 . . . annually."

Many people are concerned with the hunger of losing weight. Isn't there anything, they ask, that the doctor can do about it? A number of ways have been tried. A few, such as special hormone injections, have been highly touted in fashion and other magazines. But one can say conclusively that there is no hormone which safely produces weight loss or appetite loss.

There are some drugs which can make a patient tend to lose fat or appetite. But they tend to be dangerous, to lose any effectiveness in days or weeks, and sometimes to be prescribed without sufficient understanding and control by practitioners who have questionable ethics and knowledge.

Such a drug is digitalis, a heart stimulant which commonly causes nausea. Belladonna is another stimulant, affecting heart and lungs. Phenobarbitol—an addictive drug in the family sometimes known as "reds" or "downers"—can be given to counteract the nervous-making effects of the amphetamines. And laxatives and diuretics, as we have already seen, can be given to cause a quick drop of the scales which will have little to do with fat. Thyroid hormone has been given to speed up metabolism.

Believe it or not, some or all of these medications may be given at once, in what are sometimes called "rainbow" pills. The effects can be bizarre and dangerous. In one recent case, the pills were found to be responsible for the deaths of six women in Oregon, ages 19 to 52. Doctors have advised the public to be wary of "fat doctors" who hand out handfuls of pills after a very brief examination. One practitioner testified that he had sold some 100,000 pills for $12,000. They had cost him about $70.

The moral: if your family doctor says he has no miracles for your overweight, or he has pills which might help a little but which he does not want to give you, accept his word. He knows what he is talking about.

At this writing, only one family of drugs has any

medical acceptance for weight reduction. These drugs tend to check appetite for about four to six weeks, after which it seems to return to normal levels. Doctors usually recommend their use only when fat is a threat to health, and with the idea in mind of getting the patient off to a rewarding start on a long program of reducing.

The family is the *amphetamines* and their modifications. If the name sounds familiar, it is because the amphetamines are very big in the nation's illegal drug traffic, where they are known by such names as *bennies, uppers* and *speed.* They agitate the nervous system and can produce heart speed-up or potentiate eccentric heart rhythms; they can cause high blood pressure; they can touch off dry mouth, irritability to the point of disturbed episodes, sleeplessness, restlessness, digestive difficulties and excitability.

No one is sure just why amphetamines help curb the appetites of some people, or why they soon stop helping. But certainly they should be used only on the advice of your doctor. The warning is given because such pills are fairly easy (though not legal) to get from friends, relatives and others who have prescriptions (as for *dexedrine*) and from more questionable sources.

What if your next-door neighbor tells you how rapidly she lost weight for a few weeks with special pills? Keep in mind a weight-remedy test conducted at the New York City Health Department some years ago. Three groups of about 40 people each were put on a reducing diet. Two groups were given black coffee with the diet. Both were told it contained an appetite appeaser, though in reality the second group was getting just coffee with no appeaser. The third group was given no coffee with the diet.

Who lost weight best? Both groups who *believed* they were getting help did about as well. The third group, believing rightly that they were on their own, lost more weight than the other two groups put together.

Said the late Dr. Norman Jolliffe, who directed the experiment. "The real moral of the story may well be that people who thought they had a reducing crutch did not stay with their diets well. They trusted to the crutch, rather than to their own self-discipline. Those who knew they were on their own stayed on their diets and accomplished a weight loss."

The no-diet diet

One unconventional but realistic way to reduce fat allows you to go on eating just as you do now—but increase the output of energy from your body. This overcomes certain emotional hazards of giving up food. However, it does not mean you will get all the food you want; the additional exercise, after all, will increase your hunger.

But, and the reservation is a large one, you do have some extras going for you if you adopt this plan. Let's see what they are and why.

First, as has been explained, added exercise should make the hunger controls in your brain work more efficiently. So the first reduction in food consumption comes to you "free," without hunger. In theory, this reduction will bring you to the point at which you stop eating more than you need and stop gaining fat.

Secondly, it is the clinical impression of many experts that further step-ups in exercise sometimes do not turn on hunger quite as much as do cutbacks in eating. This *has not* been proven at this writing. But in tests with hard-to-reduce groups, such as obese children, emphasis on exercise has led to high levels of practical success.

Third, for most sedentary Americans, increased exercise so improves their sense of well-being that their emotional outlooks tend to turn up. Depression, psychiatrists say, is a common result of food withdrawal and an important cause of reducing failure. Eating is a way many people relieve depression. Conversely, the food-training of many Americans creates the deep-seated feeling, "If I am being denied food, I must be bad. I am being punished. I am not loved."

Fourth, with exercise, there are wholesome figure changes. We stand up straighter, and the pot belly retracts. We feel firmer, more physically competent, for the simple reason that we *are*. The feeling is, "I am improving myself. I am becoming more beautiful and lovable." And the plain evidence of improvement—the ability to run a few more steps each day, do another sit-up, climb stairs without huffing—creates a sense of optimism and success.

How much energy must one put out to affect weight? If you take a bus somewhere every day, and if you decide to get off ten blocks early and walk, you will burn an average of 40 extra calories. Walk the ten blocks again on the way back and you'll burn 40 more. (All these caloric output figures are averages calculated to show the energy burned beyond basal, resting need.) That's 80 calories a day. In about six weeks, if you do not increase your food, a pound will be gone. In a year, eight pounds will have disappeared. This much exercise, too, may be just enough *added* activity to make your appestat function accurately.

Dull make-work exercises are not necessary to promote energy burn. Habit changes are what count. Suppose that in your work or social life you spend 30 minutes a day on the telephone. Suppose, instead of sitting down to phone, you stood up, perhaps moved about a little. That could burn an extra ten calories in the course of the day. Piddling? In the course of a year, you're a pound lighter.

Suppose, during one hour of watching television each evening, you used your hands and arms—to knit, sew, do little repairs, whittle. You'll spend from 20 to 30 calories, which means two or three pounds a year.

Maybe a man could sacrifice an hour of television viewing to a stand-up hobby, such as woodcraft. At the *very minimum,* with the lightest task, he would burn an extra calorie a minute. Sixty calories an hour. A pound spent every two months.

(For your health's sake, doctors advise an hour a day of fairly vigorous physical activity, though even half an hour will make a marked change in physical condition, and an hour every other day is almost as good. Lungs, heart and blood vessels profit enormously. Remember, in studies in London of bus drivers [sitters] versus bus conductors [movers] the conductors had fewer heart attacks and strokes and a far better record of survival.)

How to assess the impact of activity on your weight may be seen in the chart on p. 228. But here are some general tips about exercise and fat reduction.

1. The number of calories burned per minute is related to the amount of weight being moved or supported by the muscles. A push-up moves your body only 18 inches and uses smaller and weaker muscles to do the work. Twenty push-ups—beyond the ability of most American men—move your weight ten yards and leave you pretty wrung out. You could probably walk a half mile with less fatigue, using your biggest muscles and an easy motion. So calisthenics are not a good choice for activity increases, though running in place might be an exception.

2. Dull, make-work kinds of exercise do not make good long-term programs for most of us. We stay with an activity we enjoy. Look for games, sports and hobbies that pay off calorically yet hold your interest.

3. Uphill movement, such as stair-climbing, increases the work greatly and burns calories faster. Stair-climbing burns twice the calories of walking. Climbing a steep slope doubles the output again.

4. The speed of the activity, or the vigor, also increases the caloric burn. Walking at three and a half miles an hour burns 50 percent more energy than at two miles an hour. Running, including ups and downs, doubles the burn-rate of faster walking. Typing takes some 30 extra calories an hour on a manual machine; on an electric, the burn-rate drops to 18 calories an hour.

Again, to make an effective activity program which will take down poundage, you will do best to analyze your own habits. It is a good idea to lay out on paper a typical 24-hour day, classifying what you do in each hour or half hour as sedentary, light activity, and so forth. (See p. 228.) It will quickly become apparent which hours can admit more activity. You will not only lose weight more effectively; you will tend to form habits which protect you against fatness for the rest of your life.

Most people who try increasing their activity are happy with the idea. The listless, inactive hours can be voids in one's life, or they can be times of growth and accomplishment which mark our individuality. ("We're square dancers." "I'm a golfer." "We're nature buffs.") Says one psychologist, "When we are active, we are alive. Our energy is changing something, doing something, proving that we exist and that our existence matters."

Which tricks will make you slim?

Almost everyone will tell you some tricks to make the loss of weight easier and less painful. But which ones work? To learn those which experts find pay off, test your own knowledge. Are these statements true or false?

1. *Eating before meals makes for less total food intake.*

True. A low-calorie snack, such as an orange, two carrots, or perhaps a salad, eaten 30 minutes before a meal, will make you tend to eat less. The reason? In about half an hour the carbohydrate from the food has begun to enter the bloodstream and the brain's appetite controls have been appeased to some extent. (But do not use low-bulk, high-fat foods, such as cocktail nuts, in this role.)

2. *Eating slowly, you eat less.*

True. For the same reasons as above. Often the adolescent feels stuffed after a meal because he has gobbled down his food too fast for his body to let him feel satisfied.

3. *Periodic starving is a good way to lose.*

False. The scales go down at once partly because the digestive tract is emptied. But this does not signify so much lost fat. Starving may also burn body *lean.* You don't want to lose the lean. So the deprivation which does this is wasted suffering. Starving has other dangerous aspects, as we have seen.

4. *You can lose weight while the scales stay the same.*

True. As the body loses fat and plump storage cells shrivel, water tends to fill out the tissue. The extra water you hold replaces the poundage lost, or may even exceed it. Often, the first three weeks of reducing discouragingly show nothing. Then suddenly the water is let go, in extra urination, and you seem to take a sharp drop in weight. This phenomenon is one of the chief reasons why diets are abandoned. Be patient. Stay with it.

5. *"Dietetic" foods are always lower in calories.*

False. Remember, "dietetic" refers to low-sugar content, for those such as diabetics. Calorie totals are something else. Consider dietetic cookies. In one study, the calories-per-ounce of regular oatmeal cookies were 128, of dietetic 98. But the dietetic had no raisins, so were not as complete a food. Regular coconut cookies had 140 calories per ounce, dietetic 154. Regular chocolate cookies were 82 per ounce, dietetic 109. Similar findings were made among dietetic candies. Regular ice creams are hardly different in calories from the dietetic.

6. *Low-calorie bread is markedly less caloric than regular.*

False. Some such breads are *slightly* lower in calories. But often when the label reads "fewer calories per slice," it is because the slices are thinner.

7. *A dieter should never eat the juice from roasted meat.*

False. This is a good nutrition, as is the pot liquor from stews and similar dishes. But the fat should be removed. Simply let the liquid cool and then skim off the fat with a spoon. Or for quick removal, wrap a few cubes of ice in foil or cheesecloth and swish; the fat will come out of the solution and cling to the ice bag—not all the fat, but much of it.

8. *The ad or label that reads "half the fat calories" means food is only half as fattening.*

False. It means there is less fat in the composition. In one such ad, yogurt was described this way in comparison to milk. The yogurt was less caloric, but in the amount specified, milk was 170 calories and yogurt 125—far from half. Read those labels carefully.

9. *"Two-percent" low-fat milk is much less fattening than regular milk.*

False. Regular milk is usually only 3.8 percent fat; thus, the "two-percent" milk has a little more than half the fat. But in an eight-ounce glass the calories are not greatly different, partly because milk solids are often added to this milk. The scorecard? Regular milk, 159 calories. "Two-percent" milk, 142. The reducer must beware of a false sense of security and eating freedom which he may get from supposedly low-calorie foods. He should be sure he knows the degree of reduction.

10. *Ice milk is so much less caloric than ice cream that the dieter can let himself go.*

False. Typical vanilla ice cream is 174 calories to an average serving (one-third of a pint). Typical vanilla ice milk is about 137 calories. Taking just a little more than an extra *ounce* of ice milk will make the snack the equal of ice cream. However, the reduced fat and added non-fat milk solids of ice milk add more protein and micronutrients.

11. *A pack a day of sugarless gum adds nothing to the diet.*

Regular gum is figured to have about eight calories to the stick (mainly as sugar, which dissolves out and is swallowed). "Sugarless" gum contains sorbitol and mannitol, which dissolve out and yield some five calories per stick. That is 25 calories to the pack. That would add a pound in less than five months.

12. *Reducers should go easy on salt to lose fat faster.*

False. Salt affects only fluid retention in the body. But going easy on salt during the first phases of reducing can help minimize the discouraging *appearance* of no loss, which we have seen is due to extra water being retained.

13. *Cooking methods have some bearing on cutting caloric intake.*

True. Obviously, boiling, baking and steaming are preferred to frying and sautéing. For people who need or want to watch calories, there is cooking ware (ranging from skillets to egg poachers) that is stick-proof; that is, you do not need to rely on butter, oil, shortening and so forth to start cooking your food.

14. *One can reduce on meal-in-a-can liquid formula diets.*

True. But doctors are unenthusiastic about the idea. Most such diets provide about 900 calories a day—awfully low for the larger or more active person. They are nutritively complete, except for calories, of course. Like all "monotony" diets, they are hard to stay with and teach nothing about how to maintain weight after the loss. They are also lacking in bulk, which makes them intestinally undesirable for the long pull. Finally, says Dr. Philip White: "Formula diets are an expensive source of nutrients."

15. *Eating before sleep makes the calories stay with you.*

False. The economy of the body is continuous. It does not matter what time of day you eat or exercise. If this were not so, we could not lose the fat we have built up over the years. (However, a high-fat load into the bloodstream before sleep *may* have other consequences for the circulatory system.)

16. *Snacking helps some people to want less food.*

True. No one is sure why, but the idea of spreading the day's food over more meals acquired some currency after one nutritionist noted that people on the island of Bali had very good average weights and snacked through the day.

Subsequent animal experiments, especially those conducted by Dr. Clarence Cohn of Michael Reese Hospital in Chicago, showed that total food intake did decline when subjects ate more often.

Harvard's Dr. Stare, who made the observation on Bali, sums up how he himself uses the "snacking" technique:

"On the simplest level . . . I merely borrow from my regular meals. I like to snack. If I add snack foods to my regular three meals, I will obviously gain weight. So instead I borrow food from meals.

"For a morning coffee break, I use the orange juice I didn't drink at breakfast, and perhaps a little toast or pastry I didn't have. These I enjoy with my coffee at 10:30 or 11:00 A.M.

"At lunch, I may save half a sandwich to be eaten in mid-afternoon, perhaps with some ice cream.

"Before dinner I never stay away from the *hors d'oeuvres* with the cocktails. They make nutritious snacks. Later, when I have dinner, I go right into the main course, skipping the salad or shrimp cocktail.

"And I don't eat dessert at dinner. I save it for a night snack. Sometimes my 'dessert' is a raid on the refrigerator.

"We're already moving toward six meals a day, with meals, plus morning and afternoon coffee breaks, plus evening TV snacks.

"The net result of the plan is, though I'm not hungry, I don't gain weight. I eat anything I enjoy, but not too much, simply making sure my diet remains adequate in nutrients."

17. *Alcohol taken in occasional quantity, as at a party, is a fast way to gain weight.*

False. Alcohol does provide calories, which are treated by the body like any other, when taken in small amounts. But when one consumes more than a little, as at a celebration, some goes off as vapor from the lungs and some by rapid secretion into urine. From a caloric point of view, one is better off consuming several drinks at an occasional party, instead of a drink every day. This fact, of course, does not imply a recommendation for periodic heavy drinking, which takes its toll in other ways.

18. *Most people gain weight when they stop smoking, so it is better to go on smoking rather than get fat.*

False. The typical weight-gain of a withdrawing smoker totals about seven pounds, an amount not really difficult to lose. It has been calculated that the bad physical effects of smoking are akin to those of carrying an extra 100 pounds!

One of the best adjuncts for smoking withdrawal, by the way, is added exercise, which decreases smoking desire for most people. Simultaneously, it helps to hold appetite to the level of body need, regardless of what is happening in the lungs.

19. *Reducing clubs, farms and salons can help the dieter.*

True. But the principles of such operations must conform to those of science. Be assured that any "amazing discovery" in weight control should be, in part, in the hands of your doctor, and discuss the matter with him before signing up. You may save much money and wasted, heartbreaking effort. The group ways of losing weight have only one merit, really—the added motivation of the watching eyes of others. Mirrors are cheaper.

In conclusion, none of the vast majority of people who have to deal with a weight-gaining tendency all their lives should see weight reduction in terms of one heroic effort, which will make everything right. The problem grows out of our way of life, our style of living. It continues. So the effort to reduce, if it is to be successful, must be seen as the beginning of a lifelong change in style. The reward can be life itself.

SECTION IV

The Nutritionist In The Supermarket

CHAPTER 12

What is missing from our food?

Recently, a popular national magazine printed an interview with Adelle Davis, a California lady who writes books on food which make both the bestseller lists and the *Unapproved* lists of physicians and scientific nutritionists. The article was titled, appropriately, "Adelle Davis and the New Nutrition Religion." And it began with the question, "Well, do you start with the assumption that most Americans now alive are poorly nourished?"

To this the reply was, in part: "No doubt about that. ... Watch what people buy at the supermarket. White flour, white bread, noodles and prepared stuff, overcooked and overfrozen TV dinners, soft drinks, imitation fruit juices.... What's happened to market food is just tragic! Even the best fruits and vegetables have signs of disease and soil deficiencies."

And later she adds such lines as: "Our ground has been depleted to a point where even a cow can't get adequate nutrition from the grass it grazes on.... The whole country is at the mercy of people who are making money off our food."

Adelle Davis's charges that the mainstream of our food supply is inadequate to the optimal support of life are really relatively mild. Some of her colleagues reach levels of vituperation which are Olympian in energy and invective. A few years ago, one small group issued a statement on bread which included these sentences, typical of a certain point of view: "The enriched bread fed to the American public is a national scandal. First of all, the wheat grown in poor soil and fertilized with water-soluble commercial fertilizer is of low protein content. . . . The modern flour mill removes the precious vitamins and minerals. This is then bleached with . . . chlorine dioxide (which is a poison); and to this lifeless mass, a few dead synthetic chemicals (improperly called vitamins) and inorganic iron are added. We not only think these foodstuffs are worthless; we believe that many of them are positively harmful. . . . We are a nation of sick people. Our hospitals are crowded to capacity. All the metabolic diseases are increasing by leaps and bounds. Coronary thrombosis is attacking young men in their 20's. Cancer is the leading cause of death in children under 14. Diabetes and mental disease are on the increase even in children. And dental caries are rampant!"

On an inquiry from a reader, enclosing the latter material, *McCall's* magazine referred the statements to one of the world's most respected authorities on nutrition, Dr. Fredrick Stare, who chairs Harvard's Department of Nutrition. Dr. Stare expressed opinions quite consistent with those of all medicine and nutrition science on the matter of "depleted" foods. His comments concluded, "To imply or suggest that enriched white flour can cause or contribute to the diseases listed in the clipping is a cruel and reckless fraud."

Dr. Stare was sued, in what became a landmark case, *Boston Nutrition Society* vs. *Dr. Fredrick Stare*. The trial was brief. The plaintiff called an expert witness, who had stated that white flour was "unfit for human consumption," and who related disease causes to refined and processed food. On cross-examination, this witness had to admit that he had no acquaintance with any research showing a toxicity of the bleaching of white flour, and that he did not know the chemical composition of bread or the vitamins it contained. Then he was asked what he thought about the addition of vitamin D to white bread. He said it was poisonous. The next question from Dr. Stare's attorney was: "Do you happen to know that vitamin D isn't one of the enriching articles in enriched white bread?"

The jury deliberated 15 minutes and denied the charge against the Harvard physician and biochemist.

The incident is a good example of what happens whenever fearful fantasies about food are brought to the test of cold reality. Almost all threats about the hazards hidden within our food supply are similarly unsupported, and they are advocated by men and women who, while they may be well-meaning, nevertheless lack the information and education to evaluate foods and their effect on the human body.

Dr. Stare has long been a spokesman for the reputable and trained practitioners of the nutrition sciences. So let us consider what scientific nutrition has to say about the widespread belief that industry is scurrilously stealing health values from our foods, and that those whose job it is to protect us are either indifferent to the nation's welfare, or can be bribed, politicked or intimidated into betraying their trust.

Dr. Stare sums up the views of science in two statements. First, "All the necessary foods are in the supermarket or grocery store." And second, "Goodness is still in our foods. The poisons are in the pens and tongues of those who, by peddling misinformation, half truths, statements out of context, and downright falsehoods gain some temporary notoriety, inflate their own egos, and a few make a profit, or hope to."

What is meant here by scientific nutrition? The group would include medical doctors who are interested in matters of food and health, the scientists of various disciplines who have unlocked the secrets of how food becomes life, those who direct the laboratories of universities and reputable research centers, those who teach the chemistry and technology of food and its making, growing and preparing, those who design food combinations and patterns to accomplish medical purposes for hospitals, universities, welfare programs and the like—in brief, those who have the training, the licenses, the degrees, the titles and jobs which place upon them the credible stamp of *knowledge*.

These people, uniformly, go first to their colleagues for challenge or confirmation of new ideas. They have evidence, not testimonials. And they do not keep secrets; their discoveries promptly belong to all for the benefit of all. When you read or hear statements about a huge and powerful conspiracy to cheat the nation of the food upon which it depends for life, stop and think. Who has more to lose from the truth—the promoters and idiosyncratics, or the men who devote their lives at fixed and rather unimpressive incomes to learning nutritional truth and to the guardianship of the national health? Can one really believe that a quarter of a million physicians are indifferent to the lives of their patients? Can one really believe that tens of thousands of accredited scientists would all stand still for this grand public cheat, that none would speak out, or, even more implausible, that they are all deluded, that they do not know? Commonsense can go a long way toward sorting out the fake from the genuine, the self-serving from those who serve others, the scare-mongers from the health-seekers.

If the reader here detects the author's tone of outrage and dismay, he is quite correct. For the best efforts of nutritionists cannot find evidence for commonplace horror stories of a national food suply sweepingly devitalized, depleted and debased, which is supposed to have brought the populace to the brink of debility.

There is nothing very new about the idea that value is stolen from foods. In the United States, it seems to have begun early in the 19th century with a crotchety minister named Sylvester Graham, whose name is memorialized in the graham cracker. Graham had no medical or scientific training, but he began to lay out various programs of hygiene which were rigorous and a little self-abusive. There seemed almost no medical condition for which he did not have an answer. Cholera, at the time, was a mystery to everyone but Graham. He opined that it came from the dual error of lewdness and eating chicken pie.

The "staff of life"

The core of Mr. Graham's health system involved bread. The coarse, chewy bran—the tough hull of wheat —was objected to by many consumers of the time, as it still is. So millers began to remove it from the wheat. Graham was outraged. The millers had presumed, he said, "to put asunder that which God has joined together."

Bran is the reason grains have to be milled; it is a tough, protective outer shell of the seeds. It is chiefly cellulose which we cannot break down digestively, and which, in excess, is quite irritating to the intestines. Graham pointed out that one did not remove such chaff from the diet of the horse. But we have noted that grazing animals have needs and digestive apparatus quite different from ours. They can use cellulose as a carbohydrate; we cannot.

The puritanical "Grahamite" movement became a powerful force in America of the mid-1800s. There were even riots. And when Horace Greeley was running for president of the United States, his Grahamite beliefs pervaded many of his speeches. Scientifically, of course, the program had little meaning.

Then, in the 1870s, some real problems developed. A new breed of wheat began to be grown, tough spring wheat which still fills the fields of our Great Plains. It did not crush too well under the stone wheels which had done nicely for the older, soft wheat. So steel-rollered mills were invented.

Let us look for a moment at a grain of wheat. Underneath the tough bran hull is the *aleurone layer,* a thin inner lining of the bran, which gives whole wheat bread its brownish color. Underneath the aleurone layer is the vast bulk of the grain, the starchy *endosperm.* This is the stuff from which our flour comes. At the bottom of the grain, in a little corner, is the *germ,* which surrounds the *embryo,* which in turn is the new potential wheat plant. It stands to reason that, as we have seen in other foods, this reproductive portion of the plant has a high nutritive content of a broad spectrum. The trouble with the germ and embryo is that they can make an oily mess of a mill. And if they are included in the flour, the flour has what most housewives consider to be a poor texture. It will also turn rancid very quickly.

With refrigeration, rapid transport of food supplies

from a distance and the growth of a broadly based food industry, grains have become a less important food source for Americans. In fact, we have rarely depended on grain as the chief protein source; bread has been useful and important, but not truly our "staff of life." We are meat eaters.

But in the late 19th century, fresh fruits and vegetables were much less available. So the B vitamins of the wheat germ were a more important source, and there was a short period during which the removal of germ and embryo and aleurone layer in milling seemed to have caused some nutritional problems, especially for low-income families.

Today, with our enormous variety of foods, with plenty of complete protein, and our much, much smaller consumption of bread per capita, wheat is not nearly such an important food source as it once was. And, at the same time, programs of enrichment have restored the important micronutrients removed in milling and refining wheat. One reason for this restoration of white flour is that Americans, and most other Western people, have steadfastly preferred white flours and breads over dark by overwhelming margins.

For our own purposes, let us see what the real differences are between whole wheat bread and enriched white. This will also help us to see the fallacies of the "natural" and "organic" food claims, ideas which simply have no basis in science, reason or reality. Let us compare two slices as follows:

	Slice of White Bread (enriched)	Slice of Whole Wheat Bread
Calories	60	55
Protein	2 grams	2.5 grams
Fat	.7 grams	.7 grams
Carbohydrate	12 grams	11 grams
Water	8 grams	8 grams
Calcium	19 milligrams	23 milligrams
Iron	.6 milligrams	.6 milligrams

	Slice of White Bread (enriched)	Slice of Whole Wheat Bread
Vitamin A	Only a trace	Only a trace
Thiamine (B_1)	.06 milligrams	.06 milligrams
Riboflavin (B_2)	.05 milligrams	.03 milligrams
Niacin	.6 milligrams	.7 milligrams
Ascorbic acid (C)	Only a trace	Only a trace

We can see that there is little to choose from between white and whole wheat, nutritionally. Then what is the significance of a slice of bread in our daily diet? It is about a thirtieth of the protein need, and the protein is incomplete. Its fuel value is perhaps a fortieth to a fiftieth of daily average need. It offers about a fortieth of the calcium need, about a twentieth of the iron need (for a man) and about a thirtieth for a woman. It has about a twentieth of the thiamine and a thirtieth of the riboflavin for an average adult, and less than a twentieth of the niacin.

Other vitamins and minerals are removed in the milling process, but these, as we have seen, are not involved in actual shortages; in most cases, deficiencies of these nutrients are unknown or relatively so.

But one may ask, aren't the "natural" vitamins and minerals in the whole wheat bread better for you than the "synthetic" ones in the enriched white? Let us test this common faddist proposition. Below is a molecule of niacin:

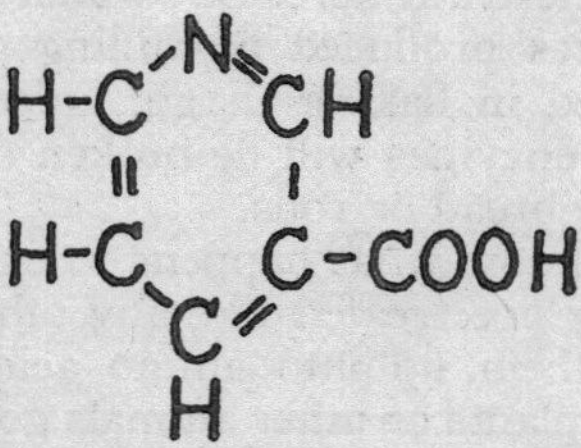

```
       N
     /   \\
H-C       CH
  ||      |
H-C       C-COOH
   \    //
     C
     |
     H
```

A molecule of niacin, exactly the same whether naturally occurring or synthesized.

Scientists identified this chemical pattern and its content of atoms. Then they found that they could take the same kinds of atoms (Cs, Hs, Os, Ns) and put them in the same pattern to form a *synthetic* niacin molecule. The two substances were identical by any known test. Both synthetic and natural molecules restored growth in deficient animal and human life forms. They provided maximal health. In short, one can find no difference between the two because the substances really are the same. That is what "synthetic" means. It is not a substitute, not an approximation.

Says Dr. Stare, voicing the opinion of anyone with scientific credentials in the field: "It has been proved that there is no difference between synthetic vitamins and natural ones."

Well, then what is the difference between the two breads, we ask the health-fooders. "Minerals," some say, "natural minerals."

We now known that a mineral is a chemical element. Iron is iron. Calcium is calcium. Sodium is sodium. These atoms—pure, single and alone—are what are needed in the body and in its chemical manufacturing. *All* minerals are "natural," that is, precisely the same as they are found in nature, whether they occur in foods, or in the earth, from which they are taken by foods.

If not vitamins and minerals, is there anything else? "Yes," say some health-fooders, "enzymes. In stone grinding, the temperatures are lower, so enzymes are not destroyed, as they are in steel grinding."

There is some truth here. But watch carefully. First, the temperatures produced in milling are much lower than those used in baking. Ergo, unless you eat your flour raw, the enzymes will be broken down before the flour gets to be bread or rolls.

Second, we know what happens to enzymes when we eat them. They are treated like any other protein. Our bodies break them up into amino acids and such. If enzymes from plants or other animals got into the bloodstream whole, we would have allergic and immune reactions to them, as we do with any foreign protein.

So if the enzymes remained in the bread, the cells would see them only as so many Cs, Hs, Os, Ns and a few other atoms. And indeed, those enzyme atoms do remain in the flour, and are eaten by us.

The facts should speak for themselves. It is interesting to note, in this context, the consumption of wheat germ and wheat germ oil, perfectly good foods if you like them. These replace any of the germ which might be removed from the wheat. The need for these foods as "health supplements" should also be clear: simply, they are not needed any more than is any other single food.

The refinement of sugar follows the wheat tale, except that sugar has never been so important a food as wheat. Sugar is a good and useful food, but the degree of its refinement is unimportant nutritionally.

Canned and frozen foods

As with bread, many people believe that our canned and frozen food products have been robbed of their nutritive value by food processors. Dr. Philip White, of the AMA's Council on Foods and Nutrition, has a full and effective response to this unfortunate conviction, and one with which all of nutrition science agrees. It is worth reading carefully and remembering:

"In the industrial canning process, the vegetable is harvested at the proper time to assure optimal size, appearance and nutritive value." (Author's note: the processors can choose much better than you and I can, and in fact control whole crops from seed to harvest, always with an eye to good nutrition.)

"The product is cooled immediately after picking and rushed to the factory, washed and blanched and immediately processed by a short-time, high-temperature process. The cooking process, followed by a very rapid cooling period, is the key to the superiority of industrial procedures over many home procedures. The food is cooked in a closed system with a minimum of air and cooking time. When the final product is prepared for home consumption, it is necessary *only* to warm the food prior to serving. Warming, rather than use of extreme heat, assures that once again the vegetables are given minimal treatment.

"In the freezing process, if vegetables are picked and then quick-frozen, the nutrient values are equal to or perhaps even higher than those of fresh vegetables which may not have been properly handled in the chain of farm to market to consumer.

"Home grown, freshly harvested vegetables cooked almost immediately generally will not have greater nutritional value than high-quality processed vegetables. Slow-cooking methods used frequently by homemakers often destroy as many vitamins as are lost during the industrial canning process. [Author's note: yes, this does mean that values are lost during canning. But do reserve judgment until the whole story is told.] Fresh vegetables which have been poorly stored at the market also may be less nutritious than those picked from a home garden. . . .

"Even though there may be significant loss of nutritive value from vegetables during both industrial and home processing, this loss is more significant to the vegetable than to the consumer. Do not be fooled by reports of 10% to 20% nutrient loss unless you know the amount of nutrient that was originally present and the amount that remains."

In other words, the food may not be an important source of the particular nutrient; or the food may be an important source of the nutrient, but the nutrient is in such large supply that small losses are unimportant; or the nutrient may be so plentiful in the general food supply that the loss form this one food is unimportant. Twenty percent would be a substantial industrial loss in processes such as canning; but in practical terms, the chances are that this loss is largely made up by the fast and expert harvesting, washing and controlled cooking. In freezing even this much loss would be rather unusual.

Concludes Dr. White, and all of responsible nutrition

science: *"Today's scientific methods used in commercially preserving foods are a guarantee that your processed vegetables, whether canned or frozen, will be safe and wholesome."*

Why do people believe the faddist claims that processed foods are nutritionally lacking? One reason is certainly taste. Flavoring factors in food often boil away at moderate heats, and can be lost in processing. However, these flavors have little to do with nutrition; in fact, in home cooking, flavors can be preserved while nutritive elements are lost. The truth is, you can't judge nutrition by the quality or quantity of flavor.

Crops are often chosen for their ability to survive processing or for their uniformity of size and color—at a sacrifice of flavor or texture. But while the author freely confesses that he has never tasted a frozen potato that he would ever care to taste again, and that frozen corn seems to him a distant relative of the tender, wormy little ears that were the elixir of his childhood, he understands that he is not being nutritionally deprived. He remains wistful, but well-fed.

Processors are constantly striving to improve flavor and texture. Anyone who thinks that processors do not leap to any advantage in flavor or food value over the products of their rivals grossly underestimates the business sense of these people. The industry's own technical personnel and our government demand that nutritive quality and, most important, safety be paramount. If we want dinner to be ready in five minutes, we can have it and it will be good and safe for survival, but there is sometimes a price in pleasure. The use of convenience foods is a personal choice.

One problem the author has repeatedly pointed out to the food industry is the hazard of unrealistic advertising. Advertisers sometimes go too far when they describe certain commercial foods such as puddings, cakes, pies and frozen dinners as "just like mother used to make." (Unless, of course, mother was a dreadful cook.) This produces a false expectation and a sense of being swindled. After all, how can the consumer be expected to accept industry's claims for *nutritive* concern and care and quality, when its advertising for a canned meatball (for which any tasteful person can feel only pity and politely concealed repugnance) falsely implies that the poor thing has been crafted with the care and attention of a Florentine chef?

Refinement of food is not the only accusation of nutrient-theft made by certain health-food enthusiasts. Many see what they like to call "degenerative diseases" as being on the rise because of nutritional deficiencies. Such diseases as cancer, heart disease and arthritis are implicated. Indeed, the caseload of such illness is rising, but medicine generally agrees that this is so because these ailments are associated with increasing age, and more and more people are living longer. Moreover, medicine is not aware of the role of nutritional deficiency as the cause of such diseases, any more than it is aware of the deficiencies.

For example, in the magazine article referred to earlier, Adelle Davis is quoted as saying, "Apparently everyone in America has a magnesium deficiency." If this is the case, why are not the federal health agencies and the faculties of medicine and nutrition able to find such deficiencies?

Where are the deficiencies supposed to come from? Says Carlton Fredericks, who has a radio program about food, "many of our foods spring from soils which have been overcultivated or underfertilized or both, yielding vegetables and fruits below standard in vitamin-mineral content."

Fredericks was once charged by the Food and Drug Administration with, among other things, making claims that vitamins and minerals could be used to treat such conditions as cystic mastitis, lowered thyroid activity, high blood pressure, strokes, damaged brain and nerve cells in children, multiple sclerosis, varicose veins, lack of resistance to cancer, epilepsy, gray hair, mongolian idiotism, muscular dystrophy, club feet and lack of menal resistance to house-to-house salesmen. The court upheld the charges against Fredericks.

Our soil is as good as our food

But what about the charge that depleted soils rob plants of needed nutrients? First, a little common sense. If our plants are deficient in vitamins and minerals, why do not these deficiencies appear in people? How is it that the health-food enthusiasts, without education or training in medicine, can find these signs when licensed physicians cannot?

Second, the nutrients in the plants are there for the sake of the plant, not for us. The carrot, for example, does not make vitamin A precursors as a generous gesture to humans; it produces the stuff for its own growth and survival. And plants take up minerals because they are needed in their own biochemistry.

So if the soil does not contain the nutrients to supply the needs of plants, the plants *simply will not grow.* Indeed, foods grown on soils which are *low* in nutrients—usually nitrogen—develop poor yields. In other words, if you can buy and eat the food, it is nutritively complete, whether the food comes from a bumper crop or a bad-year crop. The effect is similar to trying to raise 50 chickens on the food for ten. The weaker chicks die out, leaving more food for the stronger. Of course, even the stronger may not be as large—the food, becoming life, can produce just so much chicken body—but what there is to eat is chicken.

(It is interesting, in this light, to look at the "organic" produce in many a health-food store, which is usually much more expensive and is commonly undersized. It can lead one to some amusing speculations on soil management on some of the "natural" farms.)

An American Medical Association statement on our soil quality and its meaning for our food exemplifies informed opinion on this subject: "Soils on which food crops are grown in this country are analyzed frequently and are adequately fertilized to prevent nutritive depletion. No disease or abnormality in man, except endemic goiter due to a deficiency of iodine, has been traced to a deficiency in soil. The yield of the crop produced, rather than its nutritional quality, will be adversely affected if the soil is not maintained at the proper composition."

And from the American Dietetic Association comes the comment: "The nutritive value of a given crop, such as wheat, is influenced more by the kind of seed planted than by the fertility of the soil."

"But," say the health-fooders, "what kind of fertilizer is going into the soil? Isn't it chemical? Isn't it poison? Aren't they poisoning our food?" Let us look and see.

CHAPTER 13

Is there poison in our food?

Today a number of Americans, many of them well educated, are making these kinds of claims about what we eat:

"They are putting things in our food. There is no doubt about it. You can see all the forbidding names on the labels, and you hear about the sprays and the fertilizers. There is all the talk about pollution and the ecology, and there are books with ominous titles, such as *The Poisons in Our Food.* Where is the truth in this kind of talk? What can we be sure of when we buy and eat?"

The truth about chemical fertilizers

The charge is commonly made nowadays that "chemicals" are being used to fertilize the soil and that this is producing a deleterious effect on our food. For example, returning to the comments of Adelle Davis: "You can choose the best diet possible in America and be low in vitamin A because almost all our foods are grown with chemical fertilizers high in nitrates, which destroy A."

That sounds shocking. But let us look at what chemical fertilizers really are, and especially what nitrates are, and how they relate to the vitamins produced by the plants.

First, we ought to define the word "chemical." The dictionary says a chemical is a substance made by or used in a chemical process. This definition certainly includes the whole process by which food is created, digested, metabolized and its elements restructured to make and sustain life. In fact, many of the man-made chemicals we shall look at either are taken from life forms or are duplicate copies of these forms. For example, *citric acid* is one of the additives commonly found in soft drinks. It is also produced by the body from simple sugars, to become a key chemical in the Krebs cycle, the process by which fuel food gives energy to the cells. In fact, the cycle is sometimes known to biologists as the *citric-acid cycle.* So this simple chemical should not be regarded as a menace when we find it on soft-drink labels, both cola and *un*cola.

To understand chemical fertilizers, we might first reason that agriculture probably would not spend so enormous a sum of money putting fertilizer into the soil unless it were necessary. And it is necessary, because each crop consumes chemicals from the soil to grow.

Recall the explanations in chapter 3 of the ways in which plants take up very simple chemical substances and turn them into complex foods, and their need for simple nitrogen chemicals to make proteins. These nitrogen forms are usually nitrates and ammonia in combinations with oxygen or hydrogen. Where do they come from in nature? When plants, or the animals that eat plants, decay, nitrogen is returned to the soil. Also, the body wastes of animals contain nitrogen, but not in a very concentrated form.

Those who speak of "organic" farming refer mainly to the use of animal wastes and decaying organisms (such as leaves) to restore the soil after a crop has grown. True, farmers of a century ago had little choice but to spread manures, plough in rotted plants and now and then let the land lie fallow. But these processes are slow, and worse, inefficient.

Ironically, three-fourths of the air we breathe is the nitrogen that both we and plants need so urgently. But in its pure, free state it is a chemical loner, reluctant to join with any other element and so, useless to us. How did it get into the soil in usable form in the first place? Researchers believe that before life began on the earth, continual lightning storms struck through the primeval atmosphere. These storms are thought to have supplied the energy for the nitrogen to combine with free hydrogen (as ammonia) and with oxygen.

Today, this process is repeated in industry to make our fertilizers. Electrical charges are passed through air in closed containers, trapping the free nitrogen as ammonia and/or nitrates. These are added to the soil, often in water, just as primeval rains washed nitrogen compounds out of the atmosphere and into the earth's crust.

Chemical fertilizers also restore, or add, other basic elements to the soil—sulfur, iron, oxygen combinations with calcium, and so on. In one view, it may be said that modern chemical fertilization techniques follow methods which long antedate the "natural" ones of organic farming. It is difficult to understand how nitrates can be thought by anyone to destroy the vitamin A in plants (which actually use the nitrates to *make* vitamins). Besides, if they did, the plants themselves could not grow and survive.

Comments Dr. Fredrick Stare: "With agricultural chemicals we can produce the food we need. Without them, we could not. . . . The National Plant Food Institute estimates that chemical fertilizers alone save the public 13 billion dollars a year on its food bill."

Speaking to the recent Western Hemisphere Nutrition Congress, distinguished entomologist Dr. George Decker said: "One thing seems clear to all who are familiar with the facts. The agricultural production and the standard of living in the various nations of the world are proportionate to knowledge and use of chemicals in agriculture. . . . The layman remains unaware that if the use of agricultural chemicals were banned in America tomorrow, the yield of many crops would be reduced by 10 percent to 90 percent, and surplus stocks would soon disappear."

He added: "Since 1930, increased crop production has been dependent largely upon advances in technology (rather than bringing additional land under cultivation). In fact, since 1954, when the number of acres in farms decreased for the first time, all increases in production have been due to technological progress."

In other words, despite the claims of the ill-informed,

we really have no choice. Since World War II, for example, more than half our farmers have left the land. Farming is still a family business in America, despite big-business implications of some critics. If we define a family farm as one on which the family does more than half the work, then 95 percent of farms fall into this category. And the productivity of these people, for the last 20 years, has *had* to increase at a rate double that of other businesses, in order to feed our own people and also many of the world's hungry. We cannot afford to return to 19th-century farming, and there is no scientific reason why we should want to.

Facts about sprays and pesticides

Are we bound to sprays and pesticides as well as to chemical fertilizers? Experts agree that we are, and they also agree that with the knowledge and skill and controls we already have, there is no evident danger to our food supply.

When it has become so fashionable to rail against sprays, such as DDT, this may seem a surprising statement. But let us see what is involved in the pesticide question, and what is really happening.

The booming production of agriculture produces an equal boom in plant diseases, weeds and pests. Even with the use of chemicals, in California alone weeds cost the state one million dollars *a day*. Insects and plant diseases, uncontrolled, could make this sum look like a pittance. Today's technique of farming specialization, what is known as *single-crop farming*, "has created a banquet table for insects who pour into the fields in such prodigious numbers that the only way to cope with them is by chemical means," says the USDA.

And the Department of Agriculture states that without pest-killing chemicals, many familiar foods would either disappear or become luxuries. Every second or third crop of potatoes or tomatoes would be wiped out. Beef-raising and dairying in the southeastern states could not continue at their present rate. Commercial apple production would stop. Peaches would not grow in the east. Oranges and grapefruit could become curiosities.

Instead of a "silent spring," we should be very likely to face a "hungry autumn."

What many people have not clearly understood about the pesticide question is this: There is quite a difference between a wholesale use of DDT or other sprays on square miles of elm trees or lakes, and the calculated, scientific and controlled application of chemicals to crops. The former pesticide use was not wise, and there was little law or enforcement to manage the problem. On the other hand, the farm use has been and is controlled in many ways and at many levels. Putting it simply, the farmer who negligently contaminated his crop with any poisonous substance would be a ruined man. He has long used chemical controls, such as naphtha, arsenic and toxic petroleum products. The newer chemicals are in many ways safer. And, in any case, no responsible farmer ever went about spraying ripening fruit or vegetables with DDT.

But the real proof—to avoid long technological argument—is certainly in the supermarket pudding. Are we being filled with poisons by our food or aren't we? And that question is being asked ceaselessly by researchers at the U.S. Food and Drug Administration and other agencies.

While the FDA long ago was interested in such matters, an amendment to the law under which it operates was passed in 1954. This amendment directed FDA to set up tolerances for the chemicals in question and to check them in raw foods. These tolerances are very conservative, and they take into consideration the work of the Food and Agriculture Organization of the United Nations and of the World Health Organization. Moreover, if the tolerance for one chemical is one part per million, that for two chemicals in the food together is a *total* of one part per million. So we can't get excess amounts of spray because more than one is used.

To check, FDA people take shopping carts into markets in 18 cities and buy bags of typical groceries according to a statistical plan. In one three-year period, some 50,000 grocery orders were bought, including samplings of food imports. These were checked for more than 50 pesticide chemicals. FDA "market basket" studies have been very comprehensive. A diet list for a 17- to 19-year-old male, the country's biggest eater, was developed, including a two-week supply of food. This food was then prepared for the table, and then the chemists took it apart looking for poisons.

Traces of pesticides did appear. It should be noted, however, that pesticides are used for many purposes, from mosquito abatement to highway weed control, from home gardening to forest conservation. Quite a lot of the pesticide which did reach the food was not from the hand of the farmer.

The following are some of the results among the more important and common pesticides. They are given as fractions of what is called "acceptable daily intake." Such an intake, obviously, incorporates a *wide* safety margin. That margin, of course, includes all that we know about prolonged intakes over the years, and a big safety factor is used in computing this aspect.

Pesticide	Fraction of Acceptable Daily Intake Found
DDT	1/20
Lindane	1/208
Malathion	1/200
Carbaryl	1/17

Conclude Keith Dawson and Reo E. Duggan of the FDA: "Currently, the incidence and levels of pesticide residues in the nation's food supply are not approaching dangerous or even alarming levels. . . . The information on ready-to-eat foods obtained from the market survey is most reassuring . . . [but] there should not be alarm or complacency concerning pesticide residues in food."

In other words, the fear that we have been and are being poisoned by pesticides in our food is not based on fact. Moreover, no one at FDA has any intention of letting the fear become a reality. Improved controls and greater restrictions come into being with any threat, as with the ban on DDT, which for chemical and medical reasons is well out of the picture. The restrictions on the use of DDT have been a step forward, and the search for less toxic pesticides is intense.

Some facts about food additives

Chemicals added to food when it is being processed have also been the focus of many scare stories. And fears here have proven to be much less warranted than those about pesticides. The U.S. Department of Agriculture's Dr. Ruth Leverton, noted as an expert in both academic nutrition and consumer education, sums up informed scientific opinion about the distrust of our food supply this way:

"Despite the abundance and high quality of our American food supply, the charlatans are waging a persistent campaign to undermine the confidence of the public in the nutritional value of our foods. They have succeeded in raising serious doubts in the minds of many Americans about the integrity and purity of the nation's food supplies. It is vital to the purpose of the quacks to cast doubt on the honesty and decency of food growers and processors and the quality of the food they produce. How else can the charlatans sell their own special foods and supplements?"

But even without the proddings and scare talk of the fakes and faddists, there is something a little discomfiting about swallowing down foods the labels of which are long lists of ingredients with forbidding names, vague purposes and unfamiliar identities. Whose mouth ever waters for a diglyceride? Who puts on the grocery list some butylated hydroxytoluene?

It is an old and valid saw that we fear most what we understand least. So let us see what additives are, what they do to food and what they do to us.

Suppose we begin by looking at a couple of nonexistent labels. One offers us a product containing,

"Acetone, mythyl acetate, furan, diacetyl butanol, methylfuran, isoprene, methylbutanol, caffeine, essential oils, methanol, acetaldehyde, methyl formate, ethanol, dimethyl sulfide and propionaldehyde." The instructions are to soak this stuff in hot water, throw it away and drink the water. Would you do it? Well, would you reconsider if you knew the product was nothing but pure coffee?

There are no man-made chemicals added to that list. These are merely the natural chemicals found in coffee. Even worse sounding might be a label that read, "Actomyosin, myogen, nucleoproteins, peptids, amino acids, myoglobin, lipids, linoleic acid, oleic acid, lecithin, cholesterol, sucrose, adenosine triphosphate (ATP), glucose, collagen, elastin, creatine, pyroligneous acid, sodium chloride, sodium nitrate, sodium nitrite and sodium phosphate." There are some familiar names here, factors which you may recognize as essential nutrients, or as chemicals which your own body makes. We have used many of these names. This chemical parade turns out to be sugar-cured ham, again with not a man-made chemical added.

Astute readers may also notice that some of these names appear on contents labels in the supermarket as additives. For the fact is that many of the feared additives are only food substances that nature uses to preserve, enhance flavor, produce better texture or what have you.

Additives are sometimes fortification and enrichment nutrients of questionable necessity. The reader should by now be able to recognize these and to evaluate the rationality of their addition. For example, the addition of vitamin B_{12} to certain breakfast cereals is questionable if one remembers that there is no shortage of B_{12} in the average dietary and that it is not customarily found in plant products anyway. One suspects the addition might be for the benefit of sales rather than for the consumer.

As for other kinds of additives, those which do not seem to add to the nutrient values of food, some of the current talk and writing might well lead the average

American to think that chemicals arrived in foods by means something like this: A white-smocked scientist looks up from his lab bench and calls to a colleague, "Hey, Charlie, look at this! I found some powder up on the top shelf, and I tossed it in the mushroom soup, and it turned this great shade of blue and completely dissolved all the hair that falls in the soup down in the kitchen! Better call down to Production and tell them we're putting in a new additive."

Additives are more carefully thought out than this. And generally, they serve the consumer as much as or more than the manufacturer.

It is true the law was once such that manufacturers could put what they chose in food, and it was up to government agencies to learn if it was harmful, prove that it was and take action to remove the substance. But back in 1958, the process was reversed. Now manufacturers must first run tests to prove the safety of an additive, then apply to the FDA for an *order* permitting use and a *tolerance* specifying what amounts of the material shall be considered safe. This law and its procedures provide excellent protection for the consumer. In fact, protection was really pretty good even before the 1958 amendment.

At this writing, some of the law may be a little too rigid. Consider the recent *cyclamate* upset. These artificial sweeteners were banned because of what was widely reported as a cancer threat. Most scientists are confident there never was such a threat. But one clause of FDA law said that a ban *had* to be instituted if a substance appeared to produce cancer in man or any animal. Rats on tremendous quantities of cyclamates developed bladder tumors.

In practical terms, there was already a limit of 23 milligrams per pound of body weight on cyclamates, or 3500 mg. per day for the average man (154 pounds). The National Academy of Sciences found that only 2.5 percent of the population consumed more than 1000 mg. a day *at a peak.* The dose the rats were getting was roughly *150 times* that high maximum every day for their entire lives. If a man ate that much cyclamate, he would be receiving about five ounces daily, which would be quite a lot of sweetness—the equivalent of over nine pounds of sugar. It is hard to believe that any human would want so much sweet.

Sweetners which are still in use, such as saccharin, are among the *flavoring additives* one sees on labels, and almost anyone recognizes what these are on sight. But few people recognize the *preservatives,* and those who do usually view them with alarm. What are these chemicals?

Among the most common are *calcium and sodium propionate,* whose names are often on labels with the words "added to retard spoilage." These are intended to keep molds and bacteria from making foods such as bread inedible. They are not poisons. They are salts of propionic acid, which is produced naturally in Swiss cheese during its making. These salts are completely metabolized by the body, that is, simply used in the food chain as harmless building blocks.

This is one principle of additives, to use those made by nature to protect its foods. For example, we have noted that vitamin E occurs naturally with unsaturated oils; it functions in the body to slow down the oxidation of oils. E also does the same thing on the grocer's shelf; it slows down the oxidation of oil to which it is added, and thus prevents rancidity.

Citric acid (as we have pointed out, a key chemical in the energy processes of our cells) is also an antioxidant, as is ascorbic acid; both are sometimes put into processed foods to prevent oxidation and discoloration. BHA (butylated hydroxyanisole) and BHT (butylated hydroxytoluene) are even more commonly used to prevent a food from combining with oxygen, as in potatoes. BHA, BHT and *propyl gallate* (another safe antioxidant which one often sees on labels) are closely related to fairly common food substances.

Indeed, most additives are discovered doing their job naturally in foods, or as close relatives to food chemicals made by nature—close enough so that when taken into the body they are safely broken down and their atoms used in the food cycle. But whether naturally occurring or not, there must be good reason to believe that such substances will not interfere with the work of the body—followed up by tests to make sure.

Since hundreds of additives of various kinds are used, we cannot list them all. Some are such common foods as acetic acid (vinegar). Some are familiar products used to add color, like carotene or chlorophyll. Some are used to change the consistency of the product—pectin from fruit, usually apples, keeps jelly gelatinous. Some, like the natural factor lecithin, are used to make the product hardier—for example, to make cake mixes work so you can forget about tiptoeing around the oven while the cake is rising. Acidity or alkalinity is sometimes important for food, as in the case of leavening agents which cause the release of gas, to fluff up baked goods; these same ingredients you use in your own start-from-scratch baking. Do you recognize such chemicals as sodium aluminum sulphate, calcium acid phosphate and calcium silicate? They are in your own can of baking powder. There are stabilizers and thickeners, with the odd names agar agar, carragheen and guar—all are only vegetable gums.

The fact that an additive is a naturally-occurring food substance does not guarantee that it would meet the strict FDA requirements. Our controls are very conservative. For example, in the FDA's feeding studies for new additives, a factor for safety is allowed. The usual number is 100. This stands for 100 times that amount of additive which has *any biologic effect* on experimental animals. Such effect need not be threatening; it can be a slight change of blood pressure. Test animals are fed 100 times the latter quantity, to see if there are untoward health changes at such extreme levels of intake.

And if we didn't use additives? Comments Dr. Bernard Oser, of Food and Drug Research Laboratories, Inc., "Baked goods would go stale or mold overnight, salad oils and dressings would separate and turn rancid, table salt would turn hard and lumpy, canned fruits and vegetables would become discolored or mushy, vitamin potencies would deteriorate, beverages and frozen desserts would lack flavor and wrappings would stick to the contents."

Food additives are ancient, for man has always had the problem of trying to keep his food on hand without having it go bad. And understandably, the further we try to stretch that trick—with dinners on little aluminum trays on which they were placed six months before, and with the art of cookery reduced to adding boiling water or an occasional home-broken egg—it is not surprising that science must deliver some new ways of treating food. The food additives are important to our nutritional welfare. The more we become dependent on convenience foods, the more this will be true. (The prospect may be depressing, but only from an aesthetic point of view, certainly not because of any health concern.)

Says Dr. Fredrick Stare: "As a physician and student of nutrition . . . I am convinced that food additives are safe. The consumer is in far greater danger from improper food preparation, storage and plain overeating, than from food additives whose use is carefully regulated, and revised when necessary."

Fluoride, the missing additive

All of nutritional and medical science is agreed that our most important nutrient, water, ought to have one additive in most regions of the United States. The additive is fluoride, an element which becomes deposited in teeth to make them harder and more resistant to the attack of bacterial acids which cause tooth decay. The American Dental Association, American Association for the Advancement of Science, the American Medical Association and the U.S. Public Health Service are only a few of the supporters of the drive to fluoridate water to prevent needless caries (cavities).

"On the basis of available evidence," reads an AMA statement, "it appears that fluoridation decreases the incidence of caries during childhood. Other evidence indicates as well a reduction of dental caries up to at least 44 years of age."

The scientific recommendation is that the fluoride content of water supplies be tested. If they are not naturally endowed with one part per million of fluoride (about a thousandth of a gram to a quart of water) they should be brought up to that standard.

Over 60 million Americans now have this benefit. No health risk has proven to be involved, and doctors do not expect to find any in future. Fluoride is a nutrient occurring naturally in such foods as fish, cheese, meat and tea, though not in sufficient quantity to protect our teeth.

CHAPTER 14

Reading labels for health and profit

Labels and advertising should tell the consumer whether he wants something or not, whether the price is right, and whether or not he will really get what he is led to expect. The final decision can mean much in terms of both money and health. In the United States, nutritionists agree, false and misleading advertising and poor food decisions are costing the American consumer billions.

Many of these decisions are based on ads and labels that lead people to expect miracles of health from nutrients, or that make threats to the effect that buying anything but special products risks illness. This mail-order ad is a good example:

NEW ... "ACEROLA PLUS" ... MOST EFFECTIVE ALL-NATURAL VITAMIN C TABLET MONEY CAN BUY, it begins. And we may as well interrupt. Why *all-natural?* We have seen that ascorbic acid is ascorbic acid. There are no "unnatural" vitamins. Your cells will never tell any difference, for there is none. The ad continues: NOW IS THE TIME TO GIVE YOUR BODY THIS ADDED PROTECTION. Why? Because the ad appeared in winter. The implication is that one needs more vitamins at certain seasons of the year. This is generally a false concept. And of course, if the meaning is intended that vitamin C cures or prevents colds, we know that medicine has never been able to find evidence of this.

The ad lists four vitamin C sources in the one pill: NATURAL VITAMIN C FROM ROSE HIPS, HIGH SOURCE OF THIS AMAZING VITAMIN. NATURAL VITAMIN C FROM RICH GREEN PEPPERS. NATURAL VITAMIN C FROM BLACK CURRANTS—A NEW SOURCE. NATURAL HIGH-POWERED "VITALITY VITAMIN C" FROM REAL ACEROLA BERRIES.

Here we have a puzzle. Granted, there is vitamin C in all four sources. But no matter how "high-powered" the source, it is still just vitamin C, the same molecule. And why four *different* sources? It is like being offered a gasoline made from Texas, California, Alaska and Pennsylvania oils. It would be refined down to the same chemical substance.

Finally, another puff: FANTASTIC NATURAL VITAMIN C POTENCY, 80 TIMES HIGHER THAN ORANGE JUICE! This refers to the acerola berry. But all you are getting in the tablet is 100 milligrams of ascorbic acid. Don't be confused by claims that fall back on the relative potency of the source of a vitamin. All you get is what you pay for.

Or do you? This tablet sells for three times the amount charged at the corner drugstore. And you don't need the special *triple-strength* they offer which will improve nothing but the vitamin C content of your urine. Why not just get the vitamin C from the food you eat?

Do we need supplemental vitamins?

Americans spend at least $600,000,000 a year on self-prescribed vitamin supplements. Yet scientists conclude that the vast majority are not needed, and that multivitamin pills in particular include quantities of micronutrients amply supplied by ordinary food. With the possible exception of increased iron for women and girls above the age of nine, supplements are not needed, and merely teach poor eating habits, especially to children.

For example, suppose you take a multivitamin pill because you may suffer from small dietary lacks of A and B complex vitamins. You continue to eat a diet which is preponderantly, or at least in large part, fat, but take the pills, rather than add a few vegetables which would not only cover the vitamin problem but would also improve the overall composition of your dietary. You have a dietary which encourages overweight, perhaps entails a cardiovascular risk, perhaps does your digestive tract no good—but you now have A and B vitamins.

The conclusion of the medical profession on supplemental vitamins that are not prescribed is expressed by Dr. Philip White: "Foods properly selected and prepared provide all the nutrients necessary for good nutrition. Usually, the people who advise that supplemental vitamins are needed by all are the very ones who sell vitamins; their motives are based on financial self-interest, not on benefiting the public health. Only a physician can advise on a person's need for supplement or therapeutic doses of vitamins. Most persons receive adequate supplies of vitamins from ordinary foods."

Vitamin and mineral pills are often sold with the promise of providing a fast pick-up, quickly relieving a discomfort, or bestowing a sense of well-being.

Indeed, many people think they can use vitamins to feel better, as they would aspirin. But unless one is in a state of very serious vitamin deficiency, it would be a long time before the impact of promised restoration could be felt. Taking, say, calcium for the nerves is fairly silly and pointless; but it is even more pathetic to expect that in an hour or so the calcium would make its effects felt. Ads that imply instant pick-up or calm-down or discomfort-relief from nutrient supplements are doubly offensive to doctors and nutritionists. They pile one scientific fallacy on top of another.

Such ads may also suggest—falsely—that one can become deprived of micronutrients in as little as a day or a week, with immediate impact on your health or energy. But vitamins or minerals missing from your dietary in so short a time span are most unlikely to produce perceptible symptoms. When a nutritional deficiency does occur, it does not happen fast. Marked symptoms are slow to appear. And then, correction is not an overnight matter. One does not need supplements to bridge bits of carelessness with diet. The return to a sound, normal diet will take care of everything.

Hearty meals of micronutrients?

So heavily are vitamins and minerals stressed as the source of health, and so grimly is any small absence depicted to be the harbinger of disease, that many of us get a distorted impression that the essential value of a meal is its micronutrient content. In the report of the White House Conference on Food, Nutrition and Health, it is noted that many people "are lured by advertising that suggests falsely that certain cheap, widely sold products, because they contain a few added vitamins and minerals, can replace usual foods or whole meals."

Let there be no confusion between this question and the highly desirable fortification and enrichment of certain foods urged by nutritionists—of which examples are the vitamin D added to milk and the B vitamins and iron restored to wheat products. It makes sense when a widely lacking vitamin (D), with few food sources, is added to a commonly used basic food (milk), which is also the best source of a nutrient (calcium) that depends on the added vitamin for its use in the body. It also makes sense when important nutrients that are lost from wheat in processing are put back where they ought to be.

But there is another kind of fortification with micronutrients which can be commercial enhancement of a product with limited nutritional value. The product is then sold less on the worth of the basic food than on the values of the low-priced micronutrient enhancers. The food then becomes a kind of vitamin pill—often an expensive one—that provides all the promotional whack for the product.

Suppose Vita-Bubble, an exciting new chewing gum, is advertised as follows: "Every vitamin your body can possibly use, 100% of the daily requirement. Why fight with your child about breakfast? Just give him two sticks of Vita-Bubble and let him chew and pop until his teacher takes it away from him, by which time he will have *all* his vitamins for the day. Just think! You can be a good mother, yet not give a thought to his nutrition again, just fill him up as he demands. All the minerals, too. And kids love it!"

Anything wrong with that? Most nutritionists think so. The implication is that micronutrients are the main values, all we need to know or think about in a food. Also, there is an offense to logic and education, in that chewing gum cannot be considered important to nutrition.

The author has long held that the overemphasis of commerce on micronutrients is an important basis for food faddism and quackery. Such emphasis tends to suggest that the vitamins and minerals can equal the foods in which they are normally found.

An introduction to labels

Every consumer should acquire some skill in reading food labels, so that he can evaluate both the claims made in faddist promotions and the enthusiasms of conventional food advertising. Such skill is his primary key in buying the best nutrition for each dollar spent. As an example, let's look at some dry cereals in a variety pack. The first cereal is mainly sugar. How do we know? Simply because the law requires contents of a product to be listed *in the order of their importance, usually their quantity by weight.* All products which cross state lines come under this regulation, and also, it is a general principle of state food and consumer-protection laws as well.

The second largest ingredient in the cereal is wheat. (We do not know the relative proportion of these first two constituents, or any others. But there is hope that this will change, in order to give the buyer a better picture of what he is buying.) The third ingredient is corn syrup. It, too, is really sugar, except for a small amount of calcium and iron. The syrup's energy value is all carbohydrate.

So this cereal is indeed sugary. The label says a serving of the breakfast food is 89 percent carbohydrate, 5 percent protein and 1.5 percent fat. Thus a child who eats a seven-eighths-ounce serving (another fact on the label is a serving size) gets a little over one gram of protein, or perhaps a thirtieth of his RDA. The added milk will be the only significant protein source in the dish.

After corn syrup, the next ingredient is lecithin, an additive that provides and stabilizes the physical consistency of the cereal. So we know we have run out of major ingredients. Additives are good signals on the label to let us know we are examining tiny amounts. Salt is another good signal, because once salt comes up on the label, nothing else listed is of any quantity consequence. For example, in buying bakery products note how often the salt is more than the butter—even though the label boasts "made with real butter." In our cereal, lecithin is followed by honey. If we did not realize the facts about labels, we might think the honey was an important ingredient.

The next ingredient is glycine, a nonessential amino acid. So we know that the five-percent protein level has been arrived at with the help of this addition, and that an even larger part of the protein content than we might have thought is in nonessential aminos. Sodium acetate, an additive, is then followed by sodium ascorbate (C), niacinamide (for niacin), thiamine (B_1), riboflavin (B_2), vitamin A palmitate (A source) and vitamin D. The label says these vitamins are about 29 percent of MDR.

But why put vitamin D here? The cereal is going to be taken with milk. Why vitamin A, which is normally only a trace in wheat? Isn't the vitamin C quite out of place in a wheat product? And why the overload of B vitamins—for even a slice of bread, which offers a great deal more wheat, would supply perhaps a tenth of these amounts? Is it to provide something to sell? These misplaced nutrients are very likely to create a false sense of security, and encourage people to omit the foods in which they are found. For example, some people may read the presence of vitamin C as enabling them to skip breakfast juice or fruit.

There is a tendency among many people to regard dry breakfast cereals as being much alike, and as being ample foods for a morning meal. They differ. But this cereal—and it is not an especially bad example—is like less than half a slice of enriched bread with three or four teaspoons of sugar, except for the vitamin addition.

How plainly advertising conveys its message that vitamins are similar to whole foods can be seen in a number of ads. One that was long seen on television showed a man at work and a child at play, both too busy for lunch. We then see a woman who bewails, "What's a mother to do?" A disembodied voice soothes her. Her family is all right. They have had a certain dry cereal for breakfast, and it contains 100 percent of the minimum daily requirement of vitamins. The implication here that lunch is unnecessary is most unfortunate. A serving of that cereal is only 100 calories, chiefly carbohydrate. Does one really feel safe giving a child only this much food, plus some milk, to carry him through one mealtime, let alone two? And who needs 100 percent of his vitamins in so slim an amount of mediocre food? The vitamin content certainly does not mean that we can be careless of our other meals, let alone omit the meals of a growing child. Yet isn't this the inference one might make?

The object here is not entirely to excoriate cereal makers—their products have a place—but to show the consumer how important it is to read and understand the labels of products that are sold mainly on the basis of vitamins. An example is the artificial drink sold as an orange-juice substitute by virtue of its added ascorbic acid. The label will reveal that its chief ingredients are water and table sugar, with nonnutritive flavorings and vitamins. While there is nothing wrong with this pleasant, fruity-tasting drink, and others like it, we should not be misled into thinking that it really and fully takes the place of the food it resembles. (True orange juice is a much more valuable food, with a whole spectrum of important nutrients.) The label is the place where the food's true identity is revealed. The wise consumer looks here to check the glib generalities of advertising.

When should you check food labels against advertising claims? It is a good idea:

1. When a special claim for health or growth is made or implied, especially in terms of advantages over similar foods.
2. When a nutritional shortcut is stated or implied,

in terms of time or cost or substitution for conventional foods or meals.

3. When it is stated or implied that a food will give you an emotional or physical uplift, beyond that one would normally expect from any good food eaten and enjoyed.
4. When it is stated or implied that a special food has special qualities for appeasing appetite.
5. When the price seems a little low for the nutritional qualities stated or implied, as in the case of complete-meal products.
6. Whenever fear is used to motivate you, as in the case of threatened poisons, impurities or nutritive weaknesses of similar foods, or when the implication is made that any single food product is a dietary essential.

Suppose we look at a powder which is to be added to milk to prepare a quick breakfast. The ad for the powder pictures a complete breakfast, with each food item referred to in the following copy: "Each glass delivers as much protein as two eggs, as much mineral nourishment as two strips of bacon, more energy than two slices of buttered toast, and even vitamin C—the orange juice vitamin."

Sounds good, and easy, too. Breakfast in a powder. But when we read the label, all we find as the main foods in the powder are nonfat dry milk and sugar; vitamins and flavorings are added. Now we look more closely at the ad copy. "Each glass" means the powder *plus* fresh milk. So let us check up. The protein in two large eggs in 13 grams; there are 8.5 grams in this much whole milk. The "mineral nourishment" in two strips of bacon consists mainly of calcium (2.6 milligrams of the 800 recommended daily) and iron (.53 mg. of the ten to 18 recommended). Looking at whole milk, we find 285 mg. of calcium in a glass and .1 mg. of iron. Thus the unimpressive mineral nourishment of bacon can be equaled by adding only .4 mg. of iron in the manufacture of the powder.

This breakfast product has "more energy" (calories) than two slices of buttered toast, meaning more than

260 calories, of which the fresh milk supplies 160. And of course milk has very little vitamin C, so the powder must incorporate some of the vitamin as an additive.

But minerals do not equal bacon; protein does not equal eggs; vitamin C does not equal orange juice. If we merely drank a glass of fresh milk, we would get everything heralded in the ad, with the exception of about 100 calories of fuel, about .4 mg. of iron and some vitamin C. The powder now seems less impressive.

On the other hand, if we ate the breakfast pictured in the ad, this is what we would get in terms of the key nutrients:

Energy (calories), 600; protein, 23.3 grams (a third of RDA for a man of medium size); fat, 37.8 grams; carbohydrate, 63.5 grams; calcium, 118.6 milligrams (about one-eighth of RDA); iron, 4.53 mg. (a third to a fourth of average RDA); vitamin A, 1620 I.U. (about 40 percent of RDA); thiamine, .48 mg. (at least a third of RDA); riboflavin, .4 mg. (at least a fourth of RDA); niacin, 3.3 mg. (about a fifth or more of RDA); and ascorbic acid, 93 mg. (much more than RDA). Note also that RDA is always much higher than the MDR, the term for nutrients usually used on packages.

In brief, what we have here is a good breakfast; with milk added, it is a really fine breakfast. And the quick-breakfast powder can hardly bring a glass of milk to nutritional equivalence with this meal. If we look and buy carelessly, we could drink the quick-breakfast drink and think we were getting something which we were not.

What more can you learn from labels?

By knowing something of food-level law, you can make a number of other judgments. Here are some label facts, based on federal label laws, which are also models for the several states:

1. The food is what it says it is. If the label says olive oil, it cannot be any other oil. And a label must be specific; it cannot say "syrup," but must identify itself better as maple syrup, corn syrup, a blend of cane and maple syrups, etc.

2. If the food is an imitation, it will admit so promptly and clearly, as "imitation bacon bits."
3. Ingredients must not mislead, so they are listed on the label in order of predominance. And if a product is a mixture of chicken and noodles, with just a little chicken, the label must make clear that you are buying mainly noodles.
4. The label tells the *net* contents. If the product is solid, or solid and liquid, the measure is by weight. If it is liquid, it is in volume. But *net* content is not necessarily all food. For packaging, shelf-life and processing purposes, many solid foods come in a liquid medium, which is generally part of the net weight. "Net" really means everything that is contained in the can, jar or package.
5. On some labels ingredients are not listed because the name of the food tells the ingredient story. These are "standard foods," for which a compositional identity has been established under Food and Drug laws. For example, strawberry jam must have a certain relationship of fruit to sugar, or it cannot be labeled as jam. Ketchup must have a certain quantity of tomatoes.

There are three kinds of food standards—for identity, quality and fill. Products that do not meet these standards, but use the names, can be seized and destroyed and those responsible be punished by fine or imprisonment.

The food industry cooperates in the making of standards, for they protect honest foodmakers against dishonest competition, which at one time used to make fruit spreads with very little fruit, a lot of water and pectin and artificial color and flavor, with a little grass seed tossed in to make the stuff taste like jam. These products were once high-volume items, as were other fakes.

At one time cheeses were often heavily weighted with excess water. Today, Cheddar cheese must have no less than a certain minimum of milk fat and no more than a certain maximum of moisture.

Moreover, a standard food may not contain any ingredient which is not included in the standard (for example, cocoa used to be filled out with cheap starch), unless the standard allows for optional ingredients. When optional ingredients are used, as, say, an addi-

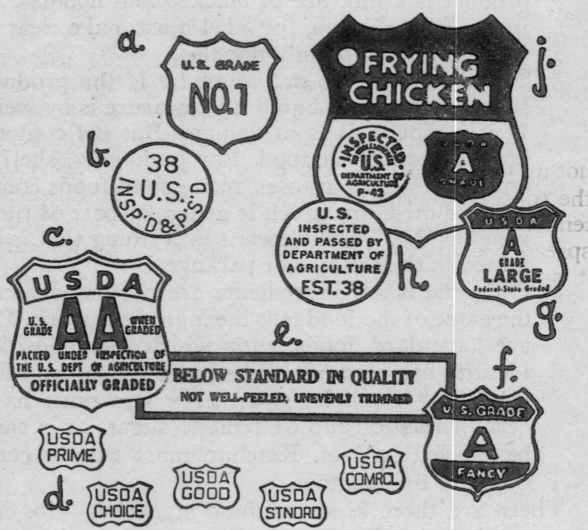

Do you recognize these government marks? (a) Seen on fresh fruits and vegetables, this indicates packing under the supervision of a U.S. government grader. It shows quality differences, but not nutritional differences. (b) Used on fresh and cured meat, showing inspection for health purposes of both the food and the packing plant. (c) Butter and Cheddar cheese grading mark. (d) Meat quality stamps. (e) A label showing that a food for which there is a standard cannot meet that standard, and the reason why; it is still good nutrition. (f) USDA grade mark for canned, frozen and dried fruits and vegetables, also used on jam, jelly, honey and a few similar items. (g) Egg grading mark. Note that both federal and state requirements are met. (h) Inspection mark for canned, frozen, dried or packaged meat and products, showing that the food is sanitary and that its label is approved by USDA as truthful and accurate. (j) A USDA poultry "wing tag." This shows three marks at once. First, it shows the age of the bird. Second (lower left), it shows the inspection mark for all poultry, fresh, frozen, canned or dried, indicating cleanliness and safety. Third (lower right) is the mark for quality, showing meatiness, for example.

tive to make noodles cook faster, such ingredients must be stated on the label.

Standards have been adopted for many foods, such as bread, rolls and buns, jams and jellies, salad dressing and mayonnaise, syrup, oils, macaroni products and many canned foods.

When quality standards for canned fruits and vegetables are not met, they must be labeled "Below Standard in Quality" followed by "Good Food—Not High Grade," or by a statement which tells why the food is not up to par, such as "Excessively Broken." Very often the contents miss a standard of appearance, ripeness or tenderness. For example, by law, cream-style corn can spread out just so far when dumped out of the can. If it spreads farther, it is too soupy, and substandard. "Stringless" canned green beans are allowed just one tough string per ounce. And there is continual laboratory checkup, as well as policing in the market.

What is meant by standard of fill of containers is fairly obvious. So are the standards for claiming enrichment, as of bread or flour. In some foods, a statement of addition, such as margarine with "vitamin A added," must have a required amount of the vitamin.

What grade and quality marks mean

Grading of food is not usually required by law, but is up to the processor. To have foods graded, a packer must meet certain standards of cleanliness and permit a government grader to make the decisions. There are things wrong with the system, and changes are being made, but the main thing is to know how to take advantage of what we have. Some grading is done under the U.S. Department of Agriculture, and some under state laws. The standards listed are federal, but are agreed with by most local authorities.

Eggs There are three grades—"AA" or "Fresh Fancy," "A" and "B." These appear in the USDA shield.

"AA" or "Fresh Fancy" eggs are produced under a strict quality-control program. When candled (held up to a light) they have little air space, well-centered yolk and thick white. When broken, they spread little and stand high.

"A" eggs cover a moderate area when broken, have a reasonably thick white and a high firm yolk. They are fine for all purposes. "B" eggs are lacking in appearance, but suited to cooking.

This is what egg sizes mean:

Size	Minimum weight per dozen
Jumbo	30 oz. (2.5 oz. per egg)
Extra large	27 oz. (2.25 oz. per egg)
Large	24 oz. (2 oz. per egg)
Medium	21 oz. (1.75 oz. per egg)
Small	18 oz. (1.5 oz. per egg)
Peewee	15 oz. (1.25 oz. per egg)

USDA counsels that if there is less than seven cents per dozen difference in price between neighboring sizes in the same grade, you get more for your money by buying the bigger ones.

Meats Over 80 percent of the meat in the nation's markets is federally inspected. For meat must be inspected if it crosses state lines. Once it is checked, it is stamped with a circle in which one finds the abbreviations, "U.S. INSP'D & P'S'D." This is an assurance of clean, wholesome meat. The mark is on each carcass, however, not each cut. You must ask the market manager if you do not see such a mark on the meat and you want to be assured that it has been inspected—which is important. State inspection is often good, too. The inspection question is an especially good one to ask about pork, since you will not find U.S. stamps of grade quality on pork.

Grading, which is done at the packer's cost and request, is essentially the same for beef, lamb and veal (calf). The grade mark appears in a purple U.S. shield, which you should see on the fat of each cut.

Luxury quality of beef, lamb and veal earns the grade "Prime." It is the most costly, tender, juicy and flavorful. The second grade is "Choice," which is a little less costly, tender, juicy and flavorful.

The third grade is "Good." Fairly tender, "Good" beef is a widely used, medium grade that does not have so much flavor and juiciness. Lamb is not awfully good at this grade, however, and not much is sold. "Good" veal is borderline at this point.

The next grading mark is "Standard" (usually young animals) and next down is "Commercial" (mostly from older animals). Moist-heat cooked, or tenderized, these lower grades can taste perfectly good. And actually, the nutritive value of some lower grades can be better, with less fat and more protein.

But the trick in all this is that packers and stores do not like to sell meat with the lower-grade labels. So commonly, they put their own grades on, such as "Super" or "Excellent."

Look out when you see such gradings. One consumer group collected some 75 different private gradings. Generally, if the meat can make "U.S. Prime" or "Choice," the store does not use its own meaningless grades.

Poultry If it crosses state lines, poultry is inspected and marked in the usual way, with the U.S. inspection circle. And you should be certain that poultry has had state or federal inspection. The inspection stamp appears on every inspected bird, usually on a wing tip or on the package, as does the grading mark.

Poultry grades are on U.S. shield marks, and they are only "A" or "B." You rarely see "B" grades in the market, though the grade does not mean lack of nutritive or sanitary qualities. Sellers usually decline to show a grade at all if the bird doesn't make "A"—or they use a private grading, such as "Premium." Ignore it. It is usually not meaningful.

The "A" grade on chickens, turkeys, geese, ducks and guinea hens refers only to meatiness, fleshiness and the quality of dressing-out. It does not say anything about tenderness, which is a function of age.

Age labeling is a bit tricky. Young chickens may be labeled as Broiler, Fryer, Roaster, Capon or Rock Cornish Game Hen. Young turkeys may be Fryer-Roaster, Young Hen or Tom. Young duck may be Broiler, Fryer or Roaster Duckling. Young geese or guinea are simply marked as such. Older birds, usable for baking, stewing, soups or salads, are equally nutritious—under labels such as Hen, Stewing Chicken, Fowl, Yearling Turkey, Old Turkey and Mature. "Mature" is a common label for older birds of other types.

Fruits and vegetables Fresh fruits and vegetables are easier for most people to judge than are meats, and do not carry disease. So there is not as much inspection or grading. But you may see crates marked "Packed Under Continuous Inspection of the U.S. Department of Agriculture," or "Packed by ——— Under Continuous Federal-State Inspection." So check crates when you can. Top grades are "U.S. Fancy" or "U.S. No. 1." Without government stamps, grades mean little.

We have seen that there are standards of quality in much canned and frozen fruit and vegetable packaging, which are musts, unlike inspection programs that are voluntary. Package labels are "Grade A" or "Fancy," "Grade B" or "Extra Standard," "Grade C" or "Standard." But on these labels nutritive quality is not the issue; the grading is for aesthetic quality. Knowing this, why pay for perfect shape and appearance if you want peas for making soup, for example? When grade labels appear, many Americans are suspicious of anything that does not sound absolutely tops in quality, but such suspicion can cheat you of good buys in processed produce.

Other grading labels Buy only "Grade A" milk, the only grade allowed in interstate commerce. Milk should also be pasteurized, for protection against disease. There is only one advantage of raw over pasteurized milk. The processing destroys some 20 percent of the ascorbic acid.

But, whatever faddists say, milk is not a good vitamin C source, and the loss of the vitamin in pasteurizing is only an insignificant two to five milligrams per glass of milk. Tuberculosis, and cattle diseases which can be transmitted to man by raw milk, *are* significant. True, the inspection of raw milk is usually quite careful. But the simple fact is, people do become ill from drinking raw milk. Doctors agree the risk is not worthwhile. Odd claims of all kinds are made by faddists for raw milk. Such claims indicate great health values in favor of it. But nutritionists are unaware of such merits. Government laboratories cannot find them.

Other dairy products, such as butter and cheese, are eligible for U.S. inspection and grading. "AA" is best quality butter, but "A" is almost as good. "B" is not much seen, and may have slight flavor flaws. Other USDA marks that are coming into wider use and are good indicators of quality are gradings like "Quality Approved" for butter or Cheddar cheese, for cottage and process cheeses and sour cream. "Extra Grade" is the USDA's best designation for nonfat dry milk.

Fish are also inspected sometimes, but not by USDA. Here the marking is USDI, for the Department of Interior.

One reason for listing all this material is to indicate that none of the official quality marks really tell much about nutritive value. Inspections are important for safety. Other government gradings are really made on an aesthetic basis.

Labels and ads tell us much more about nutrition when we look at *processed* foods. It is important nutritionally to study the label of a frozen main dish, for example, to see that water is the predominant ingredient, and that meat is only third. With some rough mental arithmetic, you may learn that there is not enough complete protein in the dish. Whatever a food label or ad says about "old-fashioned rich whatzis" or "made with AA creamery butter" or "blood-building" or "bone-making" or "hearty meal," the ingredients and their order may tell a thin nutritive story.

Great efforts are being made to develop new ideas for labeling and food identification which will tell the consumer more about what a product will do to support growth and life. But all efforts that the author has seen, or participated in, come down to one simple fact: if the consumer does not know about food values, and if he does not stop to look and think, he remains vulnerable to the faddist and the pitchman.

SECTION V

The Food Scientist In The Kitchen

CHAPTER 15

Preventing foodborne illness

Each year some two million Americans are afflicted with with a family of bacteria known as *salmonella*. For some people the result is a day or two of cramps, diarrhea and other familiar intestinal symptoms. But some of the rarer salmonella relatives are such deadly microbes as those that cause typhoid and paratyphoid fevers.

Salmonellosis, the illness which comes from being affected with such bacteria, is not the most common foodborne illness. That honor goes to *staphylococcal* (often called "staph") *poisoning*. And in sum, it and hundreds of other organisms are thought to account for some 10 million cases a year of illness from food.

Few such cases are reported—perhaps 20,000 a year of salmonellosis, for example. Most people made ill by food think they have "a bug," "a virus," "intestinal flu," or "indigestion." The discomfort goes away, and the misery is forgotten, but the more seriously afflicted do not forget so easily. And besides, the vast majority of such uncomfortable, wasted days are needless. So let us see what we can do to protect ourselves from foodborne illness—for most Americans seem to be unaware of some of the dangers and pointlessly concerned about matters which are not threatening.

We might begin with one simple but useful fact. By and large, those foodborne infections which can cause us trouble cannot be seen, smelled or tasted in food. And those microbes that produce the signs we sniff, look and taste for in food are usually fairly harmless. So to protect ourselves against foodborne illness requires more of intellectual than sensory vigilance. For most such infections are carried on eatables that our senses tell us are perfectly good.

The U.S. Public Health Service has launched a vigorous campaign to cut down the toll of foodborne illness. USPHS doctors say that while we cannot defend ourselves against all foodborne infections by personal care and hygiene, we can reduce our risk considerably with a little knowledge and effort.

How food becomes infected

Most of us think of microbes in a negative way and imagine we are getting rid of them with soap and water and smelly solutions. And when we think we are clean, and our food is clean, we try to seal out the microbes with underwear or shoes or plastic wrapping material, whichever is most appropriate.

But microbes are more plentiful and pervasive and tough than most of us suspect. Some exist 18 miles above the earth at the edge of space; others are found at the bottom of the sea, in bubbling hot springs, in polar ice or powerful acids. We are covered with microbes, inside and out. All of life and food, all of air and soil are replete with them. In fact, despite their tiny size—each is only a single cell, after all—microbes vastly outweigh man. One authority has calculated that the microbes of our planet have 25 times the weight of all animal life on land and sea.

So we can forget about trying to get rid of microbes. They are survival experts. Leave one alive and it becomes two in two or three hours at most, and usually in a fraction of that time. The consequence of this rapid doubling and redoubling is breathtaking. It has been said that if one cell of *E. coli* had enough food, in three days it could yield a mass of bacteria greater than the earth. And of course, in a matter of minutes, it would double again.

The key phrase here, of course, is *if one cell of E. coli had enough food.* What serves as food for microbes is astonishingly varied. Most can live on *our* food; some do so by living in us. And some that live in us give us back such things as vitamins or join in performing essential functions for us. In fact, microbes are an essential part of life processes on earth. And it is mainly the microbial failures that hurt us. For what successful microbe would destroy its host? So it is the rare microbe that is harmful.

Our first effort is not to allow our food to become a culture medium for harmful microbes, and to avoid eating large groups of them—or large amounts of the toxins some produce. The chief ways we can do this are: by not inoculating our food with such microorganisms, by rejecting food which has been handled so as to encourage microbial multiplication, by mechanical rather than chemical cleaning and by keeping our food in environments which are too hot or cold for microbial comfort. In a majority of cases, we can't actually kill harmful microbes without ruining our food.

Because microbes are *everywhere,* they enter food by endless routes. In a few cases we can see them, as in the case of molds, or smell them, as in sour milk. So of course we don't place a new loaf of bread against a moldy one, or allow drops of soured milk to get into fresh. But in most cases, we cannot perceive microbes. We must understand where they are likely to be. That is why you should not mix a meat loaf with your hands when you have a cut finger; there are probably *staphylococci* in the cut.

Staphylococci are thought to be the most common cause of food poisoning, with millions of cases a year. We do not want them in our food. It is not so much what the bacteria themselves will do to us. But as they eat and grow, they produce what is known as an *enterotoxin* (intestinal poison). The staph are easily killed by heat, but the toxin is not alive in the first place. It remains intact and can make us very ill.

About half of all humans are thought to carry staph at any given time. Even without cuts, you can infect food by handling yourself—touching hair is often a good way, for hair, even when seemingly clean, is a good home for bacteria—and then the food. And since there is so much staph around, you should not let that meat loaf stand, either before or after cooking, at a temperature which is not hot or cold. It is worse, by the way, to let food stand *after* cooking. For cooking breaks down protein and carbohydrate structures in such ways as to make nutrients more easily available to bacteria, so they can grow faster. Heat or cold, then, slow bacteria multiplication; moderate temperatures encourage it.

Health officials have found that certain foods, combinations of foods and certain conditions are most likely to create harmful cultures of microbes. Perhaps the best way to identify these foods and conditions is to face the practical decision, to eat or not to eat?

Which foods might make you ill?

Picture yourself in the kitchen, standing before the refrigerator, cupboard or breadbox. Try to judge which foods are safe and which are unsafe to eat under the conditions sketched below.

Milk and milk products

QUESTION: You want to use a ten-day-old carton of milk. It smells a little sour, but it is going into a recipe in which the taste would be covered up. Safe or unsafe?
ANSWER: Safe, if it has been pasteurized. Souring in dairy products is caused by *acidophilous* bacteria, which is not only harmless but desired in yogurt or sour cream. Butter is slightly different in this case. Rancid taste is a signal to discard it. For rancidity is a sign that butter fat has been decomposed.

Bread, rolls, cakes

QUESTION: You need bread for breakfast, but at the open end of your half loaf two pieces show spots of bluish mold. You can't see mold on the rest, but—safe or unsafe?
ANSWER: Safe. Even if you do get a little mold of the sort that blooms on baked goods, it won't hurt you. Cut off the mold you see and use the food.

Cheeses and jellies

QUESTION: There is mold on the surface. Safe to eat or not?

ANSWER: Again, remove the mold you can see and eat the food. If you do get a speck of the mold, it is harmless.

Cured bacon, ham and sausage

QUESTION: Bacon, ham and sausage will pick up mold spots, usually blackish or bluish. Safe or not safe?
ANSWER: Safe again. Just cut off the mold. Don't be afraid of eating some mold accidentally. But if the mold is extensive, cut well away from it.

QUESTION: You've been away for a month, and come home to find bacon left in the refrigerator. Safe or unsafe?
ANSWER: Theoretically, bacon can last up to eight weeks in the refrigerator (though ironically, only half that time in the freezer). The problem is that you cannot tell how long the bacon was refrigerated by the market before you bought it. It is really best to use cured meats in about a week. If ham is cooked, try to use it within five days.

In the freezer, cured ham and pork sausage should not be held more than two months, bacon less than a month, frankfurters less than three months.

Eggs, egg sauces and custards

QUESTION: You've had some eggs in the refrigerator for a month. You crack one to make a spicy omelet. It has a slightly off odor. You crack a second, and it has a little blood spot. Which, if either, is safe to eat?
ANSWER: Both eggs are safe, for eggs store well six months or more, and blood spots will not make you ill. However, we assume the shell is not cracked or broken, for any opening could allow microbes into this ideal culture medium.

QUESTION: Taking eggs from the carton, you notice some little dirt spots. You crack them into a bowl, since the shell is intact. Safe or unsafe?
ANSWER: Unsafe. Infected dirt on egg shells can cause

salmonella, and the cracking contaminates the egg. Since poultry is a common source of salmonella, it is wise to wash off eggs.

QUESTION: Two days before a dinner party, you make two small containers of quite eggy hollandaise sauce. One you refrigerated promptly. But, busy, you let one stand out, cooling, for a few hours. Are both safe?
ANSWER: Unsafe. Egg sauces are food-poisoning dynamite. Health officials recommend discarding them, after not more than 24 hours—even when they have been refrigerated immediately after cooking—and after two hours at room temperature. As a leftover, such sauces, or foods such as a potato salad with egg sauce, should go into the refrigerator *at once*. Such foods and sauces are considered dangerous when they have been at room temperature for two hours. On a warm day, at a picnic, the time is even less. Taste and appearance tell nothing about safety here.

QUESTION: You make a custard pie, leave it to cool, then put it in the refrigerator after three hours. Safe or unsafe?
ANSWER: Experts recommend discarding any custard which has stood at room temperature more than two hours. Custards should be refrigerated at once and not held over 48 hours.

Flour, macaroni, spaghetti, cereals, crackers, rice

QUESTION: You take some noodles or other grain food down from a warm shelf and find little black specks and insects. Is this food safe or unsafe to eat?
ANSWER: Perfectly safe. You could eat the insects, if you didn't mind. But you'll probably want to clean them out.

All acid foods (such as fruit juice, cooked fruit)

QUESTION: For a party, you have made a warm-up winter punch of fruit juices to which you will later add alcohol. But now you put it in the refrigerator in a decorative copper pitcher or bowl until party time. Safe or unsafe to drink?

ANSWER: Most unsafe. The reaction between the acids and the copper will produce a poison which can have very serious effects on those who drink it. The same is true of vessels made of sliver, silverplate-on-copper and of galvanized vessels (zinc-coated). Plastics, china, glass and other nonreactive materials make the safest acid containers.

QUESTION: You have put an opened can of grapefruit juice in the refrigerator and forgotten it for two days. The juice now seems to have a slightly metallic taste. Is it safe to drink?

ANSWER: Yes. The coating on the inside of the can will resist the acid in grapefruit and other acid foods. However, canned foods do not have long quality-survival time once they are opened; two or three days is about all you can count on in most cases. And juices are best-tasting and most nutritive when kept in covered containers.

Nonacid canned food (beans, meats, olives, etc.)

QUESTION: Someone has given you a gift of home-canned beans. You warm them up. They smell wonderful. Are they safe?

ANSWER: Maybe so, but maybe not. Eating home-canned, nonacid food can be a kind of poison roulette. The reason is a notorious bacterium, *Clostridium botulinum*. There are six varieties of this microbe, and four of them can be fatal to humans.

C. botulinum is a microbe commonly found in soil and water along with its spores, which produce a toxin as they grow. Actually, you can eat the spores and bacteria with impunity. But when they have been in food for some time, the toxin builds up in the food, and is deadly.

The bacterium needs two conditions to grow—the absence of air and a medium low in acid. Canned spaghetti sauce made with meat would *probably* be safe from botulinum because of the acidity of the tomato. But don't trust your own hunches when deciding what is safe, as which fruits are acid enough. Check with a reliable source, such as a health department or farm advisory service. Remember, in the first half of the century 89 percent of botulism incidents were due to home-canned foods. Since 1926, commercial canning has been responsible for very few incidents.

QUESTION: Suppose you open a home-canned, low-acid food and then boil it for 15 minutes. Is it safe?
ANSWER: Probably. *C. botulinum* is killed at 212 degrees (boiling) and its toxin is destroyed. But boiling must continue for *10 to 15 minutes.* The AMA reports one case of a woman who opened and tasted her home-canned beans, then, satisfied that there was no sign of infection, cooked and served them. They were infected. Her family was unscathed, for the cooking had destroyed the toxin. The woman died after eating only a small amount of toxin in the tasting.

QUESTION: A commercially canned container of low-acid food bulges or squirts when opened. However, there is no noticeable odor, such as is said to be associated with botulinum. Safe or unsafe?
ANSWER: Unsafe. A bulging can or a jar that squirts when it is opened does so because of accumulated gas, usually from decomposition caused by microbes. Botulinum can, but does not necessarily always, have this effect. Also, the odor of botulinum differs with each food and is sometimes barely detectable. As is usual with food contamination, taste and odor are rarely warnings of serious danger. The AMA points out: "Only about 50 percent of the botulism victims have lived to describe the 'suspicious odors.' "

While cooking does destroy toxins, this does not mean that foods which have been boiled before canning are safe. For to kill the spores (which will continue growth while canned) takes a temperature of 249 degrees for 10 to 15 minutes. Ordinary methods at home will not reach this temperature and hold it. A pressure canner must be used.

Few people realize that symptoms of botulism in humans can be very slow to appear. They may begin in a few hours, but sometimes may not start for several days, according to how much toxin is consumed. Symptoms are of the nervous system—fatigue and muscle weakness, then double vision, drooping eyelids, dilated pupils, dryness of mouth, swelling of tongue, difficulty in swallowing and speaking, and in fatal cases, respiratory failure. If you have eaten a food which may have contained botulinum and such symptoms appear, get help *at once.* Though there are antitoxins, they sometimes fail; the speed with which they are administered enhances their chance of working.

Pork

QUESTION: You have browned some pork chops which are about half an inch thick or less, then cooked them at a braising (low) temperature for 20 minutes. Are they safe?

ANSWER: Not really. In pan-cooking pork chops, an internal temperature of 160 degrees must be reached, so that after browning chops, about 40 minutes of braising is needed to kill the chief worrisome organism—*Trichinella spiralis,* the cause of *trichinosis.*

Trichinosis is a parasitic roundworm, which encysts itself in human muscles. Many cases are so mild as to go undiagnosed, but the infection is debilitating and can lead to chronic illness and death. Since most pork is cooked well, the danger is not terribly widespread, but it exists, and slips can happen.

Meat thermometers are urged for cooking pork. Oven temperatures of 325 to 350 degrees are recommended. So think carefully about slow-cooking recipes using lower heats, including those for ham. The thermometer should be placed with care, reaching the center of the cut and not touching bone, which conducts heat faster and deeper than the edible portions do.

QUESTION: You buy some loin pork roast and decide to freeze it. Thirty days later, you cook the roast, but because it is so solidly frozen, you are not sure that all the pink is gone when you serve it. Is it safe?

ANSWER: Yes. *T. spiralis* is killed by freezing, *but* the freezing must be completed, and at a low temperature. The AMA reports the time needed to freeze out possible trichinosis:

In a freezer at five degrees, a block of food up to six inches in any dimension needs 20 days. If the *diameter* of the block is between six and 27 inches, it needs 30 days.

If the freezer is at *minus* ten degrees, the smaller block should remain ten days, the larger 20 days.

If the freezer is at *minus* 20 degrees, the smaller block needs six days, the larger one 12.

If your freezer is not a "true" freezer, but a cold part of the refrigerator not insulated from the main compartment, it does not reach any of these low temperatures, but is probably around 30 degrees. Such freezing is inadequate for meat, and especially for killing harmful organisms. (One sign of inadequate freezing temperature is an inability to keep ice cream hard, or to harden it if it has gone soft.)

Meats

QUESTION: A roast you bought has been in the refrigerator for five days. It has no bad odor. The meat is just a little slippery to the touch. Is it safe to cook and eat it?

ANSWER: Yes. The U.S. Department of Agriculture recommends that raw meat in large pieces be kept between three and five days at most.

Stew meat, chopped or ground meat, variety meats

QUESTION: Raw hamburger has been in the refrigerator three days. Is it safe to freeze it and use it next weekend? It has no sign of bad odor or appearance.

ANSWER: Health authorities agree that *48 hours is the maximum safe storage time for ground meat,* unless it has been frozen immediately. The grinding of the meat breaks it down somewhat as cooking does, and also creates a larger surface area for microbes. During 48 hours' refrigeration, not enough contamination develops to be really harmful, but the wisest policy is to use ground meat the day you buy it. Do not let ground meat stand out of the refrigerator for two hours without discarding. The same rule applies to variety meats (heart, liver, etc.) and, though to a lesser extent, raw stew meat.

Cooked stews, ground-meat dishes, gravies, broths

QUESTION: You cooked a big meat loaf to keep on hand for lunches, but haven't used it up after four days. It tastes and looks and smells as good as ever. Safe or unsafe?

ANSWER: Unsafe. This does not mean that you are certain to become ill if you refrigerate ground-meat dishes, stews, gravies or broths longer than four days, but these foods are ideal for microbes. And *if* the meat was infected in the first place—for example, from the air during preparation—the microbes have kept growing during refrigeration. They are merely slowed, not killed. This is even true, in most cases, of freezing. So after 48 hours, the risk is there, and after 24 hours, it has begun.

In a stew, the larger the pieces of meat, the poorer the culture medium and the longer the time you have for safety. Some health officials suggest that stews may be kept 72 hours before infection becomes a good possibility.

Bear in mind that we are not speaking only of bacteria which produce toxins; we are also thinking of the whole spectrum of disease that can be transmitted by food—an enormous variety of illnesses. Often our bodies can deal perfectly well with a few "bugs," but when they are rapidly multiplied in a good culture medium, the onslaught overpowers our defenses. Furthermore, the incubation of the infection in our bodies, over a period of days or weeks, masks the source. It could, for example, be the butcher's sick child.

Such good culture foods should be refrigerated immediately after cooking. And they are a poor choice for lunchboxes, since they should not remain at room temperature for more than two hours. In fact, the temperature range from 45 degrees to 120 degrees is considered hazardous for any food with a food-poisoning potential; so food which is *just kept warm* is equally bad. (It must be *hot* to be safe.) And susceptible food kept merely *cool* is not safe. (It should be *cold.*)

Sauces and broths, having the most finely divided particles, have the shortest safe storage time. This leads to another warning. If you have cooked meat in a sauce, separate the two for storage. The meat can survive longer. The sauce should probably be discarded after 24 hours for absolute safety, and certainly after 48 hours.

Poultry, fish and shellfish

QUESTION: You buy some fresh-frozen poultry or fish, and let it stand on the cool kitchen sink for the afternoon to thaw before cooking. Safe or unsafe?

ANSWER: *Unsafe.* All fish, as well as all meat and poultry, should be thawed in the refrigerator, or put in a watertight bag or container and thawed for a time in *cold* water, or cooked frozen (the latter usually means cooking time is increased to one and a half times the normal). The reason is that the outside thaws first and can get quite warm before the inside thaws. The problem is most serious with fish and poultry, which are better culture media for bacteria than most meats, tending to be on a par with ground meats.

Because of their greater chance of bacterial infection, poultry, fish and shellfish should be used within 48 hours, and they should not remain at room temperature more than two hours.

QUESTION: You have a big, plump turkey for Thanksgiving. You want to slow-cook it for an early holiday dinner, so you stuff it the night before and refrigerate it at once. The next day you roast it thoroughly. Safe or unsafe?

ANSWER: *Unsafe.* The stuffing is a superb bacterial medium, especially if it picks up raw-meat juices while inside the bird. The same is true of stuffed-fish dishes. All must be cooked as soon as they are stuffed.

Even then, stuffing is treacherous. Few people watch its cooking temperature, so the stuffing may appear to be cooked at what are actually unsafe temperatures. If you cook a stuffed bird, the meat thermometer ought to be in the center of the stuffing—not just in the turkey meat—and the temperature should reach 165 degrees. However, this risks overcooking the turkey. Therefore, health officials recommend cooking birds without stuffing, and cooking the stuffing in a separate container. Both bird and stuffing will taste just as good.

Poultry and fish should be quick-cooled for storage. In the case of big birds, this is difficult unless the meat is removed from the carcass promptly. Experts urge removing the meat and making it into separate, meal-size packets. Then you can hold enough in the refrigerator for use within 48 hours and freeze the other packets for later use.

Fish, poultry and shellfish should be kept only a very short time in any kind of sauce. And in sauces or dressings, such as mayonnaise, they are especially poor bets for away-from-home lunches. You should think twice before taking chicken or tuna salad sandwiches on long, warm rides to picnics. You may, of course, do this 100 times without seeming to become ill—but beware the 101st. You may not even connect the sandwich with the two days of stomach upset that comes a week later.

Frozen poultry has become an American dietary commonplace, so it might be worth looking at some Department of Agriculture recommendations on *freezer* storage time:

	Storage time (months)
Uncooked chicken and turkey	12
Uncooked duck and goose	6
Uncooked giblets	3
Cooked poultry (slices or pieces) covered with broth or gravy	6
Cooked poultry not covered with broth or gravy	1
Cooked poultry dishes	6
Fried chicken	4
Poultry-meat sandwiches	1

To avoid the food poisoning which often derives from the thawing process, here is a USDA timetable for thawing poultry in the refrigerator:

	Thawing time
Chicken, 4 pounds or more	1–1½ days
Chicken, less than 4 pounds	12–16 hours
Goose, 4 to 14 pounds	1–2 days
Duck, 3 to 5 pounds	1–1½ days
Turkey, over 18 pounds	2–3 days
Turkey, less than 18 pounds	1–2 days
Cut-up turkey pieces	3–9 hours
Boneless turkey roasts	12–18 hours

Most of the health rules for fish and shellfish are much the same as those applied to small fowl, such as chicken.

Commercially frozen foods

QUESTION: You open a commercial frozen-food package to find that ice has accumulated at one side of the package, and that the food where there is no ice has darkened. Is this safe or unsafe?

ANSWER: The safety depends upon the kind of food. If it is meat, poultry or fish in sauce, it is especially risky. For these are the signs of food which has thawed in transit or in the market freezer. Don't taste. Return the package to the market, for even if it will not make you ill, it will certainly have lost quality.

Some general rules for safety in food preparation

- Always wash you hands before touching food.
- Be especially careful if you have touched any infection, especially a boil, which is probably full of staph.

- Do not allow a cut or infection on your hands to touch any food.
- Be sure to turn away coughs and sneezes while cooking.
- If you are ill, don't handle food.

No one seems to know who first said it, but almost all public-health people use the same slogan for questions concerning the possibility of foodborne illness:

When in doubt, throw it out.

CHAPTER 16

Getting the most out of our food

Some of the nutritive value of our food is lost before it ever reaches the dinner plate. How great that loss is, no one can say. But at every stage of handling food—from picking to shipping, storage to sales, preparing to cooking—there is a decline. Let us see what can be done to minimize it.

As we have seen, industry has the knowledge and special equipment to harvest and process food with a minimum of nutrient loss. But those who market our food have less information and more problems. And the average consumer has the least information and must deal with the most tricky possibilities of losing nutrients. So it is not surprising that when nutrients are lost from food, it is usually the consumer himself who loses them.

Some of the losses are minor. But there are ways we can wipe out half or more of some nutrients in foods—in the refrigerator, at the sink and on the kitchen stove. And often these nutrients are the very ones in short supply.

The problem is a significant one. In fact, the extensive loss of nutrients may invalidate much of our information on how well fed some people are. For the studies of how well Americans eat are based on a false assumption—which is that all food still has its full nutritive potential by the time it starts down our gullets.

Which nutrients are lost?

Not all food is subject to nutrient loss. Some reaches us almost perfectly intact. For example, almost the sole value of sugar is energy. And aside from burning sugar on the stove before we can burn it in our bodies, that energy value is not lost. Pure fats, such as shortenings and oils, are also almost indestructible in the kitchen, except for burning or turning rancid. On the other hand, suppose we cook broccoli in a fancy copper saucepan. Few of us know that the copper acts as a catalyst to break down fragile vitamin C. (This is true, of course, only for vessels in which copper comes in contact with the food, not for those in which copper is only a coating on the outside.)

Some common losses in food preparation are unimportant and even desirable. When we cut the fat from a steak, we lose a nutrient. But since the main value of that fat is as fuel—of which most Americans get too much—we benefit from the trimming. When more fat drips out of the meat as it broils, we again lose food value we can do without.

In charring our steak on the broiler, some of the amino acids on the outer edges are lost. But in a typical middle-class family, such a loss causes no deficiencies, since the steak eater probably gets twice the amino acids he needs anyway. So we can afford to be a little careless in the cooking, or to enjoy the luxury of leaving a little meat on the bone instead of gnawing it clean.

Plainly, in the average dietary, losses of fats, carbohydrates and proteins in the kitchen are nothing to worry about. That, of course, leaves the micronutrients—the vitamins and minerals. And it is only with vitamins that meaningful losses occur. Let us see what can be done to prevent them, and how to recognize and avoid the depletions that do occur in processing and marketing. For loss is inherent in some food processes, such as the dehydrating and reconstituting of potatoes, in which as much as 70 percent of the vitamin C can be destroyed. This does not mean that dehydrated potatoes are not good food. But nutritionists earnestly believe that in such unusual instances the consumer ought to know exactly what is missing from the expected normal value of the food, so that he can choose or reject it wisely.

How vitamin C is lost

It is generally agreed that vitamin C is the most fragile of all the nutrients. Vitamin C is susceptible to oxygen; when it combines with enough oxygen, it becomes useless to the body. Heat speeds up that process. So do alkaline substances, certain metals and even a special enzyme carried in the very foods which contain the most vitamin C.

This enzyme is the reason why we ought mentally to label vitamin C-rich fruits and vegetables "handle with care." For the enzyme does not seem to operate as long as the plant is left alone. But if we crush or cut C-rich food, the enzyme promptly becomes active. For this reason, C-rich foods should be handled as little as possible, and used quickly after handling or cooking. For example, don't cut up broccoli, green beans, cauliflower, or spinach leaves in the morning for quick cooking later in the day. (Once the enzyme has been activated, it is important not to give it time to work.) And mauling salad greens as little as you have to is not only good cooking; it is good nutrition, too.

The catalyst problem—the way in which certain metals help speed the oxidation of ascorbic acid—is especially great in the presence of heat. So commercial processors usually cook C-rich foods in stainless steel or aluminum. Copper and iron both have the catalytic effect, and so should not be used as vessels for these foods. Processors also handle C-rich foods *fast* when heat comes into the picture, and so should you. Don't cook them a minute longer than you must, and don't hold them on the stove after cooking.

As we saw earlier, processors can cook faster than the consumer can, and under more carefully controlled conditions, and so usually lose less C than you do in your own kitchen. Be sure to take advantage of this technology by following the directions on packages. In other words, don't recook canned foods which are already cooked; just heat them to eating temperature and serve right away.

Don't think of canned fruits and vegetables as having the vitamin content of fresh or frozen foods. Canned foods tend to be much lower in vitamin C, unless the label says extra C has been added or the food is quite acid, as grapefruit or orange juice. For example, a portion of cooked fresh or frozen peas has 16 milligrams of C; the same portion of canned peas has six. The difference is not always big enough to be important, however. Where it matters, you will see it spelled out in the food-composition table in Appendix A.

Your own cooking can reduce the vitamin C of a fresh or frozen food to the level of its canned counterpart. For example, by the time you have baked an apple, it will have just about the same C content as canned apple chunks or sauce, which implies a loss of about two-thirds of the C in fresh apples. So the difference between canned and fresh foods is usually felt most keenly when the fresh could be eaten raw. That is, it's too bad to eat canned peaches in summer when raw peaches, with twice the vitamin C, are available.

Since fresh and frozen foods have almost exactly the same vitamin C content, you should not feel guilty about using frozen strawberries when you don't want to bother with fresh. A two-thirds-cup serving of fresh berries has 59 milligrams of C. The same weight of frozen berries, sweetened, has only four or five milligram less—quite insignificant when you think that either serving will give you about all you need of this vitamin for the day, and that you are almost certainly getting more C from other sources.

Air is a major enemy of vitamin C, we've observed. This makes it a good idea to prepare C-rich foods *just* before you are going to use them, and to serve them at once. It also suggests that these foods should not be bought in large quantities. In most food, C fades fast, though refrigerating does slow down the loss. Even so, you will lose a lot of C by keeping cauliflower, for example, several days before cooking it, or by saving the cooked cauliflower and reheating it as a leftover.

Because of air's destructiveness to C-rich foods, home economists suggest storing such foods in plastic bags before cooking. This is also a reason that frozen-food packages direct you to pop the food right from the freezer into boiling water, rather than letting it sit out to thaw.

One C-preserving trick is to boil the cooking water for a minute or two before popping food into it. This drives some air out of the water. And C-rich foods should be cooked *covered,* not in an open pot.

Skins help to preserve vitamin C. So C-rich foods, such as potatoes, should be cooked in their skins. C is easily soluble in water; it tends to dissolve into the cooking liquid and disperse through it. Leaving skins on helps to prevent this.

The water hazard also suggests that such foods be cooked on a rack, in the steam rising from the boiling water. This method is especially desirable with leafy vegetables. Dry-cooking methods, such as baking rather than boiling a potato, can conserve much more ascorbic acid. If you must cook in water, use as little as possible. When cooking frozen foods, follow the directions about water quantity. Measure, don't guess; the processor has carefully experimented to learn how much water is needed.

As a final cooking rule, never add soda to foods rich in vitamin C. Being alkaline, soda destroys the vitamin.

Acid, on the other hand, is a preserver of vitamin C. So acid fruits and juices—such as orange, lemon and grapefruit—tend to hold their vitamin content, especially if they are kept cool, and are protected from air. When storing juices, it is a good idea to fill up the container, since a container half empty is one half full of air.

Fruit "drinks" do not have the same C-keeping qualities as genuine juices. Studies have shown that they gradually lose C on the market shelf, and still more when they are opened and kept in the refrigerator. So consume these promptly.

(It would be helpful, of course, if we had some way to tell how long solid and liquid foods have been in their containers. A consumer movement is under way at this writing to get processors to mark such dates on labels in plain English—it is sometimes on the label now, but in code—along with a statement about the shelf life the product can endure without losing nutritive value.)

To choose fresh foods which are more C-rich, simply look for the usual signs of quality. Food that is fully mature and free of bruises, cuts and tears will have more ascorbic acid.

How we lose B vitamins

Though the chemical properties of B vitamins are in many ways quite different from those of vitamin C, nutritionists find that much the same techniques of buying, preparing and storing foods rich in B vitamins are desirable to prevent nutrient losses. For example, B vitamins, like C vitamins, are water-soluble, so the same cooking techniques are recommended—very little water, as little cooking time as possible and serving promptly.

Our concern is chiefly with the "big three" of the B vitamins—thiamine, riboflavin and niacin. For, except in special cases, these are the only ones ever in short supply. The other B vitamins, in addition to being much more plentiful, are less easily harmed in food preparation. For example, boiling vegetables for up to 15 minutes can actually cause more active forms of folic acid to be freed, so that the cooked food has more folic acid activity than did the raw. The hardy pantothenic acid could be cooked at least two days, and sometimes four or five, before being destroyed. And B_6 survives except at temperatures high enough to insure sterilization.

But the "big three" B vitamins are more vulnerable. For example, the temperatures used for roasting meat can destroy half the vitamin B_1 (thiamine) the meat contains, and broiling temperatures can waste up to a third of the vitamin. One positive thing that can be said for the frying of meat is that it tends to prevent B_1 loss, holding it to perhaps a seventh of the original total.

Since the heat of boiling (212 degrees Fahrenheit) is much lower than that of meat cookery, boiling destroys very little thiamine in any food, unless the cooking is quite prolonged. But as in the case of vitamin C, the solubility of thiamine in water is great. This is why home economists suggest ways to consume the cooking liquid from B-rich foods, such as eating the sauce of a stew or pot roast.

The same problem of water-solubility accounts for some loss of B vitamins in canned vegetables that are packed in liquid. The vitamins are still in the liquid, but are thrown away unless the liquid is consumed with the vegetable or is used in a soup, stew or sauce.

Thiamine's sensitivity to *dry* heat results in some losses, especially from grains which are good sources of the vitamin. For example, long, dark toasting of bread makes a substantial inroad into its thiamine content. And a fraction of the vitamin content is lost from flours in the baking of the bread.

Riboflavin (vitamin B_2) is less susceptible to heat than thiamine. In fact, it is so heat-tough that it was first isolated by bringing foods to temperatures some 40 degrees higher than boiling, then holding them at this heat until all the thiamine was destroyed, but the riboflavin remained. Moist cooking, in fact, usually makes more riboflavin available from foods.

Riboflavin is also less soluble in water. For example, if the liquid is drained away from canned peas, the thiamine content drops from 1.8 to 0.8 milligrams, but the riboflavin goes from nine to five milligrams. In other words, about 60 percent of thiamine is lost through solubility, and about 40 percent of riboflavin.

But riboflavin has its own weakness. It is easily destroyed by light. And this fact establishes probably the most important guide for handling riboflavin-rich foods. For example, milk, a very important source of riboflavin, is packaged in cartons rather than bottles to protect the vitamin B_2.

Riboflavin's light sensitivity is great enough so that some can be lost just during the cooking process if the pot is not covered with a lid. A glass pitcher of milk sitting on the table through a meal will lose a fair amount of B_2. Dried legumes, an important source of the vitamin, may look decorative in glass jars in the kitchen, but their riboflavin is slowly being destroyed;

they should be in a dark refrigerator. Bread, rolls, cakes, and cookies should be in a light-proof container, such as a bread box or cookie jar; any of these items that has sat out all day in the light at the bakery is not as good food as that which comes in a bag or an opaque wrapper. (It is believed, however, that a dark crust also minimizes such losses, by keeping out light.) And it's best to buy and keep noodles and macaroni in light-proof containers.

Just how much riboflavin is lost to light? It is anyone's guess, but some suggestion of this loss can be imagined from one scientific test. Milk in a clear glass bottle was allowed to sit in sunlight for two hours—as on a doorstep. Then the riboflavin content was tested and was found to have declined substantially more than half.

Niacin is even tougher than riboflavin, and in practical terms, losses of this B vitamin need not worry us. For one thing, the reader may recall that the amino acid tryptophan can be used in place of niacin, and amino acids are very tough. But even without this safety factor, the ordinary storing and processing of food does not usually injure niacin. It even resists exposure to alkaline stuffs, such as soda, which will destroy thiamine and riboflavin.

Freezing is an excellent preservative for all three of the key B vitamins. So frozen foods generally show as high a B content as do fresh.

Losses of vitamins A and D

A and D vitamins are among the less perishable vitamins. In fact, though A has weak points, D is hardly lost at all in ordinary processing, handling and cooking. Since sunlight is an important factor in the *making* of D vitamins, heats in the cooking range scarcely affect the D group. And since they are not water-soluble, they do not leach away to cooking liquids.

Vitamin A and its precursors (such as carotene) also tend to be stable at cooking temperatures. And they, too, being insoluble in water, do not tend to be lost to cooking liquids. But A vitamins are unstable in two ways—they are sensitive to light, and they can be destroyed by oxidation.

The light-sensitivity of A is another reason for the opaque milk carton, or the colored-glass milk bottle. It is also the reason why *sun*-dried fruits, which in their plump state are good sources of A, are much lesser sources when we eat them. On the other hand, fruits dried by "artificial" methods lose little of the vitamin.

A-rich foods should be protected from light and air. Probably the simplest way to do this is to keep A-rich foods in the refrigerator.

No special precautions need to be taken for the other fat-soluble vitamins, E and K.

Practical tips on preserving vitamins

For the most part, animal products are protected from vitamin losses in storage by some of the same storage and handling methods used to prevent foodborne illness. Similarly, if such foods are not kept for periods of time that are unsafe, the nutritive losses will be unimportant. But other foods, particularly fruits and vegetables, can have lost food value when they are still perfectly safe to eat.

On the whole, vegetables are probably the most vulnerable losers of vitamins in the larder. Here are some storage pointers for vegetables, adapted from material prepared by Frances Cook for the University of California Agricultural Extension Service.

In storing leafy vegetables, remember that they should be kept in plastic bags or in a crisper at least two-thirds full. If the crisper is not that full, there is too much air for the greens, and for other vegetables, too. When preparing vegetables, you can avoid loss of vitamin C by the use of a very sharp knife or scissors to cut the leaves.

In cooking vegetables, be quick, use little water, and keep the cooking vessel covered. The water should be lightly salted in order to reach a higher temperature. Air should be removed by boiling for a minute or two, then

Key to "perishability"

Very high:	buy for immediate use
High:	may be stored for a few days
Moderate:	may be stored one to two weeks
Low:	may be stored two to six weeks
Very low:	may be stored two to three months

Vegetable	How to handle	Perishability
Asparagus	Wash. Break off tough parts. Refrigerate in crisper or plastic bag.	Very high
Beets, carrots, parsnips, radishes, rutabagas, turnips and other roots	Do not wash. Remove tops to prevent wilting. Refrigerate in crisper or plastic bag.	Moderate
Spinach, lettuce, salad greens, beet and other tops, green leafy vegetables	Wash. Drain well. Refrigerate in crisper or plastic bag.	High
Celery, head lettuce	Wash. Drain well. Refrigerate in crisper or plastic bag.	Moderate
Cabbage	Do not wash cabbage. Refrigerate in plastic bag.	Moderate
Broccoli, brussels sprouts, cauliflower, artichokes	Do not wash. Refrigerate in crisper or plastic bag.	High
Cucumbers, eggplant, okra, peppers, zucchini, and soft-skin squash, such as summer squash, segmented squash	Wash and dry. Refrigerate in plastic bag.	High
Green lima beans and peas	Do not wash. Leave in pods. Refrigerate in crisper or plastic bag.	Very high
Sweet potatoes, hard-rind squashes	Do not wash or refrigerate. Keep cool (about 60 degrees).	Low
Mushrooms	Do not wash. Refrigerate in plastic bag.	Very high

Vegetable	How to handle	Perishability
Dry onions	Do not wash or refrigerate. Keep cool but dry, with air circulating.	Low
Green onions, chives, leeks	Do not wash. Refrigerate in plastic bag.	High
Potatoes	Do not wash or refrigerate. Keep cool (55–60 degrees), dry, dark. Let air reach.	Very low
New potatoes	Do not wash or refrigerate. Keep cool (55–60 degrees), dry, dark. Let air reach.	Moderate
Snap and similar beans	Wash. Refrigerate in warmest part of refrigerator in plastic bag. Do not cut or break until ready to cook.	High
Sweet corn	Remove husks and silk. Refrigerate, unwashed, in plastic bag.	Very high
Ripe tomatoes	Refrigerate in crisper, unwashed. If not ripe, may be kept at room temperature out of direct sunlight.	High

the vegetables added and the heat lowered at once to gentle boiling when the water has returned to a boil.

Other than using a minimum amount of water, there are three basic ways to avoid the loss of vitamins in vegetable cookery. *Baking,* of course, is one, and can be applied not only to potatoes, but to squash, beets, carrots, parsnips and turnips. *Braising,* sometimes called panning or stir-frying, is another way. You put a little oil in a heavy pan to prevent sticking and burning. Just a touch of water, or the vegetables' own juices, makes steam, which does the cooking under a tight-fitting lid. Some of the vegetables for which braising is recommended are string beans, spinach, summer squash, asparagus, carrots, cabbage and other leafy vegetables. Simple *steaming,* using water in the bottom of a kettle with a perforated rack to keep the vegetables out of the water, is the third method.

Remember that canned vegetables need only be warmed to serving temperature, for they are already cooked. Serving canned vegetables, especially beans, peas, beets, asparagus and the like, cold in salads spares them another round of vitamin-destroying heat.

The soaking of dried beans before cooking can sap a good deal of vitamin value. Boil the beans for just two minutes, take them off the heat and let them stand for just an hour. This method is the equivalent of a 15-hour soaking.

How great are the losses when foods are *not* handled with nutrient preservation in mind? Here are examples to show the importance of good kitchen practices:

If cabbage is boiled with about four times as much water as cabbage in the pot, more than 50 percent of vitamin C is lost. If about a third as much water as cabbage is used—plenty to do the cooking—the C loss is only ten percent.

(There are limits to the usefulness of cutting down on cooking water, however. For example, some expensive "waterless" cookware is sold on the basis of nutrient conservation. With this cookware one uses only the water that remains from rinsing and the juice of the vegetable. But the USDA finds that not enough heat is transferred with so little moisture—heat is better conducted through water than through air—so the "waterless" cooking takes more time and thus does no better job of preserving nutrients.)

If cooked vegetables are held in the refrigerator, they lose about 25 percent of their vitamin C in 24 hours. And according to USDA research, cooked vegetables that are reheated after two or three days of refrigeration have lost from one-half to two-thirds of their C vitamins by the time they reach the dinner table.

Juicing is thought by many people to be a way to concentrate vitamins. But, in fact, squeezing out juices can lose food value. If you eat the sections of an orange, you get a fourth to a third more nutritive value.

Long storage of canned foods gradually destroys their vitamin content, but that destruction can be held down if you take seriously the label instructions to "store in a cool place." After a year of storage at 65 degrees only ten percent of vitamin C will be lost from most canned fruits and vegetables. But if the temperature is 80 degrees, as it may well be on a high kitchen shelf, the loss rises to 25 percent. Thiamine (B_1) is lost at about the same rate from fruits and vegetables at 65-degree storage, and at 80 degrees thiamine loss after a year goes up to 15 percent in canned fruit and 25 percent in canned vegetables.

Canned meats lose vitamins still faster. Pork luncheon meat is found by USDA to lose 20 percent of thiamine in three months, and about a third of B_1 in six months. This is at 70 degrees; higher temperature means still faster vitamin destruction.

Freezing is a much superior way to preserve nutrients. But there are a couple of important reservations. First, all freezer facts assume a temperature of zero degrees or less. If your refrigerator's freezer compartment stays just below the freezing temperature of water (32 degrees), use frozen foods immediately.

And even if you have a "zero" freezer, it is wise to use foods within a few months. In a year's frozen storage, beans, broccoli, cauliflower and spinach are found to lose from a third to three-fourths of vitamin C. Acid juices, such as orange juice, are the exception. They hold C well at 32 degrees for a year and more.

Another USDA hint for conserving nutrients includes a general rule for keeping fruits—hold them at room temperature until ripe and then refrigerate them, uncovered. When they have been cooked, canned or frozen, keep them covered.

Uncooked eggs do not lose vitamin content as long as they are kept cold. If you cook eggs in the shell, small B vitamin losses are avoided; cooked out of the shell, thiamine and riboflavin losses of up to 15 percent can occur. Dried egg stores well if kept cold and tightly covered; at room temperatures, however, dried egg loses a third of its vitamin A in six months and two-thirds in nine months.

In cooking all kinds of cereal products, there are two basic hazards—an overuse of water and overexposure to dry heat. For example, washing white rice before cooking is unnecessary and will cost you 25 percent of its thiamine. Substantial losses can also occur when grains are cooked in enough water so that some must be drained off at the end of cooking. The water should be fully absorbed by grains.

Don't bake cereal products beyond the stage of a light brown crust, or you pay a price in destroyed thiamine. And bake in containers which expose a minimal surface; for example, bake corn bread in a loaf instead of small sticks. Remember that the thicker the bread slice, and the less toasted, the more vitamin B_1 you get; a thin slice, toasted, can double the loss.

There is another aspect to the waste of nutrients, which is the common failure of consumers to choose the maximum food value for the dollars they spend. To make your money count nutritionally, you should know before you buy.

SECTION VI

The Doctor Looks At Eating And Illness

CHAPTER 17

What do you know about digestion and indigestion?

When doctors try to decide what forms of illness take the greatest toll of time and healthful effectiveness in America, they find it hard to choose between minor respiratory ailments, such as the common cold, and the miseries we speak of tactfully as "indigestion." Together, these two classes of illness account for most of the calls to the family doctor.

Most of us understand minor respiratory problems fairly well and can manage them. But the 30-odd feet of the digestive tract are as mysterious to the general public as was the surface of the moon before Apollo.

The price for that lack of knowledge is high. Many serious illnesses of the digestive tract go untreated. For example, there are as many as 30 million ulcer victims in the United States, and a majority are undetected and uncared for, a situation which can become life-threatening for some. The symptoms of intestinal cancer are so commonly neglected that it stands as the second worst killer among tumors.

So great is popular misunderstanding of digestion that the American Medical Association estimates some 100 million of us are addicted to laxatives that should usually be taken only on doctor's orders. Medical authorities agree that the public wastes hundreds of millions of dollars each year on needless digestive aids and remedies of all kinds, which often do no more than suppress the symptoms of treatable underlying ailments.

The fact is that what doctors call the "differential diagnosis" of intestinal illness is subtle and difficult. In many mild cases, the diagnosis is probably not that important; the problem will take care of itself in hours or days, if we do not worsen it with mistakes of home treatment, and perhaps even if we do. But in more serious matters, the sooner we stop alleviating symptoms and get professional help, the better off we will be. For in truth, the doctors now agree that the chief digestive villain is not infection, poisoning, allergy, heredity, or anything physical at all—but the emotional stress of everyday living.

The truth about the alimentary canal

Most of us think of the alimentary canal as an internal matter, an intimate pathway into the core of our bodies, into the world of cells and vital organs. But to scientists, the canal is a long tube passing *through* our bodies. Actually, it keeps crude foodstuffs away from the core processes of life, admitting for the most part only the key chemicals needed for energy and building materials.

From throat to anus the alimentary canal is continuous and made of essentially the same four layers of tissue. It changes shape and size here and there. But basically, it is a muscular, closed conveyor tube, undulating to move raw materials—our food—along its length while chemicals tear the foodstuffs apart and hundreds of millions of cells selectively take in the molecules demanded for living.

Because that raw material is crude and impure, the alimentary canal, which is in constant activity from birth, gets wear, tear and irritation. Yet in basic terms, there is really not a lot that we, or our doctors, can do for it. We can rest it. We can speed it up, and stimulate its chemical production. We can slow it down, and retard its chemistry. And if part of it gets into really bad shape, we can take out a piece and sew the cut ends back together. But most of what we laymen try to do to the canal, consciously, either has little effect or does more harm than good.

Perhaps the primary influence we have on the canal—

in a sense, even more than what we put into it—is through our feelings. It is as good an indicator of our emotions as are our faces. For example, doctors have watched the stomach—a wide, very muscular section of the canal—through wounds and special instruments. It flushes red with anger and becomes agitated with frustration; it sags limp with disappointment; it turns pale, gray and flaccid with depression and dismay. Yet, when we feel the untoward results within us, we are likely to say, "It must have been something I ate."

Let us look more closely at how the various parts of this emotion-sensitive canal work. And then let us see what is known about what goes wrong with it.

The alimentary canal has an outside shell of connective tissue. Within this is a layer of muscle. Inside the muscle is a thicker sleeve of connective tissue. And the inner-most layer is of mucous membranes, which produce secretions, the character of which changes along the passage. At intervals within the muscle layer, serving as closable gates between one segment of the canal and another, are *sphincters,* strong rings of muscle.

Before food enters, of course, it passes through the mouth, where digestion begins. Here chewing breaks up food into smaller particles, for better mixing with chemicals. At the same time, food is tasted.

(It is true that there are taste buds on the tongue. But they provide little information, receiving only four taste sensations: sweetness [at the tip of the tongue], saltiness [going back along the sides of the tongue], sourness [farther back along the sides], and bitterness [at the very back].

(The subtler kinds of tasting are really odor-recognition, which is done at the top of the nasal cavity. Here, in an area less than a quarter of an inch square, are tiny nerve endings which can detect tiny amounts of aromatic molecules in the air. As little as one molecule of a substance mixed with 30 million molecules of air or other gases can be identified by its size and shape, then quickly sorted out and labeled by the brain. If you wonder why dogs can smell things that we cannot, consider that their olfactory organs are about 40 times as large as ours.)

We could not taste anything if it were not moistened. The moisture comes from the salivary glands—the *parotid,* in front of the ear, the *sublingual,* under the tip of the tongue, and the *submandibular,* under the edge of the lower jaw. We are usually not aware of our salivary glands unless they become swollen in infections, such as mumps. Their main job is to produce the fluids of the mouth, and enzymes for the digestion of starch. This is why it is important to chew starchy foods well so as to give the salivary enzymes a chance to mix with them, to start breaking down the starches into double sugars. Poorly digested starches are one source of intestinal gas.

When we swallow, the broken-up food starts down the part of the canal called the *esophagus,* or, more popularly, the gullet. The trip, contrary to the belief of many, is a quick one. Liquids reach the stomach in a second. Solids enter in six to seven seconds. The salivary enzymes continue their work on the food for about 30 minutes in the stomach.

Food going down the esophagus does not simply drop, like laundry down a chute. It is pushed along by the motive pattern of the entire digestive system, known as *peristalsis.*

This phenomenon is possible because of two muscles in the canal. One set is circular; these muscles can squeeze inward, like fingers around a toothpaste tube. The other set consists of muscle fibers that run the length of the canal. The two sets alternately contract and relax. When the long fibers contract, the esophagus shortens. The effect is like pushing the top and bottom of a toothpaste tube together. Then the circular muscles squeeze again as the longitudinal muscles relax. This system works the food down the esophagus so efficiently that we can eat standing on our heads if we like.

The gland-filled lining of the esophagus, the *mucosa,* turns out a mucus which greases the way for the food, letting it slide easily. But once the food goes through the gateway into the stomach, other kinds of glands appear in the lining. These secrete *hydrochloric acid*—the same powerful acid which is strong enough to burn our skin and can be used to dissolve cement and similar compounds.

Here we may challenge some common beliefs about acid and the stomach. The stomach acid has to be strong enough to tear down meat—animal muscle. Without this acid in the stomach, we would starve. So unless you have a chronic illness, it is pointless to worry about acid in food upsetting you. And if you have such a chronic illness, you are badly advised to treat it yourself with advertised pills and potions designed to "fight acid stomach." We will soon explain about acidity and indigestion. But let us first watch the stomach in operation, with a third set of muscles. These muscles help the stomach squeeze and writhe to churn up food with the acid—and with enzymes produced by the stomach's glandular lining.

When the stomach is empty, the bag virtually closes. And despite all the talk to the contrary, stomachs do not stretch or shrink very much with one's dietary habits. A stomach will hold about two quarts of food and drink, when filled out, and no more.

Food spends an average of three hours in the stomach, being kneaded and mixed. It does not leave until it has reached a liquid or semi-liquid state known as *chyme*.

At the nether end of the stomach's hook shape is the exit from the organ, the *pylorus*. Here is another muscle-ring, which won't let very big particles through. Fluids squirt right on out. Carbohydrates, being rather easily divided, follow, then protein foods. Last to get through are the fats, which need the most working over, and whose presence always slows down the squeezing and twisting of the stomach, which is why fatty foods "stay with you" longer (one reason why the usually low-fat Oriental foods seem to leave you hungry more quickly).

Though most liquid foods escape from the stomach fast, milk does not. The reason is a stomach enzyme called *rennin.* It changes milk protein into a gel, which, being insoluble, cannot leave the stomach until *pepsin,* an enzyme which breaks down proteins, has had a chance to start taking the milk protein apart. So the milk stays awhile, but it does not "coat" the stomach, as many people think.

Food—now chyme—is squeezed out of the stomach in spurts by waves of peristalsis (the toothpaste-tube effect). These spurts land chyme in the next section of the canal, the *duodenum.* About nine or ten inches long, this narrow tube is a busy chemical crossroads. Here *bile* pours into the chyme. This brownish digestive fluid, made by the liver, contains bile salts, which have the effect of breaking up fats into small droplets. These droplets stay nicely dispersed, giving the bile and pancreatic juices a chance to work on them. The bile has other special digestive functions, as do juices from other small glands located in the duodenum. Also joining the secretory flow is juice from the pancreas, which contains enzymes for attacking fats, proteins and carbohydrates.

All of these juices are alkaline. And when things go well, their alkalinity neutralizes the acid chyme from the stomach. In fact, from this point on, digestion takes place in an alkaline medium.

The duodenum is really just the first part of the *small intestine.* About 20 feet long, looking a little like a length of rope crushed into a box, the small intestine is where most of digestion takes place. The small intestine is lined with tens of millions of *villi,* which are little projections densely packed together like the pile on a rug.

There are glands at the base of each villus, and these secrete still more alkaline digestive juices. The villi keep moving, waving back and forth and also contracting and expanding in length, helping to keep up a ceaseless mixing of chyme and enzyme-rich juices.

Villi are covered with absorptive cells that pick up the raw materials needed by all cells—the amino acids, sugars, fatty acids and the like. The villi's movement keeps circulating these needed food molecules over the walls of the cells that then take them into the body. The molecules are separated as they enter the villi. Aminos and sugars are diverted to the liver. Fat products go into the main blood circulation, a fact of major importance in the question of fats and heart disease.

Some salts and water are picked up in the small intestine, but more are taken up from the *large intestine.* This wider tube, about five feet long, is entered from the small intestine by way of a valve, which keeps the chyme—now largely waste and water—from backing up into the small intestine again. This backing up could happen because the large intestine begins with a steep climb, all the way from the area of your appendix up to the bottom of the ribs. It then makes a sharp turn, crosses the body, and finally descends in a sharp curve which ends at the rectum and anus.

The large intestine is a simple organ, with no villi and few of the folds which characterize the small intestine. What remains of the chyme moves through it very slowly. Whereas passage through the 20 feet of small intestine takes no more than ten hours, the five feet of large intestine are traveled about a fourth as fast, in about 13 hours.

The chyme has now had the vast majority of its nutrient value removed. It is largely waste, and begins to be considered fecal matter. It is compacted in the large intestine, gives up most of its water, and waits some hours to be discharged.

Only a minor part of the feces consists of undigested food and indigestible foods (such as cellulose). Most of the fecal bulk is made up of digestive secretions, bacteria, and cells shed from the intestinal lining. The feces are still formed, for example, during starvation, and its composition does not greatly change.

This thumbnail sketch of the digestive system is the backdrop against which the vicissitudes of indigestion are played. Let us try putting some different foods into the system to see what kinds of trouble arise.

Why food disagrees with you

Imagine you are a houseguest of an eccentric hos At the breakfast table you are served a glass of h orange juice and a cup of cold coffee and tea with sa added. The main course is a chocolate doughnut smotl ered with shrimp and clams in a little peanut-butt sauce, chopped chicken fat and marshmallows, and garnish of liverwurst.

Automatic indigestion? Quite possibly. But not b cause of the food, the method of preparation, or you digestion. If this perfectly good breakfast makes yo ill, it is only because you *think* it will. There is no othe reason why it should trouble you.

Let us analyze the meal a bit. Hot orange juice migl put off some people, but merely because it breaks th habitual pattern. In terms of the way digestion operate whether you eat a food hot or cold makes little diffe ence. Food is all essentially the same temperature by th time it reaches the stomach.

Then there is the cold coffee and tea with salt. A odd mixture of flavors—one which meets neither coffee expectation nor a tea expectation in the brai But the drink is only flavored water, and again, th temperature is of no concern to the alimentary cana The salt does no harm. After all, you usually salt you egg and eat it with your breakfast coffee or tea.

Now the main dish. In epicurean terms, the mixtur seems unimaginably bad because again, it takes all th foods out of context. But the shrimp and clams are see by the body mainly as protein to be treated no differ ently from bacon. In fact, every ingredient in the mai dish, while perhaps not very tasty, is perfectly edibl and digestible. To save lengthy explanation, let us con sider a basic tenet of eating which is propounded by th AMA's Council on Foods and Nutrition: *"Any tw foods that may be eaten separately may also be eate together."*

So it has never been the lobster followed by ice crean

or dessert that made you feel terrible. Contrary to popular belief, a cocktail made of Scotch, gin, bourbon, vermouth, wine and Irish whiskey would *not* make you ill. Combinations of liquors do not even make you drunker. For intoxication is solely a matter of the total amount of alcohol one consumes in any given setting or physical state. And distilled liquors are usually all about the same in their percentage of alcohol, about 40 to 45 percent.

Carrying scientific fact just a little further, no food is bad for a healthy person unless it is toxic (as a toadstool), infected (as with virus material), or is eaten too fast or in too great a quantity. So there is nothing wrong with our eccentric breakfast. Also, it would not matter whether this mess were served for breakfast, lunch or dinner. The stomach is usually largely emptied for any meal. And it does not know how to tell time.

In general, it may be said that when the healthy person is made ill by clean, nontoxic food, it is not the food that is at fault, but the emotional response of the eater to the food or to his life situation.

The doctor looks at the burp

Most of us believe that one of the first signs of stomach trouble is the burp, the bubble of gas that pops out of the stomach, rises to the troat and escapes—hopefully with a minimum of sound. We also know in a vague way that sometimes the burp is not really bad; after all, we burp babies after every meal. We become concerned when one or two burps don't seem to relieve the distended feeling of the stomach or when the eructations (to use the more elegant word) continue.

Many of the myriad chemical reactions taking place in the stomach during digestion produce gas products. The simplest, and one of the best known such reactions, is what happens when a carbonated beverage (chemically alkaline) runs into the acid climate of the stomach. If you want to see the principle in action, drop a little vinegar into a little soda pop and watch the bubbling and fizzing. The bubbles produced are like those which accumulate in the top of the stomach and finally build enough pressure to pop upward to the throat as a burp. Such gas forms with every meal, varying only in quantity. The old Chinese took it as a sign of politeness to maximize and vocalize the post-prandial bubble in order to show satisfaction.

But what if there are a number of bubbles? What if they escape before or long after a meal? Does this mean we should hurry for medication, or that something has disagreed with us?

Probably neither. Most digestive specialists agree that the primary cause of chronic or excessive burping is simply *aerophagia,* literally, air-eating. We are made so that it is almost impossible not to swallow a little air during meals. But aside from meal time, some saliva continually enters the mouth, and nasal secretions normally move slowly from the tip of the nose to the throat. All day long, usually unaware, we swallow and quite normally, we take in a little air with the swallows.

But aerophagia is also a common nervous habit. When we are nervous, we may salivate more—though we can also have an opposite, dry-mouth reaction—and so we swallow more. We may also swallow as a habit, nervous or not, though we have little or nothing to swallow except air. The gas may pop back up as a burp, or it may descend into the intestine and be emitted from the colon in a more unpleasant and embarassing form. (Some gas is also made in the intestines.) The habit can produce conditions which feel like chronic indigestion, a sense of distention of the stomach, possibly with pain, and feelings of fullness and discomfort in the abdomen.

Less often, excessive or chronic burping can be the result of faulty conditions in the stomach, or of reactions to spoiled food, which can produce more gas. Some experts also say that meals high in carbohydrate tend to have more gas-producing chemical reactions, but these are not harmful.

If it is a *physical* condition that leads to burping, often accompanied by "heartburn" (a burny sensation of the left side of the rib cage), the problem is usually too complex for the layman to diagnose, let alone prescribe a cure.

About "hard to digest" foods

Most of us feel that some foods are harder to digest than others. But we have difficulty telling why. The truth is that a healthy stomach and intestine can digest almost any food, but at different speeds. Foods that are *slowly* digested are those we think of as hard to digest. Sometimes this slowness of digestion is attributable to the food itself, but usually we ourselves are to blame.

For example, let us recall the way the pyloric sphincter muscle—at the nether end of the stomach—holds back larger pieces of food. If we gulp down big food lumps without much chewing, it will take longer for the churning, the acid and the enzymes of the stomach to reduce those lumps to a size that can escape the stomach into the duodenum. There is a physical logjam.

The adult stomach can hold about two quarts of food and liquid at any given time. (Ignore the tale about stomachs shrinking when we eat less and stretching large when we eat more. They stay about the same size.) Think of the stomach as something like a rubber hot water bottle with an extra small opening. Empty, its sides fall together. When we put food into it, we can cram in just so much before the walls begin to stretch. We feel that stretching as distention.

When we cram our stomachs with ill-chewed food lumps, little can escape except liquids. Soon there is very little room left at the top of the stomach and we have a feeling of needing to belch. Fatty foods also stay in the stomach a long time. And they tend to slow down the motility (activeness) of the stomach. So do food lumps that are coated with fat (poorly chewed fried potatoes) and protein foods that have been made phy ically tough by poor or excessive cooking.

If we are tired when we eat, overly hungry, excite or depressed, we tend not to chew well to break up th big lumps. And we do not get much of the salivary en zymes mixed with the carbohydrate, so that starche stay intact.

Obviously, in such situations no medication, food c beverage is going to help matters very much. Anythin we add to the logjam will probably only make thing worse. And we can hardly blame the food itself.

In this distress, we may leave the table and go fo a walk, which has the primary benefit of stopping u from eating. It has the secondary benefit of getting u out of a possibly cramped sitting position which put external pressure on the stomach and intestines. An finally, the activity of abdominal muscles in walkin may assist the squeezing actions of the digestive trac and help ease our feelings of tension.

But no matter what we do, for a time we are likel to be uncomfortable, and the best we can do is to leav the problem alone and be patient. In this state heartbur may also occur, to add to the fullness and gas.

It is hard to define heartburn and upset digestio with scientific exactitude. For example, the victim ma feel pain anywhere from his lower abdomen to his uppe chest, or even in his back and shoulders. The sensatio of nausea is particularly difficult to locate. Have yo ever tried to think exactly *where* you felt it? Most ex perts agree that nausea is felt first of all in the brain then in the stomach and intestine. Often one feels nau sea when the duodenum closes down and stomach con tractions cease. This closing off of the open pathway o digestion paves the way for *antiperistalsis,* a revers wave of contractions which tends to push the foo back up the way it came.

When this reverse wave occurs severely, we get vom iting. But when it happens more mildly, we may get jus a slight regurgitation from the stomach back up int the esophagus. When this splashes acid stomach juices upward, we get a burning feeling for the simple reason that the acid does burn. This burning, and the feeling of a distended stomach, are what many people seek to relieve with advertised "antacids."

Some facts and fictions about acid

We have seen that the normal state of the stomach is acid, and that the acid is quite powerful. A special mucus secreted by glands in the stomach keeps it from being digested by the acid and the protein-breaking enzymes. But the esophagus above the stomach and duodenum just below are not so well protected.

So when things go wrong, in such a way that more acid is produced in the stomach than is needed to break down the food passing through, rather undiluted acid gets splashed up or down or both onto vulnerable tissue. Alkaline substances can neutralize the acid and give temporary relief. This relief is what keeps drugstore nostrums selling.

Some people consistently produce more stomach acid than others. One large group produces about double the normal amount of acid; these people tend to get ulcers, which are craters of digested tissue in the duodenum (mainly), the stomach itself (more rarely), or in the esophagus (still more rarely). This acid-ulcer tendency appears to run in families. But many doctors who treat the ailments believe that what is "inherited" may not be so much a physical abnormality as an attitude and style of reaction toward life and stress—one in which anger and aggression are turned inward on the belly and the stomach gets red, active and acid.

Approximately one in seven people is acid-ulcer prone. And the statistics have changed since 1900. Before then, ulcers were mainly a female disorder, and mainly in the stomach itself. Today, ulcers are primarily a problem for men, by a wide margin, and are usually found in the duodenum. Why? No one knows, but cultural changes are suspected to be the reason. Some psychologists speak of a lesser need among women of today to repress their emotions.

The point, for our purposes, is that if you are chronically troubled by signs of excess stomach acid, you should not ignore the discomfort or treat it yourself. Regular use of alkalizers sold over-the-counter is roundly condemned by the nation's doctors, on the grounds that such practices frequently cover up serious illness and delay needed treatment.

Acid is generated in the stomach by other psychic factors, too. The thought of food, the smell and certainly the taste trigger the preparation of juices to digest it in the stomach. Thus long delay in getting a meal can put quite a lot of acid into the stomach with nothing for it to work on, especially if the person is anxious about his food or about becoming weak or ill by the waiting. This generally does not happen, however, if the hungry individual does not get emotionally upset. So if food is delayed or if it seems strange or unpleasant in an anxiety-promoting way (say, badly prepared in an expensive restaurant), try not to worry about it.

The idea that certain foods physically disagree with you as an individual is probably wrong, unless your digestive tract has already been damaged. There are allergies to food, with digestive reactions, but these are usually quite rare. The so-called disagreement is probably conditioned by some experience in one's past. For example, if you ate a whole lobster at the age of seven and felt very uncomfortable afterwards, you might go through life responding to lobster as being a food that does not "agree" with you.

On the other hand, if you must always watch your diet (avoiding coffee, wine, spices, pickles) to prevent upsets, you may be treating a basic disorder wrongly—suppressing signs with diet. If you cannot eat normally let your doctor find the reason. For example, in some studies when stomach X-rays were taken routinely about half of all the ulcers that turned up were "silent." That is, the patients were not aware that they had ulcers.

and the doctors could not tell they were there in a careful physical exam. In fact, in one such study the patients were themselves doctors.

Ulcers can be dangerous. Some can even be malignant. And there are dozens of other potentially crippling disorders which can masquerade as "sensitive stomach" or a "tendency to indigestion." Often these cases have gone untreated for years because the patient kept himself on a narrow, bland dietary and used patent medicines to ease the symptoms. So don't accept the fact that you "can't eat the way you used to," or that you "have to watch what you eat," unless you have undergone a doctor's examination. The same warning is given to those who suffer with symptoms much lower in the digestive tract.

About constipation and diarrhea

Down in the *colon,* the five feet of large intestine just before the end of the alimentary canal, there are continual, slow, kneading contractions, helping to concentrate the fecal matter and to take out the last of the water, salts and vitamins. But more or less regularly, this leisurely pattern of motion is replaced by a powerful set of waves known as *mass peristalsis.*

When these waves occur, a series of muscular reactions accompanies them. At the same time the *rectum,* the last five inches of the colon, is usually empty. The mass contraction pushes feces into the rectum, and the resulting distention triggers the defecation reflex. The muscles of the abdominal wall contract, and the last ring-like muscle of the alimentary canal, that of the *anus,* relaxes. The result, of course, is a bowel movement.

Unless we wish this not to happen. If so, we voluntarily clamp the anus tight and begin a pattern of shallow breathing until the rectum accommodates to the mass. We then get no more signals until the next mass peristaltic wave, which may come in a few minutes or a few hours.

This blocking of the normal reflex is thought to be the most common cause of constipation, unless there is some serious disorder that blocks the intestines, such as irritations in the rectum or anus that make defecation painful (hemorrhoids, fissures, and the like). In the main, however, the chronically constipated person has apparently learned to break the defecation reflex. (The psychological reasons for doing this take books to explain, so we will pass them by here.) And such willful breaking of the reflex makes matters worse. For as the feces remain overlong in the colon and rectum, more and more water is extracted from them, and they become hard and dry—perhaps to the point of impaction. Thus they are harder and more irritating to pass.

A common American response to habitual constipation is to take a laxative, or to eat coarse, fibrous foods that stimulate peristalsis. In this way, the intestines of the person who blocks the defecation reflex (usually unconsciously), and then uses laxatives or diet to make the urge and the peristalsis stronger, are caught in a vicious cycle. The intestines become dependent upon artificial stimulation and will not function properly without it. This is often spoken of as laxative addiction.

Chronic constipation, or occasional constipation, is often explained by what the patient has eaten. It is true that some foods, through their coarseness or their chemical properties, tend to stimulate the intestines. And it is true that others, such as low-fiber foods, tend to slow intestinal motility. But an ordinary mixed diet is not usually constipating—or the reverse.

There is a popular belief that a daily bowel movement is essential to health—a belief so strong that many people feel awful if they miss a day. Medicine says there is usually nothing to worry about if one is "irregular." If there is a serious cause—which is possible when there is a change in bowel habits that lasts two weeks—one should consult a doctor, instead of relying on laxatives or stimulating foods. For these may only mask a warning sign that is an important one, as may foods or patent medicines to reduce diarrhea.

Don't "poisons" escape from the feces into the body if the waste matter is held more than a day? This old belief is false. There are no such poisons in the colon. The bacteria there are usually harmless and even helpful, as in the making of vitamin K. Furthermore, the myth of exchanging evil bacteria in the colon for lovable ones, through yogurt and other fermented products, is a leftover from some misguided doctors of the 19th century—sadly still cherished among faddists today.

Constipation, says an AMA publication, "should be a rare symptom because the bowel regulates itself, if given a chance, through proper diet, sufficient fluids, exercise and good habits of elimination. Because of a false idea that regularity requires daily bowel action, many persons suffer from artificial constipation induced by laxatives."

Chronic constipation and laxative-dependency can be cleared up easily with the help of your doctor. Any chronic malfunction, such as this one, deserves professional attention.

As common as constipation is chronic diarrhea, that is, frequent, loose and watery stools. Diarrhea is most often associated with a condition doctors describe as "irritable colon" or "irritable gut." As defined by one textbook of medicine—that of Beeson and McDermott—irritable colon "signifies a variety of disturbances of colonic function which accompany emotional tension and which participate in the general bodily adaptation to non-specific stress." Diarrhea, the text continues, makes up about half of all digestive illness and *by itself ranks with the common cold.* Moreover, "It is recognized that disturbances of similar nature, but lesser degree or duration, occur in a large majority of healthy persons under emotional tension, as in preparing for bar examinations, in anticipation of marriage, or in leaving home for military service."

So again, it is hard to blame something you ate for

diarrhea, unless you have had a binge of overeating or overdrinking, or have eaten unclean food.

There is often a real relationship between the disturbances of the upper digestive tract and what goes on in the colon. For one thing, emotions which speed up the physical and acid activity of the stomach can also speed up the motility of the intestines. Food poorly digested in the stomach can in turn stimulate the intestine, as can acid splashed into the duodenum. And emotional states which slow the activity of the stomach may also slow down the intestines, contributing to constipation.

Physicians also point out that diarrhea empties the intestines rapidly. Then there is a fairly long pause as food starts down the quieted digestive tract—food often chosen for its bland, soft and nonstimulating qualities. The reaction may be a slowed-down motility with resulting constipation. This in turn may be treated with laxatives that overspeed motility and result in diarrhea, and so on.

When to call the doctor

Occasional gas, heartburn, diarrhea or constipation are so common as to be relatively normal. Even when the cause is not emotional—and remember that we often do not know that we are under emotional stress—there is little significance unless the discomfort persists or is chronic. Foodborne illness being a commonplace, we may all expect an attack now and then, especially if we eat out a lot.

We should rely on common sense to tell us whether such attacks are caused by emotions, by a toxin or by an infection. For example, in food poisoning or infection there is a natural body reaction to get rid of the irritant; the body may dump food by vomiting or diarrhea. But it does not take a great deal of vomiting or diarrhea to get rid of the food that caused the problem. Though we would not want to stop the dumping of food when such action is protective—perhaps even against a digestive state that is not capable of handling a meal just then—there are limits to how long such reactions are useful. They do become harmful. In a matter of hours, vomiting and/or diarrhea can dehydrate the body and rob it of essential salts.

It is important to replace the water, sodium and potassium. The abdominal cramps which follow soon after such an onslaught, and which can continue for days, are often caused by such depletion. So fluid should be drunk as soon as possible. And over-the-counter medicines to "coat the stomach" or to slow down intestinal motility will usually be of little value. In fact, they can hide serious warnings.

Liquids that can be salted, such as meat or chicken broth, should be taken soon. Milk, perfectly low-fat, can provide proteins and replace lost potassium. Rice is one of the first solid foods prescribed, and so are bananas.

When vomiting or diarrhea continue until they cause weakness, or there is much pain, by all means telephone the doctor. Often he can ask a few question and give short-term instructions. Do not count on being able to interpret the location of the problem from the sensations of pain. Even appendicitis often sends its pain away from the lower right-hand corner of the abdomen, where one would expect to find it.

Continuing changes in digestion that are uncomfortable, or changes in bowel habits, should be checked by the doctor within two weeks. Chronically recurring changes should also be checked.

Don't be insulted if the doctor suggests that stress or your emotional style is the true root of the problem. And don't be alarmed if he wants to treat the emotional problem or have it treated by a specialist.

Even though the cause of digestive difficulties is very often emotional, this does not mean that what is happening in your stomach or intestines is imaginary. The discomfort and possible damage are very real. The doctor knows this and is not accusing you of hypochondria. He merely wants to treat the true underlying cause, rather than deal with only the symptoms. He has ways to eliminate the possibility of physical causes first. And he can recognize some patterns that are typical of emotionally caused physical illness, such as recent *loss*—of an important person, money, position or whatever else is significant to you.

A basic principle for handling digestive problems is this: if you insist on managing the difficulty yourself, you will care for the digestive tract best by doing as little as possible. Self-treatment here is only for symptoms, not causes. Generally speaking, if a digestive problem requires treatment, it will take medical knowledge and medication that requires a prescription.

CHAPTER 18

Your food and your heart

For at least a dozen years the controversy had boiled in laboratories and conference rooms, in advertising and the press. Finally, in 1964, the American Heart Association reached a decision. As one of its publications headlined in that year: "All Americans Now Urged: Change Fat-Eating Habits."

At the core of the association's statement, this sentence stood out: "The reduction or control of fat consumption under medical supervision, with reasonable substitution of polyunsaturated for saturated fats, is recommended as a possible means of preventing atherosclerosis and decreasing risk of heart attacks and strokes. . . ."

The statement was not really understood by the general public—and not really agreed with by all of medicine or nutrition. Indeed, the entire Heart Association opinion contained some of the same fuzziness that today surrounds the whole subject of heart disease and diet. For example, an association explanation concluded: ". . . there is no final proof yet that dietary changes will prevent heart attacks or strokes . . . many factors influence the development of atherosclerosis. . . ." There is, it is generally believed, still no clearcut evidence that diet can cause heart disease. Yet the majority of heart experts are still urging Americans to change their diets to protect their hearts and blood vessels, thereby leaving laymen in a state of confusion.

If the dietary changes suggested by the Heart Association were minor ones, many more scientists might go along. But in fact, they are major. Addressing this point, Dr. Philip White cautions: "There is no assurance that a casual change in diet will be of any benefit and little assurance that a significant change will either."

How major are the dietary changes recommended by proponents is suggested by the foods which are *not allowed* in the Heart Association's plan for cholesterol reduction. One must not use:

Among meats, poultry or fish—beef (except very lean cuts), lamb (except for the leg), pork (except lean loin and well-trimmed ham), bacon, spareribs, frankfurters, sausage, cold cuts, canned meats, organ meats (such as kidney, brain, sweetbread or liver), visible fat from meat, the skin of chicken or turkey, fish canned in olive oil, goose.

Among dairy foods—whole milk, homogenized milk, canned milk, sweet or powdered cream, ice cream (unless homemade with nonfat dry milk powder), sour cream, whole milk buttermilk, whole milk yogurt, butter, cheese.

Among fats and oils—butter, ordinary margarine, ordinary solid shortening, lard, salt pork, chicken fat, coconut oil, olive oil.

Among breads and bakery goods—commercial biscuits, muffins, cornbread, griddlecakes, coffee cake, cake (except angel food), pie, cookies, crackers, mixes for breads and bakery goods, doughnuts, sweet rolls, pastry.

Among other desserts—pudding, custard, whipped cream desserts, homemade pie, cakes and cookies that are not made with allowed fat or oil.

Among miscellaneous foods—sauces and gravies (unless made with allowed fat or oil or made from skimmed stock); commercially fried food such as potato chips; French-fried potatoes; fried fish; creamed soups and other creamed dishes; frozen or packaged dinners; olives (except for small occasional amounts); avocado (except occasionally); candies made with chocolate, butter or cream; coconut (except small occasional amounts); foods made with egg yolk (unless counted as part of the four-eggs-a-week allowance); commercial popcorn.

These prohibitions are somewhat liberalized once the patient's cholesterol level has been reduced. But some heart doctors are maintaining much the same restrictions as a continuing dietary pattern in their personal diets and those of their families. It is plain that there are few Americans who would not have to make some very serious changes in diet, and feel a sense of deprivation, in order to meet some of these limitations.

What is the object of all this effort? In general, it is to lower the quantity of certain fat-like substances in the blood by (1) reducing the percentage of fat in the diet to a total of about one-third of the whole diet—a reduction from a typical 45 percent or so; (2) controlling the kind of fat consumed, so that polyunsaturated fats are more plentiful than saturated fats; (3) cutting down the amount of cholesterol eaten in meals to levels quite a bit below those now found in typical American dietaries. All this is mainly accomplished in two ways: by severely trimming the total of animal fats we eat—not easy to do in a nation that gets so much of its protein from animal sources, and by *increasing* the consumption of certain oils—generally those pressed from specific seeds and beans.

Let us look at the deadly trouble we are trying to deal with, and the possibility that dietary effort will succeed in preventing or minimizing that trouble. In other words, what do we really buy with the coin of dietary change?

What makes blood vessels close?

Today, when researchers look at heart attacks, strokes, senility and a host of other crippling or life-threatening ills, they see them mainly as symptoms of a single underlying disease—the narrowing and blocking of blood vessels. The ailments appear to differ largely as to *where* the circulation is closed down. If the block occurs in the vicinity of the heart, for example, we face a coronary; if it is in the brain, or the vessels leading to the brain, we have a stroke.

In general, the closing off of blood vessels is attributed to *atherosclerosis.* A condition from which every adult suffers to some extent, this is a kind of corrosion of the inner surfaces of arteries, the vessels carrying red, oxygen-rich blood to every corner of the body.

The corrosion begins with the accumulation of fat factors found in the food we eat and also made by the body itself. There are many of these fatty substances, cholesterol is only one of them. But since cholesterol is the easiest to measure, it is used as an index of how much of such fatty substances are in the bloodstream. Cholesterol is far from being an unwanted chemical. It is an important constituent of digestive juices, the brain, certain connective tissues and sexual secretions. Even if we eat no cholesterol, the liver makes rather large amounts of it.

The fatty substances are not the single contributor to atherosclerosis. Also involved are various elements of the blood, such as red and white cells, platelets (blood factors), and the fibrin (clotting material) that forms to help make coagulation possible.

As the inner face of the artery corrodes at one or more places, little rough bumps form, which cause eddies and broken patterns of blood flow. The greater the roughening, the more chance that these eccentric flow patterns, and the tendency to trap certain blood materials, will make a clot.

This clot can break loose at any time. If it then gets carried downstream to a narrower place in an artery, the pressure of the pumping heart can cause the stoppered artery to break. The clot can be quite small, yet block a tiny brain artery feeding key brain cells to cause the death of those cells. A clot the size of a pinhead can shut down a tiny artery in the retina of the eye and cause blindness. Even if the clot does not cause trouble, the narrowing of the artery itself can be great enough to cause blood-and-oxygen starvation of some body part it feeds, perhaps crippling that part.

Let us recall that cholesterol is only one of the fatty substances involved in the roughening and buildup of the artery wall. Let us also note that this buildup seems to be made possible by changes in the *collagen* (the body substance that holds together the cells of the artery wall), by changes in the elastic tissue of the wall (*elastin*), and by one of its hormones (*elastase*). We should remember, too, that the ease and rate with which fibrin is deposited from the blood changes the situation, as does the inadequacy or adequacy of a special enzyme, *fibrinolysin,* which is supposed to circulate in the blood and break down any fibrin that begins to litter and choke the blood vessels.

Every one of these factors is partly the result of hereditary tendencies. Moreover, changes in many glands can also affect one or more of the factors. For example, the thyroid and adrenal glands are profoundly involved. So, apparently, is the pancreas; diabetics are much more prone to atherosclerosis. Stress can be a big factor in narrowing the arteries and changing glandular secretions, so that certain personalities have atherosclerotic tendencies. Being overweight is thought by many to play a role, and smoking has definite effects on the whole problem.

Then why pick on fats?

Let us try to simplify a labyrinth of hundreds of research studies. When people have high levels of cholesterol in their blood serum, they have a greater chance of atherosclerosis, heart disease, stroke and related conditions. This has been shown by such landmark work as that of Dr. William Kannel's team in Framingham, Massachusetts, Dr. Ancel Keys of the University of Minnesota, and Dr. Jeremiah Stamler in Chicago.

This does not say, however, that higher levels of cholesterol *cause* heart attacks. The question is whether high cholesterol may be a symptom, a sign that some other condition is present which causes atherosclerosis. Why this seemingly fine discrimination? Because, if high cholesterol is only a symptom, reducing it may not remove the real cause, just as treating a headache and reducing it does not cure a brain tumor of which the headache might be a symptom.

All that we may now say conclusively is that high cholesterol is one of several significant predictors of a greater risk of heart attacks. The greatest predictor is heredity, a family tendency to have atherosclerosis and the diseases attendant upon it. Also significant are smoking, high blood pressure, diabetes, certain personality types, stressful life-styles, reduced lung volume, low exercise levels, and mesomorphic (husky, muscular) body types. The relative significance of any of these factors is hard to assess and seems to vary with the study.

Fats were suspected first of all because they provide both the raw materials from which the liver can make cholesterol and cholesterol itself. The next body of evidence came from an effort to cut down cholesterol levels by changing diet. This unquestionably works. One has only to lower the total of fat eaten—that is, reduce the quantity of saturated fats and increase the quantity of *un*saturated fats—to lower cholesterol.

(The reader may recall that saturation is a question of how many H atoms in fatty acids have open, unsatisfied bonds. When the bonds are all satisfied, the fat is saturated. When one bond is left open, the fat is monosaturated. When more than one bond is open, the fat is polyunsaturated. In general, saturated fats tend to be animal and solid; unsaturated fats tend to be of vegetable origin and liquid. This is not an absolute constant in nature, however—and the food industry has made solid shortenings that are largely unsaturated.)

But does the reduction of cholesterol by a change in diet actually cut down on heart attacks? Here is the tough and still unanswered question. True, atherosclerosis seems to increase when people move from one culture to another where more saturated fat is eaten. The Irish who came to Boston and left brothers in the old country have made a dramatic model for this fact. And moving populations of Yemenites to Israel, of Japanese to Hawaii, and Italians to the United States confirm it. They developed more cardiovascular disease. But diet cannot be pinned down as the focal point of such change, for such transplanted peoples are exposed to more stressful lives, get less exercise, begin to smoke cigarettes, and Heaven knows what else. We can be sure only that culture and heart disease are somehow connected.

The strongest study on cholesterol-cutting is probably that of 846 men studied for up to eight years, ending in 1969, at a Los Angeles veterans' center. About half got much less than average dietary cholesterol and fat, and their cholesterol levels dropped about 13 percent. The other half ate normally. Sudden deaths totaled 27 in the latter group and 18 in the former, which statistically is not significant. But of more significance is the fact that 70 of the normal-diet group suffered "fatal atherosclerotic events," and only 48 of the low-cholesterol group shared their fate. Yet Dr. Seymour Dayton, who directed the test, opines that "the data of this trial do not suffice for any confident conclusions as to the relative effects of the experimental diet upon different end points."

Research to date, usually with groups smaller than 1,000 persons, has found that cholesterol levels vary rather widely in the population, and that it is hard, perhaps impossible, to relate these levels to the diet consumed. But to put it in somewhat simplistic form, we may be looking here at the "natural" tendency of some people to end up with more cholesterol in the blood than others. Some people have heart attacks with rather low cholesterol, some with high. The question is: what is high for you? It is quite possible that each of us has his own safe limits of cholesterol, and that what is high for one man may be low for another. Thus, matching *everyone* against the same standard numbers, which we have been doing, may be confusing and inaccurate.

What the Heart Association doctors are saying is, in effect: "We think it is a good, worthwhile gamble for each of us to get down to his own lower limits of cholesterol. And we think the foods and dietary habits of the nation ought to be changed to help this happen." The best the individual can do is to let his doctor help him find his personal lower level of cholesterol. Generally speaking, a healthful life style tends to help the individual reach those lower levels.

It should be made very clear that the American Heart Association is not exclusively concerned with diet. It conducts an active campaign for a general revision of certain factors in American life: for the elimination of smoking, the reduction of personal stress, the regular watching and control of blood pressure, enough daily exercise to make us sweat and pant a bit, the maintenance of proper body weight and the early detection and control of diabetes. Fats are only part of the picture.

To prove that these changes, especially that of diet, will actually change the terrible toll of heart disease, stroke and other cardiovascular diseases will take years of further experiment. It will take big experiments, too, ones for which no one has yet been willing or able to find the necessary sums of money. Test groups are needed involving 50 to 60 times as many people as those used so far. Some experts have begged and pleaded for something like $100 million to begin the job. But Congress and U.S. agencies have not yet been persuaded to part with the cash, which they spend freely enough on nonessentials.

Each of us now can only make a personal decision about what will finally be learned when our government finds time to give more attention to health. (An interesting possibility is that if we can forestall atherosclerosis, we will among other things be governed by fewer senile senators and representatives.) Will a somewhat stringent and unaccustomed dietary turn out to have been a waste of effort? Or will those of us who take the gamble live extra years of healthful, useful and intellectually sound life?

Looking at the research we have so far, Dr. Jeremiah Stamler concludes: "The first sets of data from these first-generation studies all show that a change in diet, particularly a decrease in the intake of saturated fat and cholesterol, is capable of affecting and sustaining a fall in serum lipid levels (fats in the blood) and the evidence further indicates that such intervention does influence disease."

Dr. Stamler plainly does not see the proofs as conclusive. But he faces the need for decision, and the fact that in the cholesterol question, as in most other questions of life, not to decide is to decide. "My thesis," Dr. Stamler says, "is that if one takes the two alternatives our nation faces at the present time in dealing with a coronary epidemic that is killing 650,000 persons a year—to leave the American diet as it is or to make changes—then it is my best medical judgment that we must make changes. Let us go forward without waiting ten or 15 years for definitive trials. I don't think we can afford to wait. We have waited too long already." (It should be noted that, in his consideration of the numbers of lives at stake, Dr. Stamler has not included the additional hundreds of thousands of deaths each year from strokes and the other cardiovascular diseases that all share the common ground of atherosclerosis.)

Why it is that not all physicians or nutritionists jump onto the change-the-diet bandwagon? Is it just the usual conservatism of men who feel the responsibility of making life-and-death decisions?

The reluctance of many scientists, aside from Heart Association doctors, is complex. And these men do not constitute a small minority; in fact, they may make up a majority of those who are well informed. One sees the struggle in a sharp division among members of the Council on Foods and Nutrition and the Food and Nutrition Board, which has made the issuance of each statement on this subject an agony.

Let us try to summarize the position of those who question the villainy of cholesterol. First of all, there are other correlations between blood substances and atherosclerosis that look as good as that of cholesterol and arterial disease. Triglycerides, for example, which are other fatty blood chemicals.

In dietary terms, moreover, excess consumption of sugar is seen as a possible progenitor of atherosclerosis. Most experts now agree that if we ate less sugar (including table sugar, honey, brown sugar, raw sugar), the problem might be reduced. In general, the question asked is: do we really know what we are doing when, by cutting fats, we push the consumption of carbohydrates sharply upward? And do we fully know what will be the consequences of markedly changing the nation's sources of proteins? For example, one study, albeit a rather isolated one, shows that there is an exceptionally strong correlation between atherosclerosis and the consumption of foods rich in *lipoproteins* (a certain family of food substances in which proteins and fatty chemicals are joined together). Should we follow a diet with fewer lipoproteins? Furthermore, the scientists are keenly aware that they could wreak economic havoc on certain segments of the food industry. For example, what happens to poultry farmers if people who now eat two eggs each morning cut their consumption to four eggs a week? Certainly, much of our food industry could adapt, eventually, to produce foods that fit into the cholesterol-reduction plan. But is there enough evidence to justify cutting so deeply into the farm-market-processing purse?

Many scientists suspect the real seat of the problem is the function of the liver, which makes plenty of cholesterol even if we consume none. Others believe in studies showing that exercise, lowered blood pressure, not smoking and other factors are defenses against the effects of much fat in the diet. They look at vigorous populations and observe that another life-style sometimes seems to compensate for dietary error. And finally, they take a realistic look at how the populace has responded to the much more certain relationship between smoking and lung disease and early death. Because with almost universal medical agreement here, Americans continue to smoke almost as much as before. So how can we assume that Americans would substantially change their diet if cholesterol were proven to be the chief cause of atherosclerosis? In fact, doctors know that even with the impetus of the fright of a recent heart attack, many patients are unwilling or unable to stay on "heart diets." And what could we expect of younger people who are asked to give up much of their favorite foods, because 20 or 25 years from now they *may* have a higher risk of heart attack?

Those scientists who are reluctant to go along with the Heart Association's demand for immediate vigorous action on dietary changes are looking not only at the medical puzzles and contradictions, but at the realities of human habit and behavior.

The AMA has adopted the position that a cholesterol-reducing diet is a therapeutic measure. The medical organization has supplied information to the nation's doctors saying that when a risk of heart disease seems high, cholesterol reduction is advisable. And it has suggested that doctors also consider regulating dietary fat as an attempt to prevent the increase in serum cholesterol which may occur in men as they grow older.

But at this writing, the AMA's Council on Foods and Nutrition has stated firmly that "there is not yet sufficient information available on the relation of dietary fat to heart disease to justify general dietary changes by the public."

A common, reasonable way to cope with the dilemma has been for the family doctor routinely to test blood cholesterol levels during physical checkups. This should begin when a person is fairly young, since considerable atherosclerosis has been found in the blood vessels of American men in their early twenties, and since it takes 20 years and more for deposits to build to the point at which they are threatening. Furthermore, once arteries are discovered to be in serious trouble, it is very questionable whether much can be done.

If cholesterol levels are high—but especially if repeated tests show a rising trend—the doctor may want to prescribe diet changes as preventive medicine. But even this tactic has its problems. For an individual's cholesterol test results can vary widely, depending on the recent diet, the time of day when the test is made, current stresses and other circumstances.

If your doctor performs a cholesterol test, you may want to know what the resulting numbers signify. They show the number of milligrams of cholesterol in each

100 milliliters of blood. In populations that have little coronary disease, the average level is about 150 milligrams of cholesterol found in 100 milliliters of blood. This is also expressed as "150 mg%." In nations such as ours, where coronaries are common, the average level is 210 mg% or more.

One study showed that five out of six men who had experienced heart attacks between the ages of 40 and 69 had cholesterol levels above 210 mg%. In Dr. Kannel's study at Framingham, those middle-aged people with levels of 260 mg% proved to have a heart attack risk six times that of those people who had cholesterol levels under 200.

If you want to keep cholesterol low

So far, the response of the public to the cholesterol question has been unenthusiastic, worried and confused. Writing with noted cardiologist Dr. Irvine Page, Dr. Stamler has commented: "Human beings are currently presented the choice of following a daily special pattern of living, which is far from easy, or forgetting the whole thing. A great many people follow the latter choice."

If your choice is to take the preventive steps, it seems only reasonable to begin with a physical checkup, including an electrocardiogram (a recording of the heart's electrical activity that is the best early indicator of any trouble). Such a checkup includes routine exams that can suggest atherosclerosis already causing damage. For example, the small blood vessels at the back of the eye are the only place atherosclerosis can actually be seen by the doctor outside of surgery. The history and examinations will show whether you are in a high-risk group—through heredity, habits, personality or disease states such as diabetes or hypertension. Finally, ask your doctor's opinion of the value of a preventive diet for *you.* A serum cholesterol test, of course, will certainly help him to answer that question.

If the decision is to *reduce* cholesterol, the doctor will be able to give you a diet to do the job—or you can get one from your local heart association, which provides such materials. We have already looked at the dietary exclusions of this plan. There is also advice to increase deliberately your consumption of polyunsaturated fats, in order to raise their consumption above that of saturated fats. For women who are sedentary this means about four tablespoons of polyunsaturates daily. For women who are more active, and for men who are sedentary or moderately active, the total is five tablespoons. These fats come from corn, cottonseed, peanut, safflower, sesame, soybean and sunflower oils, and from mayonnaise or French dressing (made with the aforementioned oils).

On a low-cholesterol program meats are restricted to three-ounce servings of lean beef, lamb or pork at no more than four meals a week. The beef cuts should be from the round, flank steak, lean ground round, lean rump or tenderloin. Lamb should come from the leg only, and pork only from the lean loin. At ten other lunches and dinners you must choose instead poultry (except goose), seafood or veal. In buying the meat, the *raw* amount for a serving can be figured as four ounces, or five ounces including bone. As main-course substitues, you may use cottage cheese (preferably uncreamed), yogurt (from partially skimmed milk), peanut butter or nuts (especially walnuts).

The diet recommends skim milk, nonfat dry milk powder or buttermilk (from skim milk) to the tune of at least a pint each day.

You can use all and any vegetables, of course, following the normal nutritional rules concerning deep green and yellow vegetables. Fruits and fruit juices are not limited.

There are few restraints on breads, cereals, rice, macaroni, flour and other grain products. But any baked products that include much fat (such as biscuits, muffins, griddlecakes) must use an allowable oil, and this amount be counted as part of your fat allowance. Therefore, most commercially baked products are "out," except for breads. Most crackers are also banned. Desserts made at home with allowed fat and oil are permitted.

This is the general basis of the diet, with the idea plainly being to chop away at fats, and especially the saturated ones of animal products or those which use hydrogenated vegetable oils to any important extent.

For most people, such a diet is not easy, comfortable or highly palatable over the long haul. But in their personal lives, most nutritionists have begun to draw from the Heart Association's diet a kind of go-easy pattern of eating which can make surprisingly large reductions in fats, particularly in cholesterol and saturated fats.

As has been pointed out repeatedly, expert belief is that too much of our diet is fat. So modifications of the low-cholesterol diet can serve the purpose of reducing dietary fat content. And if we select wisely the fats that we eliminate, we will reduce our intake of cholesterol and saturated fats at the same time.

For instance, most people who work in the field of nutrition buy low-fat or nonfat milk. They go easy on solid fats, such as butter. They spare calories by choosing a greater variety of protein foods, to put less emphasis on beef and pork and more on fish and veal. They trim down on fatty sources of carbohydrates—for example, on flour products that are often heavily mixed with solid fats, such as cookies, cakes, mix-made biscuits and muffins.

In many instances, nutritionists' wives have found that it is just as easy to cook with polyunsaturated vegetable oils and margarines rich in polyunsaturates—in place of butter or heavily hydrogenated shortenings or lard. These commodities work just as well in pancakes or waffles, or even pie crusts, provide a perfectly good flavor and texture, and tip the fat balance toward unsaturation.

Most nutritionists also say that it is easy to cultivate one's taste for sherbet instead of ice cream, for angel-food cake instead of eggy pound cake, for grapefruit sprinkled with cinnamon instead of sugar, for salad dressing made with polyunsaturated rather than olive oil, for a sliced chicken sandwich instead of a hamburger or hot dog, for strawberries instead of chocolate mousse, for cucumber slices with a dip instead of potato chips.

As a further explanation of what Heart Association officials would like to see happen in the American dietary, here are two contrasting meal plans for one day:

For breakfast, the typical American choice might be a half grapefruit, two slices of buttered toast, four strips of bacon, a fried egg and coffee with cream and sugar. The heart men would prefer to see a half grapefruit, dry cereal with skim milk, a slice of toast with a teaspoon of low-in-saturates margarine, marmalade, and two teaspoons of sugar distributed among the cereal, the fruit and coffee.

For lunch the current choice might be a hamburger on a bun, French fries, cole slaw, cherry pie and milk. Preferred would be a lean beef sandwich with mayonnaise, cole slaw, melon, skim milk and coffee.

A popular dinner might be fruit juice, chicken basted with butter, buttered corn and another vegetable, salad with blue cheese dressing, roll and butter and chocolate ice cream. A suggested dinner would be fruit juice, chicken basted with an allowed oil, corn with special margarine, vegetable without butter, salad with oil dressing, a slice of bread and sherbet.

It is only fair to caution that in most cases the all-out reduction diet takes getting used to, and that some people never seem to feel comfortable with it. The go-easy program is less arduous. However, one does not expect more than a kind of holding action to result. Cholesterol levels rise much more easily than they fall, and the go-easy approach, while it can help you hold the line on the levels of fat in your blood, is not likely to *reduce* those levels markedly.

Since this is perhaps the only major nutritional question in which a middle-of-the-road opinion is difficult, almost impossible to find, the author feels that perhaps he should mention his own personal decision. Having listened to the arguments and watched the build-up of data for some 15 years, and being aware of his own weakness where food is concerned, he has chosen the go-easy path, but with questions, misgivings, and occasionally envy for those with more character. He hopes that by practicing other risk-reduction principles, particularly those of exercise and physical conditioning at a moderate level, he will not suffer overmuch from rejecting the all-out reduction diet for himself. Moreover, historically, dietary extremes have never in his knowledge been the solution once true causes and effective cures were finally known. The great hope is that new knowledge will resolve the atherosclerosis question soon, and that research into threatening disease will be moved higher in our national priorities to hasten the day.

SECTION VII

Food, Growth And Aging

CHAPTER 19

Food for the pregnant and nursing woman

As soon as an obstetrician has determined that a woman is pregnant, he checks her nutritional status. For this factor is an important one in the safety and health of both mother and child.

Most women believe that dietary care and change become necessary as soon as pregnancy begins. But the fact is that the care ought to have begun before the new life is started, and that if the mother has eaten well beforehand, little change is needed for the first months of carrying her baby.

How much difference does good nutrition make to the baby? One characteristic study was made at the Boston Lying-In Hospital. When the food habits of the mother were rated good, 42 percent of the babies born were judged to have superior health through pregnancy and into the first two weeks of life, and 52 percent had good health. When the mother's diet was fair, superior status was limited to six percent of the babies, and 44 percent were in the good category. When the mother's diet was poor or very poor, the good and superior groups combined fell to eight percent.

As is the case with all surveys of nutritional status, these facts are not without modifiers. For example, we know that good diet is usually related to other kinds of good health habits, and often to income and level of medical care as well. Yet enough such studies have been done to be sure that a mother's diet does have much impact on her baby's health and her own.

There are plenty of specifics to show this. Women who are substantially underweight or overweight when pregnancy begins are much more likely to develop toxemia of pregnancy, a still somewhat mysterious condition of water retention, high blood pressure and other factors, and one of the remaining causes of maternal death. Most of these conditions are successfully treated, but toxemia is still seen as a serious threat, affecting some six percent of American mothers.

We know that dietary iron is low among most young women, and that the added stress of pregnancy can tip the physical scale enough to let anemias appear. Calcium is not up to recommended levels for most young women; so many lose too much calcium as the baby develops. If the mother lives in a low-iodine region, and has ignored warnings to use iodized salt, goiter may begin in pregnancy.

We have seen that some B vitamins are low in women of childbearing age. But since these are not stored anyway, dietary correction once pregnancy begins usually takes care of any problem. And certainly, most ideas about "building-up" before pregnancy with increased protein, or with most vitamins and minerals, are spurious. Still, the mother-to-be should pay attention to her nutrient intake in anticipation of pregnancy, rather than wait until she knows she is expecting, if she wants the best chance for her child.

Pregnancy is a state that should be kept under medical supervision, and dietary management is an important part of that supervision. Obstetricians have long taken careful note of research into the effects of food on pregnancy, milk-forming and breastfeeding. The qualified specialist in obstetrics is your best dietary consultant during pregnancy, and the only one who can keep your diet closely related to your physical condition. The pregnant woman is warned not to follow the "more is better" food philosophy, or the idea of "eating for two." To do so is to risk sabotaging the doctor's plan, along with your own and your baby's welfare.

The author has heard some dismaying tales from men in obstetrics. One woman so dosed herself with magic "sea salt" that she caused serious fluid retention problems. Others have taken over-the-counter "appetite-killers" until the pregnancy was threatened. Still others, when advised to lose some weight, ignored the diets they were given and unwisely eliminated nearly all fats from their food. Some women, told of a tendency to anemia, have let health-food-store proprietors sell them on massive doses of "organic" iron, and thus badly worsened the common tendency of the pregnant to be constipated. Women trying to reduce have turned to the spurious "high-protein, low-carbohydrate" dieting fads and so loaded their meals with fats that they produced exaggerated morning sickness. Overenthusiastic ladies have been sold on "high-potency" multiple-vitamin pills by faddists, unaware that these might be packed with A vitamins, which the body will store to a point of damaging excess. "The problems we see," says one obstetrician, "are just as often caused by an overenthusiastic wish to eat well as by carelessness or indifference."

Though most nutritionists feel that nearly all the dietary needs of pregnancy can easily be met by sound diet, most obstetricians play it safe by prescribing some vitamins and minerals once pregnancy is diagnosed. The typical text in obstetrics suggests vitamins be supplemented to the tune of about half the nonpregnant woman's daily need, to play safe.

For the first three months of pregnancy, food needs do not change from those of a normal biogenic diet. The doctor uses this time to correct nutritional problems—such as overweight or iron-deficiency anemia—and to build up the mother for the last two-thirds of pregnancy, when she must supply the needs of the developing baby to an extent that increases her food requirements.

How much do food needs change?

On the average, the needs for most nutrients can be said to rise about 30 percent above normal during the second three months of gestation, and climb to about 50 percent above normal during the last three months.

The problem is that calorie needs *do not increase*—except during the last three months, and even then the calorie requirements go up only about ten percent. Any calories beyond this increase are likely to make fat mothers and, perhaps, fat babies. The overly fat baby does not have as good a chance for normal birth and survival, and may cause a more difficult and damaging birth for the mother. And the mother who becomes fat during pregnancy has a strong tendency to keep that fat and fight overweight for life.

We will look at weight control in pregnancy, but first let us see which nutrients are needed in larger quantity, and how and when to get them. Most obstetricians use the first three months for dietary correction and increase nutrients beginning in the fourth month. But your doctor may be among those who prefer to add nutrients (not calories) to the diet at once and sustain the increases through pregnancy. There are several reasons for doing so. One is that the doctor sees the first three months as an opportunity for education and adjustment in nutrition. Another is that morning sickness may cause the loss of some nutrients by vomiting. Follow your doctor's thinking.

To suggest how your own nutrient requirements are increased by pregnancy see the next page for the Food and Nutrition Board's carefully developed RDAs (including a wide safety factor) for the normal woman of childbearing age who weighs 128 pounds, and for the same woman during pregnancy and breastfeeding.

In addition, iodine requirement is thought to increase about 25 to 30 percent.

These nutrient increases do not mean they are likely to be in short supply in your food. Remember that diet can be a specific and individual matter during pregnancy, and that you have professional guidance. For example, while the phosphorus requirement rises 50 percent, there is a good chance you are already getting that much in your diet if you eat foods with adequate calcium—and an excess of phosphorus can help to produce the leg cramps of pregnancy.

So before you make any changes in your diet other than those recommended by your doctor, ask him. And that especially includes any kind of nutrient supplement or "health" food that well-meaning friends or money-hungry promoters try to sell you.

	Normal RDA	RDA in pregnancy	In lactation
Protein	55 grams	65 grams	75 grams
Vitamin A	5,000 I.U.	6,000 I.U.	8,000 I.U.
Vitamin D	(none established)	400 I.U.	400 I.U.
Vitamin E	25 I.U.	30 I.U.	30 I.U.
Vitamin C	55 mg.	60 mg.	60 mg.
Folacin (folic acid)	0.4 mg.	0.8 mg.	0.5 mg.
Niacin	13 mg.	15 mg.	20 mg.
Riboflavin (B_2)	1.5 mg.	1.8 mg.	2.0 mg.
Thiamine (B_1)	1.0 mg.	1.1 mg.	1.5 mg.
Vitamin B_6	2.0 mg.	2.5 mg.	2.5 mg.
Vitamin B_{12}	5 micrograms	8 micrograms	6 micrograms
Calcium	800 mg.	1,200 mg.	1,300 mg.
Phosphorus	800 mg.	1,200 mg.	1,300 mg.
Iron	18 mg.	18 mg.	18 mg.
Magnesium	300 mg.	450 mg.	450 mg.

Many women put their own and their babies' lives into the hands of the doctor, but then reserve their own and their friends' private ideas about eating. If you can't trust your doctor about how much milk to drink or whether or not vitamins are needed, and what kind, how can you trust him to do the right thing in a delivery-room emergency?

About weight and water

One of the great problems of pregnancy is weight control. There are two reasons why pregnant women are expected to gain. One, of course, is the weight of the baby—usually no more than seven or eight pounds at birth. The other is water, which can account for as much as two-thirds of the weight gain.

Two to four pounds of water fill the womb to guard the baby against shocks. And by the fourth month another kind of fluid retention is noticed, one which eventually adds from five to ten pounds of weight. This water seems to be intended to enlarge the blood volume of the mother, probably both to make the feeding of the fetus easier (this feeding is done through the mother's circulatory system) and to protect the mother in case of hemorrhage.

Adding the averages of these numbers, we arrive at a common rule of thumb among obstetricians: to allow a 20-to-25-pound gain to a normal woman, assuming that neither fat nor fluid is too large a proportion of this amount.

If a woman is overweight at the outset, her doctor may subtract the poundage she is overweight from the allowable gain. In order words, she must reduce in order to have a normal pregnancy. Underweight may call for a greater than usual gain.

If water accumulation is too great—as evidenced by rising blood pressure, "orange peel" skin over the abdomen or the sacrum (the bony triangle low on the spine) and persistent swellings of body parts such as the hands—sodium in the diet must be controlled to reduce water retention. That decision, however, is definitely a medical one. Self-ordered restrictions on water or weight in pregnancy can be risky. And doctors are becoming more liberal about allowing larger increases in both.

Perhaps the most important consideration about weight during pregnancy is that so many women feel they now have reason and excuse to eat more calories. Remember, there is no additional demand for calories until the last three months, and then only for ten percent more than your usual dietary. If weight gain is due to fat—a fact that can usually be determined by "pinching" fatty areas—then food cutbacks may be ordered by the doctor.

Food and comfort

Morning sickness appears to result from the burrowing of the fetus into the lining of the womb, starting in just a few days after conception, when the baby is only 100 cells or so. The doctor can prescribe medication, but he may also tell you the reassuring fact that women who experience morning sickness rarely miscarry.

Certain hormone changes in pregnancy slow down digestion, and often diminish the amount of stomach acid. These two facts can make poorly-chewed and fatty foods harder to handle, and the same slowdown can incline the mother toward constipation. Doctors often deal with these problems through bland but bulky diets with adequate fiber. Some find that more meals and smaller ones produce greater comfort, especially as the baby grows and there is physical pressure on the organs and passages of digestion.

Contrary to popular belief, a woman's instincts about food she should eat during pregnancy are not likely to be any better than at any other time. In fact, they may be more confused. No one can explain that midnight craving for pickles, but it does appear to come from the mother's brain and not the baby's needs.

Pregnancy can be a time for emotional stress, and when that stress is expressed in anxious or depressed feelings, the woman may turn to food for comfort. When emotional stress is added to the physical changes, it can make for much digestive discomfort.

The continuance of mild exercise—the nature of which should be checked out with your doctor—can be an important comfort factor in pregnancy. It aids digestion, helps to handle tension and the disposal of excess fluid, and it also allows the mother to eat more without getting fat.

Nursing

It is hard in so small a space to recite all the advantages of breastfeeding for both mother and child. But they are well-known. The milk of a human mother is much better designed for the baby than is the milk of a cow. For one thing, mother's milk provides immunities against disease whereas formulas made with cow's milk do not. Also, mother's milk does not cause infant digestive upsets. However, if you cannot breastfeed, be assured that science is now able to provide excellent nutrition for the formula baby.

Here is a comparison of human and cow's milk. The higher protein and ash of cow's milk may actually be detriments for some babies. (In actual practice, of course, the cow's milk is diluted for infant formulas and sugar is added.)

	Human milk (percents)	Cow's milk (percents)
Protein	1.2	3.5
Lactose (milk sugar)	6.6	4.0
Fat	3.5	3.5
Ash	0.2	0.7
Calories	65	65

The reader will remember that the nutritional requirements for a nursing mother are different from one who is pregnant. The biggest difference is calories; the nursing mother needs the calories to make her baby grow. And despite the infant's small size, his demand is 45 to 50 calories per pound each day, as against the mother's need of 16 to 20 calories per pound. The RDAs provide an average of an extra 1,000 calories a day for the mother to do her job.

Again, the doctor should manage your diet in nursing, and will give you a diet plan, the most notable feature of which is likely to be six glasses of milk a day. As with all other nutritional matters concerning diet and the nurturing of a new life, food becomes as much a part of medical prescription and plan as the drugs you may be given. It is, of course, far less precise, and should still allow you to choose most foods according to taste and mood. But whenever health becomes involved in your thinking, remember that only the doctor and other *qualified* professionals can answer your questions with knowledge. New life is too important to gamble on the fads, whims and superstititions of self-appointed experts.

CHAPTER 20

The things kids eat

We worry a lot about children. After all, they make such narrow food choices, with a taste for hot dogs, peanut butter, hamburgers, soda pop and whatever is fried, frosted or suitable for dipping in ketchup. All our promises and threats have so little effect on what goes into their stomachs. Small wonder that the typical parent wonders: do these foods give my child enough to live and grow on?

The answer is not a clearcut one. In part, it rests with the great paradox of American nutrition, which we talked about at the beginning of this book. We know that most children's dietaries are below the RDAs for certain nutrients. But we cannot pinpoint the price of these failures. In most cases, doctors and nutritionists have not been able to identify the health effects of minor nutritional omissions of the average American child, either during the young years or in later life.

Consider the results of a recent study by the Child Research Council of youngsters from ages one to ten. They found that some 50 percent of the boys did not meet RDA levels of important nutrients. They also learned that after age three the girls fared even worse; 75 percent of them between age six and age ten failed to get RDAs. "Yet," reports one of the researchers, Virginia Beal, of the University of Colorado School of Medicine, "repeated physical examinations and measurements confirmed that they were healthy children with satisfactory gains in both height and weight."

When the diets of 3,444 preschool children were studied, it was found that fruit and vegetable consumption was lacking, and that too much of the intake was in candy, soft drinks, bakery goods and fried snacks such as potato chips. There were marked nutrient shortages, especially among A and C vitamins and iron.

In late teenage girls, the dietary deficiencies persist. Dr. Hilda White of Northwestern University finds that two-thirds of them have "inadequate diets," commonly incorporating bizarre fads.

But only rarely can poor health states be directly attributed to poor diet among typical middle-class children in America. Anemias are among the few health problems which are thought to be diet-related; inadequacies of dietary iron are widely recorded. And when teenage girls become mothers, their babies show signs of improper maternal eating.

The conclusion of the nation's doctors is that while strong fear-talk is unjustified, many children are probably deprived of what they call "*optimal* health and development" by a few simple omissions from their food. And many nutritionists are convinced that when we know more, we will find that the dietary errors of childhood predispose to health problems of adult years.

Obesity is a good example of this kind of problem. We have seen how a long-misunderstood body phenomenon—the excess building of fat-storage cells through infant overfeeding—is now considered a common cause of an adult tendency to store too much body fat. Other childhood nutritional errors may have similar effects. Scientists are now asking such questions as whether too much fat in a child's food paves the way for later heart disease, whether inadequate calcium opens a path for arthritic disease, whether missing vitamins may somehow leave developing organs vulnerable, and so on.

On the other hand, we know that typical American children are not going to develop blatant deficiency signs, such as beriberi or *kwashiorkor* disease, because they leave their milk occasionally or pick at their vegetables. We know that if a child's eyes are weak it is almost certainly *not* because he gets too little vitamin A, that vitamins will not let him put aside his spectacles. We know that if his stature is small and he does not hit home runs, it is *not* because he gets too little protein, or eats refined flour, or has a passion for chocolate bars.

We know that serious childhood illness in America is largely the result of contagion, heredity or environmental accident—*not* wrong food, agricultural sprays, additives or chemical fertilizers.

Why, if children's diets are lacking in nutrients, are there not more resulting problems of disease? One reason is that dietary deficiencies are judged in terms of RDAs, which include wide safety margins. Another is that serious deficiency signs appear only when diets are very bad indeed. (A child can be 80 percent below his RDA for vitamin C and not develop the signs of scurvy.) But RDAs are not set by whim. They are carefully determined to allow for stresses which can and do occur. And they take into account subtle phenomena of cell growth and function which may not prosper with a bare minimum of nutrients.

So while the dietary errors of children are not cause for panic and overconcern, they are worth thinking about in order to give youngsters the best possible chance for health and growth. Nutritionists, like most parents, are unwilling to settle for less. And adequate diet is so simple a matter for the typical American youngster that it is criminal not to provide it.

Age and Sex	Intakes below RDA			
Boy and Girls (Birth to age 2)		**** Iron		
Boys and Girls (3–5)		** Iron		
Boys (9–11)	* Calcium			
Girls (9–11)	*** Calcium	**** Iron	* Thiamin	
Boys (12–14)	** Calcium	*** Iron	* Thiamin	
Girls (12–14)	*** Calcium	**** Iron	* Thiamin	* Vitamin A
Boys (15–17)	* Calcium	* Iron		
Girls (15–17)	**** Calcium	**** Iron	** Thiamin	
Girls (18–19)	*** Calcium	**** Iron	* Thiamin	* Vitamin A

* 1–10% below
** 11–20%
*** 21–29%
**** 30% or more

What is wrong with our children's food?

The USDA study of what is missing from the diets of youngsters shows deficiencies as *averages*. Remember, there are *many* middle-class children far below these averages, and quite a few above. So such studies are mainly indicators of danger areas. For example, the fact that the average boy between the ages of 12 and 14 gets one-to-ten percent less thiamine than is recommended for him does not mean that thiamine omissions are always minor. It suggests that some boys are missing much more, and some are getting all they need. It suggests that if there is a boy in this age group in your family, it is worth thinking about his diet to see what he *does* eat in the way of such thiamine-rich foods as enriched and whole grains, legumes and meats. Eating patterns, as we have seen repeatedly, are personal matters.

On the other hand, the chart for this 12-to-14-year-old boy, as for all other typical children, reveals no danger of protein insufficiency. So you can feel pretty relaxed about this question, and, for example, ignore food ads that imply a need to worry about your child's protein intake.

On p. 408, then, are the *danger* spots in children's diets which have been found in USDA research.

If we think about the foods that are the best sources of the four nutrients which seem to be in shortest supply among our youth, we can see a pattern. An increase in milk products and in deep green and yellow vegetables could easily eliminate the shortages of calcium and A and B vitamins. And those same green vegetables would, of course, help take care of minor deficiencies of iron as well. Also, the shortages suggest the importance of making sure that flour and grain products have been made with enriched or whole-grain flours. At this writing, it appears that such enrichment will include much larger quantities of iron, making it still more worthwhile to look for that "enriched" statement on labels for breads, crackers and other bakery products.

This thumbnail sketch of desirable food changes for young people is not, of course, meant to suggest that there are not other excellent sources of the needed nutrients. But it shows how simply we can bring children's diets up to a level which assures that they have all the health potential food can provide.

Nor do we mean to say that other nutrients are not missing. But we know that there is no dearth of fats, carbohydrates or proteins in the food of typical children and teenagers. (In fact, as we have seen earlier, a harmful surplus of high-calorie foods, especially fats, is a commonplace.) And the additions which eliminate the average nutrient shortages also take care of the more unusual ones.

If you are concerned about some shortage in the food of your child, check back to the earlier sections of this book which discuss that particular nutrient. And if it is hard to decide whether the child's diet is truly lacking in some nutrient, look again at the dietary analysis in chapter 2, which will provide an easy guide to finding food gaps.

What foods do the young need?

To be thorough, we include on these pages a chart of the RDAs of children, according to age and sex, as

Simplified Daily Food Guide

Food Group	Children	Teens and Preteens
***Milk or milk products** (cups)	2–3	3–4 or more
****Meat, fish, poultry, eggs** (servings)	1–2	3 or more
Green and yellow vegetables (servings)	1–2	2
Citrus fruits and tomatoes (servings)	1	1–2
Potatoes, other fruits and vegetables (servings)	1	1
Bread, flour and cereal (servings)	3–4	4 or more
Butter or margarine (tablespoons)	2	2–4

* The need for nutrients in one or two cups of milk daily can be met by cheeses or ice cream. One cup of milk approximates one and a half cups of cottage cheese or two to three large scoops of ice cream.

** A serving of meat, fish or poultry (three ounces) may be alternated with eggs or cheese, dried peas, beans or lentils.

Note: A total fluid consumption of three to five cups daily is recommended for all children. This amount includes milk, juices and the like.

(for children and teens of average height and weight)

Age Group (years)	Calories	Protein (grams)	Vit. A (I.U.)	Vit. D (I.U.)	Vit. C (mg.)	Vit. B_1* (mg.)	Vit. B_2* (mg.)	Vit. B_3* (mg.)	Calcium (mg.)	Iron (mg.)
0–⅙	480	9	1500	400	35	0.2	0.4	5	400	6
⅙–½	770	14	1500	400	35	0.4	0.5	7	500	10
½–1	900	16	1500	400	35	0.5	0.6	8	600	15
1–2	1100	25	2000	400	40	0.6	0.6	8	700	15
2–3	1250	25	2000	400	40	0.6	0.7	8	800	15
3–4	1400	30	2500	400	40	0.7	0.8	9	800	10
4–6	1600	30	2500	400	40	0.8	0.9	11	800	10
6–8	2000	35	3500	400	40	1.0	1.1	13	900	10
8–10	2200	40	3500	400	40	1.1	1.2	15	1000	10
Boys 10–12	2500	45	4500	400	40	1.3	1.3	17	1200	10
Boys 12–14	2700	50	5000	400	45	1.4	1.4	18	1400	18
Boys 14–18	3000	60	5000	400	55	1.5	1.5	20	1400	18
Girls 10–12	2250	50	4500	400	40	1.1	1.3	15	1200	18
Girls 12–14	2300	50	5000	400	45	1.2	1.4	15	1300	18
Girls 14–16	2400	55	5000	400	50	1.2	1.4	16	1300	18
Girls 16–18	2300	55	5000	400	50	1.2	1.5	15	1300	18

* Vitamin B_1 is thiamine; vitamin B_2 is riboflavin; vitamin B_3 is in niacin equivalents.
Note: Nutrients shown here are those most often in short supply. However, iodine can also become a problem if iodized salt is not used. Foods that supply these nutrients should also carry other nutritional essentials. Figures are those of Food and Nutrition Board.

determined by the Food and Nutrition Board. But to simplify matters, the AMA's Department of Foods and Nutrition has interpreted these RDAs in terms of familiar food groups for quick reference. The food groups referred to are amplified in chapter 2, as to the size of servings, possible substitutes and the like.

One of the great differences between parent and child is the quantity that each eats for his size. Among other things, this difference can help us to understand how children can include so much of what many parents call "junk" in their food, yet still get enough essentials to keep healthy and grow.

For example, let us compare the food intakes of a seven-year-old boy and his 30-year-old mother. We assume that each is of average size. He weighs 50 pounds, and she weighs 128. Yet the caloric need for each is exactly the same—2,000 calories a day. In other words, the boy consumes some two and a half times as much food for his size. This makes for some important dietary differences.

We might choose vitamin C as a sample nutrient. Mother needs 55 milligrams. Junior needs only 40 mg., some 30 percent less. This vitamin C, of course, comes from the same total daily food. So Mother must take care that C-rich foods occupy a bigger part of her dietary. Suppose that all the C either of them got came from tomato juice. Mother would need about a cup and a half. Junior would need about a cup.

Or take protein. Mother needs 55 grams; Junior needs only 35. Suppose both eat a large hamburger for lunch and a three-ounce slice of lean pork for dinner. Both get 43 grams of protein. For Junior, that is about 20 percent more than he needs for the day. But Mother still *lacks* 20 percent of her required protein.

The meat in the pork and hamburger add up to almost 400 calories. So Mother may need to consume another 80 calories worth of meat to get her protein. Junior can use those calories for more than a cup of popcorn or a small candy bar, yet still meet his protein need.

We see the pattern repeat in a number of ways. For example, the meats above give Junior 56 percent of his iron need. Mother has less than a third of hers. She needs 1.5 milligrams of riboflavin; his need is only 1.1 milligrams.

The simple truth is that Junior can *afford* to load mayonnaise onto his sandwich, and to have a little extra ice cream or cake. It is partly because Mother's nutrient need is greater and her caloric budget (for her weight) so much lower that she may fear that Junior's diet, replete with "luxury" foods, is really much poorer than it is.

However, Junior commonly stretches that extra capacity for luxury foods too far. The delicate food-control job of a parent is to make sure that foods containing the essential nutrients get first priority, and are really in adequate supply; once this is done, the child should still have plenty of dietary room for nutritively weak foods.

As a quick demonstration of how this works, let us choose a simplified essential dietary for Junior from the AMA guide. Let's give him three cups of milk or equivalents (500 calories), the meat servings above (under 400 calories), a serving of broccoli *and* one of carrots (45 calories), a glass of orange juice (80 calories), a serving of mashed potatoes with milk and butter (95 calories), two slices of bread (120 calories), some dry cereal (100 calories), and two tablespoons of butter (200 calories). (There are extras involved here. For example, he has much more protein than he needs in the meat alone, not to mention the protein of the bread, butter, potatoes and other vegetables.) The approximate total is 1,500 calories.

So it may not be important how Junior now spends the 500 calories left over. Suppose he uses it this way: a small bottle of cola, potato chips, some marshmallows, a doughnut, and an ice cream novelty. He is still receiving a completely adequate dietary, even with a fourth of his food intake in what Mother calls "junk."

Moreover, one could hardly say that Junior's options were worthless food even aside from the needed fuel they provide. The ice cream has some of the merits of other milk products, as the potato chips share other potato merits and the doughnut provides nutrients of the grain group. There is quite a lot of extra fat here, which would lead some doctors to say that the luxury choices were unwise. And there is quite a lot of sugar, which can promote tooth decay and *interfere with the consumption of essential nutrients,* as in the ancient don't-fill-up-on-candy cry of parents. But nevertheless, sugar is a food, not a poison, as some people seem to think.

How growth changes food needs

The two main factors which account for the food intake differences of adults and children are growth and activity. Activity is, of course, pretty obvious. And from what we have seen in our chapters on overweight, it ought to be clear that an inactive child—or a child entering less active years, as the teenage girl—can no longer afford some of the luxury foods of more active youngsters. If a teenage girl continues her luxury eating into the years of less active play, she is either going to get fat or be cheated of important nutrients.

Growth is a more deceptive thing. Children have a way of changing size and shape which can be puzzling. Take a look at the table below, showing average height and weight increases with age, as compiled from Metropolitan Life Insurance Company measurements of boys and girls:

How Children Grow

	Height Increase (in inches)		Weight Increase (in pounds)	
Year	Boys	Girls	Boys	Girls
1	10	9	16	14.5
2	4.5	4.5	5	5.5
3	3.5	3.5	4.5	5
4	3	3	5	4.5
5	2.5	3	4.5	5
6	2.5	2.5	5.5	6

How Children Grow

Year	Height Increase (in inches)		Weight Increase (in pounds)	
	Boys	Girls	Boys	Girls
7	2.5	2.5	6	6
8	2.5	2.5	7.5	7.5
9	2.2	2.2	7	7.5
10	2.5	2.3	8.5	8.5
11	2	2.7	9	10.2
12	2.5	2.5	9.5	12
13	2.7	2.2	10.5	10
14	3	1.5	13.5	9.7
15	2.5	0.8	13.2	6.5
16	1.7	0.3	9.7	3.5
17	0.5	0.0	5.7	4.5

If we do not think carefully about this chart, and similar ones, we can easily be misled. For it may appear that, after a booming growth in the first year, with a gain of 14 to 16 pounds in weight and nine to ten inches of height, growth takes the shape of a steadily mounting rise toward the years of adolescence.

In fact, this is not really true. The rate of growth is greatest in the first year, but it continues at never-again-to-be-equaled levels until the fifth year. From that time it proceeds at a fairly even pace until the child nears maturity. This is best seen on the chart below, on which we show the *percentage* of growth among boys for each year. Weight is used, because it is the increase of body mass which most affects nutrition.

How Fast Boys Grow

Year	Percent of Weight Increase
1	300
2	22

3	16
4	15
5	12
6	13
7	12
8	12
9	11
10	12
11	12
12	11
13	11
14	13
15	11
16	7
17	4

Perhaps the most strikingly important fact revealed by this chart is that the stresses of growth are unremitting well into adolescence. There is really no time when attention to good diet bears relaxing. The growth stress on a 15-year-old boy is scarcely different from that of a five-year-old in its intensity.

Yet, as puberty approaches, most children are given more license to make food choices. This is a necessary part of learning, but it does not mean that parental supervision can be abandoned. If we look at those times when dietary deficiencies creep in, we can see more than a little relationship to the times when youngsters assume more right of food choice. For it is a nutritional truism that children's diets tend to grow worse as they grow older.

(However, the very high total consumption of food by teenage boys helps guard them from dietary omissions. So does the fact that their growth reaches its peak and continues at a high level much later than does the growth of girls.)

The solution to the worsening food habits of maturing children and adolescents? Most nutritionists see the problem as little different from other problems of growing up. It is probably best answered by the development of desirable tastes and habits in early childhood, which usually come from modeling after those of parents.

It is sad, but apparently true, that no matter what Mother serves to her child, she will make little impression if she uses vegetables grudgingly herself, and always chooses candy before fresh fruit. Nor is it any good extolling the pleasures of fish, if Father grimaces every time it appears on the family table.

Though each age has its special nutritive requirements, nutrition is a family matter. Adults cannot impose a food double standard on their young. It is generally found that when a family's food habits are good or poor, so are those of its children.

With an understanding of what the human organism needs to take in in order to be healthy, and with the knowledge of the special needs of children, the nutrition of the young becomes fairly simple. But here are some of the special questions frequently encountered by nutritionists in regard to children.

QUESTION: *Wouldn't it be best to ban sweets and fatty snacks entirely from children's food?*
ANSWER: The question is largely academic. For as long as the culture makes these foods seem like special treats, children will value them as such. Doctors and nutritionists agree that parents can only guard against the substitution of luxury foods for dietary essentials. A child can eat some sweets and some fatty snacks without harm. Doctors and nutrition groups, however, have urged that such foods not be sold in schools, because of the implied approval of them, and the risk that youngsters will spend lunch money on less valuable food.

QUESTION: *Don't these snack foods cause complexion problems for teenagers?*
ANSWER: The AMA reports that acne is *not* caused by improper diet. Especially, it finds no proof that fat foods make the skin oily; so fried foods and nuts need not be banned. In some individuals, certain foods may

worsen skin problems; chocolate, for example, is a common problem. Acne should be checked by a physician to prevent unsightly scars and needless misery for afflicted youngsters. Skin cleanliness is thought to be the best control.

QUESTION: *Is it safe for teenagers to try popular reducing diets?*
ANSWER: Only if such diets meet the canons of good diet as outlined earlier in this chapter. The exclusion of any food group, or a major reduction, may be dangerous during growth. Doctors agree that the diets of children and teenagers should not be tampered with in any substantial way without medical advice. Particularly, there are a great many cases on record of teenage girls who damaged their health by unwise dieting. All the dangers of fad diets are multiplied in youth.

QUESTION: *Are children's digestive systems more inclined to upset?*
ANSWER: In some ways, yes. First, in young children the digestive system operates much closer to capacity than does that of an adult, for it is smaller. So smaller excesses make for the symptoms of overeating.

Second, for the same reason, foods which are slow to digest, such as fats, may cause more trouble. Also, children appear less able to handle fats efficiently.

Third, children are often less responsive to the warning signs that capacity has been reached. A wise idea is to slow a child's eating. This gives him time to recognize that he cannot manage more.

Fourth, children tend to become excited or fearful easily. These emotions, as we have seen, interfere with digestion. The excitement of a party, rather than the food, is likely to be the cause of digestive disaster.

Finally, children probably lack some of the immunities which help protect adults from foodborne illness of some kinds.

QUESTION: *Aren't certain combinations of foods likely to upset them?*

ANSWER: No. As with adults, children can eat any two foods together that they can eat separately.

QUESTION: *Should children rest after eating?*
ANSWER: Not necessarily. Unless they have eaten an exceptionally large meal, doctors see no reason why they should not swim or play as soon as they feel ready to do so.

QUESTION: *Isn't it best for children to do all their eating at meals?*
ANSWER: As long as the total dietary is a good one, no. Children are likely to feel hungry more often than adults. And they cannot handle as large meals. Remember, their total caloric needs are often as great as those of adults, yet they can manage less food at a sitting. Small sandwiches, milk, cookies, cheese, ice cream, fruit, nuts, celery, carrots and raisins are examples of good snacks. But dentists advise cleaning the teeth (if only by rinsing the mouth with water) after snacks as well as meals. One fact to remember: children's hunger between meals is likely to be very real, and there is no reason to deny it.

QUESTION: *Isn't snacking before bed likely to cause trouble?*
ANSWER: There is really no reason why it should, if the food would be tolerated at any other time. If the child has a nightmare, the cause is probably *not* a bedtime snack.

QUESTION: *Is mother's milk a complete and perfect food?*
ANSWER: Yes and no. For example, mother's milk lacks iron. This is one reason why mothers should be careful to get adequate iron during pregnancy. For if they do, their child will be born with about a three months' iron supply, needed during the early nursing period. Unhappily, many children are born without this protection, and infant anemias have become a serious problem. The infant, of course, should be under a doctor's supervision. He will prescribe foods or supplements to pro-

vide necessary iron in the later weeks of breastfeeding, as well as issue orders about when to introduce other nutrients as they are needed.

QUESTION: *Can parents trust a child's natural appetite?*
ANSWER: The normal, healthy child—partly because of his high level of physical activity—has an appetite which is a fairly good control for the *quantity* he eats. But contrary to myth, children *will not* automatically select the foods their bodies need. There is no known mechanism which signals a need for any special nutrient. Well-informed parents will make the food choices better.

QUESTION: *Do nutritionists still emphasize the importance of breakfast?*
ANSWER: Indeed they do. Many studies have shown that numbers of children are listless and inattentive during morning class hours because of poor breakfasts. And in one study, of those children who had poor breakfasts, only one in five ended the day with an adequate diet.

If left to their own devices to choose breakfast food, children tend to choose poorly, according to a University of California study. Teenage girls make especially poor choices.

QUESTION: *Is it important to encourage children to have broad and varied food tastes?*
ANSWER: Very. Research has shown that children with varied diets tended to have much better nutrition than those with narrow, restricted diets.

QUESTION: *Are there scientific reasons why teenage girls are less well nourished than boys?*
ANSWER: There are. The girls need almost as much of protein, vitamins and minerals as do their male peers. But they require, and usually wish to eat, only two-thirds to three-fourths of the quantity eaten by boys. Therefore, to eat well, they must choose more carefully. Also, menstruation increases their need for protein and iron. One *cultural* reason for poor diets among teenage

girls is a concern with overweight, and an unrealistic ideal of what their figures ought to be like. A teenage girl who can model fashions is probably a nutritional question-mark.

QUESTION: *Is it wrong to insist that children follow parental food choices based on what science knows of nutritive need?*
ANSWER: No.

CHAPTER 21

Food in the later years

No population group in America, among the middle classes, eats so poorly as do the men and women in the later years of life. And often their unfortunate eating habits help to defeat their hopes for rewarding years of retirement, for freedom and independence, adding instead to the health hazards common to their age.

While lack of money contributes to the problem, it is not really the key. Frequently, older people of wealth eat worse than do their peers among the poor. Their inadequate diets seem mainly to result from a biologic problem, which is usually met with indifference, neglect and misinformation.

The biologic problem centers about a decline of total food intake—at a time when the needs for most nutrients continue almost unchanged. To meet these needs in older folk is a little like trying to pack for a trip with a very small suitcase. It will barely hold even the essentials. So unless you know just what you really require, and take great care in choosing it, you wind up in trouble.

The problem is especially great for older women. Dr. Pearl Swanson, reporting on an Iowa State University study, found that the mean intake of such women was only 1,425 daily calories. That doesn't leave much room to go wrong. Men, of course, because of their larger size, use more food and fare better. But both men and women still tend to consume their favorite foods—haven't they reached a time when they can spoil themselves a bit?—and fill their dietaries with "luxury" foods. In the Iowa study, sweets and desserts furnished 20 percent of the day's calories.

The result? Here are the dietary deficiencies among older people as determined by the USDA from average data.

For older men there is a 21 to 29 percent omission of calcium, a one to ten percent deficit of vitamin A, an 11 to 20 percent deficit of riboflavin and a one to ten percent lack of vitamin C. And their record is good compared to that of women.

Women over 65 have dietary deficiencies as follows: calcium, over 30 percent; iron, one to ten percent; vitamin A, one to ten percent; thiamine, 11 to 20 percent; riboflavin 11 to 20 percent. And over 75, the dietary deficiencies of vitamin A and riboflavin increase markedly.

Many people believe that the slowdown of body processes after retirement diminishes many nutrient needs. But except for a desired decline in calories, this view is very wrong. If we compare some key recommended allowances at ages 35 and 75, for example, we find that those for protein, vitamins A, D, E, C, B_2, B_6, B_{12}, folacin, calcium, phosphorus and magnesium have not declined in the slightest. For men, iron need is the same, though in women, this RDA goes down when menstruation ceases. Niacin needs stay the same for women, but go down slightly for men, as do thiamine RDAs. It is hard to pack all this into a smaller dietary.

How many older people actually manage the packing trick? Very few, according to the Administration on Aging. This agency reports a study in which only one of 20 older folk were found to have diets which could be rated "good." This and other studies suggest that the USDA's findings on dietary deficiencies in the later years may be very conservative.

As with other age groups, no one can really say what is the price of this dietary failure. There are many grim guesses, however. For example, some 14 million people over the age of 55 are thought to suffer from *osteoporosis,* a loss of calcium from the bones which leaves its sufferers open to easy fractures and joint problems. And osteoporosis may be related to inadequate calcium intake.

Read the reports on the nutritive problems of older

people, and you quickly get the idea that the solutions must be more than purely nutritive ones. The words "neglect," "disinterest" and "indifference" appear again and again. You begin to suspect that the reason for these problems, as in so many of the troubles of the retired, begins with defeatism. The future, the sense of moving toward something good or better, loses its promise. The extreme of this state is the emotional dead-end of the rest home, in which the later years become merely a kind of anteroom for death.

Endless projects have demonstrated that older people need goals, reasons to look ahead and to enjoy the present, reasons to take the trouble of eating well in the hope of feeling able. Such reasons can be found. Older people themselves, or their younger relatives, can find services in the community that provide participation, friendship, goals, a meaning for life. Without such meaning, the older person may well merely snack at whatever is handy, standing by the kitchen sink, alone and uncaring.

Even company at one or more meals a day can help. One program in Idaho sponsors potluck dinners for older people in which meals become a joint effort of preparation. Some school lunch programs are being expanded to provide sound meals for elder citizens. In Brookline, Massachusetts, older folk can get a school lunch, after the children have eaten, for 50 cents.

Who can tell you about such facilities in your community? Social workers are helpful. So are churches, local health departments, senior citizens' groups, organizations of retired persons and the like.

From a nutritional point of view, the problems are really not difficult to handle. The usual dietary patterns of older folk show a lesser intake of meat, fish and poultry, and a disproportionately large one for breads and cereals. Fats, with their concentrated caloric value, tend to hold their place in the diet, as do sweets and desserts. Fruits and vegetables are often lacking.

If one looks back at the typical dietary omissions of the older person, one can quickly see how they can be remedied. Fruits and vegetables add relatively little to the tight caloric budget, but supply missing vitamins and minerals. A swing away from the emphasis on breads and cereals to more animal products also helps. Milk is important; a glass of skim or low-fat milk a day, preferably two, improves the average older person's diet enormously, with quite a small caloric penalty. Such people tend to eat less at meals and to snack, and milk makes a very good snack.

With age, one loses one's sense of taste and smell to some extent, and this is thought to be one cause of diminishing appetite. The situation is made worse by false notions that spicy, seasoned foods are not good for older folk. Unless there is some specific digestive disorder, diagnosed by a physician who then orders bland foods, there is no reason why an older person cannot tolerate seasonings as well as ever. And spicy foods can perk up his appetite.

Tooth and gum problems need not stand in the way, either. Grinding and chopping, combined with dental attention, can reduce the food-limiting effects of such problems.

What about supplements? If they are needed, the doctor will order them (and an older person who wants his days to be full ones should be under regular medical surveillance). Any number of investigations have shown that older people are prime targets for fad and supplement promoters. In a typical study of 135 older subjects who were steady users of self-prescribed vitamin and mineral preparations, 87 of the subjects were found to be lacking in dietary calcium. But only two of them were getting *any* calcium in their supplements. Seventy were short of iron. But only 21 of these people got *any* in their supplements. The example is characteristic of the worth of nutritional advice to older people from health-food-store proprietors, door-to-door salesmen and well-meaning friends. The usual result is a waste of scarce money, which might be spent more wisely on meat and milk.

One of the most important nutritional safeguards of the later years is exercise. Experts in the problems of aging conclude that few of their patients get sufficient exercise. Yet, as one such doctor puts it, "The longer you keep moving, the longer you'll be able to move."

Exercise helps to prevent or relieve many problems of heart and blood vessels, joints, kidneys, the brain and nervous system—and the simple, low-energy syndrome of those who are getting on. There are many exemplary stories of heart specialists, for example, who ride bicycles and take long walks well into their eighties and beyond.

Aside from the obvious and important medical benefits, such activity gives the older person far more room to err in his or her diet. For, as with any other age group, exercise can greatly enlarge the ability to consume calories. An extra couple of hundred calories a day can make all the difference in the quality of the older person's diet. And both the exercise and the resultant sense of well-being stimulate appetite.

In one sense, we see in the dietary hazards of older people the price of poor food habits in youth and middle age. When such people have favored good dietaries in earlier years, they tend to carry them into later life. If they are not used to fatty, sugary eating, they are not likely to begin it just because someone hands them a gold watch or sends them a Social Security check. If they have a taste for meat and milk, fondness for fruits and vegetables in youth, they are likely to keep it into age.

As a thumbnail guide, this is what the older person ought to get each day: one or two glasses of milk (preferably skim or low-fat); at least one large serving of meat, fish or poultry; at least one serving of green or yellow vegetables; one or two servings of citrus or tomatoes; possibly a serving of other vegetables such as potatoes; two to three servings of bread, flour or cereals; and one or two tablespoons of table fat (such as margarine). He should also be careful to drink enough liquids to make a total of at least three to five cups a day; many older people do not.

That so many of our older people have dietaries which contribute to their numerous health problems and to the needless emptiness of later years is a national disgrace. The change to a fuller dietary and a fuller life, it has been shown repeatedly, is too easily made.

CONCLUSION

The food in your future

Almost every day, since the first page of this book was set on paper, some new fact or idea about nutrition has come across the author's desk, tempting him toward unending revision. That pace of innovation and discovery is likely to speed up in the coming years. Some idea of what is happening in the world of food may be discerned in the statement of Dr. Richard L. Hall, who chaired the recent Third International Congress of Food Science and Technology. By 1985, predicted Dr. Hall, two-thirds of the food Americans consume will be in forms, and derived from sources, unfamiliar to us today.

What will these changes mean in terms of day-to-day decisions for you? What will guide you in making those decisions? There are some simple basic answers, which will become clear if we look at a sampler of what the changes are likely to be.

Among the more important novelties there will probably be some spillover from efforts to find cheap, plentiful protein for the hungry of the world. As we have noted, valuable animal proteins are usually rather expensive and inefficient to produce. So the scientific effort has taken two important new roads. The first is to produce new protein sources.

For example, the tropics produce a lush growth of leaves, ordinarily a source of protein only for such specialized animals as the giraffe. But a new process can concentrate the protein from these leaves in a form usable by humans. This is also possible with seaweed, abundant in our oceans. Algae, the little one-celled plants that make the green slime of ponds, are another source. And wasted fish-life resources, now rejected because of flavor, can also be harvested, to have their protein derived. Such other one-celled organisms as yeasts and bacteria produce protein with impressive speed and economy. In fact, one project has shown that such life can be grown on a food of petroleum, which, after all, is another natural substance made mainly of carbon and hydrogen. One expert has estimated that three million tons of dried yeast could take care of the protein needs of one billion children for a year—and that this much yeast could be grown on a "food" made from just one percent of the present crude petroleum production. Even common grass can yield protein, to the tune of 600 pounds of the nutrient per acre, as compared with the 54 pounds of protein per acre produced by the use of beef cattle.

The reader may wonder if some of these protein sources are complete with all the essential amino acids. Some are and some are not. One approach has been to try and change the characteristics of incomplete-protein foods genetically, as in the development of a special corn which has the *lysine* (an amino acid) very low in ordinary corn. Most often, however, the effort is to combine the proteins of such sources of incomplete protein as soybeans, cottonseed, peanuts, wheat, rice and corn, to give us complete-protein foods.

Some of the results of the latter efforts look like minor miracles of economics. One such plant-protein product, called *incaparina,* has become well accepted in Colombia, offering full protein nutrition for less than half a cent for a serving. Latin American babies are thriving on a vegetable-protein compound called *Duryea,* which gives them eight ounces for something more than a penny and can even be bottle-fed.

Dr. H. E. Robinson, president of the Institute of Food Technology, reports that the general belief is that soybean products will have the biggest impact. We are already seeing such products in our own markets, in the form, for example, of imitation bacon bits. And we are already getting soybean derivatives as nutritive boosters in frankfurters and lunchmeat products. The U.S. Department of Agriculture has high hopes for cottonseed protein, also, which, when added to ordinary bread, can bring its protein value to almost that of meat. And the USDA has been working wonders with cheese whey, a highly nutritious by-product of cheesemaking—and that whey is now nothing more than a *billion* pounds a year of discarded industrial waste!

The great problem at the moment has been to kill off-flavors in these products, to add familiar flavors, and also to put the protein stuffs in forms and textures which are acceptable and fit for our usual eating patterns. To suggest how far along are the texture developments, there are now over 100 new methods of texturing soy protein alone. And our biggest manufacturers have experimental products made of the new compounds which come out as snack foods, candy and carbonated soft drinks, thus promising to solve a problem which has long disturbed nutritionists.

Convenience, too, is expected to grow by leaps and bounds, though what will be the compromises with taste and quality no one yet can say. One new product will probably be food in "plastic" packages; toss it in boiling water, and not only does the food cook at high speed, but the package dissolves into edible, nutritive gravy. Experiments are being conducted, too, with packages which can themselves become cookers, freezers or refrigerators, and perhaps even be plugged into electrical current.

Meanwhile, farm experts are busy working with breeds of hogs to make pork leaner and with cattle which will have less fat, and also perhaps fats which are less objectionable to the heart experts. Older ideas are being taken off the shelf, too, such as "dehydrofreezing," in which the water in the food can be cut by half or more and the resulting product frozen. This method yields a package of frozen vegetables about the size of a cigarette package, but with all the content of its larger relatives. The author tasted such foods at USDA laboratories 15 years ago and found them actually more like fresh produce than any ordinary frozen food in most cases.

Won't all this complexity of combination and enrichment merely confuse the consumer? There is no reason why it should. For one thing, the reader has as his standard guide an understanding of what his body needs. This will not change, except in minor detail. Moreover, the nutritive content of processed foods will be easier and easier to know at a glance; the public demand and the industrial trend both are toward the plain marking of nutritive value on the package. And new methods are already being tried for making these labels easier to understand. For example, under one method being tested, the adult requirement for a nutrient is divided into tenths of that amount. Each of these tenths is called one unit. Ten units supply the daily need. In this way, all the confusion of grams, milligrams and micrograms is gone—left for the scientists. Moreover, one need not remember, for example, how many milligrams of riboflavin he needs, in order to compare that need with what is in the food. If he gets a total of ten or more units for the day, he is well protected.

Plainly, the curtain is going up on a new era of food and health. An enlightened industry, under the eye of a watchful government, can now make hunger—even hidden hunger—a rarity indeed. But while both industry and government have always had among their number men of knowledge and conscience, we must not forget that the new movement away from hunger did not begin until the public called for it. In a free society, the public gets only what it asks for. Our promising new era of healthful food will survive and grow only as long as a caring and informed people demands, and presses those demands at the cash register and the ballot box.

FOOD COMPOSITION: The Nutritive Values of Foods

Food, approximate measure, and weight (in grams)		Grams	Water %	Food energy *calories*	Protein *grams*	Fat (total lipid) *grams*	Carbohydrate *grams*	Calcium *milligrams*	Iron *milligrams*	Vitamin A value *International Units*	Vitamin B_1 Thiamine *milligrams*	Vitamin B_2 Riboflavin *milligrams*	Niacin *milligrams*	Vitamin C Ascorbic acid *milligrams*
Milk, Cream, Cheese; Related Products														
Milk, cow's:														
Fluid, whole	1 cup	244	87	165	9	10	12	285	0.1	390	0.08	0.42	0.2	2
Fluid, nonfat (skim)	1 cup	246	90	90	9	Trace	13	298	.1	10	.10	.44	.2	2
Buttermilk, cultured, from skim milk	1 cup	246	90	90	9	Trace	13	298	.1	10	.10	.44	.2	2
Evaporated, unsweetened, undiluted	1 cup	252	74	345	18	20	24	635	.3	820	.10	.84	.5	3
Condensed, sweetened, undiluted	1 cup	306	26	985	25	25	170	829	.3	1,020	.24	1.21	.5	3
Dry, whole	1 cup	103	2	515	27	28	39	968	.5	1,160	.30	1.50	.7	6
Dry, nonfat	1 cup	80	3	290	29	1	42	1,040	.5	20	.28	1.44	.7	6
Milk, goat's:														
Fluid, whole	1 cup	244	88	165	8	10	11	315	.2	390	.10	.27	.7	2
Cream:														
Half-and-half (milk and cream)	1 cup	242	80	330	8	29	11	259	.1	1,190	.07	.39	.1	2
	1 tablespoon	15	80	20	Trace	2	1	16	0	70	0	.02	0	Trace
Light, table or coffee	1 cup	240	71	525	7	52	10	238	.1	2,140	.07	.35	.1	Trace
	1 tablespoon	15	71	35	Trace	3	1	15	0	130	0	.02	0	Trace

[Dashes show that no basis could be found for imputing a value although there was some reason to believe that a measurable amount of the constituent might be present]

Milk, Cream, Cheese—continued

Food, approximate measure, and weight (in grams)		Grams	Water %	Food energy calories	Protein grams	Fat (total lipid) grams	Carbohydrate grams	Calcium milligrams	Iron milligrams	Vitamin A value International Units	Vitamin B_1 Thiamine milligrams	Vitamin B_2 Riboflavin milligrams	Niacin milligrams	Vitamin C Ascorbic acid milligrams
Cream—continued														
Whipping, unwhipped (volume about double when whipped):														
Medium	1 cup	239	61	745	6	78	8	196	.1	3,200	.06	.29	.1	Trace
	1 tablespoon	15	61	45	Trace	5	1	12	0	200	0	.02	0	Trace
Heavy	1 cup	238	56	860	5	93	7	164	0	3,800	.05	.24	.1	Trace
	1 tablespoon	15	56	55	Trace	6	Trace	10	0	240	0	.02	0	Trace
Cheese:														
Blue mold (Roquefort type)	1 ounce	28	40	105	6	9	Trace	122	.2	350	.01	.17	.1	0
Cheddar or American:														
Ungrated	1-inch cube	17	36	70	4	6	Trace	133	.2	230	Trace	.08	Trace	0
Grated	1 cup	112	36	455	28	37	2	874	1.2	1,510	.03	.53	.1	0
	1 tablespoon	7	36	30	2	2	Trace	55	.1	90	.02	.03	Trace	0
Cheddar, process	1 ounce	28	39	105	7	9	Trace	214	.2	350	Trace	.12	Trace	0
Cheese foods, Cheddar	1 ounce	28	43	95	6	7	2	163	.2	300	.01	.17	Trace	0
Cottage cheese:														
Creamed	1 cup	225	78	240	30	11	6	207	0.9	430	0.07	0.66	0.2	0
	1 ounce	28	78	30	4	1	1	25	.1	50	.01	.08	Trace	0

...creamed	1 cup	225	79	195	38	1	6	202	.9	20	.07	.64	.2	0
	1 ounce	28	79	25	5	Trace	1	26	.1	Trace	.01	.08	Trace	0
Cream cheese	1 ounce	28	51	105	2	11	1	18	.1	440	Trace	.07	Trace	0
	1 tablespoon	15	51	55	1	6	Trace	9	Trace	230	Trace	.04	Trace	0
Swiss	1 ounce	28	39	105	7	8	1	271	.3	320	.01	.06	Trace	0
Milk beverages:														
Cocoa	1 cup	242	79	235	9	11	26	286	.9	390	.09	.45	.4	2
Chocolate-flavored milk drink	1 cup	250	83	190	8	6	27	270	.4	210	.09	.41	.2	2
Malted milk	1 cup	270	78	280	13	12	32	364	.8	670	.17	.56	—	2
Milk desserts:														
Cornstarch pudding, plain	1 cup	248	76	275	9	10	39	290	.1	390	.07	.40	.1	2
Custard, baked	1 cup	248	77	285	13	14	28	278	1.0	870	.10	.47	.2	1
Ice cream, plain, factory packed:														
Container	3½ fluid ounces	62	62	130	2	8	13	76	.1	320	.03	.12	.1	1
Container	8 fluid ounces	142	62	295	6	18	29	175	.1	740	.06	.27	.1	1
Ice milk	1 cup	187	67	285	9	10	42	292	.2	390	.09	.41	.2	2
Yoghurt	1 cup	246	89	120	8	4	13	295	.1	170	.09	.43	.2	2

Eggs

Eggs, large, 24 ounces per dozen:														
Raw:														
Whole, without shell	1 egg	50	74	80	6	6	Trace	27	1.1	590	.05	.15	Trace	0
White of egg	1 white	33	88	15	4	Trace	Trace	3	Trace	0	Trace	.09	Trace	0
Yolk of egg	1 yoke	17	51	60	3	5	Trace	24	.9	580	.04	.07	Trace	0
Cooked:														
Boiled, shell removed	2 eggs	100	74	160	13	12	1	54	2.3	1,180	.09	.28	.1	0
Scrambled, with milk and fat	1 egg	64	72	110	7	8	1	51	1.1	690	.05	.18	Trace	0

[Dashes show that no basis could be found for imputing a value although there was some reason to believe that a measurable amount of the constituent might be present]

Food, approximate measure, and weight (in grams)		Grams	Water %	Food energy *calories*	Protein *grams*	Fat (total lipid) *grams*	Carbohydrate *grams*	Calcium *milligrams*	Iron *milligrams*	Vitamin A value *International Units*	Vitamin B_1 Thiamine *milligrams*	Vitamin B_2 Riboflavin *milligrams*	Niacin *milligrams*	Vitamin C Ascorbic acid *milligrams*
Meat, Poultry, Fish, Shellfish; Related Products														
Bacon, broiled or fried crisp	2 slices	16	8	95	5	8	1	2	.5	0	.08	.05	.8	—
Beef, trimmed to retail basis,[1] cooked:														
Cuts braised, simmered, or pot-roasted:														
Lean and fat	3 ounces	85	53	245	23	16	0	10	2.9	30	.04	.18	3.5	—
Lean only	2.5 ounces	72	62	140	22	5	0	10	2.7	10	.04	.16	3.3	—
Hamburger. broiled:														
Market ground	3 ounces	85	54	245	21	17	0	9	2.7	30	.07	.02	4.6	—
Ground lean	3 ounces	85	60	185	23	10	0	10	3.0	20	.08	.20	5.1	—
Roast, oven-cooked, no liquid added:														
Relatively fat, such as rib:														
Lean and fat	3 ounces	85	38	390	16	36	0	7	2.1	70	.04	.13	3.0	—
Lean only	1.8 ounces	51	57	120	14	7	0	6	1.8	10	.04	.11	2.6	—
Relatively fat, such as round:														
Lean and fat	3 ounces	85	56	220	23	14	0	10	3.0	30	.06	.18	4.2	—
Lean only	2.5 ounces	71	63	130	21	4	0	9	2.7	10	.05	.16	3.8	—

sirloin:														
Lean and fat	3 ounces	85	44	330	20	27	0	8	2.5	50	.05	.16	4.0	—
Lean only	2 ounces	56	59	115	18	4	0	7	2.2	10	.05	.14	3.6	—
Relatively lean, such as round:														
Lean and fat	3 ounces	85	55	220	24	13	0	11	3.0	20	.07	.19	4.8	—
Lean only	2.4 ounces	69	61	130	22	4	0	9	2.6	10	.06	.16	4.2	—
Beef, canned:														
Corned beef	3 ounces	85	59	180	22	10	0	17	3.7	20	.01	.20	2.9	—
Corned beef hash	3 ounces	85	70	120	12	5	6	22	1.1	10	.02	.11	2.4	—
Beef, dried or chipped	2 ounces	57	48	115	19	4	0	11	2.9	—	.04	.18	2.2	—
Beef and vegetable stew	1 cup	235	82	185	15	10	15	31	2.8	2,530	.13	.18	4.4	14
Beef potpie, baked:														
Individual pie, 4¼-inch-diameter, weight before baking about 8 ounces	1 pie	227	63	460	18	28	32	20	2.5	2,830	.07	.14	3.0	Trace
Chicken, cooked:														
Flesh and skin, broiled	3 ounces without bone	85	61	185	23	9	0	10	1.4	260	.04	.15	7.1	—
Breast, fried, ½ breast:														
With bone	3.3 ounces	94	52	215	24	12	—	10	1.1	60	0.03	0.06	9.4	—
Flesh and skin only	2.8 ounces	79	52	215	24	12	—	10	1.1	60	.03	.06	9.4	—
Leg, fried (thigh and drumstick):														
With bone	4.3 ounces	121	52	245	27	15	—	13	1.8	220	.05	.18	4.7	—
Flesh and skin only	3.1 ounces	89	52	245	27	15	—	13	1.8	220	.05	.18	4.7	—
Chicken, canned, boneless	3 ounces	85	62	170	25	7	0	12	1.5	160	.03	.14	5.4	—

[1] Outer layer of fat on the cut was removed to within approximately ½ inch of the lean. Deposits of fat within the cut were not removed.

[Dashes show that no basis could be found for imputing a value although there was some reason to believe that a measurable amount of the constituent might be present]

Food, approximate measure, and weight (in grams)		Grams	Water %	Food energy *calories*	Protein *grams*	Fat (total lipid) *grams*	Carbohydrate *grams*	Calcium *milligrams*	Iron *milligrams*	Vitamin A value *International Units*	Vitamin B_1 Thiamine *milligrams*	Vitamin B_2 Riboflavin *milligrams*	Niacin *milligrams*	Vitamin C Ascorbic acid *milligrams*
Meat, Poultry Fish, Shellfish—continued														
Chicken potpie														
See Poultry potpie														
Chile con carne, canned:														
With beans	1 cup	250	72	335	19	15	30	98	4.2	150	.08	.20	3.5	—
Without beans	1 cup	255	67	510	26	38	15	97	3.6	380	.05	.31	5.6	—
Heart, beef, trimmed of fat, braised	3 ounces	85	61	160	26	5	1	14	5.9	30	.23	1.05	6.8	3
Lamb, trimmed to retail basis, cooked:														
Chop, thick, with bone, broiled	1 chop, 4.8 ounces	137	47	405	25	33	0	10	3.1	—	.14	.25	4.5	—
Lean and fat	4 ounces	112	47	405	25	33	0	10	3.1	—	.14	.25	5.6	—
Lean only	2.6 ouncese	74	62	140	21	6	0	9	2.5	—	.11	.20	4.5	—
Leg, roasted:														
Lean and fat	3 ounces	85	54	235	22	16	0	9	2.8	—	.13	.23	4.7	—
Lean only	2.5 ounces	71	62	130	20	5	0	9	2.6	—	.12	.21	4.4	—
Shoulder, roasted:														
Lean and fat	3 ounces	85	50	285	18	23	0	8	2.4	—	.11	.20	4.0	—
Lean only	2.3 ounce.	64	61	130	17	6	0	8	2.2	—	.10	.18	3.7	—

Ham, smoked, lean and fat	3 ounces	85	48	290	18	24	1	8	2.2	0	.39	.15	3.1	—
Luncheon meat:														
Cooked ham, sliced	2 ounces	57	48	170	13	13	0	5	1.5	0	.57	.15	2.9	—
Canned, spiced or unspiced	2 ounces	57	55	165	8	14	1	5	1.2	0	.18	.12	1.6	—
Pork, fresh, trimmed to retail basis,[1] cooked:														
Chop, thick, with bone	1 chop, 3.5 ounces	98	42	260	16	21	0	8	2.2	0	.63	.18	3.8	—
Lean and fat	2.3 ounces	66	42	260	16	21	0	8	2.2	0	.63	.18	3.8	—
Lean only	1.7 ounces	48	53	130	15	7	0	7	1.9	0	.54	.16	3.3	—
Roast, oven-cooked, no liquid added:														
Lean and fat	3 ounces	85	46	310	21	24	0	9	2.7	0	.78	.22	4.7	—
Lean only	2.4 ouncese	68	55	175	20	10	0	9	2.6	0	.73	.21	4.4	—
Cuts simmered:														
Lean and fat	3 ounces	85	46	320	20	26	0	8	2.5	0	.46	.21	4.1	—
Lean only	2.2 ounces	63	60	135	18	6	0	8	2.3	0	.42	.19	3.7	—
Poultry potpie (chicken or turkey):														
Individual pie, 4¼-inch-diameter, about 8 ounces	1 pie	227	60	485	17	28	39	41	1.6	1,860	.07	.14	3.2	Trace
Sausage:														
Bologna, slice 4.1 by 0.1 inch	8 slices	227	56	690	27	62	2	16	4.1	—	.36	.49	6.0	—
Frankfurter, cooked	1 frankfurter	51	58	155	6	14	1	3	.8	—	.08	.10	1.3	—
Pork, bulk, canned	4 ounces	113	55	340	18	29	0	10	2.6	0	.23	.27	3.4	—
Tongue, beef, simmered	3 ounces	85	61	205	18	14	Trace	7	2.5	—	.04	.26	3.1	—

[1] Outer layer of fat on the cut was removed to within approximately ½ inch of the lean. Deposits of fat within the cut were not removed.

[Dashes show that no basis could be found for imputing a value although there was some reason to believe that a measurable amount of the constituent might be present]

Food, approximate measure, and weight (in grams)		Grams	Water %	Food energy calories	Protein grams	Fat (total lipid) grams	Carbohydrate grams	Calcium milligrams	Iron milligrams	Vitamin A value International Units	Vitamin B_1 Thiamine milligrams	Vitamin B_2 Riboflavin milligrams	Niacin milligrams	Vitamin C Ascorbic acid milligrams
Meat, Poultry, Fish, Shellfish—continued														
Turkey potpie														
See Poultry potpie														
Veal, cooked:														
Cutlet, broiled	3 ounces without bone	85	60	185	23	9	0	9	2.7	—	.06	.21	4.6	—
Roast, medium fat, medium done:														
Lean and fat	3 ounces	85	55	305	23	14	0	10	2.9	—	.11	.26	6.6	—
Fish and shellfish:														
Bluefish, baked or broiled	3 ounces	85	68	135	22	4	0	25	.6	40	.09	.08	1.6	—
Clams:														
Raw, meat only	3 ounces	85	80	70	11	1	3	82	6.0	90	.08	.15	1.4	—
Canned, solids and liquid	3 ounces	85	87	45	7	1	2	74	5.4	70	.04	.08	.9	—
Crabmeat, canned or cooked	3 ounces	85	77	90	14	2	1	38	.8	—	.04	.05	2.1	—
Fishsticks, breaded, cooked, frozen	10 sticks	227	66	400	38	20	15	25	.9	—	.09	.16	3.6	—
Haddock, fried	3 ounces	85	67	135	16	5	6	15	.5	50	.03	.08	2.2	—
Mackerel:														
Canned, Pacific, solids and liquid	3 ounces	85	66	155	18	9	0	221	1.9	20	.02	.28	[illegible]	[illegible]

and breadcrumbs), fried	3 ounces	85	59	195	16	11	6	14	1.3	50	0.09	0.10	1.7	—
Oysters, meat only:														
Raw, 13-19 medium selects	1 cup	240	85	160	20	4	8	226	13.2	740	.30	.39	6.6	—
Oyster stew, 1 part oysters to 3 parts milk, 3-4 oysters	1 cup	230	84	200	11	12	11	269	3.3	640	.12	.40	1.7	—
Salmon, pink, canned	3 ounces	85	70	120	17	5	0	159[2]	.7	60	.03	.16	6.8	—
Sardines, Atlantic type, canned in oil, drained solids	3 ounces	85	57	180	22	9	1	367	2.5	190	.02	.18	4.6	—
Shrimp, canned, meat only	3 ounces	85	66	110	23	1	0	98	2.6	50	.01	.03	1.9	—
Swordfish, broiled with butter or margarine	3 ounces	85	65	150	24	5	0	23	1.1	1,750	.03	.04	9.3	—
Tuna, canned in oil, drained solids	3 ounces	85	60	170	25	7	0	7	1.2	70	.04	.10	10.9	—

Dry Beans and Peas, Nuts, Peanuts; Related Products

Almonds, shelled	1 cup	142	5	850	26	77	28	332	6.7	0	.34	1.31	5.0	Trace
Beans, dry:														
Common varieties, such as Great Northern, navy, and others, canned:														
Red	1 cup	256	76	230	15	1	42	74	4.6	0	.13	.13	1.5	Trace
White, with tomato or molasses:														
With pork	1 cup	261	69	330	16	7	54	172	4.4	140	.13	.10	1.3	5
Without pork	1 cup	261	69	315	16	1	60	183	5.2	140	.13	.10	1.3	5
Lima, cooked	1 cup	192	64	260	16	1	48	56	5.6	Trace	.26	.12	1.3	Trace

[2] If bones are discarded, calcium content is much lower. Bones equal about 2 percent by weight of total contents of can.

[Dashes show that no basis could be found for imputing a value although there was some reason to believe that a measurable amount of the constituent might be present]

Food, approximate measure, and weight (in grams)		Grams	Water %	Food energy *calories*	Protein *grams*	Fat (total lipid) *grams*	Carbohydrate *grams*	Calcium *milligrams*	Iron *milligrams*	Vitamin A value *International Units*	Vitamin B_1 Thiamine *milligrams*	Vitamin B_2 Riboflavin *milligrams*	Niacin *milligrams*	Vitamin C Ascorbic acid *milligrams*
Dry Beans and Peas, Nuts, Peanuts—continued														
Brazil nuts, broken pieces	1 cup	140	5	905	20	92	15	260	4.8	Trace	1.21	—	—	—
Cashew nuts, roasted	1 cup	135	5	770	25	65	35	51	5.1	—	.49	.46	1.9	—
Coconut:														
Fresh, shredded	1 cup	97	50	330	3	31	13	15	1.7	0	.06	.03	.5	4
Dried, shredded, sweetened	1 cup	62	3	345	2	24	33	13	1.6	0	.04	.02	.4	0
Cowpeas or blackeye peas, dry, cooked:	1 cup	248	80	190	13	1	34	42	3.2	20	.41	.11	1.1	Trace
Peanuts, roasted, shelled:														
Halves	1 cup	144	2	840	39	71	28	104	3.2	0	.47	.19	24.6	0
Peanut butter	1 tablespoon	16	2	90	4	8	3	12	.4	0	.02	.02	2.8	0
Peas, split, dry, cooked	1 cup	250	70	290	20	1	52	28	4.2	120	.36	.22	2.2	Trace
Pecans:														
Halves	1 cup	108	3	740	10	77	16	79	2.6	140	.93	.14	1.0	2
Walnuts, shelled:														
Black or native, chopped	1 cup	126	3	790	26	75	19	Trace	7.6	380	.28	.14	.9	—
English or Persian:														

Vegetables and Vegetable Products

Asparagus:													
Cooked, cut spears	1 cup	175	92	35	4	Trace	6	33	1.8	1,820	.23	.30	2.1	40
Canned spears, medium:														
Green	6 spears	96	92	20	2	Trace	3	18	1.8	770	.06	.08	.9	17
Bleached	6 spears	96	92	20	2	Trace	4	15	1.0	70	.05	.07	.8	17
Beans:														
Lima, immature, cooked	1 cup	160	75	150	8	1	29	46	2.7	460	.22	.14	1.8	24
Snap, green:														
Cooked:														
In small amount of water, short time	1 cup	125	92	25	2	Trace	6	45	.9	830	.09	.12	.6	18
In large amount of water, long time	1 cup	125	92	25	2	Trace	6	45	.9	830	.06	.11	.5	12
Canned:														
Solids and liquid	1 cup	239	94	45	2	Trace	10	65	3.3	990	.08	.10	.7	9
Strained or chopped	1 ounce	28	93	5	Trace	Trace	1	10	.3	120	.01	.02	.1	1
Beets, cooked, diced	1 cup	165	88	70	2	Trace	16	35	1.2	30	.03	.07	.5	11
Broccoli spears, cooked	1 cup	150	90	45	5	Trace	8	195	2.0	5,100	.10	.22	1.2	111
Brussels sprouts, cooked	1 cup	130	85	60	6	1	12	44	1.7	520	.05	.16	.6	61
Cabbage:														
Raw:														
Finely shredded	1 cup	100	92	25	1	Trace	5	46	0.5	80	0.06	0.05	0.3	50
Coleslaw	1 cup	120	84	100	2	7	9	47	.5	80	.06	.05	.3	50
Cooked:														
In small amount of water, short time	1 cup	170	92	40	2	Trace	9	78	.8	150	.08	.08	.5	53
In large amount of water, long time	1 cup	170	92	40	2	Trace	9	78	.8	150	.05	.05	.3	32

[Dashes show that no basis could be found for imputing a value although there was some reason to believe that a measurable amount of the constituent might be present]

Food, approximate measure, and weight (in grams)		Grams	Water %	Food energy calories	Protein grams	Fat (total lipid) grams	Carbohydrate grams	Calcium milligrams	Iron milligrams	Vitamin A value International Units	Vitamin B_1 Thiamine milligrams	Vitamin B_2 Riboflavin milligrams	Niacin milligrams	Vitamin C Ascorbic acid milligrams
Vegetables—continued														
Cabbage, celery or Chinese:														
Raw, leaves and stem, 1-inch pieces	1 cup	100	95	15	1	Trace	2	43	.9	260	.03	.04	.4	31
Cooked	1 cup	190	95	25	2	1	5	82	1.7	490	.04	.06	.6	42
Carrots:														
Raw:														
Whole, 5½ by 1 inch (25 thin strips)	1 carrot	50	88	20	1	Trace	5	20	.4	6,000	.03	.03	.3	3
Grated	1 cup	110	88	45	1	Trace	10	43	.9	13,200	.06	.06	.7	7
Cooked, diced	1 cup	145	92	45	1	1	9	38	.9	18,130	.07	.07	.7	6
Canned	1 ounce	28	92	5	Trace	0	2	7	.2	3,400	.01	.01	.1	1
Cauliflower, cooked	1 cup	120	92	30	3	Trace	6	26	1.3	110	.07	.10	.6	34
Celery, raw:														
Stalk, large outer, 8 by about 1½ inches at root end	1 stalk	40	94	5	1	Trace	1	20	.2	0	.02	.02	.2	3
Pieces, diced	1 cup	100	94	20	1	Trace	4	50	.5	0	.05	.04	.4	7
Collards, cooked	1 cup	190	87	75	7	1	14	473	3.0	14,500	.15	.46	3.2	84
Corn, sweet:														
Cooked, ear 5 by 1¾ inches	1 ear	140	76	65	2	1	16	4	.5	300[3]	.09	.08	1.1	6

[illegible], cooked, immature seeds	1 cup	160	75	150	11	1	25	59	4.0	620	.46	.13	1.3	32
Cucumbers, raw, pared, center slice 1/8-inch thick	6 slices	50	96	5	Trace	Trace	1	5	.2	0	.02	.02	.1	4
Dandelion greens, cooked	1 cup	180	86	80	5	1	16	337	5.6	27,310	.23	.22	1.3	29
Endive, curly (including escarole)	2 ounces	57	93	10	1	Trace	2	45	1.0	1,700	.04	.07	.2	6
Kale, cooked	1 cup	110	87	45	4	1	8	248	2.4	9,220	.08	.25	1.9	56
Lettuce, raw:														
Head, loose-leaf, 4-inch-diameter	1 head	220	95	30	3	Trace	6	48	1.1	1,200	.10	.18	.4	17
Head, compact, 4 3/4-inch-diameter, 1 pound	1 head	454	95	70	5	1	13	100	2.3	2,470	.20	.38	.9	35
Leaves	2 large or 4 small	50	95	5	1	Trace	1	11	.2	270	.02	.04	.1	4
Mushrooms, canned, solids and liquid	1 cup	244	93	30	3	Trace	9	17	2.0	0	.04	.60	4.8	—
Mustard greens, cooked	1 cup	140	92	30	3	Trace	6	308	4.1	10,050	.08	.25	1.0	63
Okra, cooked, 3 x 5/8-inch	8 pods	85	90	30	2	Trace	6	70	.6	630	.05	.05	.7	17
Onions:														
Mature:														
Raw, onion 2 1/2-inch-diameter	1 onion	110	88	50	2	Trace	11	35	.6	60	.04	.04	.2	10
Cooked	1 cup	210	90	80	2	Trace	18	67	1.0	110	.04	.06	.4	13
Young green, small, without tops	6 onions	50	88	25	Trace	Trace	5	68	.4	30	.02	.02	.1	12
Parsley, raw, chopped	1 tablespoon	3.5	84	1	Trace	Trace	Trace	7	.2	290	Trace	.01	.1	7
Parsnips, cooked	1 cup	155	84	95	2	1	22	88	1.1	0	.09	.16	.3	19
Peas, green:														
Cooked	1 cup	160	82	110	8	1	19	35	3.0	1,150	.40	.22	3.7	24

[3] Vitamin A value is based on yellow corn; white corn contains only a trace.

[Dashes show that no basis could be found for imputing a value although there was some reason to believe that a measurable amount of the constituent might be present]

Food, approximate measure, and weight (in grams)		Grams	Water %	Food energy calories	Protein grams	Fat (total lipid) grams	Carbohydrate grams	Calcium milligrams	Iron milligrams	Vitamin A value International Units	Vitamin B_1 Thiamine milligrams	Vitamin B_2 Riboflavin milligrams	Niacin milligrams	Vitamin C Ascorbic acid milligrams
Vegetables—continued														
Peas—continued														
Canned, solids and liquid	1 cup	249	82	170	8	1	32	62	4.5	1,350	.28	.15	2.6	21
Canned, strained	1 ounce	28	86	10	1	Trace	2	5	.3	160	.03	.02	.3	2
Peppers, hot, red, without seeds, dried; ground chili powder	1 tablespoon	15	13	50	2	1	9	20	1.2	11,520	.03	.20	1.6	2
Peppers, sweet:														
Raw, medium, about 6 per pound:														
Green pod without stem and seeds	1 pod	62	93	15	1	Trace	3	6	.4	260	.05	.05	.3	79
Red pod without stem and seeds	1 pod	60	91	20	1	Trace	4	8	.4	2,670	.05	.05	.3	122
Canned, pimientos, medium	1 pod	38	92	10	Trace	Trace	2	3	.6	870	.01	.02	.1	36
Potatoes, medium, about 3 per pound:														
Baked, peeled after baking	1 potato	99	75	90	3	Trace	21	9	.7	Trace	.10	.04	1.7	20
Boiled:														
Peeled after boiling	1 potato	136	80	105	3	Trace	23	10	0.8	Trace	0.13	0.05	2.0	22

by 1/2 inch:														
Cooked in deep fat	10 pieces	57	45	155	2	7	20	9	.7	Trace	.06	.04	1.8	8
Frozen, ready to heat for serving	10 pieces	57	64	95	2	4	15	4	.8	Trace	.08	.01	1.2	10
Mashed:														
Milk added	1 cup	195	80	145	4	1	30	47	1.0	50	.17	.11	.2	17
Milk and butter added	1 cup	195	76	230	3	12	28	45	1.0	470	.16	.10	1.6	16
Potato chips, 2-inch-diameter	10 chips	20	3	110	1	7	10	6	.4	Trace	.04	.02	.6	2
Pumpkin, canned	1 cup	228	90	75	2	1	18	46	1.6	7,750	.04	.14	1.2	—
Radishes, raw, small, without tops	4 radishes	40	94	10	Trace	Trace	2	15	.4	10	.01	.01	.1	10
Sauerkraut, canned, drained solids	1 cup	150	91	30	2	Trace	7	54	.8	60	.05	.10	.2	24
Spinach:														
Cooked	1 cup	180	91	45	6	1	6	223[4]	3.6	21,200	.14	.36	1.1	54
Canned, drained solids	1 cup	180	91	45	6	1	6	223[4]	3.6	13,740	.04	.21	.7	26
Sprouts, raw:														
Mung bean	1 cup	90	92	20	3	Trace	4	26	.7	10	.06	.08	.5	14
Soybean	1 cup	107	86	50	7	1	6	51	1.1	190	.24	.21	.9	14
Squash:														
Cooked:														
Summer, diced	1 cup	210	95	35	1	Trace	8	32	.8	550	.08	.15	1.3	23
Winter, baked, mashed	1 cup	205	86	95	4	1	23	49	1.6	12,690	.10	.31	1.2	14
Canned, winter	1 ounce	28	92	10	Trace	Trace	2	7	.1	510	.01	.01	.1	1
Sweet potatoes:														
Cooked, medium, 5 by 2 inches, weight raw about 6 ounces:														

[4] Calcium may not be usable because of presence of oxalic acid.

[Dashes show that no basis could be found for imputing a value although there was some reason to believe that a measurable amount of the constituent might be present]

Food, approximate measure, and weight (in grams)		Grams	Water %	Food energy calories	Protein grams	Fat (total lipid) grams	Carbohydrate grams	Calcium milligrams	Iron milligrams	Vitamin A value International Units	Vitamin B_1 Thiamine milligrams	Vitamin B_2 Riboflavin milligrams	Niacin milligrams	Vitamin C Ascorbic acid milligrams
Vegetables—continued														
Sweet potatoes—continued														
Baked, peeled after baking	1 sweet potato	110	64	155	2	1	36	44	1.0	8,970	.10	.07	.7	24
Boiled, peeled after boiling	1 sweet potato	147	71	170	2	1	39	47	1.0	11,610	.13	.09	.9	25
Candied, 3½ by 2¼ inches	1 sweet potato	175	60	295	2	6	60	65	1.6	11,030	.10	.08	.8	17
Canned	1 cup	218	72	235	4	Trace	54	54	1.7	17,110	.12	.09	1.1	30
Tomatoes:														
Raw, medium, 2 by 2½ inches, about 3 per pound	1 tomato	150	94	30	2	Trace	6	16	.9	1,640	.08	.06	.8	35
Canned or cooked	1 cup	242	94	45	2	Trace	9	27	1.5	2,540	.14	.08	1.7	40
Tomato juice, canned	1 cup	242	94	50	2	Trace	10	17	1.0	2,540	.12	.07	1.8	38
Tomato catsup	1 tablespoon	17	70	15	Trace	Trace	4	2	.1	320	.02	.01	.4	2
Turnips, cooked, diced	1 cup	155	92	40	1	Trace	9	62	.8	Trace	.06	.09	.6	28
Turnip greens:														
Cooked:														
In small amount of water, short time	1 cup	145	90	45	4	1	8	376	3.5	15,370	.09	.59	1.0	87
In large amount of water, long time	1 cup	145	90	45	4	1	8	376	3.5	15,370	.07	.52	.9	65

Apples, raw, medium, 2½-inch-diameter, about 3 per pound	1 apple	150	85	70	Trace	Trace	18	8	.4	50	.04	.02	.1	3
Apple brown betty	1 cup	230	64	350	4	8	69	41	1.4	270	.13	.10	.9	Trace
Apple juice, fresh or canned	1 cup	249	86	125	Trace	0	34	15	1.2	90	.05	.07	Trace	2
Applesauce, canned:														
Sweetened	1 cup	254	80	185	Trace	Trace	50	10	1.0	80	.05	.03	.1	3
Unsweetened	1 cup	239	88	100	Trace	Trace	26	10	1.0	70	.05	.02	.1	3
Apricots:														
Raw, about 12 per pound	3 apricots	114	85	55	1	Trace	14	18	.5	2,890	.03	.04	.7	10
Canned in heavy syrup:														
Halves and syrup	1 cup	259	77	220	2	Trace	57	28	.8	4,520	.05	.06	.9	10
Halves, medium, and syrup	4 halves; 2 tablespoons syrup	122	77	105	1	Trace	27	13	.4	2,130	.02	.03	.4	5
Dried:														
Uncooked, 40 halves, small	1 cup	150	25	390	8	1	100	100	8.2	16,390	.02	.24	4.9	19
Cooked, unsweetened, fruit and liquid	1 cup	285	76	240	5	1	62	63	5.1	10,130	.01	.13	2.8	8
Apricot nectar	1 cup	250	85	140	1	Trace	36	22	.5	2,380	.02	.02	.5	7
Avocados, raw:														
California varieties, mainly Fuerte:														
10-ounce avocado, about 3⅓ by 4¼ inches	½ avocado	108	74	185	2	18	6	11	.6	310	.12	.21	1.7	15
½-inch cubes	1 cup	152	74	260	3	26	9	15	.9	430	.16	.30	2.4	2

[Dashes show that no basis could be found for imputing a value although there was some reason to believe that a measurable amount of the constituent might be present]

Food, approximate measure, and weight (in grams)		Grams	Water %	Food energy *calories*	Protein *grams*	Fat (total lipid) *grams*	Carbohydrate *grams*	Calcium *milligrams*	Iron *milligrams*	Vitamin A value *International Units*	Vitamin B_1 Thiamine *milligrams*	Vitamin B_2 Riboflavin *milligrams*	Niacin *milligrams*	Vitamin C Ascorbic acid *milligrams*
Fruits—continued														
Avocados—continued														
Florida varieties:														
13-ounce avocado, about 4 by 3 inches	½ avocado	123	78	160	2	14	11	12	.7	350	.13	.24	2.0	17
½-inch cubes	1 cup	152	78	195	2	17	13	15	.9	430	.16	.30	2.4	21
Bananas, raw, 6 by 1½ inches, about 3 per pound	1 banana	150	76	85	1	Trace	23	8	.7	190	.05	.06	.7	10
Blackberries, raw	1 cup	144	85	85	2	1	19	46	1.3	290	.05	.06	.5	30
Blueberries, raw	1 cup	140	83	85	1	1	21	21	1.4	140	.04	.08	.6	20
Cantaloups, medium, 5-inch-diameter, 1⅔ pounds	½ melon	385	94	40	1	Trace	9	33	.8	6,590[5]	.09	.07	1.0	63
Cherries:														
Raw, sour, sweet, hybrid	1 cup	114	83	65	1	1	15	19	.4	650	.05	.06	.4	9
Canned, red, sour, pitted	1 cup	247	88	105	2	1	26	37	.7	1,680	.07	.06	.4	13
Cranberry juice cocktail	1 cup	250	85	140	Trace	Trace	36	10	.5	20	.02	.02	.1	5
Cranberry sauce, sweetened	1 cup	277	48	550	Trace	1	142	22	.8	80	.06	.06	.3	5
Dates, "fresh" and dried, pitted, cut	1 cup	178	20	505	4	1	134	105	5.7	100	.16	.17	3.9	0
Figs:														
Raw, small, 1½-inch-diameter, about 12 per														

Dried, large, 2 by 1 inch	1 fig	21	23	60	1	Trace	15	40	.7	20	.02	.02	.1	0
Fruit cocktail, canned in heavy syrup, solids and liquid	1 cup	256	80	195	1	1	50	23	1.0	360	.04	.03	1.1	5
Grapefruit:														
Raw, medium, 4¼-inch-diameter, size 64:														
White	½ grapefruit	285	89	50	1	Trace	14	21	.5	10	.05	.02	.2	50
Pink or red	½ grapefruit	285	89	55	1	Trace	14	21	.5	590	.05	.02	.2	48
Canned:														
Syrup pack	1 cup	249	81	170	1	Trace	44	32	.7	20	.07	.04	.5	75
Water pack	1 cup	240	91	70	1	Trace	18	31	.7	20	.07	.04	.5	72
Grapefruit juice:														
Fresh	1 cup	246	90	95	1	Trace	23	22	.5	20	.09	.04	.4	92
Canned:														
Unsweetened	1 cup	247	89	100	1	Trace	24	20	1.0	20	.07	.04	.4	84
Sweetened	1 cup	250	86	130	1	Trace	32	20	1.0	20	.07	.04	.4	78
Frozen, concentrate, unsweetened:														
Water added	1 cup	247	89	100	1	Trace	24	25	.2	20	10	.04	.5	96
Frozen, concentrate, sweetened:														
Water added	1 cup	249	88	115	1	Trace	28	20	.2	20	.08	.03	.4	82
Grapes, raw:														
American type such as Concord, Delaware, Niagara, Scupernong	1 cup	153	82	70	1	1	16	13	.4	100	.05	.03	.3	4
European type such as Malaga, Muscat, Sultanina														

[8] Vitamin A value is based on deeply colored yellow varieties.

[Dashes show that no basis could be found for imputing a value although there was some reason to believe that a measurable amount of the constituent might be present]

Food, approximate measure, and weight (in grams)		Grams	Water %	Food energy calories	Protein grams	Fat (total lipid) grams	Carbohydrate grams	Calcium milligrams	Iron milligrams	Vitamin A value International Units	Vitamin B_1 Thiamine milligrams	Vitamin B_2 Riboflavin milligrams	Niacin milligrams	Vitamin C Ascorbic acid milligrams
Fruits—continued														
Grapes—continued														
(Thompson Seedless),														
Flame Tokay	1 cup	160	81	100	1	Trace	26	18	.6	150	.08	.04	.4	7
Grape juice, bottled	1 cup	254	83	165	1	Trace	42	28	.8	—	.10	.05	.6	Trace
Lemons, raw, medium, 2-1/5-inch-diameter, size 150	1 lemon	106	90	20	1	Trace	6	18	0.4	10	0.03	0.01	0.1	38
Lemon juice:														
Fresh	1 cup	246	91	60	1	Trace	20	17	.5	40	.08	.03	.2	113
	1 tablespoon	15	91	5	Trace	Trace	1	1	Trace	Trace	Trace	Trace	Trace	7
Canned, unsweetened	1 cup	245	92	60	1	Trace	19	17	.5	40	.07	.03	.2	102
Lemonade concentrate, frozen, sweetened:														
Water added	1 cup	248	88	110	Trace	Trace	28	2	.1	10	.01	.01	.2	17
Lime juice:														
Fresh	1 cup	246	90	65	1	Trace	22	22	.5	30	.05	.03	.3	80
Canned	1 cup	246	90	65	1	Trace	22	22	.5	30	.05	.03	.3	52
Limeade concentrate, frozen, sweetened:														
Water added	1 cup	248	89	105	Trace	Trace	27	2	.2	Trace	.01	Trace	Trace	6
Oranges, raw:														

diameter	1 orange	180	85	60	2	Trace	16	49	.5	240	.12	.05	.5	75
Other varieties, 3-inch-diameter	1 orange	210	86	70	1	Trace	18	63	.3	290	.12	.03	.4	66
Orange juices:														
Fresh:														
California, Valencia, summer	1 cup	249	88	88	2	1	26	27	.7	500	.22	.06	.9	122
Florida varieties:														
Early and midseason	1 cup	247	90	100	1	Trace	23	25	.5	490	.22	.06	.9	127
Late season, Valencia	1 cup	248	88	110	1	Trace	26	25	.5	500	.22	.06	.9	92
Canned, unsweetened	1 cup	249	87	120	2	Trace	28	25	1.0	500	.17	.05	.6	100
Frozen concentrate:														
Water added	1 cup	248	88	110	2	Trace	27	22	.2	500	.21	.03	.8	112
Orange and grapefruit juices														
Frozen concentrate:														
Water added	1 cup	248	88	110	1	Trace	26	20	.2	270	.16	.02	.8	102
Papayas, raw, ½-inch cubes	1 cup	182	89	70	1	Trace	18	36	.5	3,190	.07	.08	.5	102
Peaches:														
Raw:														
Whole, 2-inch-diameter, 4 per pound	1 peach	114	89	35	1	Trace	10	9	.5	1,320[6]	.02	.05	1.0	7
Sliced	1 cup	168	89	65	1	Trace	16	15	.8	2,230[6]	.03	.08	1.6	12
Canned, yellow-fleshed, solids and liquid:														
Syrup pack, heavy:														
Halves or slices	1 cup	257	79	200	1	Trace	52	10	.8	1,100	.02	.06	1.4	7

[6] Vitamin A value of yellow-fleshed varieties; the value is negligible in white-fleshed varieties.

[Dashes show that no basis could be found for imputing a value although there was some reason to believe that a measurable amount of the constituent might be present]

Food, approximate measure, and weight (in grams)		Grams	Water %	Food energy calories	Protein grams	Fat (total lipid) grams	Carbohydrate grams	Calcium milligrams	Iron milligrams	Vitamin A value International Units	Vitamin B_1 Thiamine milligrams	Vitamin B_2 Riboflavin milligrams	Niacin milligrams	Vitamin C Ascorbic acid milligrams
Fruits—continued														
Peaches—continued														
Halves, medium, and syrup	2 halves and 2 tablespoons syrup	117	79	90	Trace	Trace	24	5	.4	500	.01	.03	.7	3
Water pack	1 cup	245	91	75	1	Trace	20	10	.7	1,100	.02	.06	1.4	7
Strained	1 ounce	28	82	20	Trace	Trace	5	2	.2	150	Trace	.01	.2	Trace
Dried:														
Uncooked	1 cup	160	25	420	5	1	109	77	9.6	6,240	.02	.31	8.5	28
Frozen:														
Carton, 12 ounces	1 carton	340	79	265	1	Trace	69	20	1.4	1,770	.04	.10	1.8	99[7]
Can, 16 ounces	1 can	454	79	355	2	Trace	92	27	1.8	2,360	.05	.14	2.4	132[7]
Peach nectar, canned	1 cup	250	87	115	Trace	Trace	31	10	.5	1,070	.02	.05	1.0	1
Pears:														
Raw, 3 by 2½-inch-diameter	1 pear	182	83	100	1	1	25	13	.5	30	.04	.07	.2	7
Canned, solids and liquid:														
Syrup pack, heavy:														
Halves or slices	1 cup	255	80	195	1	1	50	13	.5	Trace	.03	.05	.3	4
Halves, medium, and syrup	2 halves and 2 tablespoons syrup	117	80	90	Trace	Trace	23	6	.2	Trace	.01	.02	.2	2
Water pack	1 cup	243	91	80	Trace	Trace	20	12	0.5	Trace	0.02	0.05	0.3	4
Pear nectar, canned	1 cup	250	86	130	1	Trace	33	8	.2	10	.01	.05	Trace	1

raw, seedless, 2½-inch-diameter	1 persimmon	125	79	75	1	Trace	20	6	.4	2,740	.03	.02	.1	11
Pineapple:														
Raw, diced	1 cup	140	85	75	1	Trace	19	22	.4	180	.12	.04	.3	33
Canned, syrup pack, solids and liquid:														
Crushed	1 cup	260	78	205	1	Trace	55	75	1.6	210	.20	.04	.4	23
Sliced, slices and juice	2 small or 1 large and 2 tablespoons juice	122	78	95	Trace	Trace	26	35	.7	100	.09	.02	.2	11
Pineapple juice, canned	1 cup	249	86	120	1	Trace	32	37	1.2	200	.13	.04	.4	22
Plums, all except prunes:														
Raw, 2-inch-diameter, about 2 ounces	1 plum	60	86	30	Trace	Trace	7	10	.3	200	.04	.02	.3	3
Canned, syrup pack (Italian prunes):														
Plums and juice	1 cup	256	79	185	1	Trace	50	20	2.7	560	.07	.06	.9	3
Prunes, dried:														
Medium, 50-60 per pound:														
Uncooked	4 prunes	32	24	70	1	Trace	19	14	1.0	430	.02	.05	.4	1
Cooked, unsweetened, 17-18 prunes and ⅓ cup liquid	1 cup	270	65	305	3	1	81	60	4.5	1,850	.08	.19	1.8	3
Prune juice, canned	1 cup	240	80	170	1	Trace	45	34	9.8	—	.01	.03	1.1	4
Raisins, dried	1 cup	160	18	460	4	Trace	124	99	5.6	30	.18	.13	.9	2
Raspberries, red:														
Raw	1 cup	123	84	70	1	1	17	27	1.1	160	.03	.09	.9	31

[7] Content of frozen peaches with added ascorbic acid; when not added the content is 14 milligrams per 12-ounce carton and 18 milligrams per 16-ounce can.

[Dashes show that no basis could be found for imputing a value although there was some reason to believe that a measurable amount of the constituent might be present]

Food, approximate measure, and weight (in grams)		Grams	Water %	Food energy calories	Protein grams	Fat (total lipid) grams	Carbohydrate grams	Calcium milligrams	Iron milligrams	Vitamin A value International Units	Vitamin B_1 Thiamine milligrams	Vitamin B_2 Riboflavin milligrams	Niacin milligrams	Vitamin C Ascorbic acid milligrams
Fruits—continued														
Raspberries, red—continued														
Frozen, 10-ounce carton	1 carton	284	74	280	2	1	70	79	1.7	220	.03	.12	.5	45
Rhubarb, cooked, sugar added	1 cup	272	63	385	1	Trace	98	112[4]	1.1	70	.02	—	.2	17
Strawberries:														
Raw, capped	1 cup	149	90	55	1	1	13	31	1.5	90	.04	.10	.9	87
Frozen, 10-ounce carton	1 carton	284	72	300	2	1	75	62	1.7	120	.05	.14	.5	116
Frozen, 16-ounce can	1 can	454	72	485	3	2	121	100	2.7	190	.08	.23	.8	186
Tangerines, raw, 2½-inch-diameter, about 4 per pound	1 tangerine	114	87	40	1	Trace	10	34	.3	360	.05	.01	.1	26
Tangerine juice:														
Canned, unsweetened	1 cup	248	89	105	1	Trace	25	45	.5	1,050	.14	.04	.3	56
Frozen concentrate:														
Water added	1 cup	248	88	115	1	Trace	27	45	.5	1,020	.14	.04	.3	67
Watermelon, raw, (1/16 of 10- by 16-inch melon, about 2 pounds with rind)	1 wedge	925	92	120	2	1	29	30	.9	2,530	.20	.22	.7	26

Grain Products

enriched flour, 2½-inch-diameter	1 biscuit	38	28	130	3	4	18	61	.7	Trace	.09	.09	.7	Trace
Bran flakes (40 percent bran) with added thiamine	1 ounce	28	4	85	3	1	22	17	1.1	0	.13	.07	2.5	0
Breads:														
Boston brown bread, slice, 3 by ¾ inch	1 slice	48	45	100	3	1	22	43	.9	0	.05	.03	.6	0
Cracked-wheat bread:														
Slice	1 slice	23	35	60	2	1	12	20	.3	Trace	.03	.02	.3	Trace
French or vienna bread:														
Enriched, 1-pound loaf	1 loaf	454	31	1,315	41	14	251	195	10.0	Trace	1.26	.98	11.3	Trace
Unenriched, 1-pound loaf	1 loaf	454	31	1,315	41	14	251	195	3.2	Trace	.39	.39	3.6	Trace
Italian bread:														
Enriched, 1-pound loaf	1 loaf	454	32	1,250	41	4	256	77	10.0	0	1.31	.93	11.7	0
Unenriched, 1-pound loaf	1 loaf	454	32	1,250	41	4	256	77	3.2	0	.39	.27	3.6	0
Raisin bread:														
Slice	1 slice	23	35	60	2	1	12	16	.3	Trace	.01	.02	.2	Trace
Rye bread:														
American, light (⅓ rye, ⅔ wheat):														
Slice	1 slice	23	36	55	2	Trace	12	17	.4	0	.04	.02	.3	0
Pumpernickel, dark, loaf, 1 pound	1 loaf	454	34	1,115	41	5	241	381	10.9	0	1.05	.63	5.4	0
White bread, enriched:[8]														
1 to 2 percent nonfat dry milk:														
Slice	1 slice	23	36	60	2	1	12	16	.6	Trace	.06	.04	.5	Trace

[4] Calcium may not be usable because of presence of oxalic acid.

[8] When the amount of nonfat dry milk in commercial white bread is unknown, use values for bread with 3 to 4 percent nonfat dry milk.

[Dashes show that no basis could be found for imputing a value although there was some reason to believe that a measurable amount of the constituent might be present]

Food, approximate measure, and weight (in grams)		Grams	Water %	Food energy *calories*	Protein *grams*	Fat (total lipid) *grams*	Carbohydrate *grams*	Calcium *milligrams*	Iron *milligrams*	Vitamin A value *International Units*	Vitamin B_1 Thiamine *milligrams*	Vitamin B_2 Riboflavin *milligrams*	Niacin *milligrams*	Vitamin C Ascorbic acid *milligrams*
Grain Products—continued														
Breads—continued														
3 to 4 percent nonfat dry milk:														
Slice, 20 per loaf	1 slice	23	36	60	2	1	12	19	.6	Trace	.06	.05	.6	Trace
Slice, toasted	1 slice	20	24	60	2	1	12	19	.6	Trace	.06	.05	.6	Trace
Slice, 26 per loaf	1 slice	17	36	45	1	1	9	14	.4	Trace	.04	.04	.4	Trace
5 to 6 percent nonfat dry milk:														
Slice	1 slice	23	35	65	2	1	12	22	.6	Trace	.06	.05	.6	Trace
White bread, unenriched:[8]														
1 to 2 percent nonfat dry milk:														
Slice	1 slice	23	36	60	2	1	12	16	.2	Trace	.02	.02	.3	Trace
3 to 4 percent nonfat dry milk:														
Slice, 20 per loaf	1 slice	23	36	60	2	1	12	19	.2	Trace	.02	.02	.3	Trace
Slice, toasted	1 slice	20	24	60	2	1	12	19	.2	Trace	.01	.02	.3	Trace
Slice, 26 per loaf	1 slice	17	36	45	1	1	9	14	.1	Trace	.01	.01	.2	Trace
5 to 6 percent nonfat dry milk:														
	1 slice	23	35	65	[illegible]	[illegible]	[illegible]	[illegible]	[illegible]	Trace	[illegible]	[illegible]	[illegible]	Trace

graham, entire-wheat bread:														
Slice	1 slice	23	36	55	2	1	11	23	.5	Trace	.06	.05	.7	Trace
Toast	1 slice	19	24	55	2	1	11	23	.5	Trace	.05	.05	.7	Trace
Breadcrumbs, dry, grated	1 cup	88	6	345	11	4	65	107	3.2	Trace	.19	.26	3.1	Trace
Cakes:														
Angel food; 2-inch (1/12 of 8-inch-diameter cake)	1 sector	40	32	110	3	Trace	23	2	.1	0	Trace	.05	.1	Trace
Chocolate, fudge icing; sector, 2-inch (1/16 of 10-inch-diameter layer cake)	1 sector	120	24	420	5	14	70	118	.5	140[9]	.03	.10	.3	Trace
Fruitcake, dark; piece, 2 by 2 by 1/2 inch	1 piece	30	23	105	2	4	17	29	.8	50[9]	.04	.04	.3	Trace
Gingerbread; piece, 2 by 2 by 2 inches	1 piece	55	30	180	2	7	28	63	1.4	50	.02	.05	.6	Trace
Plain cake and cupcakes, without icing:														
Piece, 3 by 2 by 1½ inches	1 piece	55	27	180	4	5	31	85	.2	70[9]	.02	.05	.2	Trace
Cupcake, 2¾-inch-diameter	1 cupcake	40	27	130	3	3	23	62	.2	50[9]	.01	.03	.1	Trace
Plain cake and cupcakes, with icing:														
Sector, 2-inch (1/16 of 10-inch layer cake)	1 sector	100	25	320	5	6	62	117	.4	90[9]	.02	.07	.2	Trace

[8] When the amount of nonfat dry milk in commercial white bread is unknown, use values for bread with 3 to 4 percent nonfat dry milk.

[9] If the fat used in the recipe is butter or fortified margarine, the vitamin A value for chocolate cake with fudge icing will be 520 I.U. per 2-inch sector; 120 I.U. for fruitcake; for plain cake without icing, 200 I.U. per piece; 150 I.U. per cupcake; for plain cake with icing, 280 I.U. per 2-inch sector; 140 I.U. per cupcake; and 300 I.U. for pound cake.

[Dashes show that no basis could be found for imputing a value although there was some reason to believe that a measurable amount of the constituent might be present]

Food, approximate measure, and weight (in grams)		Grams	Water %	Food energy calories	Protein grams	Fat (total lipid) grams	Carbohydrate grams	Calcium milligrams	Iron milligrams	Vitamin A value International Units	Vitamin B_1 Thiamine milligrams	Vitamin B_2 Riboflavin milligrams	Niacin milligrams	Vitamin C Ascorbic acid milligrams
Grain Products—continued														
Cakes—continued														
Cupcake, 2¾-inch-diameter	1 cupcake	50	25	160	3	3	31	58	.2	50[9]	.01	.04	.1	Trace
Pound cake; slice, 2¾ by 3 by ⅝ inch	1 slice	30	19	130	2	7	15	16	.5	100[9]	.04	.05	.3	Trace
Sponge cake; 2-inch (1/12 of 8-inch-diameter cake)	1 sector	40	32	115	3	2	22	11	.6	210[9]	.02	.06	.1	Trace
Cookies:														
Assorted, 3-inch-diameter	1 cooky	25	5	110	2	3	19	6	.2	0	.01	.01	.1	0
Fig bars, small	1 fig bar	16	14	55	1	1	12	11	0.2	0	Trace	0.01	0.1	0
Corn-cereal mixture (mainly degermed cornmeal), puffed, added thiamine, niacin, iron	1 ounce	28	3	115	2	1	23	6	1.2	—	.15	.04	.6	0
Corn flakes, with added thiamine, niacin, and iron:														
Plain	1 ounce	28	4	110	2	Trace	24	3	.5	—	.12	.03	.6	0
Presweetened	1 ounce	28	3	110	1	Trace	26	3	.4	—	.12	.01	.5	0
Corn grits, white, degermed, cooked:														
	1 cup	242	87	120	3	Trace	27	2	.7	Trace	.11	.08	1.0	0

[illegible]enriched	1 cup	242	87	120	3	Trace	27	2	.2	Trace	.04	.01	.4	0
Cornmeal, white or yellow, dry:														
Whole ground	1 cup	118	12	420	11	5	87	12	2.8	600[10]	.45	.13	2.4	0
Degermed, enriched	1 cup	145	12	525	11	2	114	9	4.2[11]	430[10]	.64[11]	.38[11]	5.1[11]	0
Corn muffins, made with enriched, degermed cornmeal; muffin, 2¾-inch-diameter	1 muffin	48	30	155	4	5	22	79	.9	170[12]	.10	.15	.8	Trace
Corn, puffed, presweetened, with added thiamine, riboflavin, niacin, and iron	1 ounce	28	3	110	1	Trace	26	3	.5	—	.12	.05	.6	0
Corn and soy shreds, with added thiamine and niacin	1 ounce	28	4	100	5	Trace	21	24	1.2	—	.19	.04	.6	0
Crackers:														
Graham	4 small or 2 medium	14	6	55	1	1	10	3	.3	0	.04	.02	.2	0
Saltines, 2 inches square	2 crackers	8	5	35	1	1	6	2	.1	0	Trace	Trace	.1	0
Soda, plain:														
Cracker, 2½ inches square	2 crackers	11	6	45	1	1	8	2	.1	0	.01	.01	.1	0
Oyster crackers	10 crackers	10	6	45	1	1	7	2	.1	0	.01	Trace	.1	0
Cracker meal	1 tablespoon	10	6	45	1	1	7	2	.1	0	.01	Trace	.1	0
Doughnuts, cake type	1 doughnut	32	19	135	2	7	17	23	.4	40	.05	.04	.4	0
Farina, cooked; enriched	1 cup	238	89	105	3	Trace	22	31	.8	0	.11	.07	1.0	0

[9] If the fat used in the recipe is butter or fortified margarine, the vitamin A value for chocolate cake with fudge icing will be 520 I.U. per 2-inch sector; 120 I.U. for fruitcake; for plain cake without icing, 200 I.U. per piece; 150 I.U. per cupcake; for plain cake with icing, 280 I.U. per 2-inch sector, 140 I.U. per cupcake; and 300 I.U. for pound cake.

[10] Vitamin A value based on yellow cornmeal; white cornmeal contains only a trace.

[11] Iron, thiamine, riboflavin, and niacin are based on the minimal level of enrichment specified in standard of identity promulgated under the Federal Food, Drug, and Cosmetic Act.

[12] Based on recipe using white cornmeal; if yellow cornmeal is used the vitamin A value is 240 I.U.

[Dashes show that no basis could be found for imputing a value although there was some reason to believe that a measurable amount of the constituent might be present]

Food, approximate measure, and weight (in grams)		Grams	Water %	Food energy *calories*	Protein *grams*	Fat (total lipid) *grams*	Carbohydrate *grams*	Calcium *milligrams*	Iron *milligrams*	Vitamin A value *International Units*	Vitamin B_1 Thiamine *milligrams*	Vitamin B_2 Riboflavin *milligrams*	Niacin *milligrams*	Vitamin C Ascorbic acid *milligrams*
Grain Products—continued														
Macaroni, cooked:														
Enriched:														
Cooked 8-10 minutes	1 cup	130	64	190	6	1	39	14	1.4	0	.23	.14	1.9	0
Unenriched:														
Cooked 8-10 minutes	1 cup	130	64	190	6	1	39	14	.6	0	.02	.02	.5	0
Macaroni, enriched, and cheese, baked	1 cup	220	58	475	18	25	44	394	2.0	970	.22	.46	1.9	Trace
Muffins, enriched white flour; 2¾-inch-diameter	1 muffin	48	39	135	4	5	19	74	.7	60	.08	.11	.7	Trace
Noodles (egg noodles), cooked:														
Enriched	1 cup	160	70	200	7	2	37	16	1.4	60	.23	.14	1.8	0
Unenriched	1 cup	160	70	200	7	2	37	16	1.0	60	.04	.03	.7	0
Oat-cereal mixture, with added B-vitamins and minerals	1 ounce	28	3	115	4	2	21	45	1.2	0	.22	.04	.5	0
Oatmeal or rolled oats, regular or quick-cooking, cooked	1 cup	236	85	150	5	3	26	21	1.7	0	.22	.05	.4	0
Pancakes (griddlecakes), 4-inch- diameter:														
Wheat, enriched flour	1 cake	27	53	60	2	2	8	34	.3	30	.05	.06	.3	Trace
[illegible] e mix)	1 cake	27	62	45	2	2	6	67	.3	30	.04	.04	.2	Trace

Piecrust, plain, baked:														
Enriched flour:														
Lower crust, 9-inch shell	1 crust	135	10	655	10	36	72	15	2.7	0	.29	.23	3.0	0
Double crust, 9-inch pie	1 double crust	270	10	1,315	20	73	143	30	5.4	0	.58	.47	5.9	0
Unenriched flour:														
Lower crust, 9-inch shell	1 crust	135	10	655	10	36	72	15	.7	0	.05	.03	.7	0
Double crust, 9-inch pie	1 double crust	270	10	1,315	20	73	143	30	1.4	0	.09	.06	1.4	0
Pies; sector, 4-inch, 1/7 of 9-inch-diameter pie:														
Apple	1 sector	135	48	330	3	13	53	9	0.5	220	0.04	0.02	.03	1
Cherry	1 sector	135	46	340	3	13	55	14	.5	520	.04	.02	.3	2
Custard	1 sector	130	58	265	7	11	34	162	1.6	290	.07	.21	.4	0
Lemon meringue	1 sector	120	47	300	4	12	45	24	.6	210	.04	.10	.2	1
Mince	1 sector	135	43	340	3	9	62	22	3.0	10	.09	.05	.5	1
Pumpkin	1 sector	130	59	265	5	12	34	70	1.0	2,480	.04	.15	.4	0
Pizza (cheese), 5½-inch sector, ⅛ of 14-inch-diameter pie	1 sector	75	47	180	8	6	23	157	.7	570	.03	.09	.8	8
Popcorn, popped	1 cup	14	4	55	2	1	11	2	.4	0	.05	.02	.3	0
Pretzels, small stick	5 sticks	5	8	20	Trace	Trace	4	1	0	0	Trace	Trace	Trace	0
Rice, cooked:														
Parboiled	1 cup	176	72	205	4	Trace	45	14	.5	0	.10	.02	1.9	0
White	1 cup	168	71	200	4	Trace	44	13	.5	0	.02	.01	.7	0
Rice, puffed, with added thiamine, niacin, and iron	1 cup	14	5	55	1	Trace	12	2	.3	—	.06	.01	.6	0
Rice flakes, with added thiamine and niacin	1 cup	30	5	115	2	Trace	26	9	.5	—	.11	.01	1.7	0
Rolls:														
Plain, pan; 12 per 16 ounces:														
Enriched	1 roll	38	31	115	3	2	20	28	.7	Trace	.11	.07	.8	Trace
Unenriched	1 roll	38	31	115	3	2	20	28	.3	Trace	.02	.03	.3	Trace

[Dashes show that no basis could be found for imputing a value although there was some reason to believe that a measurable amount of the constituent might be present]

Food, approximate measure, and weight (in grams)		Grams	Water %	Food energy calories	Protein grams	Fat (total lipid) grams	Carbohydrate grams	Calcium milligrams	Iron milligrams	Vitamin A value International Units	Vitamin B_1 Thiamine milligrams	Vitamin B_2 Riboflavin milligrams	Niacin milligrams	Vitamin C Ascorbic acid milligrams
Grain Products—continued														
Rolls—continued														
Hard, round; 12 per 22 ounces	1 roll	52	25	160	5	2	31	24	.4	Trace	.03	.05	.4	Trace
Sweet, pan; 12 per 18 ounces	1 roll	43	31	135	4	4	21	37	.3	30	.03	.06	.4	0
Rye wafers, 1⅞ by 3½ inches	2 wafers	13	6	45	2	Trace	10	6	.6	0	.04	.03	.2	0
Spaghetti, cooked until tender:														
Enriched	1 cup	140	72	155	5	1	32	11	1.3	0	.19	.11	1.5	0
Unenriched	1 cup	140	72	155	5	1	32	11	.6	0	.02	.02	.4	0
Spaghetti with meat sauce	1 cup	250	76	285	13	10	35	25	2.0	690	.07	.10	2.1	13
Spaghetti in tomato sauce with cheese	1 cup	250	80	210	6	5	36	45	1.0	830	.07	.08	1.0	15
Waffles, with enriched flour, ½ by 4½ by 5½ inches	1 waffle	75	34	240	8	9	30	124	1.4	310	.14	.21	1.1	Trace
Wheat, puffed:														
Added thiamine, niacin, iron	1 ounce	28	4	100	4	Trace	22	8	1.2	0	.16	.06	2.2	0
Added thiamine and niacin; presweetened	1 ounce	28	3	105	1	Trace	26	4	.5	0	.12	.01	1.4	0
Wheat, rolled; cooked	1 cup	236	80	175	5	1	40	19	1.7	0	.17	.06	2.1	0
Wheat, shredded, plain (long, round, or bite-size)	1 ounce	28	6	100	3	1	23	13	1.0	0	.06	.03	1.3	0

Wheat and malted barley cereal, with added thiamine, niacin, and iron	1 ounce	28	3	105	3	Trace	24	13	1.0	0	.13	.05	1.5	0
Wheat flakes, with added thiamine, niacin, and iron	1 ounce	28	4	100	3	Trace	23	13	1.2	0	.16	.05	1.8	0
Wheat flours:														
Whole-wheat, from hard wheats, stirred	1 cup	120	12	400	16	2	85	49	4.0	0	.66	.14	5.2	0
All-purpose or family flour:														
Enriched, sifted	1 cup	110	12	400	12	1	84	18	3.2[11]	0	.48[11]	.29[11]	3.8[11]	0
Unenriched, sifted	1 cup	110	12	400	12	1	84	18	.9	0	.07	.05	1.0	0
Self-rising:														
Enriched	1 cup	110	12	385	10	1	81	299	3.2[11]	0	.48[11]	.29[11]	3.8[11]	0
Unenriched	1 cup	110	12	385	10	1	81	299	1.1	0	.08	.05	1.3	0
Wheat germ, stirred	1 cup	68	11	245	17	7	34	57	5.5	0	1.39	.54	3.1	0
Fats, Oils														
Butter, 4 sticks per pound:														
Sticks, 2	1 cup	224	16	1,605	1	181	1	45	Trace	7,400[13]	—	—	—	0
Stick, 1/8	1 tablespoon	14	16	100	Trace	11	Trace	3	Trace	460[13]	—	—	—	0
Pat or square (64 per pound)	1 pat	7	16	50	Trace	6	Trace	1	Trace	230[13]	—	—	—	0
Fats, cooking:														
Lard	1 cup	220	0	1,985	0	220	0	0	0	0	0	0	0	0
	1 tablespoon	14	0	135	0	14	0	0	0	0	0	0	0	0
Vegetable fats	1 cup	200	0	1,770	0	200	0	0	0	0	0	0	0	0
	1 tablespoon	12.5	0	110	0	12	0	0	0	0	0	0	0	0

[11] Iron, thiamine, riboflavin, and niacin are based on the minimal level of enrichment specified in the standard of identity promulgated under the Federal Food, Drug, and Cosmetic Act.

[13] Year-round average.

[Dashes show that no basis could be found for imputing a value although there was some reason to believe that a measurable amount of the constituent might be present]

Food, approximate measure, and weight (in grams)		Grams	Water %	Food energy calories	Protein grams	Fat (total lipid) grams	Carbohydrate grams	Calcium milligrams	Iron milligrams	Vitamin A value International Units	Vitamin B_1 Thiamine milligrams	Vitamin B_2 Riboflavin milligrams	Niacin milligrams	Vitamin C Ascorbic acid milligrams
Fats, Oils—continued														
Margarine, 4 sticks per pound:														
Sticks, 2	1 cup	224	16	1,615	1	181	1	45	Trace	7,400[14]	—	—	—	0
Stick, 1/8	1 tablespoon	14	16	100	Trace	11	Trace	3	Trace	460[14]	—	—	—	0
Pat (64 per pound)	1 pat	7	16	50	Trace	6	Trace	1	Trace	230[14]	—	—	—	0
Oils, salad or cooking:														
Corn	1 tablespoon	14	0	125	0	14	0	0	0	—	0	0	0	0
Cottonseed	1 tablespoon	14	0	125	0	14	0	0	0	—	0	0	0	0
Olive	1 tablespoon	14	0	125	0	14	0	0	0	—	0	0	0	0
Soybean	1 tablespoon	14	0	125	0	14	0	0	0	—	0	0	0	0
Salad dressings:														
Blue cheese	1 tablespoon	16	28	90	1	10	1	11	Trace	30	Trace	.02	Trace	Trace
Commercial, plain; mayonnaise type	1 tablespoon	15	48	60	Trace	6	2	2	Trace	30	Trace	Trace	Trace	0
French	1 tablespoon	15	42	60	Trace	6	2	3	.1	0	0	0	0	0
Home cooked, boiled	1 tablespoon	17	68	30	1	2	3	15	.1	80	.01	.03	Trace	Trace
Mayonnaise	1 tablespoon	15	14	110	Trace	12	Trace	2	.1	40	Trace	Trace	Trace	0
Thousand Island	1 tablespoon	15	38	75	Trace	8	1	2	.1	60	Trace	Trace	Trace	2
Sugars, Sweets														
Candy:														
Caramels	1 ounce	28	7	120	[illegible]	[illegible]	[illegible]	[illegible]	[illegible]	[illegible]	[illegible]	[illegible]	[illegible]	[illegible]

…colate, sweetened, milk	1 ounce	28	1	145	2	9	16	61	.3	40	.03	.11	.2	0
Fudge, plain	1 ounce	28	5	115	Trace	3	23	14	.1	60	Trace	.02	Trace	Trace
Hard candy	1 ounce	28	1	110	0	0	28	0	0	—	0	0	0	0
Marshmallow	1 ounce	28	15	90	1	0	23	0	0	—	0	0	0	0
Chocolate syrup	1 tablespoon	20	39	40	Trace	Trace	11	3	.3	—	—	—	—	—
Honey, strained or extracted	1 tablespoon	21	20	60	Trace	0	17	1	.2	0	Trace	.01	Trace	1
Jams, marmalades, preserves	1 tablespoon	20	28	55	Trace	Trace	14	2	.1	Trace	Trace	Trace	Trace	1
Jellies	1 tablespoon	20	34	50	0	0	13	2	.1	Trace	Trace	Trace	Trace	1
Molasses, cane:														
Light	1 tablespoon	20	24	50	—	—	13	33	.9	—	.01	.01	Trace	—
Blackstrap	1 tablespoon	20	24	45	—	—	11	116	2.3	—	.02	.04	.3	—
Syrup, table blends	1 tablespoon	20	25	55	0	0	15	9	.8	0	0	Trace	Trace	0
Sugar:														
Granulated, cane or beet	1 cup	200	Trace	770	0	0	199	—	—	0	0	0	0	0
	1 tablespoon	12	Trace	50	0	0	12	—	—	0	0	0	0	0
Lump, 1 1/8 by 5/8 by 1/8 inch	1 lump	7	Trace	25	0	0	7	—	—	0	0	0	0	0
Powdered	1 cup	128	Trace	495	0	0	127	—	—	0	0	0	0	0
	1 tablespoon	8	Trace	30	0	0	8	—	—	0	0	0	0	0
Brown, firm-packed	1 cup	220	3	815	0	0	210	167[15]	5.7	0	0	0	0	0
	1 tablespoon	14	3	50	0	0	13	10[15]	.4	0	0	0	0	0

Miscellaneous Items

Beer (average 4 percent alcohol)	1 cup	240	90	([16])	1	Trace	11	10	Trace	0	Trace	.06	.4	0
Beverages, carbonated:														
Ginger ale	1 cup	230	91	80	—	—	21	—	—	—	—	—	—	—
Kola type	1 cup	230	88	105	—	—	28	—	—	—	—	—	—	—

[14] Based on the average vitamin A content of fortified margarine. Federal specifications for fortified margarine require a minimum of 15,000 I.U. of vitamin A per pound.

[15] Calcium value is based on dark brown sugar; value is lower for light brown sugar.

[16] The value excluding energy derived from alcohol is 48 calories. If the energy from alcohol is considered available, the value is 114 calories.

[Dashes show that no basis could be found for imputing a value although there was some reason to believe that a measurable amount of the constituent might be present]

Food, approximate measure, and weight (in grams)		*Grams*	Water %	Food energy calories	Protein *grams*	Fat (total lipid) *grams*	Carbohydrate *grams*	Calcium *milligrams*	Iron *milligrams*	Vitamin A value *International Units*	Vitamin B_1 Thiamine *milligrams*	Vitamin B_2 Riboflavin *milligrams*	Niacin *milligrams*	Vitamin C Ascorbic acid *milligrams*
Miscellaneous Items—continued														
Bouillon cube, ⅝ inch	1 cube	4	5	2	Trace	Trace	0	—	—	—	—	.07	1.0	0
Chili powder														
See Vegetables, Peppers														
Chili sauce (mainly tomatoes)	1 tablespoon	17	69	15	Trace	Trace	4	2	.1	320	.02	.01	.4	2
Chocolate:														
Bitter or unsweetened	1 ounce	28	2	145	2	15	8	28	1.2	20	.01	.06	.3	0
Sweetened	1 ounce	28	1	135	1	8	18	18	.8	10	.01	.05	.2	0
Gelatin, dry:														
Plain	1 tablespoon	10	13	35	9	Trace	0	0	0	—	0	0	0	0
Dessert powder, 3-ounce package	½ cup	85	2	325	8	Trace	76	0	0	—	0	0	0	0
Gelatin dessert, ready-to-eat:														
Plain	1 cup	239	83	155	4	Trace	36	0	0	0	0	0	0	0
With fruit	1 cup	241	81	170	3	Trace	42	14	.7	270	.07	.05	.5	7
Olives, pickled:														
Green	12 Extra Large or 7 Jumbo	66	78	65	1	7	1	48	.9	170	Trace	—	—	—
Ripe: Mission; other varieties, such as Ascolano,	12 Extra Large													

Pickles, cucumber:														
Dill, large, 4 by 1¾ inches	1 pickle	135	93	15	1	Trace	3	34	1.6	420	Trace	0.09	0.1	8
Sweet, 2¾ by ¾ inch	1 pickle	20	70	20	Trace	Trace	5	3	.3	20	0	Trace	Trace	1
Popcorn														
See Grain Products														
Sherbet, factory packed	1 cup	193	68	235	3	Trace	58	96	.1	0	.03	.15	.1	0
Soups, canned; ready-to-serve:														
Bean	1 cup	250	82	190	8	5	30	95	2.8	—	.10	.10	.8	—
Beef	1 cup	250	92	100	6	4	11	15	.5	—	—	—	—	—
Bouillon, broth, consomme	1 cup	240	95	10	2	—	0	2	1.0	0	0	.05	.6	0
Chicken	1 cup	250	94	75	4	2	10	20	.5	—	.02	.12	1.5	—
Clam chowder	1 cup	255	91	85	5	2	12	36	3.6	—	—	—	—	—
Cream soup (asparagus, celery, mushroom)	1 cup	255	85	200	7	12	18	217	.5	200	.05	.20	.1	0
Noodle, rice, barley	1 cup	250	90	115	6	4	13	82	.2	30	.02	.05	.7	0
Pea	1 cup	245	86	140	6	2	25	32	1.5	440	.17	.07	1.2	5
Tomato	1 cup	245	91	90	2	2	18	24	1.0	1,230	.02	.10	.7	10
Vegetable	1 cup	250	92	80	4	2	14	32	.8	—	.05	.08	1.0	8
Starch, pure, including	1 cup	128	12	465	1	Trace	111	0	0	—	0	0	0	0
arrowroot, corn, etc.	1 tablespoon	8	12	30	Trace	Trace	7	0	0	—	0	0	0	0
Tapioca, quick-cooking	1 cup	152	13	545	1	Trace	131	18	1.5	0	0	0	0	0
granulated, dry	1 tablespoon	10	13	35	Trace	Trace	8	1	.1	0	0	0	0	0
Vinegar	1 tablespoon	15	—	2	0	—	1	1	.1	—	—	—	—	—
White sauce, medium	1 cup	265	73	430	10	33	23	305	.3	1,350	.07	.42	.3	1
Yeast:														
Baker's:														
Compressed	1 ounce	28	71	25	3	Trace	3	4	1.4	Trace	.20	.47	3.2	Trace
Dry active	1 ounce	28	5	80	10	Trace	11	12	4.6	Trace	.66	1.53	10.4	Trace
Brewer's dry	1 tablespoon	8	5	25	3	Trace	3	17	1.4	Trace	1.25	.34	3.0	Trace

Appendix B
List of Recommended and Not Recommended Books*

BOOKS RECOMMENDED

Anderson, L., and Browe, J. H. *Nutrition and Family Health Service*. Philadelphia: W. B. Saunders Co., 1960.

Bogert, L. J., Briggs, G. M., and Calloway, D. H. *Nutrition and Physical Fitness*. Philadelphia: W. B. Saunders Co., 1966.

Borgstrom, G. *TOO MANY: The Biological Limitations of Our Earth*. New York: The Macmillan Co., 1969.

Burgess, A., and Dean, R. F. A., eds. *Malnutrition and Food Habits*. London: Tavistock Publications, 1962. Available in U.S. through the Macmillan Co., New York.

Carter, R. *Your Food and Your Health*. New York: Harper and Row, 1964.

Chaney, M. S., and Ross, M. L. *Nutrition*. 7th ed. Boston: Houghton Mifflin Co., 1966.

Deutsch, R. *The Nuts Among the Berries*. New York: Ballantine Books, 1962.

Fleck, H., and Munves, E. *Everybody's Book of Modern Diet and Nutrition*. New York: Dell Publishing Co., 1955.

——. *Introduction to Nutrition*. New York: The Macmillan Co., 1962.

Goodhart, R. S. *The Teen-ager's Guide to Diet and Health*. Englewood Cliffs, N.J.: Prentice Hall, 1964.

Hutchinson, R. C. *Food for Better Living*. New York: Cambridge University Press, 1958.

Kotschevar, L. H., and McWilliams, M. *Understanding Food*. New York: John Wiley and Sons, Inc., 1969.

Krause, M. V. *Food, Nutrition and Diet Therapy*. 4th ed. Philadelphia: W. B. Saunders Co., 1966.

Leverton, R. M. *Food Becomes You*. 3rd ed. Ames, Iowa: Iowa State University Press, 1965.

Lowenberg, M. E., Todhunter, E. N., Wilson, E. D., Feeney, M. C., and Savage, J. R. *Food and Man* New York: John Wiley and Sons, Inc., 1968.

McDermott, I. E., Trilling, M., and Nicholas, F. *Food for Modern Living*. Philadelphia: J. B. Lippincott Co., 1967.

McHenry, E. W. *Foods Without Fads*. Philadelphia: J. B. Lippincott Co., 1960.

* Compiled by the Chicago Nutrition Association

McHenry, E. W., and Beaton, G. *Basic Nutrition*, rev. ed. Philadelphia: J. B. Lippincott Co., 1963.

McWilliams, M. *Food Fundamentals*. New York: John Wiley and Sons, Inc., 1966.

———. *Nutrition for the Growing Years*. New York: John Wiley and Sons, Inc., 1967.

Maddox, G. *The Good Sense Family Cook Book*. New York: M. Evans and Co., 1966.

Martin, E. A. *Nutrition in Action*. 3rd ed. New York: Holt, Rinehart, and Winston, Inc., 1971.

Mickelsen, O. *Nutrition Science and You*. Vistas of Science 10. New York: Scholastic Book Services, 1964.

Mitchell, H. S., Rynbergen, H. J., Anderson, L., and Dibble, M. V. *Cooper's Nutrition in Health and Disease*. 15th ed. Philadelphia: J. B. Lippincott Co., 1968.

Nasset, E. S. *Your Diet Digestion and Health*. 2nd ed. New York: Barnes and Noble, Inc., 1962.

Robinson, C. H. *Basic Nutrition and Diet Therapy*. New York: The Macmillan Co., 1965.

———. *Normal and Therapeutic Nutrition*. 13th ed. New York: The Macmillan Co., 1967.

Rossman, I. *Nutrition for Your Family's Health*. New York: Emily Post Institute, Inc., 1963.

Salmon, M. B. *Food Facts for Teen-Agers*. Springfield, Illinois: C. C. Thomas, 1965.

Sebrell, W. H., Jr., Haggerty, J. J., and the Editors of *Life*. *Food and Nutrition*. Chicago: Time-Life Books, 1967.

Sherman, H. C., and Lanford, C. S. *Essentials of Nutrition*. 4th ed. New York: The Macmillan Co., 1957.

Spock, D., and Lowenberg, M. *Feeding Your Baby and Child*. New York: Pocket Books, Inc., 1956.

Stare, F. J. *Eating for Good Health*. New York: Doubleday and Co., 1964.

Tatkon, M. D. *The Great Vitamin Hoax*. New York: The Macmillan Co., 1968.

Taylor, C. M., MacLeod, G., and Rose, M. S. *Foundations of Nutrition*. 5th ed. New York: The Macmillan Co., 1956.

U.S. Department of Agriculture. *Consumers All: The Yearbook of Agriculture 1965*. Washington, D.C.: Superintendent of Documents, U.S. Government Printing Office, 1965.

———. *Food: The Yearbook of Agriculture, 1959*. Washington, D.C.: Superintendent of Documents, U.S. Government Printing Office, 1959.

Wayler, T. J., and Klein, R. S. *Applied Nutrition.* New York: The Macmillan Co., 1965.

White, P. L., ed., *Let's Talk About Food.* Chicago: The American Medical Association, 1967.

Williams, S. R. *Nutrition and Diet Therapy.* Saint Louis: The C. V. Mosby Co., 1969.

Wilson, E. D., Fisher, K. H., and Fuqua, M. E. *Principles of Nutrition.* 2nd ed. New York: John Wiley and Sons, Inc., 1965.

BOOKS NOT RECOMMENDED

Abrahamson, E. M., and Pezet, A. W. *Body, Mind and Sugar.* New York: Holt, Rinehart and Winston, Inc., 1965.

Adams, C. *Eat Well Diet Book.* New York: Random House, Inc., 1956.

Alexander, D. D. *Good Health and Common Sense.* New York: Crown Publishers, Inc., 1960.

Anchell, M., *How I Lost 36,000 Pounds.* Detroit: Harlo Press, 1964.

Bicknell, F. *Chemicals in Your Food and in Farm Produce: Their Harmful Effects.* New York: Emerson Books, Inc., 1961.

Bieler, H. G. *Food Is Your Best Medicine.* New York: Random House, Inc., 1966.

Brean, H. *The Only Diet That Works.* New York: Wm. Morrow and Co., 1965.

Cantor, A. J. *How to Lose Weight the Doctor's Way.* New York: Frederick Fell, Inc., 1959.

Clark, L. *Stay Young Longer.* New York: The Devin-Adair Co., 1961.

Cummings, C. *Stay Young and Vital.* Jersey City: Prentice Hall, Inc., 1960.

Davis, A. *Let's Eat Right to Keep Fit.* New York: Harcourt Brace, 1954.

———. *Let's Get Well: A Practical Guide to Renewed Health Through Nutrition.* New York: Harcourt, Brace and World, Inc., 1965.

———. *Let's Have Healthy Children.* New York: Harcourt Brace, 1959.

Davis, Helen A. *The No Willpower Diet.* New York: David McKay Co., Inc., 1969.

DeGroot, R. *How I Reduced with the New Rockefeller Diet.* New York: Horizon Press, 1956.

Donaldson, B. F. *Strong Medicine.* Garden City, N.Y.: Doubleday and Co., 1962.

Eiteljorg, S. *The Sweet Way to Diet.* Garden City, N.Y.: Doubleday and Co., 1968.

Elwood, C. *Feel Like A Million.* New York: The Devin-Adair Co., 1956.

Fiore, E. L., ed. *The Low Carbohydrate Diet.* New York: Ridge Press, 1965.

Fredericks, C. *The Carlton Fredericks Cookbook for Good Nutrition.* Philadelphia: J. B. Lippincott Co., 1960.

———. *Dr. Carlton Fredericks' Low-Carbohydrate Diet.* New York: Award Books, 1965.

Hauser, G. *The New Diet Does It.* New York: G. P. Putnam's Sons, 1960.

———. *New Guide to Intelligent Reducing.* New York: Farrar, Straus and Young, 1955.

Hunter, B. T. *The Natural Foods Cookbook.* New York: Simon and Schuster, 1961.

Jarvis, D. C. *Arthritis and Folk Medicine.* Greenwich, Conn.: Fawcett Publications, Inc., Crest Books, 1962.

———. *Folk Medicine: A Vermont Doctor's Guide to Good Health.* New York: Holt, Rinehart and Winston, Inc., 1956.

Kordel, L. *Eat Your Troubles Away.* Cleveland: The World Publishing Co., 1955.

Lederman, M. *Slim Gourmet, or The Joys of Eating.* New York: Simon and Schuster, 1955.

Lindlahr, V. H. *Calorie Countdown.* Englewood Cliffs, N.J.: Prentice Hall, Inc., 1962.

Little, B. *Recipes for Allergics.* New York: Vantage Press, 1968.

Longgood, W. *The Poisons in Your Food.* New York: Simon and Schuster, 1960.

Lydon, J. E. *How to Live 150 Years.* New York: Vantage Press, 1963.

Mackarness, R. *Eat Fat and Grow Slim.* Garden City, N.Y.: Doubleday and Co., 1959.

Munro, D. C. *Man Alive—You're Half Dead.* New York: McFadden Bartell Corporation, 1950.

Nidetch, J. *Weight Watcher's Cook Book.* New York: Hearthside Press, Inc., 1966.

Rienzo, G. R. *Slim Down.* New York: Vantage Press, 1964.

Righter, C. *Your Astrological Guide to Health and Diet.* New York: G. P. Putnam's Sons, 1967.

Rodale, J. I., and Staff. *Our Poisoned Earth and Sky.* Emmaus, Penn.: Rodale Books, Inc., 1964.

Rose, I. F. *Faith, Love and Seaweed.* Englewood Cliffs, N.J.: Prentice Hall, Inc., 1963.

Shefferman, M. *Food for Longer Living.* New York: Whittier Book Co., 1958.

Small, M. *Reduce with a Low-Calorie Diet.* New York: Pocket Books, Inc., 1964 (new printing).

Stillman, I. M., and Baker, S. S. *The Doctor's Quick Weight Loss Diet.* New York: Dell Publishing Co., Inc., 1968.

Taller, H. *Calories Don't Count.* New York: Simon and Schuster, 1961.

Toms, A. *Eat, Drink and Be Healthy: The Joy of Eating Natural Foods.* New York: The Devin-Adair Co., 1963.

Trop, J. D. *You Don't Have to Be Sick.* New York: Julian Press, 1961.

West, R. *Stop Dieting! Start Losing!* New York: Bantam Books, 1957.

———. *The Teen-age Diet Book.* New York: Bantam Books, 1958.

Williams, R. J. *Alcoholism: The Nutritional Approach.* Austin: University of Texas Press, 1959.

———. *Nutrition in a Nutshell.* Garden City, N.Y.: Doubleday and Co., Dolphin Books, 1962.

Wilson, M. *Double Your Energy and Live Without Fatigue.* Englewood Cliffs, N.J.: Prentice Hall, Inc., 1961.

Wood, H. C. *Overfed But Undernourished: Nutritional Aspects of Health and Disease.* 8th ed. New York: Exposition Press, Inc., 1962.

INDEX

INDEX

ATP, 105, 106, 150
Acerola Plus, 308
Acetic Acid, 47, 305
Acidophilous Bacteria, 330
Acid(s)
  Unsafe to store in copperware, 332, 333
    See also individual names: e.g., Amino Acids; Fatty Acids; etc.
Acne, 417, 418
Additives
  See: Food—Additives
Adipose Storage Cells
  See: Cells
Adrenal Glands, 383
Advertising, 7, 291, 308, 310, 311, 312, 314
Aerophagia, 368
Agar Agar, 305
Aging, 94
  See also: Old Age
Air, 296
  See also: Atmosphere
Air Force Academy Diet, 245
Alcohol
  Amount of water to metabolize, 100, 244
  Cause of dehydration, 99, 100
  Calories, 242, 276
  Combinations of, 367
  Effects after exercise, 100
  Effects at high altitudes, 100
  Social drinking in hot weather, 100
Algae, 71, 428
Alimentary Canal, 360-378
Alkalizers, 371, 372
All-in-One Diet Annual, 247
Allaway, Dr. W. H., 164, 165
American Academy of Pediatrics, 147
American Dental Association, 114
American Heart Association, 379, 380, 389, 393
American Medical Association, 9, 30, 31, 98, 102, 145, 188, 248, 254, 306, 334, 359, 366, 413
  Council on Foods and Nutrition, 18, 220, 389
  Department of Foods and Nutrition, 12, 412
Amino Acids, 47, 57-96
  Arginine, 76
  Choice groupings in reproduction process, 82
  Common to all forms of life, 66
  Essential, 72-77
  Excess, 93, 94
  Glutamic Acid, 74
  Glycine, 47
  Histidine, 76
  Lysine, 75
  Non-essential, 73, 74
  Possibility of consumption in powder and liquid form, 71
  Safe levels of, 77, 86, 87
  Threonine, 76
  Tryptophan, 75, 87, 349
  Typical male and female intake, 78, 86, 87
Ammonia, 47, 50, 296, 297
Amphetamines, 267, 268
Anemia, 102, 159, 398
  Pernicious anemia, 124, 133
Antiperistalsis, 370
Antirachitic Vitamin
  See Vitamin(s) D
Anus, 365, 373
Appendix, 365
Appestat
  See: Brain
Appetite
  Automatic controls, 204, 205, 206
  Medicines to control, 266-269
Apples, 236, 254

Arachadonic Acid
  See: Fatty Acids
Arginine
  See: Amino Acids
Arteries, 382, 383
Arthritis, 155
Ascorbic Acid, 137, 138, 139, 140, 344
  See also: Vitamin(s) C
Asparagus, 85
Atherosclerosis, 379-394
  Heredity factors, 383, 384
  Physical factors, 382, 383
Athletes, Protein Need, 88, 89
Atmosphere, Change in Components, 39-41
Atoms, 41
Avocado, Protein Content, 85

BHA, 304
BHT, 304
Babies
  Basal metabolism, 227
  Protection against obesity, 191, 208, 209
Bacon
  Frozen, 331
  Imitation bits, 429
  Mold, 331
  Refrigerated, 331
Bacteria, 327, 329-341, 429
  See also: Microbes
Baking Powder, Chemical Content, 305
Balanced Diet
  See: Diet(s)—Balanced
Bananas, Use After Vomiting or Diarrhea, 377
Barley, Malting, 112
Basal Metabolism, 198, 224-227, 233
  Normal, 226
  Rate declines from childhood, 198, 226, 227
Beal, Virginia, 406
Bean(s)
  Lima, protein content, 87
  Protein content, 85
Beaudoin, Dr. R., 175
Beef
  Considered fat meat, 23
  Frozen, sliced, with gravy, nutritional content, 26
  Protein content, 87
Beer, 112
Beets, 111
Belches
  See: Burps
Belladonna, 267
Beriberi, 30, 120, 124, 407
Beta-Carotene, 143
Better Homes and Gardens (magazine), 263
Bile, 364
Biochemistry, 37-51, 52-70
Bioflavenoids, 141
Biogenic Diet, 37, 75
Biogenic Range, 95
Biotin, 135
Blood, 159, 381, 382
  Cells in cubic millimeter of, 53
  Clots, 382
  Pressure, 384, 386, 402
  Vessels, blocking, 381-383; elements contributing to atherosclerosis, 382
  Vitamin K, for clotting, 149
Blood Sugar
  See: Sugar(s)
Body types
  See: Ectomorph; Endomorph; Mesomorph
Bologna, Fat content, 24
Bones, 150, 151, 155
  Growth and food consumption, 194
  Growth in men and women, 195
Boston Nutrition Society vs. Dr. Fredrick Stare, 282, 283
Botulism, 333-335
  AMA statement on, 334
Bowel
  Changes in habits, 374, 375
  Movements, 373
Boys
  Dietary lack of thiamine, 129
  Leanness in adolescence, 194
Brain, 204, 205, 207, 225, 361, 370
  Appestat, 205, 206
  Cortex, 204
  Hypothalmus, 204
  Number of cells, 53
    See also: Stroke
Bran, 284, 285

Bread, 14, 284-286
Enriched White, 9, 281, 282, 286, 287; protection against Vitamin B deficiencies, 129, 130
Low-calorie, 273
Mold, 330
Nutritional content of white and whole wheat, 286, 287
Protein content, 84
White, 8
Whole wheat, 8, 286
Breakfast, 7, 23, 24, 25, 258, 259, 314-316, 420
See also: Cereals, Breakfast; School Breakfast Programs
Breastfeeding, 398-400, 403-405, 419, 420
Broccoli
Cooked in copper pan, 343
Protein content, 85
Brookline, Massachusetts, School Lunch Program Expanded to Include Older People, 424
Broth, Use After Vomiting or Diarrhea, 377
Brown, Elfriede, 80
Brussels Sprouts, Protein Content, 85
Burma, 132
Burps, 367-369
Butter, 258, 259
Calories, 116, 258
Rancid, 330
Butylated Hydroxyanisole
See: BHA
Butylated Hydroxytoluene
See: BHT

CO_2
See: Carbon Dioxide
Cadmium, 165
Cake, Chocolate Layer, Calories, 203
Calciferol, Ultraviolet-Radiated Yeast Yield, 147
Calcium, 6, 8, 9, 15, 16, 50, 150-155
Deficiencies by age and sex groups, 151
Food preservative, 304
Most plentiful of minerals, 150
In pregnancy, 398
Sources, 151, 152
Supplements, 155
California, Weeds, Cost to State, 298
Calipers, 220, 221
Calories, 49, 81, 116, 223-238, 243-277
Amount and activity, 226-234
Amount needed, by age and sex, 198-200, 223, 224, 225, 227, 230-234
Correlating with food consumption, 234
Counting, 234-238
Outside factors affecting burning, 228, 229
Calories Don't Count Diet, 245
Calorimeter, 236
Calvin, Melvin, 46
Cancer, Intestinal, 359
Candy, 417
Carbohydrates, 8, 9, 42, 102, 103, 108-113, 166, 363, 364
Mold, 330, 331
Amount needed, 103
Fuel for the body, 37, 38, 48, 102, 103
High carbohydrate diet, 249, 250
Low carbohydrate diet, 247, 248
One gram yields four calories, 45
See also: Starches; Sugars
Carbon, 50
Carbon Dioxide, 40, 41, 46, 47, 48, 50
Molecule, 41, 42
Cardiovascular Diseases
See: Heart; Stroke
Carotene(s), 142, 143, 305
Accumulation can tint skin yellow, 143
Characteristic green and yellow colors, 142, 143
Depth of color indicative of vitamin richness, 142, 143
Sources, 142-145
Carragheen, 305
Carrots, 111, 120
Nutritional content, 27

Casein, 74, 75
Catalase
See: Enzymes
Cauliflower, Protein Content, 85
Celery, 82, 110, 254
Cells, 52-70
Adipose storage, 109, 177
Description of typical, 55
Separate lives of, 53, 54
See also individual names: e.g., Blood; Goblet; Muscle; etc.
Cellulose, 82, 110, 111
Cereals, Breakfast, 14, 102, 121, 302
Label-reading, 312-316
Protein content, 84, 85, 121
Charts
See: Height-Weight Charts
Cheese(s)
Cheddar—protein content, 84, 87; standard, 317
Cottage—protein content, 84
Mold, 330, 331
Protein content, 84
Uses of whey, 430
Chemical(s), 50, 295-307
Definition, 295, 296
Fertilizers, 295, 296, 297, 298
See also individual names: e.g., Nitrogen; Oxygen; etc.
Chewing, 101, 361, 362, 369, 370
Chewing Gum, Sugarless, 274
Chicken
A la King, canned, nutritional content, 26
Protein content, 87
Child Research Council, 406
Children
Digestive systems, 418
Family energy style influence on, 211
Fluid consumption, 107
Food, 406-421
Growth, 414-416
Ideal weights for, 222, 415, 416
Importance of varied food tastes, 420
Nutrition, 28-30, 406-421; pattern set by family, 211, 212, 417
Obesity in, 5, 171, 191, 192, 193, 210-214, 407
Reducing diets, 213, 214
Resting after eating, 419
Children's Hospital, Boston, 179
Chili Con Carne, Canned, Nutritional Content, 26
Chlorophyll, 41, 305
Cholesterol, 379-394
American Heart Association statement, 385, 386
American Medical Association position on, 389
Menu suggestions, 391
Tests, 389
Choline, 135, 136
Sources, 136
Chromium, 165
Chromosomes, 58, 93
Chyme, 363, 364, 365
Citric Acid, 296, 304
Citric Acid Cycle
See: Krebs Cycle
Citrin
See: Vitamin(s) P
Clostridium Botulinum
See: Botulism
Co-Enzymes, 121, 122
See also: Vitamins
Cobalamin
See: Vitamin(s) B_{12}
Cobalt, 163
Excess amounts hazardous, 163
Coffee, 257, 302
Chemical composition, 302
Coffee Breaks, 25
Cohn, Dr. Clarence, 275
Colds, Use of Vitamin C in Prevention or Cure, 139
AMA comment, 140
Collagen, 383
Colombia, 429
Colon, 368, 373, 374, 375, 376
Irritable, 375
Constipation, 110, 373-376
AMA statement on, 375
In pregnancy, 403
Convenience Foods
See: Food(s)—Canned; Food(s)—Frozen

Cook, Dr. Frances, 350
Cookware
  Copper, 163, 343, 344
  Iron, 162, 344
  Non-stick, 274
  Waterless, 353
Copper, 162, 163
  Cookware, 163, 343, 344
  Utensils unsafe for fruits, 333
Corn, 45, 75, 76, 79, 80
Coronary Attacks
    See: Heart
Cortex
    See: Brain
Cottage Cheese
    See: Cheese(s)
Cows, 82
    See also: Milk
Custards, Refrigeration, 332
Cyclamates, 303
Cystic Fibrosis, 68
Cytopalsm, 56

DDT, 298, 299, 300, 301
DNA, 58-70, 93, 94, 133, 150
  Comparison to computers, 60, 61
  Spiral, 58, 63; "unzipping," 62
  Triplets, 59, 60, 62, 63, 64
Dates, Protein Content, 85
Davis, Adelle, 281, 292, 295
Dawson, Keith, 300
Dayton, Dr. Seymour, 385
Death Rate
  Infant, 30, 31
  Obesity, 172
Decker, Dr. George, 297
Defecation Reflex, 373
  Voluntary blocking, 374
Dehydration, 98, 99, 100
Dehydrofreezing Food, 430
Deoxyribonucleic Acid
    See: DNA
Deoxyribose, 57, 62
Dexidrine, 268
Dextrins, 111, 112
Dextrose
    See: Glucose
Diabetes, 108, 117, 384, 386
  Incidence in America, 248
Diarrhea, 375, 376, 377
  Calling doctor when prolonged, 377
  Replacing fluids after attack, 377
Diet(s), 77, 79, 80, 81
  Balanced, 37, 38, 74, 88
  Biogenic, 37, 75
  Catabolic foods, 253
  Cholesterol reduction, 380, 393
  Custom-tailored, 256-263
  Distorted crash, 249, 265
  Doctor's Quick Inches-Off, 250, 251
  Doctor's Quick Weight Loss, 244-248
  Drinking Man's, 245, 248
  High Carbohydrate, 77, 249-251
  High Fat, 248, 249
  High Protein, 92, 246, 247, 248
  Lack in American, 21-23
  Liquid formula, 275
  Low carbohydrate, 247, 248
  Low cholesterol, 379-394
  Macrobiotic, 77, 78
  Monotony reducing, 247, 248
  No-Diet, 269-272
  Nutritionally sound, 265, 266
  Reducing, 244-277; Children, 213, 214; Teenagers, 418
  USDA findings on average adult, 18, 19
  Varying diets of man, 48, 49
Digestion, 66, 67, 101, 359-378
Digitalis, 267
Dinner, 25, 26
    See also: School Dinner Programs
Diseases
  Supposed, due to nutritional deficiencies, 281-294
    See also: Illnesses—Foodborne
Diuretics, 240, 267
  AMA statement on, 240
Doctor's Quick Inches-Off Diet, Dr. Irwin Stillman and Samm Baker, 250, 251
Doctor's Quick Weight Loss Diet, Dr. Irwin Stillman and Samm Baker, 244, 245, 246, 247, 248
  AMA statement, 248

Doctors, Calling When Vomiting or Diarrhea are Prolonged, 377
Dressing and Stuffing, Cooking and Refrigeration, 338, 339
Drinking Man's Diet, 245, 248
Drinks
See: Alcohol; Beer
Du Pont Diet, 248
Duggan, Reo E., 300
Duodenum, 364, 371
Duryea, 429

E. coli (bacterium), 61, 328
Eating
Personal preferences, 12
Slowly to consume less, 272
Ecology, 44
Ectomorph, 182, 191
Appetite cut-off, 185
Restlessness, 185
Eggs, 82, 84, 388
Bad odor, 331
Blood spots, 331
Dirt on shell, 331, 332
Grading, 318, 319, 320
Perfection as amino acid food, 82
Sauces—unrefrigerated, source of food poisoning, 332
Storage, 331, 354, 355
Washing shells, 331, 332
Elastase, 383
Elastin, 383
Electrolytes, Body, 157
Embolism
See: Blood Clots
Emotions
Affecting digestion, 361
Nutrition, 20, 21
Endomesomorph, 180
Endomorphs, 180
Appetite cut-off, 185
Indolence, 185
Energy, 40, 41, 45, 46, 47, 48, 49, 104-113
Family style influence on children, 210-212
From sun to plant to make food, 40, 41, 43, 44, 48, 49
Storage, 43, 44, 45, 46, 107-109
Weight affected by, 230
See also: Basal Metabolism; Calories
Enterotoxin, 329
Enzymes, 38, 67, 68, 69, 93, 121, 122, 288, 289, 344
Active sites, 67, 68
Catalase, 69
Missing cause of hereditary illness, 68
Epiphyses, 150
Ergosterol, 147
Eructations
See: Burps
Esophagus, 362, 370
Estrogens, 194
Exercise, 193, 207, 213, 214, 215, 241, 269, 270, 271, 272, 384, 386
Habit changes, 205, 206, 269, 270
Machines, 252, 253
Older people, 426
In pregnancy, 403
See also: Calories
Eyes, Blood Vessels Show Atherosclerosis, 390

Farming, 297-299
See also: Organic farming
Fat(s), 17, 23, 24, 25, 44, 45, 46, 48, 49, 95, 102, 103, 166, 343, 363, 364, 365
Amounts needed, 103, 119
Animals, hardness of, 114, 115, 384
Calories, 258, 259, 260
Consumption, 119; atherosclerosis, 379-394
American Heart Association statement on, 379
Content in food, 114-119
"Fat doctors," 267
Fuel for the body, 37, 45, 46, 48, 49, 102, 103, 116
High fat diets, 248, 249
Human, cells, 177, 178, 184, 185; description, 177
Hydrogenated, 116

Fat(s) (*continued*)
Incomplete metabolism, 117
Monosaturated, 384
One gram yields nine calories, 45
Polyunsaturated, 115, 116, 384, 391, 392
Saturated, 115, 379, 384, 391, 392
Storage cells
See: Cells—Adipose storage
Unsaturated, 384
Vegetable, liquid form as oil, 115, 384
See also: Butter; Cholesterol; Margarine
Fat-Indicator areas
Subscapular, 181
Triceps skinfold, 181
Fatness
See: Obesity
Fatty Acids, 44, 45, 48, 115, 117, 118
Arachadonic Acids, 117
Essential, 117, 118
Linoleic, 117; content in foods 117
Linolenic, 117
Fecal matter, 365, 373, 374, 375
Fertilizers, Chemical, 295, 296, 297
Fibrin, 382, 383
Fibrinolysin, 283
Fineberg, Dr. S. K., 241
Fish
Grading, 323
Thawing frozen, 338
Flour, 14, 67
Enriched white, 129, 281, 282; protection against Vitamin B deficiency, 129
Fluids, 14, 17
See also: Alcohol; Water; etc.
Fluoride, 306, 307
AMA statement, 306
Folate
See: Folic Acid
Folic Acid, 134, 347
Deficiencies in pregnancy, 134
Derivation of name, 134
Sources, 134
Food(s), 3-11, 12-34, 97-167
Additives, 296, 301, 302, 303, 304, 305, 306
American pattern of choices, 18, 19, 22, 23, 24, 25, 26, 27
Avoid letting stand after cooking, 330
Calculating needs, 223, 224, 227
Canned, 289, 290, 291, 292, 333, 334; container bulging or squirting, 334; low in Vitamin C, 345; nutrition, 289, 290, 291, 292; overcooking 344; storage, 354
Carbohydrate content, 109, 110
Catabolic, 253
Chemicals, 295-307
Children, 406-421
Comparison of intake of Adults and Children, 412, 413
Creation, 37-51
Dietetic, 273
Eaten raw, 111
Effect of being cooked, 330
Enrichment, 129, 130, 302, 311
Faddists, 281-294, 301
Fat content, 114-119
Fattening, 254, 255, 256
Forbidden in reducing cholesterol, 379, 380, 381
Frozen, 25, 26, 289, 290, 291, 354; accumulation of ice at one side of package, 340; dehydrofreezing, 430; nutrition, 289, 290, 291; storage, 354
Future, 428-431
Grading, 319, 320, 321, 322, 323; U.S. Government marks, 318
Groups, 12-19
Hard to digest, 369-371
And the heart, 379-394
Home-canned, 290, 333, 334; source of botulism, 333, 334
Labels, 7, 8, 129, 154, 308-324; law, 312, 316, 317;

Labels (*continued*)
reading, 312-317; when to check against advertising claims, 314, 315
Linoleic acid content, 117, 118
Loss of nutrients, 342-355
Method of determining adequacy of personal dietary, 12, 13, 14, 15, 16, 17
Older people, 422-427
Pregnancy, 397-405
Preservatives, 304
Progress in alimentary canal, 110, 361-365
Rules for safety in preparation of, 340, 341
Serving sizes, 12, 13, 14
Sources of thiamine, riboflavin, niacin, 127, 128
Standards control, 317-319
Storage, 327-341; proper temperatures, 337, 338
Stress affecting needs, 20, 21
Supposed nutrition hazards in food supply, 281-294
Water content, 97, 98, 99
Weights and measures deceptions, 7
See also: Calories; Health Foods; Illnesses–Foodborne
Food and Drug Research Laboratories, Inc., 305
Food and Drug Administration
See: U.S. Food and Drug Administration
Food Poisoning
See: Illnesses–Foodborne
Formaldehyde, 41, 46
Formic Acid, 46
Frankfurters, Fat Content, 24
Fredericks, Carlton, 292, 293
Freezers, 354
Sign of inadequate temperatures, 336
Frozen Food
See: Food(s)—Frozen
Fructose, 42, 43
Fruits(s), 5, 14, 16, 17, 83
Citrus, 14
Grading, 322
Juice in copper utensils unsafe, 332, 333
Protein content, 80, 84, 85
Storage, 354
Fruit Sugar
See: Fructose
Funk, Casimir, 121
Future, Food, 428-431

Gas, 40, 41, 50, 367, 368
Genetic Code, 59, 60, 61, 62
Girls, Weight Gain with Onset of Menstruation, 193, 194
Gliadin, 75
Glucose, 42, 43, 45, 57, 107, 248
Glutamic Acid
See: Amino Acids
Gluten, 74
Glycerin
See: Glycerol
Glycerol, 44, 45, 48, 115
Glycine
See: Amino Acids
Glycogen, 45, 108, 109
Goblet-Cell, 55
Goiter, 6, 30, 164, 398
Belts, 6, 164
Goulash, Frozen, Nutritional Content, 26
Graham, Sylvester, 284, 285
Graham crackers, 284
Grahamite Movement, 285
Grain Products, 14, 16, 17
Insects in, 332
Protein content, 81, 84, 286
Grapefruit
Juice stored in opened can in refrigerator, 333
Use in diets, 67, 253, 254
Greeley, Horace, 285
Green Bay Packers, 181
Guar, 305
Gullet
See: Esophagus

HCHO
See: Formaldehyde
H_2O
See: Water Molecule
Haddock, Frozen with Cream Sauce, Nutritional Content, 26

Hair, Bacteria on, 329
Hall, Dr. Richard L., 428
Ham
  Frozen, 331
  Chemical composition, 302
  Mold, 331
Hamburger, Length of Refrigeration, 336, 337
Hands, Skin Grafts Growing Fat, 176, 178
Harvard University Department of Nutrition, 175, 213
  See also: Stare, Dr. Fredrick
Health Foods, 6, 7, 8
  AMA Council on Food and Nutrition statement, 18
  Prices, 7
Heart, 379-394
  Coronary attacks, 381, 382
  Relationship of culture and heart diseases, 384, 385
Heartburn, 369, 370
Height-Weight Charts, 17, 179, 183, 216, 217, 218, 219, 221, 414-416
Hemoglobin, 60, 159
Heredity, 38, 58, 60, 383, 384
Hesperiden, 141
Hidden Hunger, 32, 33
Hirsch, Dr. Jules, 176, 177, 184, 190
Histidine
  See: Amino Acids
Hollandaise Sauce, Refrigeration, 332
Honey, 43, 112
Hormones, 38, 69, 70
  Activity during adolescence, 194; during pregnancy, 69
Hunger
  How man satisfies, 52, 53, 201, 202, 203, 204, 205
  Patterns by Age and Sex groups, 201, 202
  Signals, 202, 248
  See also: Hidden Hunger
Hydrochloric Acid, 363
Hydrogen, 41, 50, 296, 297
  Smallest and most plentiful atom, 41
Hydrogen Peroxide, Enzyme Display When Put on Cut, 69
Hydroxyl Radical, 42, 46
Hypoglycemia, 9, 108
Hypothalmus
  See: Brain

I.U.
  See: International Units
Ice Cream, 274
Ice Milk, 274
Illnesses, 292
  Foodborne, 10, 327-341, 376
  Heredity, 68
  Vitamin deficiency, 120, 124, 125, 407, 408
  See also: Botulism; Indigestion; Obesity
Incaparina, 429
Indigestion, 359-378
  Self-treatment, 372
  Stress a cause, 360
Inositol, 136
Insects
  Control by chemicals, 298
  Grain products, 332
International Units
  Measurement of Vitamin A, 143, 144, 145; Vitamin D, 146, 147
Intestinal Poison
  See: Enterotoxin
Intestine(s)
  Large, 365
  Small, 364, 365
Intoxication
  Causes, 367
Iodine, 163, 164
  Amount needed, 164
  Deficiency, 163, 164
  Lack causes goiter, 164
Iron, 158-162
  Cookware, 162, 344
  Deficiencies, 158; in infants, 158; in women, 159, 160, 398
  Low in pregnancy, 158, 159, 398
  Requirements by age and sex, 160
  Sources, 158, 160, 161, 162
  Supplements, 160, 162, 309

Jellies, Mold, 330, 331
Joint Committee on Biochemical Nomenclature of the American Society of Biological Chemists and the American Institute of Nutrition, 141
Joint problems, 155
Jolliffe, Dr. Norman, 253, 268, 269
Journal of Nutrition Education, 20

Kcal.
See: Kilocalories
Kale
Protein content, 85
Kannel, Dr. William, 383, 390
Kempner Diet, 249, 250
Ketones, 117
Ketosis, 117
Keys, Dr. Ancel, 383
Kidneys, 94
Kilocalories, 224, 225
See also: Calories
Knittle, Dr. Jerome, 184, 190
Krebs Cycle, 104, 105, 106, 132, 296
Kwashiorkor, 407

Labels
See: Food—Labels
Lactation
See: Breastfeeding
Lactose, 43, 109
Laxatives, 267, 359, 374, 375
Lecithin, 136, 305
Legumes
Protein content, 81, 83, 85
See also: Beans
Lettuce, 83, 110, 236
Leukemia, 134
Leverton, Dr. Ruth, 29, 256, 301
Life, Interdependence of, 52-70
Expectancy, 92, 93
Planetary, 58
Lightning, 296
Lime, Juice to Cure Scurvy, 137
Linoleic Acid
See: Fatty Acids
Linolenic Acid
See: Fatty Acids
Lipoproteins, 388
Liquid(s)
Drunk before and during meals, 100, 242, 243
See also: Alcohol; Milk; Water; etc.
Liquor
See Alcohol; Beer
Liver, Role
In producing cholesterol, 384, 388
In producing glycogen, 108, 109
In storing niacin, 126
Liverwurst, Fat Content, 24
Low Blood Sugar
See: Hypoglycemia
Low-Gram Diet, 245
Lunch, 24, 25
Expense-Account, 25
See also: School Lunch Programs
Lungs, 384
Water vapor evaporated from, 241
Lysine
See: Amino Acids

MDR
See: Minimum Daily Requirement
MSG
See: Monosodium Glutamate
McCall's (magazine), 282
McCollum, Dr. Elmer V., 34
Macrominerals
See individual names: e.g., Calcium; etc.
Magnesium, 156, 157
Malt, 112
Maltose, 43, 111, 112
Man
Biochemical make-up, 49, 50, 52-70; systems for managing any safe food, 123
Dietary changes, 154
Necessity of balancing weight and water, 17
Omnivorous, 134
Manioc, 109

Manufacturers, Food
  Bound by law requiring proof of safety of additives, 303
Manure, 296
Margarine, 14, 116
Mayer, Dr. Jean, 172, 175, 178, 179, 181, 183, 184, 185, 186, 195, 205, 206, 247, 249, 255, 256, 266
Mayo Diet, 248
Mayonnaise, Care in Use in Picnic Foods, 339
Meat(s)
  Calories, 235
  Early belief that proteins made animals and man combative, 38
  Fat, less protein per pound, 83, 84
  Grading, 320, 321
  Ground, effect of grinding, 336
  Lean, more protein per pound, 83, 84
  Muscle main source, 82
  Length of refrigeration, 336, 337
  Luncheon, fat content, 24
  Protein content, 80, 81, 82, 83, 84
  Thawing frozen, 338
  Variety meats, length of refrigeration, 337
  Virtual lack of carbohydrates, 109
    See individual names: e.g., Beef; Pork; etc.
Meat Loaf
  Avoid letting stand in moderate temperatures, 329, 330; mixing with cut finger, 329
  Length of refrigeration, 337
Medical Progress, 247
Medicines, Appetite Control, 266-269
Membrane, Cell, 55, 56
Men
  Dietary lack of Vitamin C in men over 75, 136
  Dietary lack of calcium, 151
  Ulcer-prone, 371
Mendel (Pioneer nutrition researcher), 75, 76
Menopause, Weight Gain During, 197
Menstruation, 193, 194
Mental Retardation, 68, 74
Mesomorphs, 180, 182, 183, 191
  Appetite cut-off, 185
  Activity with rest periods, 185
Methane, 47, 50
Metropolitan Life Insurance Company, 216, 217
  Children's height and weight table, 414-415
Microbes, 54, 327-341
  In mouth, 113
Micronutrients, 102, 310, 311, 312
    See also: Minerals; Vitamins
Milk, 13, 16, 28, 311
  Action in stomach, 363, 364
  Comparison of human and cow's, 404
  Dietary replacements, 154, 155
  Eight-ounce glass protein content, 88
  Grading, 322, 323
  Low-fat, 273, 274
  And obesity, 5, 6, 255
  Pasteurized, 322, 323
  Perfection as amino acid food, 82
  Raw, 322, 323
  Skim, 155
  Sour, 329; use of, 330
  Source of calcium, 16, 152, 153, 154, 155; Source of Vitamin D, 16, 146, 147
  Use after vomiting or diarrhea, 377
Miller, Elna, 80
Miller, Stanley, 47
Minerals, 38, 149-167
  Supplements, 165, 310
  Synthetic, 287, 288
    See also individual names: e.g., Calcium; Iron; Phosphorus; etc.
Minerals, Trace
    See individual names e.g., Iodine; Selenium; etc.

Minimum Daily Requirement, 8, 21, 155
Mitochondria, 56
Molasses, 112
Molds, 329, 330
Monosodium Glutamate, 74
Morning Sickness, 399, 400, 403
Mouth, 361
  Microbes in, 113
  Rinsing after eating, 114
Mouth Washes, 114
Mucosa, 362
Muscles
  Affecting obesity, 252
  Cells, 55
  Tonus, 225
Mushrooms
  Protein content, 85
Mustard Greens, Protein Content, 85

National Academy of Sciences, 303
National Nutrition Survey, 3
National Plant Food Institute, 297
National Research Council Food and Nutrition Board, 20, 85, 103, 131, 133, 135, 145, 160, 199
Nausea, 370
Negative Nitrogen Balance, 21
Nerve(s), Cells, 55
Newsweek, (magazine), 139
Niacin, 124, 125, 126, 127, 128-129, 349
  Molecule, 287, 288
  No dietary deficiency, 126
  Sources of, 126, 127-128
  Stored in the liver, 126
Nitrates, 295, 296
Nitrogen, 39, 40, 48, 50, 94, 296, 297
Nose
  Nasal cavity used in smelling, 361, 362
  Nasal secretions move to throat, 368
Nucleoproteins, 56
Nucleotides, 57, 58, 59, 62, 93, 106
  Chains, 58
  Triplets, 62
Nucleus, Cell, 38, 56, 62, 63
Nursing
  See: Breastfeeding
Nutrients
  Biogenic range, 165
  Loss in foods, 342-355
  Old age, 422, 423
Nutrition, 3-11, 12-34
  Children, 28-30, 406-421
  Education key to good diet, 4, 22
  Effects of stress on, 20, 21
  Errors cause of suffering in middle and late life, 33
  Minimal, 19-21
  Older people, 422-427
  Pattern set by family, 211, 212
  Physical signs of good nutrition, 30, 31; of poor nutrition, 31, 32
  Pregnancy, 397-405
  Supposed hazards in food supply, 281-294
    See also: Diet(s); Food; Minimum Daily Requirement; Recommended Daily Requirement
Nuts, 46
  Cashews, 173
  Protein content, 81, 83, 84

OH
  See: Hydroxyl Radical
O_2
  See: Oxygen Molecule
Obesity, 33, 171-187, 188-200, 239-277, 383
  Adults, 6, 171, 172
  Ages when vulnerable to, 172, 188-198
  Appetite control, 204, 205, 206
  Bodily changes, in, 189, 190, 191
  Causes, 190, 191
  Children, 5, 171, 191, 192, 193, 210-214, 407
  Death rate, 172
  Decline of basal metabolism, 198, 199
  Difficulty in maintaining weight loss, 172, 173

Obesity (*continued*)
- Fat people eating less than thin people, 184, 185
- Gaining weight without realizing it, 195, 196, 197
- Girls, adolescent, 193, 194
- Guilt feelings, 180, 203, 204
- Heredity, 172-180, 183, 184, 185, 186, 191
- Hunger satiety, 184, 185, 202, 203
- Hunger signals, 202
- Illnesses caused by, 33, 172
- National consciousness of, 171
- Overeating, 190, 191, 192
- Prevention, 189, 204-215; in adolescents, 214; in adults, 215
- Protecting babies against, 190, 191, 208, 209
- Protecting children against, 210, 211, 212, 213, 214
- Self-disapproval, 183
- Weight-gain in menopause, 197; in pregnancy, 197

Odor-Recognition
- See: Smelling

Oil(s), 45, 46, 115, 118
- See also: Fats

Old Age, 422-427
- Dietary deficiencies, 423
- Diminishing sense of taste and smell, 425
- Emotional needs, 424
- Exercise, 426
- Food, 422-427
- Protein need, 89

Optimal Health Development, 407

Orange(s)
- Juice, artificial, label-reading, 314
- source of Vitamin C, 137

Organic Farming, 296

Oro, Juan, 46

Osborne (nutrition researcher), 75, 76

Oser, Dr. Bernard, 305

Osteoporosis, 33, 423

Overweight
- See: Obesity

Oxygen, 37, 39, 40, 41, 43, 44, 45, 50, 125, 159, 296, 297
- Molecule, 41

PKU, 74

Page, Dr. Irvine, 390

Pancreas, 68, 364, 383

Pantothenic Acid, 132, 133, 347
- Foods with most, 132
- Found in all living cells, 132

Partoid Gland, 362

Pauling, Linus, 139, 140

Pectin, 305

Pea(s), Protein Content, 85

Pellagra, 30, 124

Pennington Diet, 248

Pepsin, 364

Peristalsis, 362, 364
- Mass, 373

Pernicious Anemia
- See: Anemia

Perspiration, 157, 241, 242, 243

Pesticides, 298, 299, 300, 301

Phagocytes, 54, 55

Phenobarbitol, 267

Phenylalanine, 74

Phospholipids, 136

Phosphoric Acid, 57

Phosphorus, 50, 57, 149, 150, 155, 156
- Excess in pregnancy, 400
- Sources, 156

Physical Examinations, 389, 390

Pills
- "Rainbow," 267
  - See also individual names: e.g., Calcium; Mineral(s) Supplements; etc.

Pinching Fat-Indicator Areas, 181, 182, 220

Planets, Life on, 57, 58

Plants
- Leaves, 41, 82, 83
- Limited protein value, 82
- Roots, 41, 83
- Seeds, 83
- Stems, 82
- Use of carbon dioxide, 41, 43, 44
- Use of sun energy to make food, 40, 41, 43, 44

Platelets, 382

Pollack, Dr. Herbert, 229, 230, 252
Pork, 335, 336
  Cooking, 335, 336
  Freezing, 335, 336; AMA statement, 336
  Source of trichinosis, 336
Potassium, 156, 157
Potato(es), 14, 45, 83, 111
  And obesity, 5, 254, 255
  Protein content, 85
  Source of Vitamin C, 5
Poultry
  Freezer storage time, 339
  Grading, 321, 322
  Roasted, with stuffing, 338, 339
  Thawing, frozen, 338, 340
    See also: Chicken; Turkey
Pregnancy, 397-405
  Change in food needs, 399, 400, 401
  Constipation, 403
  Emotional stress, 403
  Exercise, 403
  Homone activity during, 69, 403
  Morning sickness, 400, 403
  Nutrients needed in larger quantity, 399, 400
  Nutrition in, 397-405
  Unwise self-prescribing during, 398, 399
  Water retention, 401, 402
  Weight gain, 197, 401, 402
Propyl Gallate, 304
Protein(s), 8, 13, 15, 16, 20, 21, 52-70, 71-96, 166, 363, 364
  Animal complete, 80
  Basic rule for safe levels, 85
  Body's needs and use as result of infection, injury, surgery, 86
  Chains of amino acids, 47
  Content of foods after cooking, 90, 91
  Contractile, 67
  Diets, 92, 246, 247
  Essence of life, 52, 66, 93
  Excess, 89, 95, 96
  Fuel for the body, 37, 38, 48, 49
  Human body content, 66, 81
  Kinds of, 67
  Needs of patients in certain illnesses, 86
  Pregnant, nursing mothers' needs, 86
  Sources, 79, 80, 81, 82, 83, 90
  Structural, 67
  Timing of consumption, 91, 92
  Transport, 67
  Vegetable, incomplete, 80, 81
Prothrombin, 149
Provitamin, 142, 143
Provitamin D_3, 146
Purpura, 140
Pylorus, 363, 369
Pyridoxal, 130
Pyridoxal Phosphate, 130
Pyridoxamine, 130
Pyridoxine, 130

RDA
    See: Recommended Dietary Allowance
RNA, 63-68, 93, 94, 125, 133, 150
  Chain, 63
  Messenger, 63, 64, 65, 66
  Transfer, 64, 65
  Triplet, 64
Radioactive Particles, 46, 165
Raspberries, Black, Protein Content, 85
Recommended Dietary Allowance, 20, 21, 22, 24, 28, 126, 127-128, 137, 139, 147, 155, 156, 400, 401
Rectum, 365, 373
Reducing, Spot Reducing, 251, 252
    See also: Diet(s); Weight Reduction
Reducing Clubs, Farms, etc., 276-277
Rejuvenation, 94
Rennin, 364
Riboflavin, 124, 125, 126, 348, 349
  Dietary deficiency in certain age groups, 126

Riboflavin (*continued*)
Dietary lack in women, 129
Light sensitivity, 348, 349
Sources of, 127-128
Ribonucleic Acid
See: RNA
Ribose, 57, 63, 125
Ribosomes, 56, 63, 64, 65, 66
Rice
Cooking to preserve nutrients, 355
Use after vomiting or diarrhea, 377
Rickets, 30, 147
Robinson, Dr. H. E., 429
Rockefeller Diet, 249, 250
Rose, Dr. William, 76
Rumen, 82
Rutin, 141

SDA
See: Specific Dynamic Action
Saccharin, 304
Sacrum, 402
Salami, Fat Content, 24
Saliva, 368
Salivary Glands, 362
Salmonella, 9, 327, 332
Salmonellosis, 327
Salt
In reducing diets, 243, 274
Iodized table salt, 6, 163, 164, 398
Tablets, 157
See also: Sodium
Sauces, Length of Refrigeration, 338
Sausage(s)
Frozen, 331
Mold, 331
See also individual names: e.g., Bologna; Frankfurters; etc.
Scales, use at same time each day, 244
Schaefer, Dr. Arnold, 3, 31
School Breakfast Programs (experimental), 28
School Dinner Programs (experimental), 28
School Lunch Programs, 5, 28
To include older people, 424
Type A lunch, 28, 29
Scotch Whiskey, 112
Scurvy, 120, 137, 139
Sea Salts, 165, 398
Sea Water, Cause of Faster Body Dehydration, 99
Seaweed, 428
Seeds, 46
Selenium, 163, 164, 165
Seltzer, Dr. Carl, 180
Senility, 381
Senses, No Defense Against Food-Borne Illness, 327
Shellfish, Thawing Frozen, 338
Shivering, 229
Shortening, 384
Shrimp, Frozen, Newburg, Nutritional Content, 26
Skin
Cells, 55
Grafts, abdominal tissue causing fat hands, 176, 177, 178
"Orange Peel," 402
Sleep
Eating before, 275
Energy used during, 225
Smelling, 361, 362
Smoking, 276, 383, 385
Snacks, 5, 23, 173, 175, 259, 260, 261, 275, 276, 406, 407, 412, 413, 417, 419
Before meals to reduce food intake, 272
Before sleeping, 275, 419, 420
Soda, Destroys Thiamin and Riboflavin, 349
Sodium, 8, 156-158, 402
Increases need for water, 99, 100, 101
Used in water-softening, 157, 158
Sodium Propionate, 304
Soil
Basic elements restored by chemical fertilizers, 297
Quality, 281, 292, 293, 294; American Dietetic Association comment on, 294; AMA statement on, 293, 294

Somatype
See: Ectomorph; Endomorph; Mesomorph
Soy Beans, 429, 430
Specific Dynamic Action, 237, 238, 248
Sphincters, 361
Spinach, Protein Content, 85
"Sports Drinks," Commercial, 101, 102
AMA comment, 102
Sprays, 298, 299, 300, 301
Stamler, Dr. Jeremiah, 383, 386, 390
Staph
See: Staphylococcal poisoning
Staphylococcal Poisoning, 327, 329
Starch(es), 16, 43, 44, 45, 47, 48, 110, 111
Cooking starchy foods, 111
Granules, 110, 111
Poorly digested cause of intestinal gas, 362
Stare, Dr. Fredrick, 140, 247, 251, 275, 276, 282, 283, 288, 297, 306
Stews
Length of refrigeration, 337
Stillman, Dr. Irwin, 245, 246
Stomach, 361, 362, 363, 364, 367, 368, 369, 370, 371
Acid, 363, 371; causing ulcers, 371, 372, 373
Amount of time to digest food, 363
Capacity, 363, 369
Chemical reactions producing gas products, 367, 368
Digesting foods at different speeds, 369
Distention, 368, 369
Effect of emotions on, 361
Strawberries, 45
Vitamin C content, 345
Stress
Affecting food needs, 20, 21
Factor in atherosclerosis, 383, 384, 385, 386
Factor in indigestion, 360, 368
Stroke, 379, 381, 382, 383
Sublingual Gland, 362
Submandibular Gland, 362
Sucrose, 43, 112
Sugar(s), 14, 17, 111, 112, 113, 343
Blood, 108, 109
Brown, 112, 113
Excess consumption and atherosclerosis, 387, 388
Raw, 113
Refinement, 289
Storage, 43, 47, 48, 49
Double
See: Lactose; Maltose; Sucrose
Simple, 47, 48, 49
See also: Fructose, Glucose
Table, 112
Sulfur, 73, 149, 150
Sun
Source of energy, 40, 41, 43, 44, 46, 48, 49
Source of Vitamin D, 145, 146, 147
Supermarkets, 281, 283, 299, 300
Swallowing, 368
Swanson, Dr. Pearl, 422
Sweating
See: Perspiration
Sweeteners
See: Cyclamates; Honey; Sugar; Syrups; etc.
Syrups, 112

TV Dinners, 25, 26
Table Sugar
See: Sucrose, Sugar(s)
Taste
Buds, 361
Sensations, 361
Teenagers
Prevention of obesity in, 214, 418
Reasons for poor nourishment, 420, 421
Teeth, 155
Cleaning, 114
Effect of Carbohydrates on, 113
Microbes on, 113, 114
Need for fluoride, 306, 307
Termites, 82
Thermometers, Meat, 335

Thiamine, 124, 347, 348
  Deficiency, 124, 125; in certain age groups, 126
  Dietary lack in boys, 129; in women, 129
  Sources of, 128-129
Third International Congress of Food Science and Technology, 428
Thirst, 97, 98, 100, 101, 102
Threonine
  See: Amino Acids
Thyroid
  Gland, 164, 383
  Hormone, 267
Tomatoes, 14
Tongue, 361, 362
Toxemia, 397, 398
Toxicity, 96
Toxin, 329
Trabeculae, 150
Trichinella Spiralis
  See: Trichinosis
Trichinosis, 335, 336
  Killed by freezing, 336
Triglycerides, 387
Triplets (biochemical), 59, 62, 63, 64
Tryptophan
  See: Amino Acids
Turkey
  Frozen, with dressing and gravy, nutritional content, 26
  Roasted with stuffing, 338, 339
Turnip(s), 111
  Greens, protein content, 85
Twins, Identical
  Weight, 178, 179

Ulcers, 359, 371, 372, 373
Ultraviolet Light, 46, 146, 147
United States Bureau of Standards, 7
United States Department of Agriculture, 18, 22, 23, 136, 158, 203, 298, 339, 340, 353, 354, 408, 409, 423, 429, 430
  Agriculture Research Service, 28, 29, 254-255
  Height-Weight Table, 219, 221
United States Food and Drug Administration, 21, 137, 292, 299, 300, 303
United States Public Health Service, 328
Urea, 73, 94, 98
Urey, Harold, 47
Urine, 94, 98, 140, 240, 250, 309
Utah State Nutrition Council, 80

Valence (atoms), 41
Vegetables, 5, 14, 16, 17, 26, 27, 28, 290, 291
  Cooking to avoid vitamin loss, 342-355
  Grading, 322
  Oils, 115, 116, 118; best source of linoleic acid, 117, 118
  Protein content, 80, 81, 85
  Serving size, 27, 28
  Storage, 351, 352, 353
Vegetarians, 77, 132, 133, 156
Villi, 364, 365
Vinegar, 47, 305
Viosterol, 147
Vitamin(s), 38, 119-149, 166, 167
  Deficiency illnesses
    See: Illnesses
  Definition, 119-121
  Excess, 122
  Fat-soluble, 122, 141-149
  Function, 121, 122
  Loss in cooking, 342-355
  Methods of preserving, 342-355
  Named, 121
  Supplemental, 309, 310
  Synthetic, 287, 288
  Water-soluble, 122, 142
  A, 20, 31, 120, 142-145, 297, 349, 350; can be seen in food sources, 142, 143; loss in cooking, 349, 350; measurement by 143, 144, 145; international unit, sources, 144; toxicity, 145
    See also: Carotenes
  B, 20, 21, 124, 125-136, 398; loss in cooking, 347, 348; methods of preserving, 347-349

Vitamin(s) (*continued*)
See also: Folic Acid; Niacin; Pantothenic Acid
B Complex, 124
B_1
See: Thiamine
B_2
See: Riboflavin
B_6, 130-132
Sources, 131, 132
See also: Pyridoxal; Pyridoxamine; Pyridoxine
B_{12}, 102, 133, 134, 163
Stored in kidneys and liver, 133
See also: Biotin; Choline
C, 14, 124, 136-140, 353, 354
Air detrimental to, 344, 345; loss in cooking, 343, 344-346; medical uses, 140; methods of preserving in cooking, 344-346; RDA for children, adults, 137, 139; signs of deficiency, 139; source in potatoes, 5; sources, 137, 138; use in prevention or cure of colds, 139; AMA comment, 140
D, 31, 145-147; danger of excess amounts, 147; deficiencies, 145, 146; food sources, 146; fortified, 145; functions, 147; "irradiated" foods, 147; loss in cooking, 349; milk only truly rich source, 146, 147; recommended number of international units, 146; source in exposure to sunlight, 145, 146, 147
See also: Calciferol; Ergosterol; Provitamin D_3
E, 147-148; appears in foods carrying unsaturated fats, 148; function, 304; no known deficiency in U.S., 147, 148; sources, 148
K, 149; derivation of name, 149; sources, 149
P, 141

Vomiting, 370, 376, 377
Calling doctor when prolonged, 377
Replacing fluids after attack, 377

Water, 39-41, 46, 47, 48, 50
Adult needs, 97, 98
Amount to metabolize alcohol, 100
Body content, 17, 50, 97, 241; and reducing, 240, 241, 242-244
Content in food, 98, 99
Drinking before meals, 101; during exercise, 98, 99
Increased need due to sodium consumption, 99, 100-101
Molecule, 41-43
Vapor evaporated from lungs, 241
Water-based drinks, 14
See also: Alcohol; "Sports Drinks"; Sea Water
Water Pill
See: Diuretics
Waterless Cookware, 353
Watermelon, Caloric Content, 116
Weight
Affected by energy, 230
Charts
See: Height-Weight Charts
Human flexibility, 219, 220
Ideal, 217-238; for children, 222
Reduction, 239-277; success motivation for control, 223; tricks to achieve, 272-277
Western Hemisphere Nutrition Congress, 297
Wheat, 284, 285, 286
Description of grain, 285
Germ, 46, 148, 285, 286, 289
Refinement of, 8
White, Dr. Hilda, 407
White, Dr. Philip L., 12, 18, 209, 210, 236, 237, 248, 254, 275, 289, 290, 291, 310, 379, 380

White House Conference on Food, Nutriton, and Health, 3, 4, 5, 6, 7, 30, 311
Withers, Dr. R. F. J., 178
Women
  Born with all eggs she will produce, 82
  Dietary lack of calcium, 151; of riboflavin, thiamine, 129
  Fewer ulcer-prone since 1900, 371, 372
  More body fat than men, 186
  Pregnancy, 397-405
  Weight gain in pregnancy and menopause, 197, 198
World Health Organization, 171, 299

Yeast, 94, 429
  Ultraviolet-radiated yields calciferol, 147
Young, Dr. Charlotte, 33

Zein, 75

ABOUT THE AUTHOR

Since graduation from Columbia in 1949, RONALD M. DEUTSCH has devoted his time to explaining to the public the scientific truths and discoveries that people can use to protect themselves against needless illness, needless worry, needless confusion and expense. An author and lecturer with special interest in the fields of medicine and public health, Mr. Deutsch has written six books—including *The Nuts Among The Berries, The Key to Feminine Response in Marriage and Pairing*—and over 200 articles for major magazines, such as *Better Homes and Gardens, Reader's Digest, Redbook, Family Circle* and *Ladies' Home Journal*. He is also a frequent speaker to groups of professional nutritionists, physicians, home economists and food technologists. In 1969 Mr. Deutsch served on the President's White House Conference on Food, Nutrition and Health.

Bantam Book Catalog

Here's your up-to-the-minute listing of ove 1,400 titles by your favorite authors.

This illustrated, large format catalog gives description of each title. For your convenienc it is divided into categories in fiction and nor fiction—gothics, science fiction, westerns, mys teries, cookbooks, mysticism and occult, biogra phies, history, family living, health, psycholog art.

So don't delay—take advantage of this specia opportunity to increase your reading pleasure

Just send us your name and address and 50¢ (to help defray postage and handling costs).

BANTAM BOOKS, INC.
Dept. FC, 414 East Golf Road, Des Plaines, Ill. 60016

Mr./Mrs./Miss______________________________
(please print)

Address______________________________

City____________State________Zip________

Do you know someone who enjoys books? Just give us their names and addresses and we'll send them a catalog too!

Mr./Mrs./Miss______________________________

Address______________________________

City____________State________Zip________

Mr./Mrs./Miss______________________________

Address______________________________

City____________State________Zip________

FC—9/78